About the American Hotel & Lodging Association (AH&LA)

Founded in 1910, AH&LA is the trade association representing the lodging industry in the United States. AH&LA is a federation of state lodging associations throughout the United States with 11,000 lodging properties worldwide as members. The association offers its members assistance with governmental affairs representation, communications, marketing, hospitality operations, training and education, technology issues, and more. For information, call 202-289-3100.

LODGING, the management magazine of AH&LA, is a "living textbook" for hospitality students that provides timely features, industry news, and vital lodging information.

About the American Hotel & Lodging Educational Institute (EI)

An affiliate of AH&LA, the Educational Institute is the world's largest source of quality training and educational materials for the lodging industry. EI develops textbooks and courses that are used in more than 1,200 colleges and universities worldwide, and also offers courses to individuals through its Distance Learning program. Hotels worldwide rely on EI for training resources that focus on every aspect of lodging operations. Industry-tested videos, CD-ROMs, seminars, and skills guides prepare employees at every skill level. EI also offers professional certification for the industry's top performers. For information about EI's products and services, call 800-349-0299 or 407-999-8100.

About the American Hotel & Lodging Educational Foundation (AH&LEF)

An affiliate of AH&LA, the American Hotel & Lodging Educational Foundation provides financial support that enhances the stability, prosperity, and growth of the lodging industry through educational and research programs. AH&LEF has awarded millions of dollars in scholarship funds for students pursuing higher education in hospitality management. AH&LEF has also funded research projects on topics important to the industry, including occupational safety and health, turnover and diversity, and best practices in the U.S. lodging industry. For more information, go to www.ahlef.org.

SECURITY and LOSS PREVENTION MANAGEMENT

Educational Institute Books

SECURITY and LOSS PREVENTION MANAGEMENT

Third Edition

David M. Stipanuk
Raymond C. Ellis, Jr.

**American
Hotel & Lodging
Educational Institute**

Disclaimer

This publication is designed to provide accurate and authoritative information in regard to the subject matter covered. It is sold with the understanding that the publisher is not engaged in rendering legal, accounting, or other professional service. If legal advice or other expert assistance is required, the services of a competent professional person should be sought.

—*From the Declaration of Principles jointly adopted by the American Bar Association and a Committee of Publishers and Associations*

The authors, David M. Stipanuk and Raymond C. Ellis, Jr., are solely responsible for the contents of this publication. All views expressed herein are solely those of the authors and do not necessarily reflect the views of the American Hotel & Lodging Educational Institute (the Institute) or the American Hotel & Lodging Association (AH&LA).

Nothing contained in this publication shall constitute a standard, an endorsement, or a recommendation of AH&LA or the Institute. AH&LA and the Institute disclaim any liability with respect to the use of any information, procedure, or product, or reliance thereon by any member of the hospitality industry.

Project Editor: Jim Purvis

Editors: Peter Morris
        Tim Eaton

Contents

Preface

THE LODGING INDUSTRY HAS LEARNED a great deal about effective safety and security programs since the first edition of this text was published. The industry has also benefitted from technological advances in security equipment. Statistics on hotel employee safety show that the lodging workplace is a much safer workplace today than in years past. Changes in design and equipment as well as managerial practices have contributed to a more secure environment for guests as well. At the same time, new threats from natural disasters, infectious diseases, and terrorists have also arisen and required further developments of technology and increased managerial attention. It is hoped that this text has made a contribution to the security and safety improvements made by the industry in the last few decades and that this new edition will continue to do so.

The third edition of *Security and Loss Prevention Management* covers several new topics; it also retains material of continuing importance from the previous editions. New chapters have been developed on the legal aspects of hotel security and safety, the day-to-day safety issues in hotels, and employee safety. Other chapters have been extensively reorganized and updated. Emerging issues in the areas of infectious diseases, natural disasters, and terrorism are addressed in this edition.

Resources are provided via web links that greatly expand upon the issues discussed in the book. Some of these links are provided in the text, while others are located on the Educational Institute's website at www.ahlei.org. (Once there, search for *Security and Loss Prevention Management,* and with a few clicks you will arrive at the textbook's web page, which contains support materials for the book under the "Instructor Resources" tab. You can also access the relevant page using the QR code at the end of this preface.) The goal of this text is not to repeat the content of all of these resources but rather to present key information and then give readers a convenient way to pursue more information if they wish to do so.

Material has been retained from the previous edition where a careful review indicated that it continues to reflect current industry practice. Also retained have been some exhibits and sidebar material (such as Tony Marshall's classic "At Your Risk" columns) that continue to be useful and thought-provoking. Some material that was present in the last edition (for example, the appendix at the back of the book titled "A Guide to OSHA Regulations for the Lodging Industry") has been omitted from this new edition, but can still be found among the bonus material provided on the Institute's website under the "Instructor Resources" tab for this textbook.

Chapter 1, "Security and Safety in the Lodging Industry," has been revised and updated with new material that familiarizes the reader with the security and safety issues facing the lodging industry and explains how hotels can manage the risk management process. As alluded to earlier, this edition has consolidated the legal aspects of security and safety in a new chapter (Chapter 2, "Legal Aspects of Loss Prevention") that has been shaped in part by material found in the American Hotel & Lodging Educational Institute's textbook *Understanding Hospitality Law.* The result is a somewhat briefer but still comprehensive discussion of the legal aspects of security and safety; the lengthy law cases included in the previous edition can now be found on EI's website for those interested in referencing them.

Chapter 3, "Security Programs, Training, Design, and Equipment," also has been reorganized and updated with new material (for example, there is a new section on biometrics). "Security Procedures Covering Guest Concerns" (Chapter 4) features a new section on how guests view certain security and safety systems and procedures that hotels are either now implementing or may be implementing in the future.

Chapter 5, "Lodging Safety," is another new chapter for this edition that covers slips, trips, and falls; fire safety; water safety issues; emergency power issues; indoor air quality; foodborne illness; and bed bugs. Chapter 6, "Departmental Responsibilities in Guest and Asset Protection," looks at hotel security issues on a department-by-department basis.

"Employee Safety," Chapter 7, is a new chapter that summarizes the business case for employee safety as well as addressing how hotels can effectively manage their operations with employee safety in mind. Chapter 8, "The Protection of Funds and Information," has been updated to include new information about asset and information security, including a section on PCI (payment card industry) compliance.

Chapter 9, "Emergency Management and Media Relations," discusses a wide range of emergencies that a hotel might face, from bomb threats and terrorism to fires, natural disasters, and blackouts. A new section within the chapter also addresses how infectious diseases can impact hotels. The book concludes with a look at insurance issues of interest to hotels (Chapter 10, "Insurance").

Acknowledgments

As a third edition, this book must recognize the contributors to previous editions as well as those who have made more recent contributions. Earl J. Bleser, Chad Callaghan, William G. Cox, Thomas G. Davis, and Mark Hamilton all made significant contributions to the second edition. Adding their insights for this new edition have been David M. Bleser of Bleser and Associates, Jim Stover of A. G. Gallagher, and Chad Callaghan. Mr. Callaghan retired from the Marriott Corporation and is currently a safety and security consultant for the American Hotel & Lodging Association.

Jim Purvis of the Educational Institute must be acknowledged for his contribution to making this book happen. His quick editing, his clarification of the materials he received, and his shepherding of the book through the EI publishing process is greatly appreciated. The author also wishes to extend a general thank you to the Educational Institute and its staff for a great relationship that has lasted over several projects for almost twenty years.

David M. Stipanuk
Ithaca, New York

About the Authors

David M. Stipanuk

David M. Stipanuk is an Emeritus Professor of the School of Hotel Administration at Cornell University. During his time teaching in the School he taught courses in hospitality risk management, facilities management, hotel development and construction, and sustainability. He also taught courses in the School's industry executive programs for a number of years. Professor Stipanuk has a B.S. from the University of Wisconsin–Milwaukee and an M.S. from the University of Wisconsin–Madison. Until his retirement, he was also a registered professional engineer in the state of Wisconsin. Professor Stipanuk is the author of *Hospitality Facilities Management and Design*, published by the American Hotel & Lodging Educational Institute.

Raymond C. Ellis, Jr. (1921–2012)

The third edition of *Security and Loss Prevention Management* is dedicated to Raymond C. Ellis, Jr., who was the author or co-author of the previous two editions. Ray passed away in May 2012 after many years of important contributions to the lodging industry and to hospitality education. Ray was a wonderful person and truly a dedicated servant to the lodging industry and to his fellow man. Below is a brief sketch of some of the highlights of Ray's distinguished career.

The first seventeen years of Ray's career were with Marshall Field's. In 1955, he joined the staff of the National Safety Council and began pro bono consulting for the American Hotel Association (AHA) on safety, security, and fire protection. From 1967 to 1977, Ray administered the Howard Johnson Motor Lodge Safety Group and the hotel safety groups for New York City, New York State, New Jersey, and Massachusetts. After twenty-two years of pro bono consulting for AHA, in 1977 he joined the paid staff of the renamed American Hotel & Motel Association (AH&MA). Upon retirement from AH&MA in 1994 (today's American Hotel & Lodging Association), Ray joined the University of Houston's Hilton College, where he taught facilities management and loss prevention management. He also headed the college's Loss Prevention Management Institute. Ray retired from the university in 2008.

Ray earned a Ph.B. and MBA from the University of Chicago, a graduate certificate in Personnel Psychology from Ohio State University, and a graduate certificate in Organization Management from Syracuse University.

In 1986, Ray received the National Safety Council's Distinguished Service to Safety Award. He was named to the Hospitality Financial & Technology Professionals' Technology Hall of Fame in 1989. In 1999, the American Hotel & Lodging Association's Educational Institute presented him with the Lamp of Knowledge Award. He received the American Society of Industrial Security's President's

Award in 2000. In September 2001 he was named an Honorary Life Member of the National Safety Council. In May 2002 Ray received the Dean's Award for Excellence in Teaching for the 2001/2002 Academic Year. In 2004, he was elected Director Emeritus of the National Fire Protection Association's Lodging Section Executive Committee. Also in 2004, Ray received an etched "In Appreciation" crystal piece from the Council on Practices and Standards, American Society of Safety Engineers.

Chapter 1 Outline

Risk Management: The Business Case
Security and Safety: An Ongoing (and
  Ever-Changing) Concern
The Risk Management Process
  Four Steps of the Risk Management
    Process
  Benefits of Risk Management to a
    Business
Hotel Security Requirements
Lodging Safety and Security: Today and
  Tomorrow
Major Loss Events Involving Hotels
  Fires
  Structural Failures
  Earthquakes
  Floods

Competencies

1. Explain the importance of a comprehensive approach to risk management and outline the business case for managing risk. (pp. 3–5)

2. Discuss in general terms the security and safety responsibilities of hotels. (pp. 5–6)

3. Review the four steps of the risk management process and explain how risk management benefits a business. (pp. 6–15)

4. List hotel security requirements and discuss how lodging safety and security considerations have changed over the years. (pp. 16–17)

5. Describe major loss events involving hotels. (pp. 17–19)

1

Security and Safety in the Lodging Industry

LODGING PROPERTY STAFF, managers, and owners have a wide range of security and safety responsibilities. Protecting guests, employees, and other people from crimes and injuries is one crucial concern. Securing the physical assets of the business, including inventories, equipment, and the building itself, from theft or other loss is also important. Awareness is also needed of the potential legal requirements and liabilities that the business may face.

The importance of all of these issues necessitates the use of a comprehensive risk management approach to safety and security. In such an approach, the selection of appropriate loss control methods (such as locking systems, alarm systems, lighting systems, and many others) is complemented by risk avoidance and risk transfer activities (such as insurance purchases). Taking such a comprehensive approach enables hospitality businesses to be well-prepared to deal with any security and safety issues that may arise. As the saying goes, proper preparation prevents poor performance!

With the variety of lodging products on the market, the diverse physical settings in which they operate, and the various legal and political systems throughout the world, a "one size fits all" approach to hotel security and safety is neither possible nor recommended. This chapter discusses a number of potential areas of concern in safety and security, and some of the actions hotel managers can take to address them.

Risk Management: The Business Case

The business case for investing in risk management is a very strong one; so much so that managers should look at such expenditures as investments rather than simply as expenses. At both the corporate and the property level, it is essential for managers to recognize that prudent risk management is the foundation upon which a good business is built.

Many risk management activities focus on the protection of the **physical assets** and **human assets** associated with the business. Multi-million-dollar hotels must be designed and managed to protect their physical assets from damage by everything from storms to arson. Should damage occur, there needs to be a means of financing the repair/replacement of these assets. A hotel's human assets must also be protected. The daily operation of the business needs to be done in a manner that provides a safe work environment for employees. An important workplace benefit and protection for employees is the health insurance and other types of employee benefits provided for them by the hotel (some of which are mandated by government).

A farsighted approach to risk management also takes into account the legal elements involved in running a business. There are many laws that hotels need to comply with in the course of daily operations. While the penalties for legal noncompliance are usually monetary, they can also involve penalties that hamper a hotel's ability to do business. In unusual cases, there is even the potential for criminal charges. A hotel must also be mindful of the possibility of a lawsuit from a dissatisfied guest or business partner. Even if a lawsuit is defended successfully, the expenses can be considerable.

The magnitude of the potential financial losses that may occur if security and safety issues are not dealt with effectively means that there is a general operational benefit to having effective risk management. In practical terms, this means that the potential for security- or safety-related incidents and losses to disrupt the business have been identified and actions taken to prevent them or to reduce their severity. Examples of these actions range from the installation and maintenance of fire protection and locking systems to having emergency plans in place to cope with severe weather events or even terrorism. Managers and owners can sleep at night more easily when they know that a good risk management program is in place.

It is relatively easy to identify risk-related items on the financial statement. These expenditures include security staff (and lifeguards), a number of insurance payments for both the physical and human assets (including property insurance and workers' compensation), and some maintenance costs (such as elevator maintenance contracts, trimming palm fronds and coconuts for properties in tropical locales, and snow removal for properties in northern regions). In addition, there are a number of costs incurred in the construction of a hotel's physical assets that clearly are aimed toward loss reduction (such as the money spent for fire sprinkler systems, security cameras, and guestroom locking systems).

In addition to the direct costs associated with loss reduction, it also needs to be recognized that risk management can indirectly influence revenue and profits. For example, a number of customers require minimum safety and security levels in order to do business with a hotel (those employed by the federal government, for instance). In a worst-case scenario, a major safety or security incident can result in large amounts of lost business—either due to resulting damage to the facility or due to adverse publicity. Other indirect costs include the time spent coping with the media and reassuring the public as the result of a security or safety incident at the property. The monetary value of such indirect factors is not easy to quantify on a financial statement but it is very real. Continuing to invest in loss prevention programs can seem unnecessary, since incidents rarely occur. Yet a major value of these programs can be in what does *not* occur.

On the other hand, savvy risk management can yield an indirect benefit, especially among guests who are security-conscious. Although electronic locking systems, surveillance devices, fire protection equipment, and other security-oriented features are designed to prevent losses, they may also attract additional business from those who are concerned about their safety and privacy.[1] Hotels that are able to cater to the unique security needs of guests whose careers are in the fields of politics, sports, and entertainment may find themselves doing a lot of business with such guests.

Individual guests and meetings and convention groups may also have other safety and security concerns that go beyond the basic expectations. For example, some guests do not want to stay in ground-floor rooms whose doors open directly to the outside, while others do not want to be on upper floors in high-rise buildings because of evacuation concerns. In addition, the safety and security provisions found in hotels can vary substantially in different regions of the world. In South Korea, for example, the guestrooms in some hotels are equipped with smoke hoods for guests to use when evacuating the hotel because of a fire; some of these guestrooms also have an evacuation harness and rope for guests to use to lower themselves to the ground, should some emergency (such as a fire blocking their normal exit from the guestroom) make it necessary for them to exit the room via a sliding glass door or window.[2] Smoke hoods can be found in hotels in China as well. These are not safety features that are found in U.S. hotels.

The broader issue of social responsibility must also be taken into account when considering issues of security and safety. The history of hotels shows they were places of security and safety for travelers. Hotels do more than just deliver services; they are a home away from home for travelers, a place of employment and even identity for staff, and an element of identity and pride for the local community. An illustrative (and extreme) example of a hotel demonstrating social responsibility can be seen in the movie *Hotel Rwanda*, which chronicles the efforts of hotel general manager Paul Rusesabagina to shelter not only his guests and staff but also refugees during the Rwandan Genocide.[3]

Security and Safety: An Ongoing (and Ever-Changing) Concern

> *In an age when hotel and guest security is paramount, it is unfathomable to think that hotel guestrooms at one time had no locks on their doors whatsoever. Even more unimaginable is the fact that most travelers were unable to afford a private room, and so they slept in a common room and shared a bed with one or more snoring strangers…. The concept of using locks with keys to secure private hotel rooms was introduced in 1829, but it took many years before those metal contraptions were accepted as a means of safeguarding personal effects and even one's life.*[4]

Security and safety concerns at hotels are not new—many of them have been around since the earliest days of hotels. These hazards are similar to the ones that people face while in their homes, while in their workplaces, and while running errands or enjoying themselves. However, hotel guests often find themselves especially vulnerable because of being in unfamiliar surroundings and having cash or other valuable assets in their possession, while often being in a "celebratory" mood.

For hotels, concerns about loss prevention start with the potential losses that guests may face. To better provide for the physical safety of guests while in their guestrooms, the locking systems for guestrooms have evolved from simple locks with metal keys to quite sophisticated electronic locks. In addition, hotels have responded to guests' desires to secure their assets in the guestroom by providing in-room safes. Many of these safes have been modified so that personal computers can be secured and, in some instances, even charged while in the safe. Food safety is another area of increased attention as management seeks to provide a safer and higher-quality food and beverage experience for guests. Better workplace safety programs and equipment, and better management of injuries and illnesses have all contributed to a reduction in employee injuries and improved working conditions in hotels. Finally, the combination of better technology and procedures has led to a significant reduction in the number and seriousness of hotel fires.

Even as these positive steps have been taken, new issues have emerged. *Legionella* bacteria (the cause of Legionnaires' Disease) were first identified in a hotel in 1976. Subsequent years have revealed that *Legionella* bacteria exist in many settings in addition to hotels. Incidences of terrorism have increased in the past few decades, and among the targets of terrorism have been hotels in major cities across the globe. In recent years, hotels have been chosen by criminal elements as locations for the manufacture of methamphetamines. Hotels have also been affected by outbreaks of SARS (Severe Acute Respiratory Syndrome), swine flu, and food poisoning, either directly or indirectly. Most recently, the spread of bedbugs in a number of locations (including some hotels) has surfaced as another threat. Each of these emerging issues represents potential new losses and requires the development of new methods of management.

In addition to their efforts to reduce and eliminate security/safety issues and losses for guests, hotels must also be aware of the potential property losses and legal liabilities that they face. Theft of hotel property by guests, employees, and other parties is a real concern, as is damage from natural disasters. In most states, innkeepers face legal liability if they fail to provide "reasonable care" for the protection of their guests and their guests' invitees. Additionally, innkeepers may be held responsible for injuries to guests caused by their employees in the course of their employment. Each year, innkeepers pay millions of dollars in court judgments and out-of-court settlements as a result of negligence claims. An understanding of fundamental legal principles is necessary in order to avoid legal exposure.[5]

In order to be ready to deal with all of these issues, a hotel must implement a risk management process that identifies and prepares for all foreseeable risks.

The Risk Management Process

Author Stephen Rushmore sums up risk management this way:

> One of the most important aspects of owning and operating a hotel is minimizing the various physical and liability risks associated with this type of business. Risk management is the process of evaluating a hotel's risk exposure and developing strategies for mitigating it. It incorporates a program for reducing exposure, supplemented by insurance protection should an incident occur. Hotel owners and operators would be far better off if they could eliminate all the possibilities of an incident occurring on their properties. Since this is not always possible, particularly incidents

they have no control over, adequate insurance protection provides a way to reduce exposure to a financial loss.[6]

Risk management is the protection of people and assets through the identification and management of the risks a business faces. The goal of the risk management process is to achieve the most economical use of resources to minimize or control risk. As hospitality businesses have grown in size, the field of risk management has responded to provide solutions to the wide variety of complex security and safety issues that can arise at lodging properties. Large hotel chains employ staff members who are devoted solely to risk management. Smaller operations that rely more on contract risk management services need to be knowledgeable purchasers of these services.

Four Steps of the Risk Management Process

The four steps in the risk management process are identification of risk, assessment of potential losses, selection of proper risk management instruments, and finalizing and implementing the plan (see Exhibit 1).

The goal of risk management is to reduce to acceptable levels the company's exposure to risk. This doesn't mean that the lowest theoretical levels can be achieved, but that the hotel has taken responsible action to safeguard the economic survival of the hotel should an unfortunate or even tragic event occur. By taking a responsible and logical approach to risk management, businesses can avoid potentially catastrophic levels of loss and keep the overall cost of risk management at reasonable levels.

Exhibit 1   The Risk Management Process

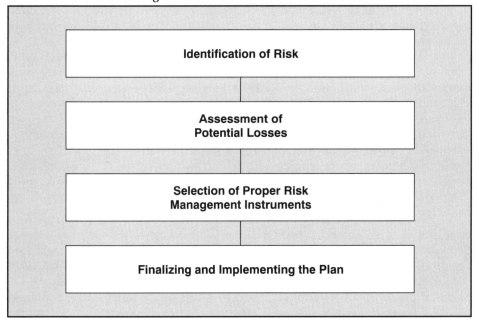

Identification of Risk

Assessment of Potential Losses

Selection of Proper Risk Management Instruments

Finalizing and Implementing the Plan

Identification of Risk. The risk management process begins with an **identification of risk** that involves not only the people who may be vulnerable but also the assets that may be subject to loss and the factors that may increase the probability and severity of loss.

Standardized checklists, walk-through audits, and balance sheets can assist in identifying physical assets. All such assets should be identified and their value established. Various options exist to establish value, including cost, book value (cost less depreciation), and replacement cost. Consideration of possible losses of cash and receivables should also be part of a property analysis.

Hospitality firms also have a major investment in people. These human assets are at risk in several ways. Some people, such as the hotel's owner or its world-renowned chef, might be particularly critical to the ongoing success of the business. Their injury or death could severely affect the hotel. Other individuals, although possibly less critical to the business, are still subject to injury or illness that could lead to operating difficulties, decreased morale, and increased costs for insurance or workers' compensation programs.

Businesses also need to recognize the potential risk to income and profits. For example, a hotel that experiences a fire may not only lose physical assets and incur injuries to employees; it is also likely to face a loss of income (and profits) during the time necessary to rebuild and reopen following the fire. Income losses during this time could be severe enough to threaten the hotel's survival even if the physical and human losses are fully compensated.

Perils and hazards. Once the assets of a hotel are identified, the next step is to determine what factors might contribute to the potential loss of those assets. The factors that might cause a loss are referred to as **perils;** the factors that might create or increase the chances of loss are known as **hazards.** Fire, for example, is a peril common to all hospitality businesses. Failure to regularly and properly clean the ductwork in kitchen ventilating equipment is a hazard resulting from poor maintenance procedures.

Peril identification is relatively straightforward. A major challenge occurs when new perils emerge or when the perception of perils on the part of the community changes. For example, in the 1970s the discovery of the *Legionella* bacteria in a hotel cooling tower resulted in the introduction of a new peril associated with the operation of this and similar equipment. As far as physical assets are concerned, the peril of global climate change in the twenty-first century is clearly on the minds of those who operate low-lying coastal resorts.

While peril exposure is widespread—and in some instances unavoidable—hospitality managers can do a great deal to manage hazards. For example, good maintenance practices in cooling tower operation can reduce or eliminate the *Legionella* hazard.

Assessment of Potential Losses. Once the risk management process has identified perils and hazards, it is necessary for managers to engage in two activities: the **assessment of potential losses**—to include the severity of impact as well as the probability of occurrence—and the determination of **risk comfort levels.** For a coastal property, the severity of impact of a category 4 hurricane is extremely high; the frequency, fortunately, is low. The assessment of potential losses process can be relatively straightforward, especially for small operations. The maximum potential losses, or costs, can be estimated by considering such factors as the value of the property, the amount of a day's receipts (when considering theft losses), the legal system (for example, limits on innkeeper's liability for guest belongings), and the cost of the insurance premium.

However, the assessment of potential losses can have its complications. Determination of liability losses in cases where someone has been injured represents a larger uncertainty for both small and large operations. For large corporations with hotels in multiple locations, the assessment of potential losses also becomes more difficult. It involves the consideration of severity of losses (What is the magnitude of potential losses?) along with the frequency of these losses (How often are they expected to occur?), coupled with the complexity of dealing with multiple locations.

Having assessed potential losses, hospitality managers (and owners) must then make some decisions related to risk comfort levels, or the amount of risk to be taken by the business. Management's risk-related comfort level involves the question of how much risk is too much risk. The answer to this question will vary depending on the individuals involved. Some investors are averse to risk and choose secure investments, while others invest their funds in highly speculative ventures where the potential returns (and potential losses) are much greater. In some instances, a false comfort level—caused by ignorance—results in an unknowing assumption of risk. This is a very dangerous situation; ideally, the comfort level has been achieved via a clear understanding on the part of management and ownership of what is at risk, the factors that place these items at risk, and the probability and likely cost of a loss.

Many companies have saved untold sums by looking past first impressions to seriously weigh all of the risk-related variables at stake. For example, one franchisor was considering offering a franchise to a large and successful hotel in a major U.S. market. It appeared to be a sound business decision—the hotel had existing contracts providing a large base of group business, an excellent location, and, overall, was a very attractive business venture—yet the franchisor ultimately walked away from the deal due to risk issues. Why? The hotel did not have a fire sprinkler system installed (as an existing building, the code stated it did not need to comply with the same standards as new construction) and the owner was unwilling to install such a system. The franchisor felt it could not jeopardize itself by having a major hotel fly its flag without fire sprinklers. The risk was too great.

Selection of Proper Risk Management Instruments. After identifying the risks an organization is exposed to, managers must determine how to handle those risks. One important way to deal with risks is via loss control. Risks can also be avoided completely in some instances, or they can be insured, self-insured, or passed on contractually to another party (other than an insurance company). It is often the case that responses to certain combinations of perils and hazards involve a combination of actions, including loss control, avoidance, risk reduction, risk assumption, loss financing, and shifting loss.

Loss control. Loss control involves actions to reduce the frequency and/or the severity of the various losses that can occur. Effective loss control requires excellent knowledge of perils and how they may affect the hotel. For example, in order to deal with loss control regarding fires, managers need to understand key issues associated with fires, such as points of origin, physical characteristics, flame spread, and elements of interactions with physical assets and human beings. Knowledge is also required of various hazards that increase the hotel's fire risk, such as the role that physical structure and design plays in creating fire hazards, as well as the contribution of operating techniques to increasing this risk.

Loss control professionals recognize that actions to address loss control will involve the reduction of frequency and the reduction of severity. Some risk issues lend themselves to both actions, while others are affected by only one. Loss control activities during the past several decades, for example, have reduced both the frequency and severity of hotel fires. On the other hand, while no risk manager can reduce the likelihood of a hurricane at a given location, actions by managers can reduce the severity of losses that occur when a hurricane hits. In all instances, the key elements of an effective loss control program embrace both education and training. Employees must be educated concerning workplace hazards, and constantly trained to respond appropriately to them.

Loss control actions are sometimes grouped into those involving physical factors and those involving human behavior. Loss control involving physical factors focuses on the elimination or reduction of unsafe physical conditions through redesign or modification of the physical elements themselves—such as the installation of electronic locking systems. Instructing housekeeping staff about guest-room security procedures deals with human behavior; it is an unseen loss control initiative and requires an ongoing managerial effort. By contrast, actions involving physical factors are visible evidence of a loss control program and may not need a significant ongoing managerial effort. Physical modifications may continue to function long after employee training about risk is forgotten. However, not all risks can be managed by physical measures alone. That is why ongoing staff training in this area is so important.

Most loss control experts agree that, once the property's physical hazards have been identified and mitigated, mature loss control programs should focus on identifying and modifying unsafe staff behaviors. Behavior-based safety training is based on the premise that unsafe behaviors are the root cause of most accidents—with some estimates as high as 85 percent. An effective behavior-based program has two critical elements: (1) top management support, and (2) goals that are clearly defined and embraced by both management and staff.

The easiest approach to behavior observation and modification is to incorporate the behavior observation cycle (see Exhibit 2). This tool can be easily taught to the line-employee members of the hotel's safety committee by role-playing, practical application, and mentoring. For example, two managers on the safety committee might role-play a peer-to-peer safety observation. For the first role-play, the "employee" involved in the unsafe behavior might readily agree with the arguments put forth by the "employee" performing the part of the safety observer and decide to stop the unsafe behavior. For the second role-play, the "employee" might push back, using typical excuses: "I've always done it this way"; "I'm too busy to do what you ask"; "You're not my boss." This gives the "safety observer" a chance to counter each objection calmly and rationally,

Exhibit 2   Behavior Observation Cycle

Managers and others can use the behavior observation cycle to improve worker safety at their properties. The behavior cycle consists of five steps:

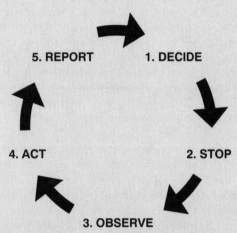

1. **Decide** where in the hotel you are going to observe staff members at work.

2. **Stop** out of your normal work flow and focus your attention on the staff member(s).

3. **Observe** staff member behavior while routine work is being performed.

4. **Act.** If a staff member is performing the work safely, reinforce that behavior by praising the employee. Conversely, if the employee is working unsafely, take the employee aside and explain your concerns. Do not leave until you have received the employee's buy-in and commitment to stop the unsafe behavior. If the employee pushes back, do not engage in an argument but seek out the employee's immediate supervisor for support.

5. **Report.** Make some kind of record of the behavior observation and the inter-action. If the unsafe behavior is observed during subsequent observations, appropriate action should be taken (retraining, disciplinary measures, etc.).

and show that, if compliance cannot be obtained, the last resort is to notify the employee's supervisor.

Another portion of behavior observation training might involve breaking into small groups to visit various parts of the hotel—for example, the kitchen, laundry area, and guestrooms (to observe room attendants in action). Each group should be accompanied by a manager. After observing staff members at work (usually for about fifteen minutes or so), the groups can return to home base to discuss any unsafe staff behaviors they might have witnessed and come up with suggestions for better work practices. Managers involved in the observations should pass along the groups' suggestions to the appropriate managers or supervisors for follow-up.

Avoidance. Avoidance is taking a preventive loss control action because the risk associated with a certain activity is unacceptable or because the action necessary to avoid the risk is so readily achievable that it would be foolish not to take the action. For example, removing diving boards from swimming pools is an avoidance action, to cut back on the chance of guests and others injuring themselves at the pool. Not serving alcohol at events where minors might be present would be another avoidance action relating to liability. It is also possible that avoidance might be undertaken for activities other than those having unacceptable risks. For example, the purchase of pre-cut chicken parts by a hotel restaurant eliminates the potential for employees to cut themselves preparing certain chicken dishes for cooking. This avoidance tactic might result in a more economical way of doing business, with the economics driven, in part, by reductions in workplace injury costs.

Risk reduction. Risk reduction focuses on reducing the severity of a loss or the likelihood of it occurring. For example, fire sprinklers are used to reduce the risk of fire and the potential for injuries or lost lives.

Risk assumption. Risk assumption means that few or no loss control actions are taken because the risk associated with a certain activity is very low. While this may mean the potential costs are low and no loss control action is considered warranted, it could also mean the nature of the risk is such that no action can be taken. For example, hotel managers would probably take little loss control action related to the common cold. They also would take little loss control action related to a meteor striking the property. In the first instance, although the frequency is high, the severity is slight; in the second instance, the severity is extremely high, but the frequency is, fortunately, extremely low. In both instances, the risk is assumed.

Assuming a risk may still require some method of financing. However, because of the nature of various assumed risks, the expenses in these areas may not even be accounted for as risk-related expenses. Towels stolen from guestrooms, for example, may only show up as linen shortages, and the cost of replacement may be treated the same as towels discarded due to wear or damage.

Loss financing. Even when loss control efforts are applied, risk—and therefore loss—is generally not completely eliminated. Therefore, there needs to be some means available to pay for a loss when it occurs, and insurance, or **loss (risk) financing,** is a very common method.

Those managers involved in hotel operations, especially at the department-head level and below, may find themselves relatively uninvolved in insurance purchases. However, they have a responsibility to their employees and guests as well as to their role as stewards of the facility and its equipment, so, even though they are not responsible for purchasing insurance, they still should be aware of the types and limitations of insurance coverage. In deciding whether to purchase an insurance plan with large deductibles (or other forms of **retentions**), hotel owners must take into account their own risk comfort levels and any linking coverage with other properties they may own. For hotel chains, insurance decisions typically are made at the corporate level to take advantage of economies of scale. Another reason to leave insurance decisions to specialists at the corporate office is that the language of insurance can be daunting and viewed as relatively arcane by property-level managers without familiarity with this field.

Despite the remoteness of the insurance purchase decision from the duties of most managers, managers should not assume that they can get by without any knowledge of insurance. Knowledge of the fundamentals of insurance and claims management will benefit managers in their business careers. First, as prospective managers are receiving their education, they do not know what the future holds; those with entrepreneurial goals may quickly find themselves as owners who must make insurance decisions for their personal business ventures. In any event, most managers will likely find themselves at times working for owners who will want to rely on them for recommendations about insurance.

Shifting loss. Shifting loss is an attempt to shift the risk from one party to another by legal contract. This involves a number of common business activities, such as contractual agreements (including leasing and subcontracting). In addition, risk is often transferred via clauses in other contracts (examples being hold-harmless agreements, indemnity agreements, and requirements for insurance purchases). Since both parties to contracts will be attempting to shift risk to the other, awareness of risk issues in contracts is an important element of a good risk management program.

In addition, the provisions of various laws of innkeeping at the state level limit the potential loss for hotels in some situations—in effect shifting the loss for the hotel. For example, if the Hollyhock Hotel hires Joe's Plumbing to make some repairs and Joe drops a wrench and injures himself, the hotel would not be held liable under state law.

Finalizing and Implementing the Plan. Each of the risk management practices just discussed should be integrated into a comprehensive risk management plan for the property. Prior to its implementation, the plan should be studied by management and legal consultants. Management should be comfortable with the specific actions that are outlined for loss control and avoidance, risk reduction, the levels of risk assumption that are made, the proposed levels of insurance, and the approaches outlined to shift loss. Legal consultants should review the proposed plan in light of existing labor agreements; local, state, and federal regulations; and general legal compliance. Once the plan is finalized, the real work of risk management begins—that of implementing the plan.

In large corporations, there is a full-time risk management department that helps guide the implementation process. It brings particular skills to this process in areas such as loss prevention training programs, knowledge of the insurance marketplace, and the details of insurance purchase. Smaller operations may find some of this responsibility is in the hands of consultants or brokers, which is why their selection should be based on industry experience as well as insurance knowledge. However, even with a strong corporate staff, much of the responsibility for implementation lies in the hands of hotel managers at the property level. For example, it is typically the property's general manager (or the general manager's designee) who ensures that security policies are developed, understood, and followed. The general manager is also in a position to provide feedback to the risk management department when elements of the corporate program are difficult to follow. The implementation of any plan also requires appropriate adjustments to local conditions and situations. For example, due to local regulations regarding security guard qualifications and training, it may not be financially feasible for a hotel to have its own security guard force—even if the corporate policy prohibits contract service.

One potential problem with risk management efforts is neglect. Once actions are implemented and success is achieved, it is sometimes easy to neglect ongoing fine-tuning and re-training to keep the program successful. The result is that loss-producing situations recur—along with additional costs. Risk management is ongoing, not a "do it and forget it" effort. That is why the most effective programs take a proactive approach.

Benefits of Risk Management to a Business

When exploring the benefits of risk management for a hospitality operation, discussions should include benefits that exist pre- and post-loss, as well as direct and indirect benefits.

Pre-Loss Benefits. The pre-loss benefits of a risk management program include the reduced cost of risk, reduced anxiety, and increased efficiency in meeting externally imposed obligations.

Reduced cost of risk. By implementing a good risk management program, companies are able to minimize the cost of risk—the combined costs of losses incurred, insurance, and risk management measures to reduce losses.

Reduced anxiety. By having a risk management program in place, management can be assured that losses will not be catastrophic, consequently allowing them to focus on the business itself. This provides an overall reduction in worry for the hotel's owners, managers, and employees.

Increased efficiency in meeting externally imposed obligations. A well-run risk management program will ensure that externally imposed obligations—ranging from government regulations to contractual requirements—are met in a cost-effective manner. For example, risk managers at chain hotels might arrange to purchase insurance coverage for multiple hotels rather than for each hotel individually, thus saving costs. Since elevator inspections are required by most building codes, risk managers might negotiate cost-effective contracts with outside vendors for these services.

Post-Loss Benefits. The post-loss benefits of a risk management program include the survival of the business, continued operation, stable earnings, continued growth, and social benefits.

The survival of the business. In the face of catastrophic events, it is possible that hospitality businesses without sufficient risk management programs may be unable to sustain themselves. It is not unusual, for example, for an independent restaurant with insufficient insurance to be forced out of business by a major fire. In other instances, an event such as a severe and well-publicized bedbug infestation may result in a slow strangulation of a lodging business due to negative public perceptions. A good risk management program can help a business survive either type of catastrophic event.

Continued operation. Effective risk management programs will ensure that a business has enough resources to keep operating, if at all possible, despite a catastrophic event.

Stable earnings. Risk management is particularly important when dealing with the financial community and outside investors. Even if a hotel can, in the long run, survive a series of hits, the resulting erratic earnings that may occur can cause a lowered credit rating in the financial community, which could jeopardize the hotel's continued operation, growth, and even survival. Therefore, it is prudent for managers to purchase business interruption insurance. Sold as an add-on to a property insurance policy or a package policy, this coverage offers protection in the event that a catastrophe (such as a fire) causes the hotel to close temporarily.

Business interruption insurance covers: (1) operating expenses such as rent, electricity, staff wages, etc., that occur even though the hotel is not open to guests; and (2) lost income. The price of business interruption insurance is based on the likelihood of a fire (or some other disaster) damaging the hotel. Other factors that influence the price include the hotel's location, mitigation measures, and **probable maximum loss (PML).** PML is usually defined as the anticipated value of the largest loss that could result from the destruction of the hotel and the loss of its use.

Property underwriting decisions are based on a PML survey. Much of this survey is completed by the property owner, and it is vital that this information be complete and accurate. The rating system automatically defaults to the "worst" category if the information is missing. For instance, if the information for the roof system is missing, the rating program defaults to "wood shingles," which can have a large detrimental effect on the property's insurance premium.

Continued growth. A good risk management program can help a business continue to grow after a catastrophic event occurs. Unless a hotel can regroup and rebuild—sometimes both literally and figuratively—in the aftermath of a catastrophic event, its ability to achieve continued growth can be seriously impaired.

Social benefits. A business's risk management program can contribute to the general welfare of society as well as to the business itself. Via wages and benefits received for their work, a hotel's employees make a living and receive medical and other care. A hotel's physical facilities and its profits are sources of tax revenue for the community. If a hotel can recover more quickly from a catastrophic event because of its risk management program, and therefore (to name just one social benefit) avoid laying off staff members, the community as a whole will benefit from the hotel's risk management program.

Direct and Indirect Benefits. A direct benefit of a risk management program is the reduction in loss expenses that the hotel incurs; a good risk management program can cut down on the number of loss events and therefore loss expenses. An indirect benefit of risk management comes in the form of better relationships with suppliers, customers, and employees. For example, companies that provide a safe workplace not only have the direct benefits of reduced workers' compensation costs but may also experience the indirect benefits of lower turnover and higher job satisfaction among its employees.

Hotel Security Requirements

The good news regarding crime in the United States is that the rate of occurrence for almost all crimes has declined from the year 2000 to the present.[7] The rate declines have been in the 7 to 10 percent range for many crime categories, and the actual number of crimes has declined in almost all categories. The lodging industry has the potential to benefit from this overall drop in the crime rate. At the same time, lodging industry growth has meant that there are more hotels and more guests in hotels, so even a decreasing national crime rate does not necessarily mean fewer crimes against guests or hotels.

Large hotels often have full-time staff devoted to security and safety management and have more resources to devote to addressing loss prevention in their design and operation than do smaller hotels. Hotels of all sizes are often franchised and therefore benefit from corporate input about safety and security issues and operational procedures. A variety of lodging markets have emerged or have experienced robust growth in recent years, including casino, limited-service, extended-stay, and boutique hotels. Safety and security programs need to be customized for each of these types of hotels.

To address the wide range of security issues and property types requires managers to pay attention to many details. The following list indicates general elements that should be considered for inclusion in any property's security program:

- Locks and key control
- Guestroom security
- Control of persons on premises
- Perimeter control
- Protection of assets (money on hand, guests' assets, equipment, inventories)
- Emergency procedures
- Communications
- Security records

Occasionally, attempts are made to introduce uniform security standards for the lodging industry. While such efforts are undoubtedly well-intentioned, the lodging industry understandably tends to view them as unrealistic and ultimately counterproductive. Instead, each hotel company should develop or adapt security programs to meet its own unique security needs. If necessary, hotel managers should seek outside assistance from local law enforcement agencies or qualified lodging industry security consultants to address the security issues at their hotels.

Lodging Safety and Security: Today and Tomorrow

Lodging safety and security is a rapidly changing field, especially when it comes to safety and security technology. No hotel manager working in the 1950s would have believed that a guestroom door lock would ever need batteries, or that a guestroom lock could change its combination automatically! A manager working in the 1990s would have been surprised to learn that in the near future a guest-room door could be unlocked by a guest without the guest touching the door. Smartphone, RFID, biometric, and facial recognition technologies are all in use at a limited number of hotels today, with more hotels likely to embrace this technology in the future. Not only has locking technology changed, but so too has its integration with other hotel functions, such as housekeeping.

In the 1970s, U.S. hotels experienced a number of catastrophic hotel fires. Few hotels had fire sprinklers and smoke detectors in the early 1970s, yet today these are found in the vast majority of U.S. hotels. Code changes, upgraded hotel company construction specifications, and an increased awareness of the risks associated with fires have resulted in a dramatic decrease in the number of U.S. hotel fires and their severity. Many hotels also took the further step of prohibiting smoking. In addition to reducing the fire risk, this measure took away the health risks associated with secondhand smoke for guests and employees, and reduced the costs associated with cleaning rooms.

It is safe to assume that guests, employees, lodging companies, and other stakeholders will continue to expect hotels to offer the latest in safety and security technology. Striving to address these expectations, while still providing the hospitality environment that is desired, will be challenging. At some point in the future will hotels adopt security measures similar to what air travelers face today? It seems unlikely, but a significant increase in terrorist incidents at hotels might trigger a significant increase in hotel security.

The lodging industry has a number of safety and security training materials available through AH&LA's Educational Institute, which also offers security certifications. It is expected that there will be increased efforts by the private sector to create hotel safety and security certifications as well. Increased efforts in the areas of code requirements and government regulation is also to be expected in the future. One example of current efforts to bolster model codes in the safety and security area is *NFPA 730: Guide for Premises Security.*[8]

Major Loss Events Involving Hotels

Hotels have been the scene of some major catastrophes over the years. These have at times involved a large loss of life as well as the destruction of valuable property. These types of events underscore the need for managers to make sure that they have good risk management programs in place at their hotels.

Fires

In 1946 there were 119 people killed at the Winecoff Hotel in Atlanta, Georgia, in the deadliest hotel fire in U.S. history. Many people were trapped in the hotel, since there was only one stairway to evacuate the fifteen-story building. Earlier in 1946, sixty-one people (many of them children) were killed at the La Salle Hotel in Chicago. Both of these fires resulted in changes in building codes and fire-fighting procedures.

In the 1980s there were a number of hotel fires that once again caused fire safety guidelines and codes to be reviewed and updated. The Las Vegas MGM

Grand fire in 1980 killed eighty-five people, due primarily to smoke inhalation. Also in 1980, the Stouffer's Inn in Harrison, New York, had a fire that killed twenty-six people. **Egress** issues as well as the lack of an adequate fire suppression system were noted in the accounts of these tragedies.

In 1982, a Hilton hotel in Houston had a fire limited to just one room that produced toxic smoke, resulting in the death of twelve people. Egress issues as well as hotel staff members who prevented information from being transmitted to the fire department were cited as contributing causes to this tragedy. In 1986, the Dupont Plaza Hotel in San Juan, Puerto Rico, experienced a fire that killed ninety-seven people and injured 140. Stored furniture provided the fuel for the fire, which was made worse by the lack of fire suppression equipment and by egress issues.

A major hotel fire at the Royal Jomtien Resort in Thailand in 1997 resulted in the death of ninety-one hotel guests and staff members. Leaking propane used for cooking was ignited and the resulting fire and smoke spread throughout the hotel. Lack of compartmentalization, egress issues, and the lack of a fire suppression system all contributed to this tragic event.

Not all hotel fires result in a large loss of life. In 2009, the nearly completed Mandarin Oriental Hotel in Beijing (part of the Television Cultural Center building) found itself in the path of a massive Chinese New Year fireworks display set off nearby; the fireworks started a fire that led to extensive damage to the building but only one death (one of the responding firefighters). In 2008, portions of the exterior of the Monte Carlo Hotel and Casino in Las Vegas suffered a fire that resulted in considerable damage and required closing the hotel for over two weeks. The fire was contained an hour after it began, and no one was hurt. Total losses due to the fire and loss of business were nearly $100 million.

Structural Failures

In 1981, the Hyatt Regency Hotel in Kansas City experienced the collapse of suspended walkways in the hotel's atrium. With 114 killed and 216 injured, this was the deadliest structural failure in U.S. history at the time (only surpassed by the collapse of the World Trade Center's Twin Towers in 2001). Investigators determined that the design of the walkways was faulty. Settlement costs are believed to be well in excess of $100 million. In 2011, MGM Resorts International announced that it planned to demolish the Harmon Hotel in Las Vegas before it ever opened for business, due to structural deficiencies that made it unsafe. The uncompleted Harmon cost the company $275 million in construction costs, with demolition costs expected to be $30 million more. As of this writing, the hotel still stands, unoccupied, as the legal wrangling over its fate continues.[9]

Earthquakes

Earthquakes can bring death and destruction to hotels. In the 2010 earthquake in Haiti, the Hôtel Montana, a popular tourist hotel, collapsed and injured or killed hundreds of people. In 2006, in the aftermath of an earthquake on the Big Island of Hawai'i, the Mauna Kea Beach Hotel was forced to close due to structural damage. It reopened in 2008 after spending $150 million on a major renovation.

Floods

Floods can devastate a hotel. In perhaps the most spectacular recent example, the Gaylord Opryland property in Nashville was flooded in May of 2010. The resulting damage closed the hotel for almost six months. The cost of repairing the flood damage was estimated to be in excess of $200 million, with other costs during the repair period amounting to almost $60 million.

Endnotes

1. T. W. Hilliard and S. Baloglu, "Safety and Security as Part of the Hotel Servicescape for Meeting Planners," *Journal of Convention & Event Tourism,* Vol. 9, Issue 1, 2008, pp. 15–34.

2. A video showing smoke hoods in use for a hotel evacuation in Korea can be found at http://www.youtube.com/watch?v=j2pviTIqtZM. A photo showing an evacuation rope in a Korean hotel can be found at http://www.bobmay.info/july022001.htm.

3. http://www.imdb.com/title/tt0395169/.

4. Stephen Rushmore and Carolyn Malone, "Keys and Hotel Security—From Metal to Plastic," *Cornell Quarterly,* December 1998, p. 91.

5. For readers desiring more information about hotel legal issues, see Jack P. Jefferies and Banks Brown, *Understanding Hospitality Law,* Fifth Edition (Lansing, Mich.: American Hotel & Lodging Educational Institute, 2010).

6. Stephen Rushmore, "Hotel Risk Management Is Critical," *Lodging Hospitality,* February 11, 2010.

7. http://www.disastercenter.com/crime/uscrime.htm; http://www.census.gov/compendia/statab/2011/tables/11s0302.pdf.

8. http://www.nfpa.org/catalog/product.asp?pid=73006&order%5Fsrc=B484.

9. http://www.reviewjournal.com/news/las-vegas/judge-gives-ok-demolish-harmon-hotel, July 19, 2012; http://www.nytimes.com/2013/01/23/us/unfinished-tower-in-las-vegas-is-symbol-of-a-reversal.html?_r=0.

 ## Key Terms

assessment of potential losses—An estimation of a lodging property's maximum potential losses, or costs, which can be calculated by considering such factors as the value of the property, the amount of a day's receipts (when considering theft losses), the legal system (for example, limits on innkeeper's liability for guest belongings), and the cost of the insurance premium.

avoidance—Taking a preventive loss-control action because the risk associated with a certain activity is unacceptable, or because the action necessary to avoid the risk is so readily achievable that it would be foolish not to take the action.

egress—A means of escape from a building or structure.

hazards—Factors that might create or increase the chances of loss.

human assets—The employees of a business.

identification of risk—The stage in the risk management process at which management identifies both the assets of the hotel that may be subject to loss and the relevant perils and hazards that may increase the probability and severity of loss.

loss control—Actions taken to reduce the frequency and/or the severity of various losses that might occur.

loss (risk) financing—The utilization of sources of funds to pay for losses; sources of funds can be classified as internal (for example, a retention program is established to use funds from within the organization to pay for losses) or external (a transfer program is established, generally through the purchase of insurance, to use funds from outside the organization to pay for losses).

perils—Factors that might cause a loss.

physical assets—An asset class that includes the hotel's inventories, equipment, and the building itself.

probable maximum loss (PML)—The anticipated value of the largest loss that could result from the destruction of the hotel and the loss of its use.

retentions—Those portions of an insurance claim that are paid by the insured party, rather than the insurance company.

risk assumption—Taking few or no loss control actions because the risk associated with a certain activity is very low or the assumed risks have small financial costs.

risk comfort levels—The magnitude and nature of risk that a hotel's management and investors are willing to accept.

risk management—The protection of corporate assets through the identification and management of the financial risks a corporation faces.

risk reduction—Efforts to reduce the severity of a loss or the likelihood of it occurring.

shifting loss—The attempt to transfer risk from one party to another by legal contract.

 Review Questions

1. What is the business case for investing in risk management?
2. What are some of the security and safety concerns that hotels face?
3. The risk management process consists of which four steps?
4. What is the difference between a hazard and a peril?
5. What are some actions a hotel can take to control its losses?
6. What are some of the benefits of risk management to a business?
7. What are some general elements that should be included in any hotel's security program?
8. What are some major loss events involving hotels?

Internet Sites

For more information, visit the following Internet sites. Remember that Internet addresses can change without notice. If the site is no longer there, you can use a search engine to look for additional sites.

AH&LA Educational Institute
www.ahlei.org

American Hotel & Lodging
  Association
www.ahla.com

American Society of Travel Agents
www.asta.org

International Association of Chiefs of
  Police
www.theiacp.org

International Association of Professional Security Consultants
www.iapsc.org

International Foundation for Protection Officers
www.ifpo.com

National Crime Prevention Council
www.ncpc.org

National Fire Protection Association
www.nfpa.org

National Institute of Justice
www.nij.gov

U.S. Department of State, Overseas
  Security Advisory Council
www.osac.gov

Chapter 2 Outline

Loss Prevention and the Law
    Legal Definitions
The Hotel's Duty to Protect Guests
    Reasonable Care Rule
    Acts of Hotel Employees
    Acts of Guests and Patrons
    Assault by Third Parties in Restrooms
    Assault by Third Parties in Hotel
        Parking Lots
    Acts by Third Parties at Hotel
        Entrances
The Hotel's Liability Regarding Guests'
    Property
    State Statutes Limiting Liability
    Unclaimed Property
    Liability for Handling Mail for Hotel
        Guests
    Liability for Automobiles of Guests
        and Others
The Hotel's Liability for Loss of Property of
    Non-Guests
    General Nature of Liability
    Bailments for Non-Guests
    Hotel Liability for Restaurant Patrons'
        Property
    Hotel Defenses to Liability Claims of
        Non-Guests

Competencies

1. Describe the American legal system and define basic legal terms. (pp. 23–27)

2. Summarize the meaning of reasonable care, describe how a hotel's duty to exercise reasonable care may not be delegated, and cite cases illustrating the reasonable care rule. (pp. 27–34)

3. Explain how a hotel might be held liable for the acts of its employees. (pp. 34–36)

4. Explain how the hotel might be held liable for injuries a guest receives at the hands of other guests, patrons, or third parties. (pp. 36–39)

5. Identify steps a hotel must take to limit its liability for loss of guest valuables, and cite cases illustrating a hotel's liability for guests' property. (pp. 39–44)

6. Explain how a hotel can limit its liability for loss of a guest's personal property other than valuables, and describe a hotel's liability if guest property disappears from a guest's room, hallways of the hotel, the hotel lobby, checkrooms, baggage rooms, and storerooms, or is lost by fire. (pp. 44–45)

7. Describe a hotel's liability with regard to unclaimed property, and summarize a hotel's liability for handling guests' mail. (p. 46)

8. Describe a hotel's liability for automobiles belonging to guests and explain the theory of bailment. (pp. 46–48)

9. Describe a hotel's liability for loss of a non-guest's property. (pp. 48–51)

2

Legal Aspects of Loss Prevention

THE LEGAL ASPECTS of loss prevention is a very large topic, so this chapter can only provide an overview of legal issues of importance to hotels. Within the United States, there are numerous federal, state, and local laws and regulations pertaining to loss prevention that are applicable to hotels. This chapter addresses primarily those laws and regulations that pertain to a hotel's relationship with its guests. After a brief introduction to the American legal system and an explanation of basic legal terms, the chapter takes a look at a hotel's duty to protect its guests before moving on to discuss the hotel's liability regarding the property of guests as well as non-guests (those individuals who are on the property but are not registered guests—patrons of the hotel's restaurant, for example). While the concepts and legal cases discussed in this chapter will be helpful to hotel owners and managers, obviously company attorneys should be consulted if an incident with legal ramifications occurs at a hotel.

Loss Prevention and the Law

Every state has its own **statutes** and court rulings on innkeeper laws. These laws deal with the rights and responsibilities of innkeepers and can be fairly extensive. Although such laws almost invariably deal with the same general topics, they can differ from state to state. Lodging management and security personnel should read the innkeeper statutory laws of their state. The understanding gained from this information can contribute to the development of a more effective security program.

Also, in determining what elements might be included in a particular security program, it may be wise to review recent court and jury decisions that deal with hotel security matters. Many recent cases have addressed one or more of the following issues: locking systems, key control, security personnel on the premises, lighting, door viewports, police liaison, crime in the community, security efforts tailored to the needs of a specific property, and the involvement of employees as the hotel's "eyes and ears" with regard to the security function. These areas of concern are frequently stressed in depositions by expert witnesses for the plaintiff.

Before diving into the legal aspects of loss prevention, it is important to gain a basic understanding of the workings of the American legal system. In

Understanding Hospitality Law, Jack P. Jefferies and Banks Brown provide a brief explanation of this system:

> The laws governing hotels and motels in the United States are myriad. They include many common law rules that have evolved from early English judicial decisions and social customs. Law derived from such sources is known as **common law** or the common law system. It was developed in England during the Middle Ages as **courts** sought to resolve disputes between individuals by applying generally accepted rules and principles of justice. As society evolved from the feudal into the industrial era, courts under the common law system continued to apply many of the rules and principles enunciated by courts in earlier, similar cases. Within this developing common law system, special common law rules regarding the rights and liabilities of innkeepers and their guests also evolved. This special body of rules applicable to innkeepers under the common law resulted from what was considered to be the public nature of the occupation....
>
> Examples of old common law rules uniquely applicable to innkeepers are: (i) innkeepers as operators of public places must as a general rule provide available accommodations to travelers who are willing and able to pay for such accommodations, and (ii) an innkeeper under common law would be **liable** as an **insurer** for the loss of guests' property brought to the inn, with certain exceptions.
>
> Throughout the years, the common law rules governing innkeepers have been refined by court decisions, and modified by federal, state, and municipal legislation and administrative agency rules and regulations, which, in turn, have been further defined by federal, state, and municipal court decisions and administrative agency rulings.
>
> In addition, hotels and motels today are subject to numerous federal, state, and municipal statutes and administrative rules and regulations governing a multitude of subjects never covered by common law. These governing statutes, rules, and regulations have, in turn, been further defined by federal, state, and municipal court decisions and administrative agency rulings....
>
> It is important for the layperson to note ... that since the United States is a federation of states, each state through its state court system develops its own case law and judicial precedent on issues involving state laws. State courts generally decide issues involving local and state laws and disputes between citizens of the state. In this respect each state court system is independent of other state jurisdictions. Thus, for example, the decision of the highest state court in California may be binding on lower courts in California, but is not binding on the courts in another state, such as New York. This is true even though a New York court, in interpreting a New York State statute, could indeed look at a California State court decision interpreting a similar California statute and find the California court decision reasoning to be "persuasive" or "interesting" or "of no effect whatsoever" in New York. It is thus that a New York court can reach a different result from California courts on the same general issue. Consequently, when you become concerned with a legal problem, you must use care to consult, or have your lawyer consult, the state and local laws in the state in which your hotel is located, as well as federal law.

The layperson should also be aware that the federal court system includes 94 district courts and a court of **appeals** for each of the 13 judicial circuits, and the Supreme Court of the United States.... Federal courts generally decide disputes involving federal laws and disputes between citizens from different states (subject to certain jurisdictional requirements). One federal circuit court of appeals may reach a decision different from that of another federal circuit court of appeals on the same type of legal problem. It is left to the U.S. Supreme Court to determine which of the circuit courts is correct (or to decide to leave the different decisions of both circuit courts standing).

This is an oversimplification in your introduction to the laws governing hotels, motels, and restaurants, but it is intended to help you understand why a decision in California may differ from a court decision in New York, Iowa, or Hawaii, and understand why two federal circuit courts render what appear to be directly contrary decisions on apparently the same question when the courts are both part of the same federal court system.

It is important that the layperson also recognize that the law is a continually changing body of rules and cannot be viewed as frozen in time and space. For example, common law rules established a standard of absolute liability of the hotel operator for the loss of a guest's property. The state legislatures in most states then limited this common law liability, often to $500. In some states, the legislatures then increased the amount of this liability to more than $500. Moreover, some state courts today appear to exercise a quasi-legislative function in redefining and modifying the meaning of said statutes, with the effect of increasing liability. Many other laws (common law, statutory, and regulatory) affecting hotel and motel operators are also undergoing constant evolution and change over the years.

Thus, from both a historic and national perspective, the laws affecting hotels and motels present a slowly changing kaleidoscope of legislation, regulations, rules, and court and administrative decisions affecting the legal rights, responsibilities, and liabilities of hotel and motel operators.[1]

The frequency of all types of lawsuits is increasing annually, and hotels, motels, inns, clubs, restaurants, and resorts are not immune from this danger. Management cannot afford to ignore the financial ramifications associated with costly settlements. The hospitality industry, with its special emphasis on people and personal services, represents an area where the possibility for litigation is very great.

Legal Definitions

Generally, in a suit alleging negligence, the plaintiff must show that the defendant innkeeper had a duty to use reasonable care to protect the plaintiff or victim from foreseeable acts; that the defendant failed to perform this duty; that this failure was the proximate cause of the incident; and that the plaintiff actually suffered loss or injury.

The central legal issue is that innkeepers owe a duty of care to all persons on their properties. Failure to meet this duty may result in security-related liability.

In most states, the innkeepers' duty or standard of care is legally defined as taking reasonable care to protect against foreseeable acts. There is probably no concept that has affected the lodging industry more than the court interpretation of **reasonable care.** Unfortunately for the innkeeper, there is no concise and clear-cut determination of what a court or jury may consider to be reasonable care in any given case. Whether reasonable care is exercised depends on the facts and circumstances in each case. Because such an uncertain legal climate exists, this text considers various cases which may have long-term implications (sometimes contradictory) for the industry.

Like reasonable care, **foreseeability** is an imprecise term. Courts and juries may consider certain consequences to be foreseeable at some properties and not at others. Factors that may help determine foreseeability at a given property include the prior incidence of that type or similar types of crime on the premises, the prior incidence of all types of crime on the premises, and (in an increasing number of cases) the crime rate of the surrounding community. The practical result of many court and jury decisions as they relate to foreseeability has been to expand the innkeeper's duty to include being aware of criminal activities both on- and off-premises. For example, if certain crimes are taking place in a community, a court or jury might decide that a reasonable innkeeper should foresee the possibility of a similar crime happening on-premises; if such a crime does indeed occur on-premises and the victim alleges negligence on the innkeeper's part in not taking reasonable steps to prevent such a crime, it may be difficult for the innkeeper to plead successfully that he or she did not know about the crimes in the community if they were generally known.

Simply failing in a duty does not in itself establish liability for negligence. The breach of a duty to exercise reasonable care must be shown to be the underlying **proximate cause** of an incident. Proximate cause, sometimes called **legal cause,** is usually defined as that primary moving predominating cause from which an injury follows as a natural, direct, and immediate consequence, and without which the injury would not have occurred. It is not sufficient that the defendant's conduct has been one of the causes of the plaintiff's injury. It must be the proximate cause, which is sometimes said to depend on whether the conduct has been so significant and important a cause that the defendant should be legally responsible. A proximate cause of an incident need not be its only cause.

Foreseeability is again a factor. **Negligence** involves a foreseeable risk, a threatened danger of injury, and an injury that is caused by conduct unreasonable in proportion to the foreseeable danger. For example, if someone carelessly leaves a can of gasoline near an open flame and the gas then explodes, causing injury, a jury might find that such an act created a foreseeable risk of harm and that the injury was caused by conduct unreasonable in proportion to the foreseeable risk.

Suits alleging negligence request that the defendant be required to pay **damages.** There are two types of damages: compensatory and punitive. **Compensatory damages** are awarded to compensate the plaintiff for pain and suffering, loss of income during a period of absence from work, medical and hospital expenses, and recuperative facility or home-service expenses. Compensatory damages may sometimes be covered, perhaps after the payment of a deductible, by an individual's or corporation's liability insurance policy. In recent years, there has been a trend within the courts for juries to assess punitive damages in addition to compensatory damages. **Punitive damages** are damages awarded against a person to punish him or her for outrageous conduct. The chief purpose of punitive damages is to inflict punishment as an example and a deterrent to similar conduct. Some courts have allowed insurance coverage for punitive damages under certain circumstances, while other courts have disallowed insurance coverage of punitive damages as a matter of public policy. The size of punitive damage awards can be substantial, sometimes totaling several million dollars.

The court in which a suit or case is first tried is often called the **trial court.** The suit is filed by the **plaintiff** against the **defendant.** At the commencement of a lawsuit, the defendant can ask for dismissal of the complaint. If the allegations in the plaintiff's complaint fail to establish a valid legal claim or the defendant has an absolute affirmative defense, the complaint should be dismissed. After each party has had an opportunity to discover the facts of the case, but before the case is tried, either the plaintiff or the defendant can ask for a **summary judgment.** A defendant can be granted summary judgment if, upon undisputed facts, the plaintiff fails to meet the factual and legal requirements to establish its case. A plaintiff can be granted summary judgment if, upon undisputed facts, the defendant's liability is absolute; that is, the plaintiff has a valid legal claim supported by the facts and no defense is possible. The jury will then deliberate only the amount of damages to be awarded.

After the close of proofs offered in evidence, either the plaintiff or defendant can ask for a **directed verdict.** The defendant can contend that it should be granted a directed verdict because the plaintiff failed to prove its cause of action. The plaintiff can request a directed verdict claiming that the defendant has been unable to establish a defense. Directed verdicts are rendered by judges, not juries.

If the case goes to the jury and the jury returns a decision, the losing party can ask for **judgment n.o.v. (notwithstanding the verdict)** and/or a new trial. In granting judgment n.o.v., the trial judge overrules all or part of the jury **verdict.** The judge can also grant a new trial.

Whichever party loses the suit can appeal the decision. The party appealing is the **appellant;** the party appealed against is the **appellee** or **respondent.**

The Hotel's Duty to Protect Guests

Now that we have covered some background information about the American legal system and have defined some legal terms, it is time to talk about some of the specific legal aspects of a hotel's duty to protect its guests. In this section we will cover the "reasonable care" rule in some detail before discussing how hotels may be held liable for the actions of its employees, guests/patrons, and third parties.

Reasonable Care Rule

As mentioned earlier, hoteliers owe their guests a duty of reasonable care. What this means, legally speaking, is that a hotel is not the *insurer* of its guests (that is, it does not have to pay an injured guest unconditionally); rather, the injured guest collects from the hotel only if he or she can prove that the injury resulted from a failure by the hotel to use reasonable care.

If, when reading the preceding paragraph, you recognized that you were going in a circle, you just joined the millions of judges, lawyers, jury members, and law students who have run around that same circle for hundreds of years. "Reasonable care" is a centuries-old legal term, but, as we pointed out earlier, it is a very imprecise term. What it really means is that a judge or a jury, after hearing all the evidence in a lawsuit, will be asked to determine if the hotel acted or failed to act in a way that a reasonable hotel would have acted (or would have failed to act).

A simple example: There is a big puddle of water in a hotel lobby, and the lobby has marble floors that are slippery when wet. The hotel knows about the puddle for quite a while but just leaves it there. Unreasonable? You bet. Guest John Doe slips, falls, and breaks his leg. Did the hotel's unreasonableness cause the accident? Yes. If the hotel had cleaned up the puddle in a timely fashion, John would not have slipped in it. Now change the facts a little: the same puddle is in the same place, but it had only just formed there because a hotel employee just broke a vase, and the employee was rushing to grab a bucket and mop to clean it up when John comes in and falls. Was the hotel unreasonable? Maybe. Maybe John's lawyer will argue in court that the hotel should have put something around the puddle or in front of the puddle so that John would have been warned it was there. That question goes to the jury. Here is what the judge would tell the jury: "Ladies and gentlemen of the jury, thank you for your patience. You have heard all of the evidence. It is now up to you to decide whether the hotel was negligent. If you find that the hotel failed to meet the standard of reasonable care, then you must find it was negligent. 'Reasonable care' is the care that a reasonably prudent hotel would have used under the circumstances. If you find by a preponderance of the evidence that a reasonably prudent hotel would have put something in front of the puddle while the hotel employee was off getting a mop and bucket, then you must find the hotel to be negligent."

It is a very frightening prospect for any business to be sued by an injured person and then have a jury apply a standard as vague as "reasonable care" in judging whether it is liable. True or not, it is widely believed that juries will favor an injured individual over a business, if at all possible. This is one of the reasons that hotels carry insurance.

Because injuries can be caused by many things, it is impossible to make any one statement that covers all of the guest-protection situations hoteliers face. There are cases in hotels involving fires, falls from windows, falls in lobbies, falls in parking lots, attacks by intruders in guestrooms, attacks in hallways, drowning in pools, diseases caught in spas, bedbugs—the list is endless. We will give you some representative examples from cases in just a moment. But, before we do, there is one thing you must always remember: the hotel may not delegate its duty to exercise reasonable care in order to relieve it from liability. For example, in an early New York case a hotel was held liable for injuries a woman received when an elevator fell due to the breaking of a corroded piston rod, even though the hotel had employed experts to examine and repair the elevator before the accident.[2] This example is important for two reasons. First, it tells hotel managers and staff that they can't rely on some other company or vendor to keep their hotel safe—the duty to use reasonable care is the hotel's. Which means it is the hotel that will be sued should an incident occur. (This does not mean that the hotel cannot turn around and sue the vendor it trusted, but the hotel is the entity that the guest has a right to look to.) Second, this example highlights how the law and the business of running a hotel intersect. Unless the hotel is at least reasonably safe, in a very short time it will not have any guests, because safety is the one thing guests depend on.

In the following paragraphs, we will take a look at some court cases involving hotels and their guests in which the "reasonable care" rule was an issue, and see the types of judgments and awards that are handed down when judges and/ or juries find that the hotel in question did not meet the reasonable care standard.

In *Kiefel* v. *Las Vegas Hacienda, Inc.*,[3] the hotel was found liable for failure to provide a reasonably safe sleeping room accommodation to the plaintiff, who was attacked in the early morning by an unknown person who entered her room. In *Splawn* v. *Lextaj Corporation, d/b/a Lexington Hotel*,[4] a TWA stewardess was raped by an intruder in her room at the Lexington Hotel in New York City. A jury awarded the woman $1,800,000 for past pain and suffering and $200,000 for future pain and suffering over a five-year period. An appeal was denied.

In another intruder case that was famous in its day, the entertainer Connie Francis was awarded $2.5 million (and her husband $150,000) against Howard Johnson's Motor Lodges, Inc., by a jury in a federal district court. The award stemmed from an alleged criminal assault that occurred while Ms. Francis was a guest at a Howard Johnson hotel in Westbury, Long Island, New York. In this case, the rapist entered her room through a sliding glass door. The door gave the appearance of being locked, but was capable of being unsecured from the outside without much difficulty. Howard Johnson filed a motion in federal court asking that the damage award be set aside as "excessive." Eventually the court upheld Ms. Francis's $2.5 million damage award, but reduced her husband's award to $25,000.[5]

In a case involving a Motel 6 in Fort Worth, Texas, a woman guest who was a professional photographer was leaving for the hotel to go to dinner one night. Two ex-convicts allegedly bullied their way into her room, raped her repeatedly, stole her photographic equipment, and drove off in her car. Motel 6 settled her negligence lawsuit for $10 million.[6]

In *Orlando Executive Park, Inc. (OEP)* v. *P.D.R.*,[7] a Florida appellate court upheld an award of $750,000 as compensatory damages against the hotel operators and franchisor. In this case, a guest was allegedly beaten, robbed, and sexually attacked by an unidentified man. The guest was accosted as she was returning to her room and was dragged to a secluded stairwell in the building. The guest claimed that the hotel's duty to exercise reasonable care for her safety was breached by allowing the building to remain open to anyone who cared to enter, by failing to have adequate security on the premises to deter criminal activity against guests, by failing to install TV monitoring equipment in the hotel's public areas, by failing to establish and enforce standards of operation that would protect guests from attack, and by failing to warn of previous criminal activity. The appellate court upheld the jury's conclusion that the hotel operators did not provide adequate security, noting that there were reasonable measures in this case that could have been taken to deter the incident.

A registered guest at a Days Inn in Rome, Georgia, walked next door to the Shoney's Restaurant with two co-workers. On the way back to the hotel, they were jumped by four men, beaten, and robbed. The guest's left eye socket, cheekbone, and nose were broken, and the injuries were permanent. He sued the Days Inn. The evidence at trial showed that there had been prior incidents of vandalism and trespassing, as well as an assault on a security guard. The evidence also showed that the Days Inn had hired a security guard, but that his shift did not begin until 11:00 P.M., and, therefore, he wasn't on the premises when the attack occurred. Further inquiry revealed that the security guard had very little training, had a criminal record, and had assaulted one of the other security guards in the past. There was no video camera or other monitoring system for the parking lot. Nevertheless, the trial judge threw the case out. He held that a motel owed its guests a duty of reasonable care, and that part of that duty had to do with whether a particular injury was foreseeable. The judge reasoned that since there was no prior history of violent attacks on guests at the motel, the motel had no reasonable basis to anticipate that one of its guests might be jumped in the parking lot. The appeals court reversed the decision. It reasoned that, in order for a particular incident to be foreseeable, there need be no history of precisely the same type of incident on the premises. Rather, it is enough that there is evidence of similar types of problems.[8]

In *Stahlin* v. *Hilton Hotels Corporation*,[9] a guest, while hurriedly dressing in the room of the defendant hotel in Illinois, got his foot tangled in his shorts and fell backward, banging his head against the wall. The injury caused some pain and a large bump. His roommate called the hotel later that evening to report that the guest had a large bump on the back of his head and was vomiting. The hotel responded by sending up a woman to offer assistance and medical help who claimed to be a licensed practical nurse but who was, in fact, unlicensed. She did not diagnose serious injury, whereas the guest was suffering a subdural hematoma. As a result, when the guest finally did seek the services of a doctor, it was too late to prevent major surgery and permanent brain damage. This allegedly could have been prevented if an immediate diagnosis had been made. The hotel was found liable to the guest and his wife for $210,000. The court stated that the hotel had no duty, under Illinois law, to provide medical aid or assistance in this case, but that if the hotel did come forward to offer to assist with medical help, it must exercise reasonable care in providing such medical assistance. The hotel, in the opinion of the court, had volunteered to come forward and supply medical aid, but had failed to supply a competent person to administer the medical aid.

In *Estate of Hutchins* v. *Motel 6 Operating Company*,[10] it was decided that a case against a Motel 6 hotel had to go to trial because of evidence that the hotel had not acted with reasonable care when a guest died in a hotel room. Mr. Hutchins had checked into the hotel, and was there to meet his friend Ms. Hillis. According to the court:

> Hillis knocked on Hutchins' door but she did not hear anything. She went to the front desk and got a key from the desk clerk. She went back to the room, knocked on the door, and then opened it, but the security latch was on and she could not fully open the door. She saw Hutchins lying on the bed with his hand on his head. She thought he may have gotten drunk and passed out. He appeared to be breathing normally. Hillis decided to

let Hutchins "sleep it off," and she went shopping for about an hour to an hour and a half. She went back to the motel and called Hutchins from her cell phone but he did not answer. She did not knock on the door because she did not want to awaken other guests. Hillis called Hutchins a few more times and then fell asleep in her car.

Hillis woke up around 5:00 A.M. on February 28, 2003, when someone parked next to her shut an automobile door. She could not find her cell phone so Hillis went back to the room, knocked, and opened the door as far as she could. She called Hutchins' name but he did not respond.... Hillis panicked and ran to the motel office. She asked the clerk to call 911 because something was wrong; Hutchins would not answer the phone.

Hillis testified that the clerk told her she had to call her boss first, that he lived ten minutes away, and would be there shortly. Hillis testified it was at least thirty minutes before the manager arrived. Hillis stayed in the lobby while waiting on the manager, and when he arrived, they went to the room together. When the manager opened the door, he told Hillis that Hutchins was dead. The manager then instructed the clerk to call 911.

The coroner's office received the call at 7:00 A.M., arrived at the scene at 7:19 A.M., and pronounced Hutchins dead at 7:25 A.M.

Mr. Hutchins' estate claimed that the hotel should have acted with more dispatch, which the hotel denied:

[The hotel] argues that it had no notice of any problem with Hutchins until Hillis came to the front desk sometime after 5:00 A.M. on the morning of February 28, 2003. Hillis did not tell any Motel 6 employee how long Hutchins had been lying in his bed in the same position or provide any other information from which the desk clerk could reasonably conclude that Hutchins was in a medical emergency. Hillis testified she told the desk clerk she could not get into Hutchins' room and could not get him to answer the telephone. She asked the clerk to call 911 because something was wrong. [The hotel] contends there is nothing in the record to establish that Motel 6 was on notice that Hutchins was in mortal danger and time was of the essence. It points out that Hillis never asked to use the motel telephone to call 911 herself, never attempted to locate her cell phone to make a call to 911, and never left the lobby as she waited for the manager to come.

Nevertheless, the court held that a trial was necessary because "there are genuine issues of material fact as to whether the Motel 6 employee acted in a negligent manner. The evidence raises a jury question as to how a reasonably careful person would act under the circumstances."

In another case,[11] the Missouri Court of Appeals similarly held that a case had to be tried despite the hotel's claims that there was not enough evidence of wrongdoing to go to a jury. The plaintiff, Mr. Stafford, was staying in the defendant hotel. There was a knock on the door. Mr. Stafford opened the door and two men entered who subsequently hit Stafford with a bottle, stabbed him several times, and then robbed him. When Stafford sued, he claimed that the hotel failed to warn him of danger, failed to make sure that safety devices were functional, failed to install the proper security devices, and recklessly disregarded the safety of its guests.

The court concluded that even though Stafford voluntarily let the assailants in the door and chatted with them for ten minutes, there were still questions for a jury to resolve. The court said that "Drury [Inns, Inc.] may not have had a duty to rescue Stafford within his hotel room when no employee saw the two assailants enter his room and Stafford did not yell for help. However, even though Drury may not have had a duty to rescue, that does not absolve Drury of its underlying duty of care as an innkeeper to make the premises safe. In his petition, Stafford alleged Drury failed to provide a safe place and did not provide the proper security measures or ensure that security devices within the hotel were functional and operational."

Recreational Facilities, Exercise Rooms, and Health Clubs: Liability for Guests' Injuries. Many hotels provide recreational sports facilities, exercise rooms, and health clubs for guests' use. As guests utilize such facilities, injuries may occur. What is the hotel's liability, if any, for such injuries? The duty a hotel owes to the guest is the duty of reasonable care under the facts and circumstances of the case.[12]

Should a guest become injured while using the exercise room or recreational facilities, the guest's own negligence may in some cases be a valid defense for the hotel. The guest's contributory negligence is a question of whether the guest exercised reasonable care in the circumstances. In *Luftig* v. *Steinhorn*, the plaintiff was injured when he tripped on a plainly visible hole in a baseball field owned by the hotel. At trial, the plaintiff admitted that he saw the holes in the outfield, and he failed to prove that the hotel was negligent. Therefore, the plaintiff could not recover any damages from the hotel.

Another possible defense is that the injured guest assumed the risk of his or her activities. For instance, in *Luftig,* the court stated that one reason the plaintiff could not recover was that he was playing the outfield with knowledge of hazards, and therefore, he assumed the risk of the accident.[13] Posting notices warning users of recreational facilities or exercise rooms that there are dangers (i.e., heart attacks, pulled muscles, etc.) involved may not exonerate the hotel. However, such notices may put the guest on notice of the risks involved, and thereby facilitate the hotel's invoking the defense of assumption of risk by the guests.[14]

In *Hooks* v. *Washington Sheraton Corp.,*[15] a federal court upheld an award of $4.6 million to a hotel guest injured in a diving accident at the hotel swimming pool. The guest dived off the pool's diving board and landed in such a manner as to break his neck and injure his spine so severely that he became a quadriplegic. Evidence introduced at trial indicated that the Sheraton Park Hotel's diving board was not of the standard fiberglass design generally used for hotel swimming pools. Employees of the Sheraton had arranged to replace an aging board with a "duraflex" diving board, made of extruded aluminum that was used generally in competitive swimming events. Testimony showed that the duraflex board was designed to throw a diver higher and farther than a fiberglass board. The Sheraton's employees allegedly were aware of these properties when they purchased the duraflex board.

A federal jury in the Virgin Islands awarded $6.8 million to a guest injured in an American Motor Inns (AMI) swimming pool at the chain's Frenchman's Reef Holiday Inn. The guest charged AMI with negligence in construction and maintenance of the pool where he broke his neck in a dive and subsequently became a quadriplegic. A settlement for $4.4 million was reached while the case was being appealed.

Pool drains can also be involved in tragic incidents. In one case, a swimmer's hair became caught in a malfunctioning drain and, despite valiant rescue efforts, the individual drowned. In another case, a 16-year-old New Jersey girl was held underwater by drain suction in a hot tub and drowned. At the Medfield Area Recreation Club in Cary, North Carolina, five-year-old Valerie Lakey was in a wading pool whose drain cover had been pried off earlier in the day by other children. When she sat down, the resulting suction held her to the bottom of the pool and literally disemboweled her. Although the child survived, she must now take nourishment intravenously and may require several organ transplants in the future. The Lakeys subsequently sued the pool's manufacturer, the pump's manufacturer, the county (which certified the pool), and the recreation club. After three years of lawsuits, the family finally received payments of $25 million from the pool's manufacturer (a record in North Carolina), $2.5 million from the county, $2.9 million from the pump manufacturer, and $500,000 from the club itself. This and similar judgments have led to the recommendation that an emergency switch be visible and readily accessible in the pool area to turn off the pump. Furthermore, dual drains, which reduce the suction at any given drain, are becoming more common.

Vermont[16] and New Hampshire[17] have enacted laws that serve to limit the liability of ski area operators for injuries to skiers using the area. As a safeguard against possible negligence suits against the ski area operators, the laws establish that persons participating in the sport of skiing assume the risk and accept, as a matter of law, the dangers inherent in the sport, and therefore may not maintain an action against a resort based on injuries suffered as a result of these inherent dangers. These laws followed a judgment by a Vermont court in the case of *Sunday* v. *Stratton Corporation*.[18] The plaintiff, a novice skier, was awarded $1.5 million for injuries sustained as a result of what the court found to be negligent trail maintenance, resulting in his skis becoming entangled with underbrush on the edge of the trail. Although the new laws in Vermont and New Hampshire were designed to prevent further awards along the lines of the *Sunday* case, operators of ski facilities in both states will continue to be responsible for guarding against risks to skiers in their ascent of the ski trail and are held to official standards in the operation of mechanisms such as uphill passenger tramways.

In New York State, the Industrial Commissioner promulgated a new Downhill Skiing Safety Code[19] that set forth responsibilities for skiers and safety rules for ski facility operators. The rules included, among others, rules regarding snowmaking equipment, marking trails, equipping trail maintenance vehicles with flashing or rotating lights, and inspecting trail conditions. Violation of the code is punishable by fines and imprisonment.

The Michigan Ski Area Safety Act protects ski resorts from liability for skiing accidents. Skiers assume the risk that they could be injured by variations in terrain, surface or subsurface snow, or ice conditions. The Act was passed to reduce litigation and provide economic stabilization to the ski industry. In *Shukoski* v. *Indianhead Mountain Resort, Inc.*, the court rejected the argument that the Act did not pertain to a snowboarder, noting that snowboarders are exposed to identical risks as traditional alpine skiers.[20]

In 1977, the New York Appellate Division reversed a judgment that Kiamesha-Concord, Inc., was guilty of negligence in connection with an accident occurring on its ice skating rink.[21] On June 4, 1972, the defendant's employee had checked the rink every ten or fifteen minutes to make sure it was suitable for skating. At trial, the Supreme Court of Kings County charged the jury that if the rut or hole in the ice alleged to have caused the personal injuries existed for more than fifteen minutes, then the defendant should have corrected the condition. The Appellate Division held that this charge was erroneous and stated that: "Under the circumstances, defendant's failure to discover the hole within fifteen minutes does not necessarily establish negligence."[22] The Appellate Division then reversed the judgment based on the jury verdict and granted a new trial, holding that the verdict was contrary to the weight of the evidence and was based upon an erroneous charge that was highly misleading in its suggestion of an arbitrary time as a criterion of constructive negligence.

In *Gallo* v. *Buccini Group*, the court upheld a trial verdict in a case where a guest alleged that a hotel had failed to warn that a spa was not operational, and that the guest had contracted a bacterial infection of the digestive tract from using the spa. When she was treated, she suffered complications that included a blood infection. The jury awarded the plaintiff $150,000 after a three-day trial.

As you can see, laws and court judgments regarding recreational facilities and hotel liability vary from state to state. Hotel managers should be aware of the laws in their own state.

Agreements seeking to relieve hotels from liability. Some states' statutes address the validity of "exculpatory" clauses in contracts of membership or admission to recreational facilities such as ski areas, health clubs, exercise rooms, and so on. An exculpatory clause is an agreement whereby one party seeks to absolve itself from liability even if negligent. In New York State, however, § 5-326 of the General Obligations Law states:

> Every covenant, agreement, or understanding in or in connection with, or collateral to, any contract, membership application, ticket of admission, or similar writing, entered into between the owner or operator of any pool, gymnasium, place of amusement, or recreation, or similar establishment and the user of such facilities, which exempts the said owner or operator from liability for damages caused by or resulting from the negligence of the owner, operator, or person in charge of such establishment, or their agents, servants, or employees, shall be deemed to be void as against public policy and wholly unenforceable.

This statute overrules the earlier court ruling in *Ciofalo* v. *Vic Tanny Gymnasium*,[23] which upheld the validity of an exculpatory agreement between the owner of the gymnasium and a user of the facilities. Therefore, a hospitality operation should consult local counsel to see if similar state statutes exist which void any exculpatory agreements.

Acts of Hotel Employees

A hotel employer may be held liable for the acts of his or her employee acting within the course of employment under the doctrine of *respondeat superior*. Under this doctrine, the act of the employee becomes the act of the employer by operation of law. Once the employer hires the employee and has the power to control his or her acts, the employer becomes liable for any wrongful acts of the employee.[24] Therefore, if an employee commits a wrongful act while working within the scope of employment, the employer will be deemed liable whether or not he or she exercised reasonable care in hiring that employee.

A lawsuit was brought against a Louisville, Kentucky, hotel by a plaintiff-guest stemming from an incident in which the hotel clerk allegedly gave the plaintiff-guest the key to a room that was already occupied. According to the plaintiff, when he attempted to open the door to the room with the key, he was shot in the chest when the person occupying the room fired a gun through the door. Criminal charges were not prosecuted against the occupant who fired the gun, and the hotel was sued for damages resulting from the plaintiff's injuries. In a San Francisco case, a hotel was held liable for $250,000 in an assault case. The assailant admitted that he heard the newly trained desk clerk call out to bell personnel the room number of the female guest; he then followed her to the eighth floor where he committed the assault on her person.

It should be noted that in some jurisdictions there is some authority for holding the hotel liable to guests for the **tortious** acts of its employees *committed outside the scope of employment.*[25] For example, in *Crawford* v. *HotelEssex Boston Corp.*,[26] the guest recovered damages on the theory that the hotel breached a plaintiff-guest's contractual rights of "immunity from rudeness, personal abuse, and unjustifiable interference." In *McKee* v. *Sheraton-Russell, Inc.*,[27] the Second Circuit Court of Appeals, applying New York law, held that a hotel may be liable for a bell-person's improper advances toward a female guest in her room. The court noted that this would be so even if the bellperson by making such advances was acting outside the scope of employment. The action was based upon the breach of the hotel's contractual requirement of decent and respectful treatment implied from the relationship of hotelkeeper and guest.[28]

Certain cases have shown some of the outer reaches of a hotel's liability for the acts of its employees. Consider the following: In *Tobin* v. *Slutsky*,[29] the United States Court of Appeals for the Second Circuit discussed the liability of a New York hotel for failure to protect a guest from an assault by one of the hotel's employees. In this case, an employee at a family resort in upstate New York molested a fifteen-year-old guest at knife point. The court decided that the hotel was not an "insurer" of the guest's safety but must exercise "reasonable care" to prevent such harm. This federal court declared:

> We construe the law of New York to oblige an innkeeper to use reasonable care, commensurate with the quality of the accommodations offered, to see that his guest is not abused, injured, or insulted by his employees. In the case of a first-class family resort, reasonable care would mean a high degree of care. Indeed, examination of the New York cases leads us to believe that the duty of reasonable care has generally been interpreted to be a severe one.

The federal court held that the hotel, being a first-class family resort, had a high degree of care, and that whether the resort had met this degree of care was a jury question. Accordingly, the Court of Appeals remanded to the trial court for a decision on this issue. The Court of Appeals held that $30,000 would not be excessive under the facts, but that punitive damages could not be awarded in this case.

In another case, a lounge paid a male patron $115,000 because he was assaulted by one of the lounge's door attendants. It appears in this case that the door attendant made advances to the patron's girlfriend. The patron objected and an argument ensued, during which the door attendant struck the patron and fractured his jaw. The medical bills were $23,000. The pre-trial discovery proceedings allegedly revealed that the door attendant had never been specifically trained with regard to the security and safety of guests, and that there was negligence in the supervision of the attendant and in the delegation of authority by the employer to the attendant.

A Tennessee woman sued the posh Essex House hotel in New York City for $16 million, charging one of the hotel's security guards with groping her and "sucking and biting her breast" while she lay ill waiting for an ambulance.[30]

In *Zivojinovich* v. *Barner,*[31] the plaintiff claimed that a hotel caused him injury when the hotel manager lied to the police. The evidence was that the plaintiff was drunk and rowdy at a New Year's Eve party at the hotel. The hotel called the police to have him and his party removed from the hotel. According to the plaintiff, the hotel manager lied to the police by giving the impression that the plaintiff had threatened violence. As a result, the plaintiff claimed, the police had repeatedly tasered him. The court held that the hotel had the right to remove the guest from the hotel, and to seek police assistance, but held that the hotel could be held negligent if it found that the manager had indeed lied to the police.

Acts of Guests and Patrons

In New York, a hotel may be held liable for injuries received by a guest that were reasonably foreseeable and that might have been prevented through the exercise of reasonable care. Thus, when a football team made a hotel its headquarters and the lobbies were crowded with celebrating people, the hotel was held liable for injuries an elderly woman received when two of the crowd ran through a revolving door at great speed. This was because the hotel had not provided a door attendant to supervise the door. In its opinion, the court said that if the hotel had exercised reasonable care and diligence for the safety of its patrons, it could have readily foreseen that without precautions to control the use of the door, some patron might be injured by the unrestrained cavorting of some celebrant.[32]

The matter of a restaurant's liability for injuries to patrons by other patrons is addressed in *Kimple* v. *Foster.*[33] A jury awarded three plaintiffs $6,500 each in damages for personal injuries sustained during a violent episode in a tavern.

In a famous case, in October 1994 a jury ordered the Las Vegas Hilton Hotel and its parent company, Hilton Hotel Corporation, to pay former Navy Lt. Paula A. Coughlin $1.7 million in compensatory damages[34] for emotional distress plus $5 million punitive damages for failure to provide adequate security at the hotel, where she was allegedly groped by drunken male aviators in a crowded third-floor gauntlet during the infamous Tailhook Association convention at the hotel. This was the notorious gathering at which some eighty-three women were allegedly assaulted or harmed by Navy aviators at the Las Vegas Hilton Hotel.

In *Adams* v. *Starwood Hotel & Resorts,*[35] the plaintiff claimed that he was injured at a banquet at the hotel when he became involved in an altercation with another guest. Adams claimed that the other guest was drunk. The hotel claimed that two security guards were on duty, and that they had broken up the first fight but reached the second fight too late to break it up. The hotel also claimed that there was no record of fights on its premises. The court refused to let the case go to the jury, finding that there was no evidence that additional security guards would have made any difference. In stark contrast, in *Kuehn* v. *Pub Zone,*[36] the court upheld a $300,000 verdict in favor of a plaintiff injured in a bar by members of a motorcycle gang, who attacked him in the men's room. The court found that the bar's owner knew that the gang was dangerous, and had signs stating that those wearing the gang's "colors" would not be permitted in the bar. The court's logic was that the violence the gang engaged in was foreseeable, and that the bar should have provided more security (such as calling the police) when gang members showed up.

Assault by Third Parties in Restrooms

Somewhat similar to the *Kuehn* v. *Pub Zone* case just mentioned, in which a customer was attacked in the men's restroom and the bar was held liable, the Missouri State Supreme Court found a St. Louis hotel liable when a woman was raped in one of the hotel restrooms.[37] The court upheld the jury award of $100,000 to the plaintiff, even though there had been no such previous incidents at the hotel. In this case, the plaintiff was a patron of one of the restaurants in the hotel. An apparently neat, well-dressed man followed her down into a restroom in the hotel's lower lobby (where convention meeting rooms and offices were located) and there assaulted her.

In a New York case,[38] a man was attacked by an unidentified assailant in the restroom of a restaurant. The restaurant patron was stabbed in the neck and suffered other injuries. He sued the restaurant, alleging negligence in maintaining adequate security. The appellate court held that the plaintiff failed to demonstrate that the restaurant owed a duty to protect the patron from a sudden, unforeseeable, and unexpected attack, despite a similar attack five months earlier. The court stated:

> The mere fact that a single similar incident, involving different patrons, may have occurred in the defendant's restaurant approximately five months prior to the instant incident does not, without more, render the present incident any less unexpected and sudden. The plaintiff has failed to establish that the defendant owed a duty to protect the plaintiff against such an unexpected and sudden assault.

Because the court held that the restaurant in this case had no duty to protect patrons from unforeseeable, unexpected, and sudden attacks on its premises, the plaintiff could not recover damages for any of the injuries sustained in the restroom assault. The result of this case would have been quite different if the plaintiff had been able to demonstrate that the restaurant knew or should have known of the potential for danger in the unattended restroom and subsequently failed to take preventive measures.

Assault by Third Parties in Hotel Parking Lots

In *McCoy* v. *Gay*,[39] the Georgia Court of Appeals affirmed the trial court's directed verdict in favor of a hotel sued by a patron for alleged negligence in protecting patrons from assaults by third parties. In this case, the patron alleged that an assault occurred in the hotel's parking lot. The plaintiff claimed that poor lighting and inadequate security in the parking lot was the proximate cause of the plaintiff's injuries, and alleged that previous criminal assaults on the hotel premises constituted notice to the hotel of the allegedly dangerous condition. The trial court and the appellate court disagreed. The Court of Appeals held that evidence of two assaults within the hotel building a couple of years before the incident, and one criminal assault of a guest in the parking lot ten years before the incident, would not constitute a "reasonable apprehension" of danger by the hotel, alerting it to act to prevent the injury to the plaintiff.

In *Lienhart* v. *Caribbean Hospitality Services, Inc.*, the plaintiff, Janice Lienhart, was vacationing in Aruba. She situated herself in a lounge chair provided by the hotel on a public beach beside the Aruba Grand Resort and Casino, and fell asleep there, right beside the Tiki hut that the hotel also provided on the beach. She was then struck by a pickup truck and boat trailer that were backing up on the beach. The hotel did not own the pickup, the trailer, or the boat. The owner, Unique Sports, which ran a concession out of the resort, did nothing to warn the resort's guests about any possible danger. The lower court dismissed the case against the hotel, reasoning that while the hotel had established a zone of control over part of the beach, it had no responsibility to warn about the activities of Unique Sports, particularly since there had been no similar accident. Not so, said the appellate court. The hotel either knew or should have known that its tenant, Unique Sports, was creating possible dangers by its vehicles used on the beach. The court concluded:

> The record does not support the district court's holding. As noted above, Lienhart admitted only to general knowledge that the vehicles periodically moved to and from the beach. She was not aware that they would be driven into that part of the beach where the Aruba Grand placed chairs for its guests' use. The Aruba Grand, however, rented space to Unique Sports in a building adjacent to the resort, advertised its beach and water sports activities right on the premises, and derived income from its guests' use of those activities. Viewing the facts in the light most favorable to Lienhart, we cannot conclude that her knowledge of the risk was equal or superior to that of the Aruba Grand. The hotel thus owed Lienhart a duty to warn, and the district court erred in concluding otherwise.

Acts by Third Parties at Hotel Entrances

In *Banks* v. *Hyatt Hotel Corp.*,[40] the plaintiffs sued the hotel operators as well as the operators of a shopping mall that was part of the building complex in which the hotel was located. The action was a derivative claim brought by the family of a guest who was murdered in a robbery attempt as he was returning to the hotel after walking through sections of New Orleans. The assault occurred on a public sidewalk only four feet from entrance doors that led to the shopping mall and the hotel. On appeal, the Fifth Circuit Court of Appeals affirmed the lower court's decision in holding the defendant hotel operators liable for damages of $975,000, while absolving the shopping mall operator from any liability. In discussing the geographic area for which the hotel could be found liable for inadequate security, the court indicated that such an area would extend only to the hotel's own premises and the area immediately surrounding its entrance. The court indicated that it was not prepared to say that a hotel had a duty to provide security beyond this limited area or to warn guests of crime hazards in other parts of the city.

In *Zerangue* v. *Delta Towers, Ltd.,*[41] the United States Court of Appeals for the Fifth Circuit upheld the jury verdict of the lower court, which held the Ramada Hotel in New Orleans liable for damages resulting from personal injuries sustained by an invitee of a hotel guest when she was sexually assaulted on a public sidewalk outside the hotel.

The Hotel's Liability Regarding Guests' Property

In this section, we will look at a hotel's liability regarding the property of its guests. First we will cover state statutes limiting a hotel's liability, then discuss what hotels should do when a guest's property is left at the hotel and goes unclaimed. Next comes a discussion about a hotel's liability for handling mail for its guests. The section concludes with a look at a hotel's liability for the automobiles of guests and others.

State Statutes Limiting Liability

As noted in the previous section, guest safety is paramount if a hotel hopes to be successful. Safety of guest property is also crucial. Guests will not stay in a hotel if they think there is a good chance their property will be stolen. As a result, hotels should, as a matter of good business sense, take the steps necessary to secure their guests' property. Hotels should endeavor to hire honest employees, control who has access to the hotel and its rooms, and investigate complaints of theft.

But what if the hotel's efforts fail? What if a guest leaves, say, $1.2 million worth of jewelry in her guestroom and it gets stolen? (As you will see, that actually happened.) Does the hotel have to reimburse the guest? Maybe, maybe not. When it comes to property, there is a key question that hotel managers need to ask: "What does my state law say about limiting my liability?"

Most states in fact do have statutes that may limit the amount a guest may recover from a hotel for loss of personal property. In some states where hotels are not so protected, the common law rule applies. In many of these common law states, the hotel is considered practically an insurer and held strictly liable for loss of a guest's property—unless the loss is caused by a guest's negligence, an **act of God,** or an act of a common enemy. Unless there is a modification or limitation of common law liability in the state statutes, the common law liability for the full value exists.

States that have enacted protective legislation did so because they realized that to hold a hotel strictly liable would be to encourage guests to be sloppy with their property and dishonest with their claims, not to mention put a hotel at risk of immediate bankruptcy. The protective statutes are considered to be in **derogation** of the common law and will be strictly construed. Thus, hotels in states having such protective statutes must be very careful to comply fully with the terms of the statutes, particularly with requirements concerning the posting of "Notices to the Guest on the Limitations of Liability." The limitations set forth in the state statutes are usually conditioned upon the posting of such notice.

Space prohibits reviewing the legislation of all the states. This discussion will deal primarily with New York State statutes, since many other states have adopted statutes similar to New York's. Local counsel can advise hotel managers about whether their hotels' procedures strictly comply with the applicable statutes in their states.

Liability for Valuables. In order to limit its liability for the loss of a guest's valuables, a hotel in New York must provide a safe or safe-deposit boxes in the hotel office or other convenient place for the deposit of valuables, and must post notices to the guests regarding the existence of the safe or safe-deposit boxes. This notice must be posted "in a public and conspicuous place and manner in the office and public rooms, and in the public parlors of such hotel, motel, or inn" (§ 200, N.Y. General Business Law; see also Exhibit 1). If a New York hotel satisfies the statutory prerequisites, it will normally be free of all liability in the event that guests neglect to deposit valuables in the safe or safe-deposit boxes during their stay.

Similar statutes exist in other states. In *Walls* v. *Cosmopolitan Hotels, Inc.*,[42] a case in the state of Washington, a watch valued at $3,685 was allegedly taken from the guest's hotel room. After the guest discovered the loss, he noticed that the door to his room had been severely damaged previously and one could "easily" obtain entry by pushing on the door, even if it appeared to be locked. The court, however, refused to impose any liability on the hotel, because the guest had not deposited the watch in the hotel safe, as required by the Washington statute.

A guest of a hotel in New Orleans sued for a diamond ring that the guest reported missing from the guest's room. The guest sued for the alleged loss of the $10,000 value of the ring.[43] The Louisiana Innkeepers' Statute specifies that the hotel's liability for the loss of a guest's property from a guestroom is limited to $100 absent some proof that the hotel was negligent. The plaintiff claimed that the ring was stolen due to the hotel's negligence. However, various pieces of valuable jewelry, some traveler's checks, and cash were all left intact in the guest's room. The ring was reportedly the only item missing. The court held there was no evidence to support a finding of negligence on the part of the hotel. Therefore, the court upheld the innkeepers' statutory liability limit of $100 (in New York, this would now be $1,500; note, however, that in New York the hotel would arguably not be liable).

In New York, a well-known actress was robbed in a hotel elevator of a reported $253,000 worth of jewelry.[44] Although the hotel had complied with the statutory requirements to provide a safe and post notices, the guest sued on the ground that the loss of valuables was caused by the hotel's negligence. The jury, however, found in favor of the hotel, reportedly deciding that the guest had had a reasonable amount of time in which to deposit the jewelry in the hotel safe, but had failed to do so.

Exhibit 1   Sample Guest Notice

NOTICE TO GUESTS

A Safe is Provided in the Office for the Safekeeping of Money, Jewels, Ornaments, Bank Notes, Bonds, Negotiable Securities and Precious Stones Belonging to Guests.

DAILY RATES FOR ROOMS			MEALS*	
Single from	$ . . . . to $		Table d'hote Breakfast from	$ . . . . to $ . . . .
Double from	$ . . . . to $		" " Luncheon "	$ . . . . to $ . . . .
Extra Persons		*SUBJECT TO APPLICABLE TAXES		
(each) from	$ . . . . to $		" " Dinner "	$ . . . . to $ . . . .
Suites from	$ . . . . to $		A la Carte as per menu	

GENERAL BUSINESS LAW—SECTIONS 200, 201, 203-a, 203-b, 206, 206-d

SECTION 200. SAFES; LIMITED LIABILITY. Whenever the proprietor or manager of any hotel, motel, inn or steamboat shall provide a safe or safe deposit boxes in the office of such hotel, motel or steamboat, or other convenient place for the safe keeping of any money, jewels, ornaments, bank notes, bonds, negotiable securities or precious stones, belonging to the guests of or travelers in such hotel, motel, inn or steamboat, and shall notify the guests or travelers thereof by posting a notice stating the fact that such safe or safe deposit boxes are provided, in which such property may be deposited, in a public and conspicuous place and manner in the office and public rooms, and in the public parlors of such hotel, motel or inn, or saloon of such steamboat; and if such guest or trav-eler shall neglect to deliver such property, to the person in charge of such office for deposit in such safe or safe deposit boxes, the proprietor or manager of such hotel, motel, or steamboat shall not be liable for any loss of such property, sustained by such guest or traveler by theft or otherwise; but no hotel, motel or steamboat proprietor, manager or lessee shall be obliged to receive property on deposit for safe keeping, exceeding one thousand five hundred dollars in value; and if such guest or traveler shall deliver such property, to the person in charge of such office for deposit in such safe or safe deposit boxes, said proprietor, manager or lessee shall not be liable for any loss thereof, sustained by such guest or traveler by theft or otherwise, in any sum exceeding the sum of one thousand five hundred dollars unless by special agreement in writing with such proprietor, manager or lessee.

SECTION 201. LIABILITY FOR LOSS OF CLOTHING AND OTHER PERSONAL PROPERTY LIMITED. 1. No hotel or motel keeper except as provided in the foregoing section shall be liable for damage to or loss of wearing apparel or other personal property in the lobby, hallways or in the room or rooms assigned to a guest for any sum exceeding the sum of five hundred dollars, unless it shall appear that such loss occurred through the fault or negligence of such keeper, nor shall he be liable in any sum exceeding the sum of one hundred dollars for the loss of or damage to any such property when delivered to such keeper for storage or safe keeping in the store room, baggage room or other place elsewhere than in the room or rooms assigned to such guest, unless at the time of delivering the same for storage or safe keeping such value in excess of one hundred dollars shall be stated and a written receipt, stating such value, shall be issued by such keeper, but in no event shall such keeper be liable beyond five hundred dollars, unless it shall appear that such loss occurred through his fault or negligence, and such keeper may make a reasonable charge for storing or keeping such property, nor shall he be liable for the loss of or damage to any merchandise samples or merchandise for sale, unless the guest shall have given such keeper prior written notice of having the same in his possession, together with the value thereof, the receipt of which notice the hotel or motel keeper shall acknowledge in writing over the signature of himself or his agent, but in no event shall such keeper be liable beyond five hundred dollars, unless it shall appear that such loss or damage occurred through his fault or negligence; as to property deposited by guests or patrons in the parcel or checkroom of any hotel, motel or restaurant, the delivery of which is evidenced by a check or receipt therefor and for which no fee or charge is exacted, the proprietor shall not be liable beyond two hundred dollars, unless such

value in excess of two hundred dollars shall be stated upon delivery and a written receipt, stating such value, shall be issued, but he shall in no event be liable beyond three hundred dollars, unless such loss occurs through his fault or negligence. Notwithstanding anything hereinabove contained, no hotel or motel keeper shall be liable for damage to or loss of such property by fire, when it shall appear that such fire was occasioned without his fault or negligence.

2. A printed copy of this section shall be posted in a conspicuous place and manner in the office or public room and in the public parlors of such hotel or motel. No hotel, motel or restaurant proprietor shall post a notice disclaiming or misrepresenting his liability under this section.

SECTION 203-A. HOTEL AND MOTEL KEEPER'S LIABILITY FOR PROPERTY IN TRANSPORT. No hotel or motel keeper shall be liable in any sum exceeding the sum of two hundred and fifty dollars for the loss of or damage to property of a guest delivered to such keeper, his agent or employee, for transport to or from the hotel or motel, unless at the time of delivering the same such value in excess of two hundred and fifty dollars shall be stated by such guest and a written receipt stating such value shall be issued by such keeper; provided, however, that where such written receipt is issued the keeper shall not be liable beyond five hundred dollars unless it shall appear that such loss or damage occurred through his fault or negligence.

SECTION 203-B. POSTING OF STATUTE. Every keeper of a hotel or motel or inn shall post in a public and conspicuous place and manner in the registration office and in the public rooms of such hotel or motel or inn a printed copy of this section and section two hundred three-a.

SECTION 206. RATES TO BE POSTED; PENALTY FOR VIOLATION. Every keeper of a hotel or inn shall post in a public and conspicuous place and manner in the office or public room, and in the public parlors of such hotel or inn, a printed copy of this section and sections two hundred and two hundred and one, and a statement of the charges or rate of charges by the day and for meals furnished and for lodging. No charge or sum shall be collected or received by any such hotel keeper or inn keeper for any service not actually rendered or for a longer time than the person so charged actually remained at such hotel or inn, nor for a higher rate of charge for the use of such room or board, lodging or meals than is specified in the rate of charges required to be posted by the last preceding sentence; provided such guest shall have given such hotel keeper or inn keeper notice at the office of his departure. For any violation of this section the offender shall forfeit to the injured party three times the amount so charged, and shall not be entitled to receive any money for meals, services or time charged.

SECTION 206-D. POSTING OF RATES OF VARIOUS TYPE ACCOMMODATIONS. In addition to other provisions in this article relating to posting of rates, every keeper of a hotel, motel, or inn shall post publicly and conspicuously at the place maintained for the registration of guests so that it can be easily and readily seen and read by guests registering, a statement of the charges or rate of charges by the day indicating the standard rates for rooms or suites of different accommodations, and for meals furnished. The standard rates shall be that schedule of rates available to guests who do not qualify for special discounts or rate deductions.

NEW YORK STATE HOTEL & MOTEL ASSOCIATION, INC.
(HOTELS)

Check Out Time . . . .

In *Hisako Nagashima* v. *Hyatt Wilshire Corporation,* a bag of jewelry was stolen from a guest while she was standing at the checkout desk in the lobby of a California hotel. The guest had just taken possession of the small bag of jewelry *after* checking it out from the hotel safe. She had not informed hotel personnel about the value of the jewelry or the fact that the bag held jewelry. While the guest was in possession of the bag, and still at the checkout counter, an unidentified person stole the bag of jewelry from her.[45]

The guest sued the hotel. The parties stipulated that the reasonable value of the jewelry was $72,000. However, the hotel had not agreed with the guest to assume any liability greater than the $500 limit specified by California statute. The hotel had complied with the California statutory requirement to post printed notices in each hotel room informing the hotel's guests that a safe was available and that the hotel would not be liable for property of unusual value unless it was placed in the hotel safe.

The appellate court found that the trial judge committed error in holding the California innkeeper statute not applicable to the case. The California innkeeper statute provides that if an innkeeper "keeps a fireproof safe and gives notice" about the safe to hotel guests, the innkeeper "is not liable, except so far as his own acts shall contribute," for loss or damage to a guest's property unless deposited with the innkeeper, but in no case is an innkeeper liable for more than $500 for each guest's property "unless he shall have given a receipt in writing… to such guest."

The California appellate court ruled that if a guest wants property protection greater than the $500 limit, then the guest should declare the value of the property in order to give the innkeeper the chance to confirm the estimated value. The innkeeper can then refuse to assume the higher liability or, if he or she decides to do so, the innkeeper can take added precautions to protect such property. Thus, liability over the $500 limit is based on the hotel's agreement to assume the higher limit.

In this case, the hotel was protected by the California innkeeper statute because it maintained a fireproof safe and gave notice to guests about the availability of the safe as required by the California statute. Also, the hotel did not agree to assume any liability over the $500 limitation. *The California court then noted that the statute does not restrict the $500 liability limitation to the period of time in which a guest's property is actually located inside the safe. The limitation of liability therefore applied in this situation, where the valuables had been withdrawn from the safe and were stolen from the guest while she was checking out of the hotel.*

Accordingly, the appellate court reversed the trial judge's decision and remanded the case to him with direction to enter judgment in favor of the guest, *but limiting the amount to $500.*

Two cases have made it very clear that rules relating to notices that limit liability have to be complied with strictly. In the first, *Paraskevaides, et al.* v. *Four Seasons Washington,* the court decided that technical non-compliance with the notice provisions voided the limits of liability. The guests left $1.2 million worth of jewelry in the guestroom safe. The safe had a sign on it that said the hotel would not be liable unless the guests put their valuables in a safe-deposit box kept by the hotel. The jewelry was stolen. The hotel claimed that it had complied with the notice provision that governs District of Columbia hotels. The court said no, because that law required posting in the public rooms of the hotel and this was not done. Thus, there was no limitation on liability. The court said bluntly:

> Perhaps the Paraskevaides had notice; perhaps not. But whether they did is irrelevant to our disposition of this case. The statute says what it says: a hotel must "display conspicuously in the guest and public rooms of [the hotel] a printed copy" of the statute in order to limit its liability to guests. (D.C. Codes 30-101[a].) The Four Seasons undoubtedly displayed a copy or summary of the statute in its guestrooms. It may even have done so "conspicuously," although that remains unclear. What is clear is that the Four Seasons did not display, conspicuously or otherwise, a copy or summary of the statute in its public rooms. Therefore, when we strictly construe this statute, as we must, we conclude that the Four Seasons failed to comply fully with the statute's requirements for limiting its liability to the Paraskevaides.

Similarly, in *Ippolito* v. *Hospitality Management Associates and Holiday Inns, Inc.*, the appeals court upheld a verdict for guests who claimed to have had cash and jewelry stolen from their room. The registration card they signed clearly said that the hotel would not be liable unless valuables were deposited in the hotel safe. The court noted that the statute required that the notice be posted in a conspicuous place in the room, and that there was conflicting testimony as to whether the notice was so posted. Since the jury decides who is right when there is conflicting evidence, its decision on that point ruled the day. Once the jury decided against the hotel on that point, it then followed that there was no limitation of liability. As the court said: "…[I]f an innkeeper fails to post notice, then [the law] is not applicable, and the innkeeper's liability is not limited."

A Days Inn hotel was held liable for the entire contents of a room safe stolen from one of its guestrooms. The front desk clerk was told that the guest was a jewelry salesman and that the guest's bag contained sample jewelry. The clerk recommended that the guest use the safe in his room to store the bag. The court stated, "Where an innkeeper misleads its guest into believing that the latter's property may be safely placed at a particular location in the inn, this [statement] leads a guest to disregard whatever posted statutory procedures there might be for safeguarding a guest's property generally." The judgment was in the amount of $142,834 plus $46,606 in interest.[46]

If a hotel offers in-room safes, the safes should contain a conspicuous notice that the hotel also provides a safe in the front office for the safekeeping of jewelry and other valuables.

In a New York case, *Spiller* v. *Barclay Hotel*,[47] the hotel was held liable for the full value of valuables lost while the guest was checking out. In this case, the guest gave the bellperson her bags to take to the hotel cab area and watch over while she checked out of the hotel. When she went to the cab area, she noticed that one bag containing jewelry and other articles was missing. The court awarded the plaintiff over $1,700 for the lost articles, holding that the New York statutory limitations did not apply in these circumstances, and that the hotel's bellperson was negligent in failing to watch the guest's bag after leaving it in the cab area.

A final word about guest valuables. Hotel managers should be aware that a hotel may not be obligated to receive all valuables proffered by a guest for safekeeping. For example, in New York, a hotel need not accept valuables that exceed $1,500 in value. The hotel's right to refuse to accept such guest valuables are discussed in detail later in the chapter.

Personal Property Other Than Valuables. In New York, the General Business Law, § 201, permits the hotel to limit its liability vis-à-vis the guest's personal property other than valuables, provided that the hotel posts "in a public and conspicuous place and manner in the office or public room, and in the public parlors of such hotel or inn a printed copy" of the applicable statutes. The limits of liability vary, however, depending upon the nature of the property lost and the general location where the property was lost.

Guestrooms, hallways, and lobbies. If the property is lost from the guest's room, the hallways of the hotel, or the hotel lobby, the New York statute provides that the hotel is not liable for the loss of wearing apparel or other personal property in excess of $500. However, if the guest is able to prove that the hotel's negligence resulted in the loss of such personal property, the $500 limitation may not be binding. In that event, the guest could recover the full value of the property—unless the guest was also negligent.

In *Cohen* v. *Janlee Hotel Corp.*,[48] a guest in a large metropolitan hotel went to bed leaving the guestroom door unlocked so that her girlfriend, who was sharing the room, could get in without awakening her. The next morning a valuable coat was missing from the room. The New York court refused to find the hotel liable on the ground that the guest's negligence was a contributing factor in the loss.

Checkrooms. Hotels usually provide a place to keep the belongings of guests and of patrons who are not guests but are using hotel facilities such as a restaurant or banquet room. Although under common law the hotel will only be liable as a **bailee** to patrons, and, therefore, must be proven to be negligent if it fails to redeliver their belongings, a bailee nevertheless generally bears a heavy **burden of proof** to avoid liability. Many states have thus passed legislation limiting the hotel's liability under such circumstances.

The New York Court of Appeals in *Weinberg* v. *D-M Restaurant Corp.*[49] summarized the rules of liability relating to a restaurant's checkroom in New York. The court stated that § 201 of the New York General Business Law limits recovery by a patron who sues for negligence:

1. To $75 if the restaurant does not charge a fee for the checkroom service, and if the person checking the garment does not declare a value that exceeds $75 and obtain a written receipt when delivering the coat to the checkroom;

2. To $100 if a value in excess of $75 is declared, no charge or fee is exacted for checking the coat, and if negligence cannot be proved to be the cause of the loss;

3. To the full value of the garment if a value in excess of $75 is declared and a written receipt stating such value is issued when the coat is delivered to the checkroom attendant and either (i) negligence is shown or (ii) a fee or charge is exacted for checking the coat.

In *Aldrich* v. *Waldorf=Astoria Hotel, Inc.*,[50] a hotel permitted an independent contractor to operate a checkroom on its premises. The independent contractor charged a $.35 gratuity for checking services. The plaintiff was attending a ball at the hotel. She checked her mink jacket at the checkroom. When she returned, the mink jacket was gone.

The court held the independent contractor liable on the grounds that he was not a hotel, motel, or restaurant, and therefore not entitled to the limitations of liability set forth in the New York statute, § 201 of the General Business Law. The court stated the statute was in derogation of common law liability and therefore must be strictly construed. The court then held the hotel liable under principles of **agency** and pointed out that the hotel had failed to disclose to the plaintiff that the checkroom was not operated by the hotel. So far as the plaintiff was concerned, she was entrusting her coat to the safekeeping of the hotel. When the hotel attempted to assert the statutory limits on liability in this case, the court rejected such limitations, asserting that the $75 limitation applied only where no fee or charge was exacted, and that in this case the $.35 "gratuity" was actually a "fee" for checking the coat. The court thus held that the New York statute was inapplicable in this case and awarded the plaintiff judgment against the defendant independent contractor and hotel for $1,400.

Therefore, if a hotel's checkroom is operated by an independent contractor, the hotel would be wise to indicate in a posted notice and on claim tickets that the checkroom is operated by an independent contractor that is not an agent of the hotel. Moreover, the hotel's agreement with the independent contractor should include a clause to the effect that the independent contractor will **indemnify** and hold the hotel harmless against any claims by a guest or patron for loss of property from the checkroom, and that proper insurance will be provided that also covers the hotel's liability.

Baggage rooms and storerooms. The New York statute (§ 201) also limits the hotel's liability for losses from baggage rooms and storerooms to a maximum of $100, unless the guest, at the time of delivery, obtains a written receipt from the hotel agreeing that the value of the guest's property is in excess of $100. Even if the guest obtains a receipt stating a higher value, the hotel's liability is still limited to a maximum of $500 unless the loss occurs as a result of the hotel's negligence.

Merchandise samples. The New York statute (§ 201) also limits the hotel-keeper's liability for loss of or damage to merchandise samples or merchandise for sale (whether the property remains in the guest's possession or has been given to the hotel for storage). In connection with these items, the hotelkeeper is under *no liability whatsoever* unless the guest has given written notice stating the value to the effect that he or she has the samples or merchandise, which written notice the hotelkeeper *must* acknowledge in writing. Even in that event, the hotelkeeper's liability is limited to $500 unless the guest can show that the loss or damage occurred through the hotel's fault or negligence.

Loss by Fire. The New York statute (§ 201) also deals with the loss of a guest's personal property by reason of fire. This statute will only free the hotel from liability if the hotel can prove that the fire occurred without any fault or negligence of the hotel. This means that there is an initial presumption that the hotel is negligent, and the hotel must disprove this presumption of negligence in order to limit liability.

Unclaimed Property

Some states have statutes which provide that any hotel that has any unclaimed baggage or other property in custody for six months may sell the same at public auction. The statutory requirements may differ in each state. This procedure applies only to *unclaimed* property. Before selling the property, the hotel must be certain that no agreement was made to hold it for a period of time, or that at least six months have elapsed since the expiration of an agreed time. The statutory procedure for a sale must be strictly followed.

If the hotel has no record whatsoever of the address of the owner of the unclaimed property and does not know the name of the property's owner, it should not make the sale under such statute. This is because the hotel cannot mail the notice required by the law. This failure to comply strictly with the statutory procedure may make a hotel liable if the owner subsequently appears and asks for the property.

Note that in some states, such as New York, the hotel's right to sell unclaimed property has been questioned. In New York, the *ex parte* sale of guest property was declared unconstitutional in *Blye* v. *Globe-Wernecke Realty Co.*,[51] and guests must be afforded notice and the opportunity to be heard prior to permanent deprivation of the property.[52]

In light of the foregoing, the simpler course is to turn over all such lost or mislaid property to the police.

Liability for Handling Mail for Hotel Guests

If a hotel accepts delivery of guests' mail from the post office, it may be liable for negligence for any failure to deliver such mail to the guest, to forward such mail, or to return such mail to the post office. Section 508 of the United States Postal Services Domestic Mail Manual states, in part: (1) when delivery is not restricted at the sender's request, mail addressed to a person at a hotel, apartment house, etc., may be delivered to any person in a position to whom mail for that location is usually delivered; and (2) mail addressed to a person at a hotel, school, or similar place is delivered to the hotel, school, etc. If the addressee is no longer at that address, the mail must be redirected to the addressee's current address, if known, or endorsed appropriately and returned to the Post Office.

Liability for Automobiles of Guests and Others

Many hotels provide space for parking guests' automobiles. The hotel may operate its own garage or parking space or have a working agreement with an independently owned garage. In either case, where the hotel has been entrusted with the automobile, it may be liable for its loss or damage. The scope of the hotel's duty and the legal standard of care to which a hotel may be held with respect to guests' automobiles and contents vary from state to state. For example, in some states a hotel may be held liable under the common law rule as an insurer against loss or damage, while in other states the hotel is required to exercise ordinary and reasonable care under the circumstances.

In a few states, the hotelkeeper's liability for loss of a guest's car and property and requisite standard of care may be determined by statute. For example, in *Kushner* v. *President of Atlantic City, Inc.*,[53] the court held that under the state's hotelkeeper statute an automobile was considered "personal property" for which a hotel would not be liable unless the loss was caused by fault or negligence of the hotel. The hotelkeeper was thus absolved from any common law liability as insurer.[54]

Under the common law rule, hotels are liable as insurers for guests' property that is on the hotel premises, or *infra hospitium*.[55] This common law concept defining the scope of the innkeeper's liability itself may depend on various factors. For example, in *Merchants Fire Assurance Corp.* v. *Zion's Security Corp.*,[56] the hotel was held liable because its bellperson kept the key to the car. In cases in which the automobile was held not to be *infra hospitium*, factors such as the guest's keeping the keys, the lack of a fee charged by the hotel, and the lack of control exercised by the hotelkeeper over the guest's car were all considered relevant.[57]

The courts have held that even when the car was placed in a public garage, the garage company was the agent of the hotel in performing its contract for the safekeeping of the car. Therefore, the guest was entitled to sue the hotel for damages to the automobile, the hotel being liable for the acts of its agents.[58]

In a case in Virginia,[59] the trial judge refused to render summary judgment in favor of the defendant-hotel when a guest's automobile and its contents were stolen from the hotel's own outdoor parking lot. The judge's order apparently was based on the principle that the hotel did have some duty to protect guests' property on the hotel premises. Therefore, a jury should decide at trial whether the hotel took necessary and reasonable precautions in this case. The judge also refused to limit the hotel's liability for the loss of the guest's personal property contained in the vehicle under the Virginia hotelkeeper's statute, since "the alleged loss did not take place from a room or rooms or the office of" the hotel, as required by that statute.

In *Garratt* v. *Impac Hotels 1, LLC*, the court held that the hotel was not liable for the theft of a guest's vehicle where it was left for eighteen days in the hotel parking lot as part of the hotel's "Park and Fly" package (where the hotel invited guests to stay overnight and leave their vehicles for up to two weeks in the lot when they were flying to another destination). The guests claimed that the hotel was liable because it failed to warn about criminal activity in the parking lot. The court held that when the guests checked out, the "special relationship" of guest to innkeeper was terminated, and hence the hotel had no ongoing duty of care. It also held that since the guests were free to obtain their car and drive away at any time, the hotel did not have custody or control of the car and thus there was no **bailment.** Finally, the court held that there was no contractual duty because the "Park and Fly" program only applied to parking for two weeks, and the guests had left their car there for eighteen days.

In contrast, in *Helton, et al.* v. *Glenn Enterprises, Inc.*, the court held that where a guest parked close to but not on hotel property, and was assured that it was safe to park there by the front desk attendant, and the vehicle was stolen, the hotel could be held liable. This case is an excellent example of how statements made by a hotel's employees can create liability where otherwise there would be none.

Theory of Bailment. Hotels have also been held liable for loss or damage to a guest's automobile and/or its contents on the theory of bailment. Again, the question of whether a hotel is liable may depend on the amount of control the hotel exercises over the automobile and parking facilities. Some jurisdictions may distinguish between gratuitous bailments and bailments for hire. If a fee is charged for parking, if a fee is included in the guest's bill for the hotel's parking service, or if the hotel benefits from "free" parking, the bailment may fall within the category of bailment for hire, for which the standard of care in most states is generally that of ordinary and reasonable care. On the other hand, if the arrangement is classified as a gratuitous bailment, in some jurisdictions the hotel may have a lesser duty of care—namely, to be free of **gross negligence.** However, hotel managers should be cautious, because in a number of jurisdictions, the distinction is not clear, and the **gratuitous bailee**–hotel may be held to the standard of ordinary and reasonable care.[60]

The Horseshoe Hotel & Casino in Tunica, Mississippi, required its employees to park their cars in a particular lot. An employee had her car stolen from the employee's lot. Because the casino required that the cars of its employees be parked in a particular designated lot for the employer casino's own convenience and interests, a special relationship—a bailment—arose. Thus the court held Horseshoe Hotel & Casino liable.[61]

The Hotel's Claim When the Hotel Does Not Own or Manage the Garage. In certain circumstances, a hotel may be able to bring a separate legal action against the garage operators for indemnification or a cross claim against the garage for contribution, alleging that the garage's negligence caused the loss or damage to the guest's car. For example, in *Governor House* v. *Schmidt*,[62] the hotel was held directly liable to a guest for property stolen from the guest's automobile in a connected and adjacent garage facility on the common law doctrine of *infra hospitium.* However, the appellate court held that the hotel could maintain an action against the garage operators for contribution or indemnification in which the garage's negligence, if proven at trial, would be the basis of liability.

The hotel might also obtain an indemnity agreement from the outside garage. In this case, even if a claim were made against the hotel, it could seek recovery from the garage for losses or damages. One sample indemnity agreement form appears in Exhibit 2.

The hotel should consider obtaining insurance against liability for loss or damage to guest cars. In all cases, insurance should be obtained to cover the hotel's liability if its door attendants drive guest cars to and from the garage.

As a matter of public policy, courts in a number of states may not give any effect to the fact that the hotel has posted a notice to guests attempting to absolve it from liability for loss or damage to guests' automobiles or personal property therein, unless it is a statutory notice pursuant to state statutes limiting such liability.[63]

The Hotel's Liability for Loss of Property of Non-Guests

In this section, we will discuss a hotel's potential liability when people who are not guests of the hotel suffer a loss of property while at the property or through the

Exhibit 2   Sample Garage Indemnity Agreement Form

Garage Indemnity Agreement

Date _____

In consideration of the storage in the garage owned and/or operated by the undersigned at _____ of automobiles belonging to guests at   (address of garage)

the HOTEL _____ which automobiles may have been
        (name of hotel)

delivered to the garage either by Hotel employees or by the guests themselves upon recommendation from the Hotel and in consideration of payment of the agreed charges for such storage, either by the guests or by the Hotel, the undersigned agrees

(1) To pay to the Hotel the following commissions or other compensation [insert details of arrangement for payment to Hotel, if any. If no compensation is paid, this paragraph may be omitted].

(2) To indemnify and hold the Hotel harmless from any and all claims, suits, judgments, or demands from the owners of said automobiles based upon or arising from loss of or damage to the said automobiles, the accessories thereto or property in said automobiles, occurring while the said automobile, accessories, and contents are in the possession of the undersigned, his agents, servants, or employees or under their operation or control, or otherwise, during the period subsequent to the delivery of said automobile to the undersigned, its agents, servants, or employees and prior to its redelivery to the Hotel or to the owner of said automobile.

(3) Concurrently herewith the garage has furnished a surety bond in the sum of $ ____ to cover the faithful performance by the garage of this agreement of indemnity.

In Witness Whereof, the undersigned has affixed his hand and seal the day and year first above written.

In the presence of:

_____ (LS.)

_____

---

alleged negligence of the hotel. After looking at the general nature of liability, bailments for non-guests and a hotel's liability for restaurant patrons' property will be covered. The section concludes with a look at hotel defenses to the liability claims of non-guests.

General Nature of Liability

As previously discussed, most states have statutes limiting the common law liability of hotels as insurers of guests' property. Many of the state statutes relate to a hotel or restaurant's liability for the property of persons who are not technically "guests" of the hotel (i.e., persons who are attending social functions at the hotel, bar and restaurant patrons, visitors of registered guests, etc.). Hotels and restaurants often provide checking facilities for such persons to deposit their coats, briefcases, and other personal belongings. In New York State, the General Business

Law provides a statutory schedule of liability for the loss of personal property of guests or patrons from checkrooms of any hotel, motel, or restaurant. (See the earlier discussion on checkroom liability.)

Bailments for Non-Guests

In the absence of any state statute limiting liability, hotels may be liable for loss of property under a theory of bailment. When the hotel agrees to accept the non-guest's property for safekeeping, the hotel is legally a "bailee" and is generally bound by the applicable legal standard of care. For example, in *Crosby* v. *20 Fifth Avenue Hotel Co., Inc.,*[64] a court held that upon checking out of the hotel and leaving property checked in storage, a person no longer is a guest. However, the relationship between that person and the hotel with respect to the stored property is that of **bailor** and bailee, respectively. In this case, the guest checked out of the hotel leaving two trunks in storage. He returned to claim the trunks after two years and four months. During this time, the hotel had sold the trunks pursuant to a state law then in effect that allowed hotels to sell "unclaimed chattels" at auction after following certain notice procedures. The court held that as a gratuitous bailee, the hotel would be held to the duty to be free of gross negligence. However, the court went on to say that under the common law, a bailee had no right to sell goods without the bailor's consent. Therefore, because of the "unauthorized" sale, the court rendered a judgment in favor of the plaintiff-bailor for the value of the trunks and their contents. On appeal, the appellate court modified this judgment by reducing the award by the value of an antique item left in the trunk because the hotel should not be expected to know that such an extraordinary item was left in the trunk.

In another case, a departing guest stored a trunk at a hotel while she was temporarily absent. It was held that the hotel was not liable for the loss of a diamond pendant from the trunk on the ground that the hotel never agreed to assume liability for a diamond pendant, but only for such articles as are *"ordinarily* contained" (emphasis added) in a trunk.[65]

Rosin v. *Central Plaza Hotel, Inc.,*[66] a case in Chicago, involved the loss of luggage delivered to the hotel *before* the plaintiff's arrival. The Illinois court held that the hotel was merely a gratuitous bailee, and, under Illinois common law, liable only for any loss of bailed property caused by the hotel's gross negligence or **fraud.**

The hotel's custody of the property may be actual or constructive. It is actual custody if a hotel employee takes possession of the property. It may be constructive custody if the property is brought upon the premises with the hotel's consent. In either case, the hotel as bailee may be liable for loss caused by its negligence.[67]

The Supreme Court of Minnesota, in *National Fire Insurance Company* v. *Commodore Hotel, Inc.,*[68] held that the hotel will not be considered a bailee if it or its agent has no knowledge of the presence of the property on the premises or the acceptance of such property for safekeeping. The court held that the defendant-hotel was not a bailee of a mink jacket placed in an *unattended* cloakroom by a person attending a luncheon party at the hotel. The court held that on the facts of this case the hotel was not informed that the coat would be left in the unattended room. Therefore, the plaintiff maintained custody and control over the fur coat.

Likewise, there was no evidence showing constructive (or implied) delivery of the coat for the hotel's safekeeping.

Hotel Liability for Restaurant Patrons' Property

In Washington, D.C., a case was brought by two patrons of a major hotel restaurant, claiming $35,680 in damages for jewelry that disappeared from their hand luggage while they ate lunch.

When the couple entered the hotel, a bellperson offered to check their bags. The couple turned the bags over to the bellperson, making no mention of the bag's contents. Allegedly the hotel failed to post any notice setting forth the statutory limits on the hotel's liability in such a case. The courts held that, under Washington, D.C. law, the relationship between restaurant and patron could not be considered the relationship of innkeeper and guest, and therefore the patrons could not premise their actions on strict liability imposed on innkeepers.

The court of appeals held that under the "bailee-for-hire" theory there was a question of fact to be determined by the jury as to whether the hotel had constructive knowledge that the patrons' hand luggage might contain valuable jewelry (or less valuable items). The court of appeals, therefore, remanded the case to the trial court for the jury's determination as to the contents of the bag. The jury rendered a verdict for the hotel.[69]

Hotel Defenses to Liability Claims of Non-Guests

In the event of a suit against a hotel as bailee, the hotel has the burden of proof to show that it complied with the required standard of care with respect to the property. The degree of care required may vary, depending on the state law governing the hotel. Even if the hotel has received no payment for holding or storing the property, it may still be liable, depending on the particular state law.

In *Coykendall* v. *Eaton*,[70] the trial court held the innkeeper not liable for property of a non-guest because the court ruled that the non-guest turned the property over to an unauthorized clerk, and the hotel never agreed to become a bailee. On appeal, the court reversed and remanded the case to the trial court, holding that the question of the clerk's authority should have been presented to the jury. It was held that the hotel clerk had no authority to receive property of persons who were not guests. In *Booth* v. *Litchfield*,[71] it was held that since there was no evidence of authority for a clerk to receive property after the guest had surrendered his room, the hotel was not liable for such property.[72]

It should be noted that the negligence of the property owner, if such can be shown to be the cause or a contributing cause to the loss, may be asserted by the hotel to reduce (or, in some states, to eliminate) its liability.

Endnotes

1. Jack P. Jefferies and Banks Brown, *Understanding Hospitality Law,* Fifth Edition (Lansing, Mich.: American Hotel & Lodging Educational Institute, 2010), pp. 3–6.

2. *Stott* v. *Churchill,* 15 Misc. 80, 36 N.Y.S. 476 (1895), *aff'd,* 157 N.Y. 692, 51 N.E. 1094 (1898). See also *Blansit* v. *Hyatt Corp. of Delaware,* 874 F.2d 1015 (5th Cir. 1989), involving

a fall on a hotel escalator. See also *Kauffmann* v. *Royal Orleans, Inc.,* 216 So.2d 394 (La. 1968), involving a hotel restaurant's duty of reasonable care.

3. 404 F.2d 1163 (7th Cir. 1968), *cert. denied,* 395 U.S. 908, (1969) *reh'g. denied* 395 U.S. 987 (1969).

4. 197 A.D.2d 479 (1st Dept. 1993), 83 N.Y.2d 753 (1994).

5. *Garzilli* v. *Howard Johnson's Motor Lodges, Inc.,* 419 F.Supp.1210 (E.D.N.Y., 1976). On appeal, the case was settled for $1,475,000.

6. Unreported case. *Wall Street Journal,* July 18, 1991, p. 1A.

7. 402 So.2d 442 (Dist. Ct. of App., 5th Dist. 1981). See also *Wassell* v. *Adams,* 865 F.2d 849 (7th Cir. 1989).

8. 230 Ga. App. 786, Ga. App. LEXIS 281 (Feb. 26, 1998).

9. 484 F.2d 580 (7th Cir. 1973). See also *Gingeleski* v. *Westin Hotel Company* (1998 U.S. App. Lexis 10535, 9th Cir., May 22, 1998) on the duty of care that a hotel owes its guests once it is known or there is reason to know of a patron's illness.

10. No. 4:05 CV 01304 SWW, E.D. Ar. August 14, 2006.

11. *Stafford* v. *Drury Inns, Inc.,* No. ED84555 (Mo. Ct. App. 2/15/05).

12. *Luftig* v. *Steinhorn,* 21 A.D.2d 760, 250 N.Y.S.2d 354 (1st Dept. 1964), *aff'd mem.,* 16 N.Y.2d 568, 260 N.Y.S.2d 840 (1965). See also *Jungjohann* v. *Hotel Buffalo,* 5 A.D.2d 496, 173 N.Y.S.2d 340 (4th Dept. 1958); *Kane* v. *Ten Eyck Co.,* 10 Misc.2d 398, 175 N.Y.S.2d 88 (1943).

13. See also *Kulaga* v. *State of New York,* 37 A.D.2d 58, 322 N.Y.S.2d 542 (4th Dept. 1972), *aff'd,* 31 N.Y.2d 756, 338 N.Y.S.2d 436 (1972).

14. *Olsen* v. *State of New York,* 30 A.D.2d 759, 291 N.Y.S.2d 833 (4th Dept. 1968), *aff'd* 25 N.Y.2d 665 (1969), 306 N.Y.S.2d 474 (1969).

15. No. 76-1958 (D.C. Cir. 1977). See also *Wiegman* v. *Hitch-Inn Post of Libertyville Inc.,* 308 Ill. App. 3d 789, No. 2-98-1494 (Ill. Ct. App. 1999) where the jury awarded a guest $52,500 when she slipped on a wet floor at the swimming pool.

16. 12 V.S.A. § 1037.

17. R.S.A. 225-A:24(I).

18. 136 Vt. 293, 390 A.2d 398 (1978).

19. 12 NYCRR Part 54.

20. 166 F. 3d 848, No. 97-2241 (6th Cir. 1999).

21. *Bushman* v. *Kiamesha-Concord, Inc.,* 58 A.D.2d 638, 396 N.Y.S.2d 44 (2d Dept. 1977).

22. *Id.* at 44.

23. 10 N.Y.2d 294, 220 N.Y.S.2d 962 (1961). See also *Wurzer* v. *Seneca Sport Parachute Club,* 66 A.D.2d 1002, 1003 (4th Dept. 1978).

24. 53 Am. Jur. 2d. § 417.

25. *Clancy* v. *Barker* 71 Neb. 83, 98 N.W. 440 (1904), *aff'd* 71 Neb. 91, 103 N.W. 446 (1905).

26. 143 F.Supp. 172 (D.C. Mass. 1956).

27. 268 F.2d 669 (2d Cir. 1959).

28. *Id.* at 672.

29. 506 F.2d 1097 (2d Cir. 1974). See also *Crawford* v. *Hotel Essex Boston Corp.,* 143 F.Supp. 172 (D. Mass. 1956). See also *Moore* v. *Florida Innkeepers, Inc., et al.,* 20 ATLA Newsletter 152-54 (1977), where a hotel was charged with falsely advertising the hotel as a safe place. This case was settled.

30. *New York Post,* March 18, 1998, p. 22, Col. 5.

31. No. 07-11903 (11th Cir. April 23, 2008.

32. *Schubart* v. *Hotel Astor, Inc.,* 168 Misc. 431, 5 N.Y.S.2d 203 (1938), *aff'd* 255 A.D. 1012, 8 N.Y.S. 2d 567 (1938).

33. 205 Kan. 415, 469 P.2d 281 (1970).

34. See *New York Times,* Oct. 29, 1994, p. 1, col. 4; and Nov. 1, 1994, p. A-24; and Nov. 6, 1994, p. 46, col. 1.

35. No. 54418-7-I (Div. 1, Washington Ct. of Appeal, 10/17/2005).

36. 364 N.J. Super. 301, 835 A.2d 692 (2003).

37. *Virginia* v. *Madesco Investment Corp., d/b/a Bel Air Hilton Hotel,* 648 S.W.2d 881 (Sup. Ct. Mo. 1983).

38. *Lindskog* v. *Southland Restaurant, Inc.,* 554 N.Y.S.2d 276 (Sup. Ct. App. Div., 2nd Dept. 1990).

39. No. 65117, slip opin. (Ga. Ct. App., March 2, 1983).

40. Docket No. 81-3377 (5th Cir., January 9, 1984). See also *Holland* v. *Days Inn Motel* 705 So. 2d 1126, KA 5474 (La. Ct. Apps 1997) aff'd in material part, rev'd on another point, 747 So. 2d 1133 (Sup. CT. LA. 1999) 262 A.D. 2d 193, where the court denied hotel liability when the attack was 150 yards from the hotel or on public property not adjacent to the hotel. See also *Joseph McAndrew* v. *Pierre Hotel* (199 N.Y. App. Div. Lexis 7426, June 22, 1999) where the court said that the "hotel's duty to keep its business secure" extended to guests, not to the non-guest plaintiff, who "was assaulted on a public sidewalk." Moreover, said the court, the "duty" to keep a sidewalk safe "applied only in trip and fall cases and we decline to extend it." But see the Alamo Rent A Car case, where the jury found the company acted negligently in not warning the customer of dangerous areas in Miami. (*Estate of Tosca Dieperink* v. *Alamo Rent A Car,* case number: 98-4124 CA [25] [Fla. Cir. Ct., Miami Dade Co., 05-11-2000].)

41. U.S. Court of Appeals (Fifth Circuit No. 86-3357, June 25, 1987).

42. 13 Wash. App. 427, 534 P. 2d 1373 (Wash. Ct. App. 1975).

43. *Phillip* v. *Fairmont-Roosevelt Hotel, Inc.,* 469 So. 2d 1140 (La. 1985).

44. *Gabor* v. *Hotel Waldorf=Astoria Corp.,* 70 Civ. 4310 (S.D.N.Y. 1973). See also *H.K. Mallak, Inc.* v. *Fairfield FMC Corp.,* 33 F. Supp. 2d 748, No. 96-C-1207 (E.D. Wis. 1999).

45. 279 Cal. Rptr. 265 (Ct. App. 1991).

46. *Charles Bernard, Ltd. d/b/a Days Inn Art Deco/Convention Center* v. *Tobias Jewelry Ltd.,* 751 So. 2d 711, No. 3D98-3150 (Fla. Dist. Ct. App. 2/16/00).

47. 68 Misc. 2d 400, 327 N.Y.S. 2d 426 (Civ. Ct. N.Y. Co. 1972).

48. 276 App. Div. 67, 92 N.Y.S. 2d 852 (1949), reversed on other grounds, 301 N.Y. 736, 95 N.E. 2d 410, confirmed to 277 App. Div. 1097, 101 N.Y.S. 2d 622 (1st Dept. 1950).

49. 53 N.Y. 2d 499, 426 N.E. 2d 459 (1981).

50. 74 Misc. 2d 413, 343 N.Y.S. 2d 830 (Civ. Ct. N.Y. Co. 1973).

51. 33 N.Y. 2d 15, 20, 300 N.E. 710 (1973).

52. See also *Sharrock* v. *Del Buick-Cadillac,* 45 N.Y. 2d 152, 379 N.E. 1169 (1978); *People* v. *Lerhinan,* 90 A.D. 2d 74 (2d Dept. 1982); *U.S.* v. *Rahme,* 813 F. 2d 31 (2nd Cir. 1987).

53. 251 A. 2d 480, 105 N.J. Super. 203 (1969).

54. See also *Park-O-Tel Co.* v. *Roskamp,* 203 Okla. 493, 223 P. 2d 375 (Supreme Ct. Okla. 1950); *Savoy Hotel Corp.* v. *Sparks,* 57 Tenn. App. 537, 421 S.W. 2d 98 (1967).

55. See *Dispeker* v. *New Southern Hotel Co.,* 52 Tenn. App. 379, 373 S.W. 2d 897 (1963), *cert. denied,* 213 Tenn. 378, 373 S.W. 2d 904 (1963).

56. 109 Utah 13, 163 P. 2d 319 (1945).

57. See, for example, *Cloward* v. *Pappas,* 79 Nev. 482, 387 P. 2d 97 (1979); *Sewell* v. *Mountain-view Hotel, Inc.,* 45 Tenn. App. 604, 325 S.W. 2d 626 (1959).

58. See *Kallish* v. *Meyer Hotel Co.,* 182 Tenn. 29, 184 S.W. 2d 45 (1944); *Savoy Hotel Corp.* v. *Sparks,* 57 Tenn. App. 537, 421 S.W. 2d 98 (1967). See also cases in Annot., 156 A.L.R. 233 (1945).

59. *Coates* v. *Second Richmond Motel Enterprises, Inc.* (Docket No. LC-1138).

60. See *Edwards Hotel Co.* v. *Terry,* 185 Miss. 824, 187 So. 518 (1939).

61. *Robinson Property Group Limited Partnership* v. *Debra Rodman.* (1998 Miss. LEXIS 359, Sup. Ct. Miss., July 23, 1998).

62. 284 A. 2d 660 (D.C. Ct. App. 1971).

63. See *Savoy Hotel Corp.* v. *Sparks,* 57 Tenn. App. 537, 421 S.W. 2d 98 (1967). See also 1999 Iowa Code Ann. §§ 671.7 and 671.8.

64. 173 Misc. 595, 20 N.Y.S. 2d 227 (1939), *modified on other grounds,* 173 Misc. 604, 17 N.Y.S. 2d 498 (1940).

65. *Waters* v. *Beau Site Company,* 114 Misc. 65, 186 N.Y.S. 731 (1920). See also *Crosby* v. *20 Fifth Avenue Hotel Company, Inc.,* 173 Misc. 595, 20 N.Y.S. 2d 227 (1939), *modified on other grounds,* 173 Misc. 604, 17 N.Y.S. 2d 498 (1940); *Ticehurst* v. *Beinbrink,* 72 Misc. 365, 129 N.Y.S. 838 (1911).

66. 345 Ill. App. 411, 103 N.E. 2d 381 (App. Ct. Ill. 1952).

67. *Adelphia Hotel Co.* v. *Providence Stock Co.,* 277 F. 905, 76 A.L.R. 213 (3rd Cir. 1922) (applying Pennsylvania law); *Bean* v. *Ford,* 119 N.Y.S. 1074, 65 Misc. 481 (1909).

68. 259 Minn. 349, 107 N.W. 2d 708 (1961).

69. *Blakemore* v. *Coleman,* 701 F.2d 967 (D.C. Cir. 1983).

70. 55 Barb. 188, 37 How. Pr. 438 (1869).

71. 201 N.Y. 466, 94 N.E. 1078 (1911). See also *Arcade Hotel Co.* v. *Waitt,* 44 Ohio St. 32, 4 N.E. 398 (1886).

72. *Adelphia Hotel Co.* v. *Providence Stock Co.,* 277 F. 905, 76 A.L.R. 213 (3rd Cir. 1922).

🔑 Key Terms

act of God—A casualty, loss, or event caused by direct, immediate, and exclusive operation of the forces of nature, uncontrolled or uninfluenced by the power of human beings.

agency—Presupposes a directing principal and a directed agent under delegation of authority to the agent, either by contract, express or implied, or by operation of law, estoppel, or ratification.

appeal—The removal of a cause from an inferior court to one of superior jurisdiction for the purpose of obtaining a review. The term "appeal" indicates a re-examination by a higher tribunal of issues determined in original trial. The term "appeal" has a double significance and may be used to designate the act of lodging the action in the appellate court and also the action itself, when in the appellate court.

appellant—The party appealing a previous court decision.

appellee—The party appealed against. Also known as the respondent.

bailee—A person with whom personal property is entrusted; generally bears a heavy burden of proof to avoid liability.

bailment—The delivery of personal property for some particular purpose, or on mere deposit, upon a contract, express or implied, that after purpose has been fulfilled it shall be redelivered to the person who delivered it, or otherwise dealt with according to his or her directions, or kept until he or she reclaims it, as the case may be.

bailor—A person who entrusts his or her property to another.

burden of proof—The burden or duty of satisfying the minds of the jury of the truth of all the material facts alleged by the plaintiff and denied by the defendant.

common law—The general Anglo-American system of legal concepts and the traditional legal technique that forms the basis of the law of the states that have invoked it. While there have been conflicting theories as to the origin of the common law in the North American Colonies, it is generally settled that the Law of England, as it existed at the time of the colonial settlements, is the basis of the common law in this country (with the exception of Louisiana). The common law is a system of unwritten law not evidenced by statute, but by traditions and the opinions and judgments of courts of law.

compensatory damages—Damages awarded to compensate the plaintiff for pain and suffering, loss of income during a period of absence from work, medical and hospital expenses, and recuperative facility or home-service expenses.

court—A tribunal empowered to hear and determine questions of law and fact, either with or without a jury, upon pleadings either oral or written and upon evidence to be adduced under well-defined and established rules according to settled principles of law.

damages—Monetary awards paid by the defendant to (1) compensate the plaintiff, to (2) punish the defendant, or to accomplish both.

defendant—The person or side that a lawsuit is brought against.

derogation—The partial repeal or abolishing of a law.

directed verdict—An immediate decision rendered by a judge after the close of evidence, because either side failed to prove its cause.

foreseeability—The reasonable likelihood that a specific future incident could have been foreseen—and, therefore, prevented—based on knowledge of past similar incidents on the premises or in the surrounding community.

fraud—An action calculated to deceive (including acts, omissions, and concealments) involving a breach of a legal or equitable duty, trust, or confidence that results in damage to another.

gratuitous bailee—A person who comes into possession of the personal property of another, receives nothing from the owner of the property, and has no right to recover from the owner for what he or she does in caring for the property. A gratuitous bailee is liable only to the bailor for bad faith or gross negligence.

gross negligence—Negligence that is substantially and appreciably higher in magnitude and more culpable than ordinary negligence. Gross negligence is equivalent to the failure to exercise even a slight degree of care. It is very great negligence, or the absence of slight diligence, or the want of even scant care; and a disregard of consequences that may ensue from the act; and indifference to the rights of others.

indemnify—To secure against loss or damages.

infra hospitium—Means "within the inn." Under the doctrine of *infra hospitium,* the innkeeper's liability for loss of a guest's property attaches only where property was within the walls of the inn itself, or, if outside, was in the care and under the charge of the innkeeper.

insurer—One who undertakes or is obligated to compensate the other for loss or damage to person or property.

judgment n.o.v (notwithstanding the verdict)—A judgment by a trial judge that overrules all or part of the jury verdict.

legal cause—The primary or predominating cause from which an injury follows as a natural, direct, and immediate consequence, and without which the injury would not have occurred. Also known as proximate cause.

liable—Obligated in law or equity to make satisfaction, pay compensation, or make restitution.

negligence—Failure to exercise the care that a reasonably prudent person would exercise under like or similar circumstances.

plaintiff—The side that initiates and files the suit.

proximate cause—The primary or predominating cause from which an injury follows as a natural, direct, and immediate consequence, and without which the injury would not have occurred. Also known as legal cause.

punitive damages—Damages awarded against a person as punishment for outrageous conduct which also acts as a deterrent to similar conduct.

reasonable care—Taking actions that are ordinary or usual to protect against a foreseeable event—the central legal issue being that innkeepers owe a duty of care to all persons on their property. Failure to meet this duty may result in security-related liability.

respondent—The party appealed against; also known as the appellee.

statute—An act of the legislature; a particular law enacted by the legislative branch of the government.

summary judgment—A judgment granted (1) to the defendant when the plaintiff fails to meet the factual and legal requirements to establish its case, or (2) to the plaintiff when a valid legal claim exists supported by the facts with no possible defense.

tortious—Wrongful.

trial court—The court in which a suit or case is first tried.

verdict—A decision made by a jury and reported to the court on matters lawfully submitted to the jury in the course of the trial of a case.

 Review Questions ———————————————————————

1. What is common law?

2. What does "reasonable care" mean?

3. What is the doctrine of *respondeat superior?*

4. What is the hotel's responsibility in the case of an assault on a guest by other guests/patrons and third parties?

5. Under common law, what is the innkeeper's liability for losses of a guest's property?

6. In what ways do states limit a hotel's liability with respect to the loss of guest property?

7. Why is it important to post notices to the guest concerning the statutory limitations of liability?

8. How should a hotel handle unclaimed property?

9. What are some of the ways in which a hotel may be liable for loss or damage to guests' automobiles?

10. How might a hotel be liable for the property of non-guests?

 Internet Sites ———————————————————————

For more information, visit the following Internet sites. Remember that Internet addresses can change without notice. If the site is no longer there, you can use a search engine to look for additional sites.

American Hotel & Lodging
  Association
www.ahla.com

AH&LA Educational Institute
www.ahlei.org

FindLaw
www.findlaw.com

HospitalityLawyer.com
www.hospitalitylawyer.com

Hotel and Restaurant Law
http://topics.law.cornell.edu/wex/
hotels_and_restaurants

International Association of Chiefs of
  Police
www.theiacp.org

International Association of
  Professional Security Consultants
www.iapsc.org

International Foundation for
  Protection Officers
www.ifpo.com

National Crime Prevention Council
www.ncpc.org

National Institute of Justice
www.nij.gov

Chapter 3 Outline

Competencies

1. Explain the key issues in developing and setting up a security program, including liaison with law enforcement and security staffing. (pp. 61–71)

2. Identify the elements of security training that are critical to an effective security program. (pp. 71–78)

3. Describe the critical security concerns related to the design of the hotel's building(s) and the layout of the grounds. (pp. 78–85)

4. Identify common components of guestroom security and describe their uses. (pp. 85–90)

5. Explain the importance of closed-circuit television, communication systems, alarm systems, and elevator security to hotel security. (pp. 90–95)

3

Security Programs, Training, Design, and Equipment

SECURITY REMAINS A PRESSING CONCERN for the lodging industry, which faces both long-standing and newly emerging security issues. Criminals still target the traveling public as well as targeting hotels. Innkeepers continue to bear the legal and ethical responsibility to provide **reasonable care** for their guests and their guests' invitees. Cybercrimes have now been added to the list of industry security concerns. Internationally, hotels have become a target of terrorists, resulting in the deaths of guests and employees as well as significant loss of property.

To address these security concerns, the industry has developed a number of managerial methods and has utilized a wide array of security equipment. It is highly unlikely that any single property would ever have to implement every security procedure or use every device that is discussed in this chapter. Hotel owners and managers should identify those items that are applicable to their property and then consider how to apply them to their property's existing or potential security exposures. In recognition of the rapidly changing legal and technological landscape, hotel owners and managers should seek assistance from their attorneys, local law enforcement officials, and industry security consultants to help them address their security needs.

Developing the Security Program

Some important points relating to the development of a hotel's security program need to be made at the outset. First, a security program should stress the *prevention* of security problems. It is far more desirable to keep security incidents from occurring than it is to catch a criminal after a crime has been committed. Certain actions and procedures, properly implemented, may help to prevent or discourage security incidents. Nonetheless, it must be recognized that *not all crime is preventable*. A facility's security program, therefore, should be designed to train hotel staff to prevent security incidents whenever possible and to react quickly, appropriately, and effectively to any unpreventable security incidents.

Each property should continually review its security procedures. Whenever necessary, the property should update its procedures to meet its changing security needs. General areas that should be considered for inclusion in a property's security program include locks and key control, guestroom security, control of persons on the premises, perimeter control, protection of assets, emergency procedures, communications, and security records. In addition, a property's design and layout can greatly affect its security program. For lodging establishments still at the planning stage, security concerns should be considered at the architectural level.

The Need for Effective Management

Providing appropriate security for any lodging establishment is a never-ending activity. Because of crime against guests, employees, lodging properties, and the assets of each, management is continually challenged to develop and support an effective security program. Without ongoing vigilance at the management level, a property's security may suffer.

All members of the property's management and supervisory team should be involved in the development of security guidelines. The special needs of the particular hotel must be incorporated in the guidelines. While in draft form, all security guidelines and procedures should be reviewed by legal counsel. Upon approval, this information should be provided to all employees. However, it may be best to customize the guidelines and procedures for each department, so that employees can focus their attention on the portions that directly affect their job duties. Employee turnover and changes in job assignments necessitate a regular review program to keep all employees aware of their security responsibilities.

While recognizing the need to protect guests, employees, and their assets, managers must also recognize that guests and employees may themselves create security problems by stealing property and services from the hotel.

Security should be recognized and used as a management tool. Whether the size of the property requires a large security staff or allows for the security function to be assigned to one or several on-premises supervisory staff, the security role should be clearly defined and implemented. The protection of guests, employees, and assets requires managers (and, indeed, all staff members) to be constantly alert to possible security breaches.

Areas of Vulnerability

A hotel's security procedures must take into account the worst-case scenarios—crimes such as violent assault, armed robbery, rape, and even murder. Such attacks upon guests, even if few in number, can generate adverse publicity, can seriously damage the reputation of the property, and may be extremely costly during subsequent litigation. One problem in designing a security program, however, is that the precautions used to prevent crime must take into consideration the property's image. The lodging industry is, after all, a service industry; a hotel markets an image of hospitality as its main product. Over-the-top security procedures may be good for safety, but they will be bad for hospitality. Poorly thought-out security procedures may offend or inconvenience guests and drive them away altogether.

Another area of vulnerability results from the use of inadequate procedures for checking and extending credit to guests. Such procedures may lead to losses by permitting the unauthorized or fraudulent use of payment cards, personal checks, and traveler's checks. This type of security incident is less visible to the public than crimes against persons and is therefore less likely to greatly affect public relations efforts. When establishing credit procedures to protect a property from incurring losses through bad debts, care must again be taken to avoid offending one's guests.

A high degree of vulnerability exists in the protection of the physical assets of a lodging establishment. All too often, expenses due to theft are ignored and written off as a cost of doing business. Very little effort may be spent in trying to control the loss of tableware, linens, and towels—to name but a few of the items whose theft results in a monetary loss to the organization; however, when an organized crime team is concentrating on stealing television sets from the rooms of a hotel, the extent of the dollar loss becomes immediately evident. Whether dealing with an organized crime effort or with the theft of assets by guests or employees, management has a responsibility to take preventive action.

Studies by the U.S. Small Business Administration have indicated that business failures can often be directly related to employee theft, which may appear in numerous forms within the hotel and may combine to constitute a major concern.

Setting Up the Security Program

A lodging property's management should consider many factors in evaluating its property's security requirements and in determining whether a special security presence is warranted. If it is, management must decide how that presence may best be integrated with the operation of the hotel. The management team must be committed to the concept of security as a vital function within the hotel in order to integrate security into the day-to-day operation and administration of the property.

Setting up such an integrated security system is a process that involves many elements. These may include establishing working relationships with local law enforcement agencies, choosing whether to use in-house or contract security personnel, and creating an appropriate and effective security training program for all hotel staff members.

The Importance of Law Enforcement Liaisons. Because hotels are affected by the communities in which they are located, a property's management may gain insight into potential security problems by looking at the crime rate and past experiences of the property and surrounding community. Liaisons with local law enforcement agencies and neighboring lodging properties can help management gain an understanding of the nature and extent of local crime problems.

Developing such liaisons often results in clear benefits. In some residential communities, local organizations have developed community crime watch programs in their areas; such programs attempt to promote neighborhood or block activities to develop an awareness of suspicious persons or actions. Some lodging properties have adopted a similar concept that involves developing a telephone network that notifies both police and participating lodging properties when a crime has happened. Each property notified, in turn, may call other properties in the network. Some properties find that such a program may aid the security efforts of the participating lodging establishments. However, such a program should be cleared with the property's legal counsel to ensure that the information disseminated does not violate Federal Trade Commission regulations or other federal or local laws, or result in a suit for defamation or libel.

Public safety is, of course, the specific responsibility of law enforcement agencies. A hotel's managers should cultivate and maintain a close and cooperative relationship with the local branches of these agencies. Law enforcement personnel should be invited to visit the property in order to become familiar with it. If possible, it is also a good idea to review security procedures with the local authorities. Managers should request police guidance in crime prevention and should document such efforts.

A good relationship with local law enforcement agencies can often encourage a prompt response to security incidents and more frequent police patrols. In turn, a greater police presence can be a deterrent to crime; measurable reductions in total crimes have been noted in some cases in which liaison relationships have been developed. Good relationships may also be very helpful following a security incident or during an emergency.

Frequently, community police budget limitations within a jurisdiction do not permit an evaluation of crime as it relates to a specific hotel. Where a crime unit does exist within a law enforcement agency, a full report about local community and lodging industry crime may be available. Such a report will usually include data on homicide, rape, robbery, assault, burglary, theft, and auto theft, as well as a general category of "Other."

The liaison relationship may also overcome the problem of guests reporting incidents to the police but not to the management of the hotel. This results in discrepancies in the reports of incidents on the premises and hampers the security program, because employees may be unaware of some incidents. In a close working relationship, it is more likely that the police will alert management when they are called directly regarding a guest complaint. This permits management to respond to the guest and to be aware of areas where corrective action may be required. It also prepares management for possible litigation and facilitates the preparation of necessary information for legal and insurance review.

A potential problem. Unfortunately, law enforcement agencies and private security personnel have not always cooperated well with each other. Police have sometimes viewed private security efforts as being staffed with poorly trained older (or retired) law enforcement personnel who are largely ineffective and even fairly apathetic. In today's changing security scene, this stereotype often does an injustice to a lodging property's security personnel or function, because private security has become more professional and sophisticated. Better communication is the key to educating local law enforcement agencies about the broad scope of a lodging property's security program and about the growing professionalism of the industry's security personnel.

The most effective cooperation results when both the police and the property understand the needs of the other. The police should know enough about a property and its security program to be able to offer appropriate assistance in a given situation. They should be informed of any special events or visitors (for example, political or entertainment figures) that may involve an unusual security risk at the property. On the other hand, the property's staff should have a basic understanding of police procedures so that they can be of greatest assistance to the police once they arrive after an incident has occurred. Local law enforcement authorities will be able to explain the type of assistance they would find most helpful. This information should be included in a property's security training program.

In one positive development, some police departments have gone so far as to assign a number of detectives to work directly with hotel security directors. These detectives can teach a property's personnel about police procedures and needs, offer guidance to the staff about what to watch for, and share information about any crime patterns in the area that may affect the property. At the same time, they learn about the property and its security system, improving the likelihood of effective police response in times of need.

Security Staffing. In developing a security program, a hotel will need to consider whether to hire staff as full-time personnel, to contract with a local security company, to arrange for part-time protection with local off-duty police personnel, or to use any combination of these or other options.

Because of a facility's size and organizational structure, it may be appropriate to assign security responsibility to a member of the management staff, such as a resident or assistant manager, a chief engineer, or the human resources director. If management decides the property needs a security department, it must determine whether the department should be a proprietary unit with in-house staff functions or a security program run through a reputable, licensed contract security company. In some situations, it may be feasible to employ off-duty police to cover certain hours of operation while the property's staff provide daytime coverage as one of their responsibilities. If the security department or function is run by the hotel, additional considerations include determining whether the staff will wear uniforms, whether certain or all members of the security staff will be armed, and whether there are shifts on which security personnel need not be assigned. (Unless mandated by a local or state jurisdiction, the senior security executives of the lodging industry are unanimously opposed to the use of firearms by security staff. The rare instance where an armed security officer would have been of value in a specific security incident is far outweighed by the insurance costs and the potential for accidental injury or death of innocent bystanders in a shoot-out.)

All decisions concerning security deserve careful thought and should be discussed with legal counsel. Each option has its adherents.

Contract security. The proponents of contract security organizations argue that such organizations can provide sophisticated services to hotels at considerable savings. In addition, they assert that a reputable contract security company will provide thoroughly screened, tested, and trained personnel. It may also provide consulting services, including in-depth surveys of hotel security requirements, electronic audio countermeasure sweeps (a debugging tactic), data processing security, and assistance in contingency planning for bomb threats and natural disasters. Finally, they contend that an in-house security staff may become too familiar and friendly with the other employees. If a guard catches a friend stealing, he or she might hesitate to report that friend. Some people believe that this situation may be less likely to occur if security personnel are supplied by an outside agency.

In selecting a security company, make sure that extensive guard training, geared specifically to each facility, is provided. Review contract and insurance

AT YOUR RISK

BY ANTHONY MARSHALL

Hotel Security Should Wear Appropriate Uniforms

Frank J. Moran plays the snare drum for the Law Enforcement Emerald Society of South Florida Pipe and Drum Band. As the security manager for Wackenhut Corp., he is putting his weight behind getting hoteliers to properly uniform their security officers.

"Anyone who believes that a uniformed security officer isn't a deterrent to crime is nuts," he said.

Moran, a security professional, told me a "blazer" story. Recently, at an urban, city hotel in Miami, the property's sixteen full-time security officers were dressed in dark blue blazers, gray flannel pants, and white button-down shirts. No security emblems or badges adorned the uniforms. The security officers looked very preppie instead of looking like security officers.

Unfortunately, the hotel had a problem—criminal acts against property and guests were on the rise. In an attempt to lower the crime rate, the director of security decided to abandon the "soft" dress code and go "high profile" instead. He wanted his security officers visible and dressed to be seen. His rationale was that most criminals prefer to do their business at hotels where there are no security officers watching them.

Finally, the officers looked like security officers. Moran told me all of the security officers liked looking more like a law enforcement official rather than taken for reception desk personnel.

Hotel guests expressed their comfort to management for the visible security presence. From the guests' standpoint, the more para-military looking, the better. Today's hotel guests do not want to become another hotel crime statistic; guests want competent security protection.

Lastly and most importantly, in the first ninety days after the introduction of the new uniforms, the hotel's crime rate plummeted. Crimes of distraction, such as stolen luggage from the lobby and briefcases from the restaurant, abruptly stopped. Other types of hotel crime significantly decreased, too.

I asked Moran to describe to me an ideal hotel security officer's uniform. He said it would consist of a military-style light colored shirt with epaulets and button-flap chest pockets. He suggested long sleeves for formality. He recommends a conservative, dark, single-colored clip-on tie (the tie should pull off during an altercation rather than becoming a choking hazard).

Moran said security officer designation arm patches should appear on both sleeves. An officer's identification name tag should be attached over the right side pocket. Moran suggested a security badge be worn over the left shirt pocket, and he likes large, wide-brimmed Stetson cowboy hats or the traditional "Smokey the Bear" style ones.

"I don't like baseball hats on security officers," Moran said. "They lack command appearance and aren't professional."

Pants, he says, should be dark in color and have no cuffs to get tangled up in during an altercation or chase. Military-style, pant-leg piping, he claimed, adds

At Your Risk *(continued)*

additional command appearance. He recommends plain black belts and socks, and shoes with rubber soles.

"Blue blazers are great for hosts greeting guests, but not security officers greeting criminals," Moran said.

"What about mace or other sprays?" I asked.

"Never!" said Moran. "Sprays are chemical weapons and require training before use, and, in hotels, the likelihood of spraying guests as well as criminals is too high of a risk to take."

"What about a radio?" I asked.

"An excellent communication device, enabling the officer to communicate with his superiors as well as other appropriate authorities, is an essential part of an officer's uniform," Moran said.

Understand, Moran said, the uniform is one of the tools that enable security officers to successfully accomplish their tasks.

Once the hotel's director of security had issued the new uniforms for his security officers, he then ordered an electric golf cart as part of his crime reduction program. Today, a uniformed security officer patrols the hotel's outside property seven days a week, twenty-four hours a day. The results: No criminal activity. Will such spectacular results last forever? No, but it works like magic now.

Uniformed hotel security officers are a deterrent to crime. Don't deter your deterrent with improper uniforms.

Courtesy of *Hotel & Motel Management,* June 1, 1998. Used with permission.

requirements (i.e., named insured clauses and requirements for proof of insurance) with legal counsel. If your state or community requires security agencies to be certified, verify that the agency you choose meets this legal requirement. Be clear and specific regarding the services to be provided by the contract organization. Require the security firm to conduct frequent unannounced inspections, day and night, by supervisory personnel to ensure that its guards are in compliance with company regulations. Determine whether the security service can provide a sufficient number of personnel on short notice in the case of a large-scale emergency. Insist that security officers be required to file daily and unusual-incident reports. Determine the percentage of the security firm's hotel customers retained on an annual basis; rates of retention are an excellent indication of a company's service level.

Carefully construct the contract so there will be no misunderstanding as to the supervision of the contract security officers; supervision should be provided by the contract security organization while the contract staff is on the premises. The management of the lodging facility should carefully establish exactly what the contract employee is to do under most conceivable circumstances.

When hotel management gives orders or instructions to the contract employee, a different relationship is established. The responsibility for the actions of the contract security officer becomes blurred, and there are instances in which the contract employee has been considered as a workers' compensation case for the property rather than for the contract security company. Contract companies have held and prevailed that the instructions from the hotel executive may have placed the contract employee in jeopardy and may have been contributory to the workers' compensation incident. In other instances, the contract employee has turned to his or her company for the workers' compensation relief, but has sued the lodging establishment under general comprehensive liability, which affords the opportunity for a much greater settlement than would be available through workers' compensation alone.

A contract security organization will almost always be willing to perform an in-depth security survey for a property if the property has not already performed one for itself or had one performed by another agency. Remember, however, that a contract security organization is selling services. This fact may sometimes lead such an organization to overstate a property's security needs, which can pose an unfortunate problem for an innkeeper. Suppose a property implements some (perhaps even most) of a contract security organization's recommendations, yet despite such efforts, a security incident occurs on the premises. It is possible that a plaintiff might subpoena and use the security organization's written recommendation in court as evidence of the innkeeper's knowledge of alleged "inadequate security." Even though the recommendation may have overstated the needs, if the innkeeper failed to implement every suggestion, a jury may be more likely to judge the innkeeper negligent.

In-house security. Proponents of proprietary or in-house security departments point out a number of advantages to this system. They emphasize the fact that the hotel has greater control over its own security officers. They also argue that training for in-house security staff members can be much more directly related to the lodging industry. They believe that the peculiarities and special needs of the industry are more effectively addressed by those within the industry than by those in a contractual relationship with the industry. In addition, they emphasize that the quality of in-house security personnel is under the direct control of the hotel rather than under the control of a contract security company, and that the director and staff of an in-house department are more effectively integrated with the property's other departments and personnel. Serious consideration should be given to including the security director as a member of the property's executive committee, an action that would not be possible with a contract security staff. Finally, they point out that a greater sense of loyalty may be developed among an in-house staff, since career paths can be established that move security personnel into other roles within the organization.

Off-duty police. Some properties use off-duty police officers for their security staff. There are certain benefits associated with this practice. Such officers have superior training in reacting to and dealing with crimes and other emergencies, they understand the law, they are used to dealing with people, they may be better able to identify known criminals, they are immediately recognized as authorities, and they often do in fact have more authority than ordinary citizens (as a deputized individual, they are not limited to a "citizen's arrest"). In addition, police liaison and response may be enhanced. However, there may be potential drawbacks as well. First, police officers may be oriented more toward apprehension functions than toward prevention. Second, some jurisdictions require off-duty officers to be armed, and this may not be desirable (if they are armed and injure somebody, the property may be liable). In addition, off-duty officers may not be permitted

AT YOUR RISK

BY ANTHONY MARSHALL

Senseless Shooting Shows Danger of Armed Security Guards

Abraham Oliden was shot in the chest and stomach on Friday afternoon, January 2, 1998. Oliden was killed by Miguel Valdes, over an argument in the parking lot.

Witnesses said that Valdes, an armed security guard, lost his temper when Oliden, a delivery man, blocked some parking spaces with his van. Irrational? Absolutely. Negligent? Sure.

"It's one of those things that happens in this world that you never expect," said Valdes' mother.

It's illogical to never expect that a shooting misadventure can occur where armed security guards are involved. It's not farfetched: The arming of security guards always involves risks of an accidental or irrational shooting.

Hoteliers owe it to themselves to consider all the implications of taking such a step in their hotels. To arm hotel security guards is to risk misadventure, devastating publicity, and millions of dollars in lawsuits for the shooting of a hotel employee or guest.

Today's hoteliers must focus on security to win today's customers. It's a fact of life. Travelers want a safe haven, and many travelers ask reservation agents if the hotel is safe.

Security questions often make hoteliers squirm, but they shouldn't. The common law requires hoteliers to exercise "reasonable care" for the security of their guests. The law doesn't require "best care" or "the finest care."

Reasonable care is that care that a reasonable hotelier would exercise after prudent consideration of the size, type, and location of the hotel, as well as the history of criminal activity at or in the vicinity of the hotel.

Reasonable security practices include having a good key-control system. One such system issues each registrant a new key, invalidating all previously used ones. All security experts expect hotels to provide guestroom doors with peepholes, chain or bar guards, and sturdy bolt locks.

It always is a plus to have brightly illuminated public areas, walkways, hallways, and parking lots. Enclosed and secured guestroom hallways are becoming common, and the presence of visible, uniformed security guards is always favorable.

Don't arm hotel security guards with firearms, grenades, and flame-throwers, though. That's the stuff of movies—not real life. Do dress security guards in military-style police uniforms, however, as a flashy deterrent to crime. It's common sense: Most criminals don't commit crimes in front of witnesses, especially uniformed security officers.

The law does not require—nor do guests have the right to expect—hotels to become armed fortresses. Common law simply requires hotels to exercise reasonable care for their security.

Hiring uniformed, armed, off-duty policemen as security guards is one option.

One advantage to this is that they arrive qualified for security work. Their training and experience cannot be successfully challenged in court by complaining plaintiffs in a lawsuit.

(continued)

At Your Risk   *(continued)*

One disadvantage, however, is that some off-duty police officers lack the diplomacy and tactfulness to interact well with hotel guests. They may take the Rambo approach with guests: too tough and rough.

Some hotels may employ off-duty police officers in security as well as non-security jobs, but there's a catch to that. Hotel managers may be unaware that many police departments throughout the United States require off-duty police to carry their weapons. I was once introduced to an off-duty police officer, in civilian clothes, wearing a concealed ankle holster with his loaded pistol in it. I felt uncomfortable.

When should off-duty police officers, employed by the hotel, leave their guns at home? That's a policy issue for management to establish and enforce. While I like the badge and the honorable men and women wearing it, I don't like off-duty officers' guns in hotels.

An off-duty police officer working for a hotel is classified as a hotel employee, and the hotel would be liable for that officer's negligent acts.

Valdes shot Oliden in a fit of temper for which his employer may have to pay dearly. Imagine the horror if this asinine shooting had occurred at your hotel—surrounded by reporters and television cameras trying to answer the unanswerable.

Perhaps you would hear yourself say: "It's one of those things that happens in this world that you never expect!"

That's not a thoughtful, nor a sufficient, answer to such a senseless tragedy.

Courtesy of *Hotel & Motel Management*, February 16, 1998. Used with permission.

to wear uniforms in some jurisdictions. Finally, an officer may be working at the hotel following a full-duty police shift and the fatigue factor must be considered.

Personnel practices. While security concerns should be addressed during the selection and hiring of all employees, personnel screening is an especially critical consideration in hiring a member of the security department, given that this person will be responsible for the protection of guests, employees, and property assets. The use of an authorization statement and affidavit should be considered, if approved by legal counsel. Such a statement, signed by the job applicant, allows the property to more easily investigate the applicant's background. Bonding (insuring for protection from employee theft) through an insurance company permits more effective screening of applicants and is certainly warranted in the case of security staff members who, by virtue of their function, have access to most areas of the hotel.

Scheduling security staff on the property is another important consideration. During daytime operations, involving all employees as the "eyes and ears" of the property may make it possible to reduce the security staff to a few key persons able to respond to a security-related call from an employee. In setting schedules, special programs and activities that may affect the number of security staff needed during a particular work shift should be taken into consideration. In many properties, additional security staff members are assigned during the nighttime hours.

Supervision. Supervision of the security function is a critical element in the successful administration of the lodging establishment's security program. At small hotels, the resident or assistant manager, chief engineer, or human resources director may take on the role of security supervisor in addition to their other duties, but in large properties it may be more effective to assign a full-time director

---

A Security Officer's Typical Day

A typical day's schedule for a security officer might look like this:

- Sign in at your department or with the manager on duty
- Pick up your equipment
- Check for activities from the previous shift that might need your attention
- Check daily function sheets for upcoming events
- Begin your patrol, covering guestroom areas, public and recreation areas, perimeter, parking lot, and service areas
- Repeat patrols hourly
- Complete your patrol log at regular intervals
- Check employee packages
- Monitor employee time clocks
- Investigate guest claims
- Respond to emergencies
- Investigate disturbances
- Report suspected controlled substance abuse
- Complete daily log and report incidents that may need attention on the next shift
- Return equipment
- Sign out with manager on duty

A security officer might complete numerous rounds of the property during an eight-hour shift.

Source: *Lodging Security Officer Training* (Lansing, Mich.: American Hotel & Lodging Educational Institute, 1995).

to the security department. As previously noted, the director of security should be a member of the management or executive planning committee in order to facilitate maximum cooperation and exchange of information. To do otherwise may allow problems to arise that could have been anticipated and prevented—concerning, for example, the arrival of a special group, exhibit, convention, or conference.

The supervisor of the security function must take special care to prevent possible **collusion** between the security staff and other members of the hotel staff. This problem is usually addressed by rotating the security staff through various assignments within the property on a regular basis.

The Elements of Security Training

Training for security personnel is critical to an effective security program, regardless of the source of the security staff on the premises. Although a contract security guard is usually trained by the contract security company, he or she still needs an orientation to the philosophy and special service needs of the hotel. Orientation is also necessary for off-duty police officers, since they are shifting from an apprehension role to a prevention role. In addition, a careful analysis must be undertaken of the limits of an on-premises security officer's authority under local codes and regulations. Procedures to follow in a citizen's arrest, the arrest authority of a deputized security guard, and the legal limits placed upon an off-duty police officer are all factors to review in such an analysis.

In addition, since every employee of a lodging facility may act as an integral part of its security program, all employees should be given a thorough security orientation at the time they are hired and should be regularly exposed to an ongoing security education program throughout their term of employment. Such continuing security education programs can occur in conjunction with departmental or staff meetings. Records of attendance and minutes of such meetings should be maintained and preserved for possible future reference.

Surveillance plays a role in most aspects of guest and property protection. Awareness and observation by all members of the hotel staff is a key element of surveillance, as are more formal measures. One major lodging company used the phrase "Care and Be Aware" for their safety and security training some years ago. The current "If You See Something, Say Something" campaign by the Department of Homeland Security and the American Hotel & Lodging Association is a further example of the surveillance role of all hotel staff.[1]

Training should be comprehensive and should include all aspects of the protection of guests, the general public, employees, and the assets of guests, employees, and the property. Depending upon a particular facility's needs, training may be expanded to include the special concerns of emergency management and interconnections with other departments in the hotel. The key point is that the unique needs of every property call for the development of individually designed security systems and individualized security training programs. Of course, different properties may have some similar security needs as well, and thus their security systems may feature common elements.

A training program, including training documents such as a security manual or employee handbook, should be developed to meet very specific needs. While security textbooks are important training documents in their own right—they can point out problems common to the lodging industry and can discuss the various ways different properties have dealt with them—they cannot offer a specific series of steps that will invariably solve all properties' security problems. Nor can they relieve management of its responsibility to investigate and determine its property's unique security requirements. General information can create a general awareness that must then be applied to a specific situation or property. The practical insights gained from a careful examination of the security needs of a given property should be included in a customized security training program.

Security personnel should also keep abreast of the latest thinking and developments in the security field by reading the various security publications available. Because new security equipment is regularly being introduced and approaches to security are constantly being refined, such periodicals can provide important supplemental information that may help management keep its particular security program up-to-date.

A security training program might cover such topics as the nature and role of private security, the nature and extent of crime, and an examination of the criminal justice system. It should deal with such specific topics as the legal powers of, and limitations on, security personnel in the property's jurisdiction. It should also inform employees about patrol techniques, access control procedures, report writing, fire prevention, alarm systems, communication systems, and any other specific information that they should know in order to perform their jobs effectively.

In some cases, the lack of security training may be part of an overall lack of emphasis on training at a property. The manager of such a property may have accepted certain myths about training that need to be dispelled. Common training myths include the following:

- "Positions turn over so fast, it doesn't pay to train." High turnover is sometimes used to argue against implementing an extensive training program. The problem with this kind of thinking is that the lack of a training program, or the ineffectiveness of an existing training program, may itself be one cause of the high turnover.

- "Experienced employees don't need training." Not all experience is good experience. Some experienced applicants may have been poorly trained and may have developed poor work habits. Also, it is difficult to evaluate experience. An applicant with ten years of experience may in reality have one year of experience repeated ten times.

- "Training is simple. Anybody can do it." Managers or supervisors who have been promoted from the same job for which they are now training others often feel that they know everything about the job and that they can teach others spontaneously or as the need arises. This kind of hit-and-miss training may produce haphazard results.

- "Employees always resist training." While employees sometimes resist training, this is not inevitable. They resist when their trainers are poorly prepared, when the training is poorly presented, and when their training is never followed up by performance appraisals or on-the-job coaching.

Admittedly, it takes time—and therefore money—to develop an effective security training program. Management needs to carefully examine its operation and premises to discover potential security exposures. It then must decide how to best use its resources (systems, procedures, and personnel) to deal with the exposures. Finally, every aspect of management's plan that relies on the performance of personnel needs to be explained through training.

The cost of developing a security training program should be seen as an investment in the future of an operation that will reap significant benefits. An operation in which all employees are attuned to security concerns can create a safer environment for its guests, visitors, and employees. Guests will respond positively to the feeling of safety and security experienced on the premises, making them more likely to return, and the employee turnover rate may drop, because effective training generally reduces turnover and because fears of being assaulted or victimized will be alleviated. Both of these factors can make the operation more profitable.

The financial benefits of a security training program also include the reduction of losses due to criminal activity. The presence of an organized security effort is likely to make criminals less apt to target a hotel and can also reduce employee theft. Legal costs are likely to fall as well, since every prevented crime against guests represents an averted potential lawsuit. Even when a crime does occur, the existence of a well-trained security staff will help a lodging establishment defend itself in a lawsuit. In numerous cases, presenting evidence of an effective and well-organized security program has helped to persuade a jury that a hotel provided the reasonable care mandated by law.

An important part of preparing a security training program is determining not only what should be learned, but also who should learn it. The training for security department personnel needs to be more extensive than the security training for personnel in other departments. For example, a room attendant or bellperson probably does not need to know the design of the entire security system. Rather than unnecessarily overloading all employees with security information they will not need (which can discourage and alienate them), trainers should focus their efforts on providing employees with the security information they need to know.

Another important point is that each property should write down its security standards and procedures in a security manual that can be used to help train employees. A carefully written manual helps ensure consistency in employee training and performance. Just as important, actually having to write the manual forces managers and trainers to think carefully and organize their thoughts about security in a way that often does not happen if they are allowed to rely merely on their memories and on oral instruction. The formats of security manuals can vary; regardless of the format used, the contents of a security manual should cover the broad range of the property's security concerns in *specific* terms.

In addition, with the input of many of the lodging industry's corporate security executives, the Educational Institute of the American Hotel & Lodging Association developed a very effective training program for security officers. Successful completion of *Lodging Security Officer Training* provides the individual with a "certificate of completion."[2]

Who Is Responsible?

When a property uses an in-house security staff, it is obvious to all concerned that the property is responsible for the actions of its staff—if the security officers are negligent, the property may be held liable. The property cannot evade this responsibility merely by using off-duty officers or a contract security service, because in legal matters these security officers are usually considered to be the hotel's agents. In other words, hiring such services does not relieve a property of its legal responsibility to provide reasonable care.

One legal case that deals with this topic is *Vacation Village* v. *Burns International Security Service*. Vacation Village hired Burns International Security Service to provide security officers for its 44-acre hotel complex. Early one morning, four armed men used a master key to enter a guestroom. The men sexually assaulted a woman and her teenage daughter while holding the husband and teenage son at gunpoint. Responding to a noise complaint, the sole Burns security officer knocked on the door, causing the assailants to flee.

The victims filed suit against Vacation Village and Burns for failure to provide adequate security. The plaintiffs settled out of court for $1 million, which was paid entirely by Vacation Village. Meanwhile, Vacation Village had sued Burns for negligence, contending (among other things) that Burns had promised to provide fully trained and supervised security officers, when in fact it had provided untrained and largely unsupervised personnel with little security background. Burns defended itself by contending that Vacation Village knew it was missing master keys but did not want to spend the money to re-key the property; that Vacation Village had a bad attitude about security, revealed by its repeated refusals to discuss security problems with Burns personnel; and that any negligence on Burns's part was not the **proximate cause** of the plaintiffs' injuries. The jury voted that Burns was negligent, but decided that this negligence was not the proximate cause of the incident. Vacation Village had to pay the entire $1 million out-of-court settlement.

The use of off-duty police officers poses certain potential legal problems as well. If an off-duty officer uses his or her legal authority to make an unwarranted arrest, whose agent is the officer: the community's or the property's? In some cases, the officer is considered the property's agent. This means the property could be held liable for false arrest and false imprisonment. Similar liability could result if an armed officer injures someone.

The Authority of a Security Officer

In the eyes of some citizens, a uniformed security officer has the same authority as a public law enforcement officer. Indeed, some security officers—once outfitted with a uniform, badge, and, at times, weaponry—sometimes wrongly believe themselves to possess the privileges of public law enforcement officers. This attitude must be changed if the police, the public, and the individual security officer are to understand and accept the role and authority of the private security officer in crime prevention.

In fact, a hotel security officer, in the absence of any special commission, deputization, ordinance, or state statute, possesses no greater authority than any other private citizen. However, because the security officer can be involved in protective functions on a daily basis, he or she may be in a position to use certain powers more than most other private citizens. The exercise of these powers may involve nothing more than simply stopping undesirable conduct, or it may involve making a citizen's arrest.

Most security officers will, at some point in their careers, be faced with situations in which they must determine the appropriate legal action to be taken, such as calling the police, questioning a suspect, or making a citizen's arrest. Because of the limits of their authority, however, security officers should *never* interfere with the rights of a person without trying to obtain that person's consent and voluntary cooperation. To prevent improper acts that could result in a liability suit against the security officer and/or the employer, an officer must understand what constitutes a crime according to the appropriate criminal law so that he or she may be more specific in communicating with public law enforcement agencies.

Criminal statutes set limits on the behavior of lodging security officers. Activity beyond these limits may result in criminal charges being filed for assault, battery, manslaughter, or other crimes. **Tort law**, which provides bases for actions permitting one person to remedy a wrong committed against him or her by another, also restricts the actions of the security officer. Tort law permits an injured party to bring a lawsuit for damages against the security officer, as well as the employing property, for such unreasonable conduct as false arrest, false imprisonment, malicious prosecution, defamation, and slander. Those charged with responsibility for security should be familiar with applicable state and local laws regulating private security, particularly those relating to citizen's arrests.

Citizen's Arrests. Normally, the task of arresting criminal offenders is one for a sworn police officer. Most U.S. states, through state statutes, judicial pronouncements, or common law, permit a private citizen to make a **citizen's arrest** under certain circumstances. Even where the law permits a security officer to make a citizen's arrest, however, he or she should do so only if a sworn police officer cannot respond in time *and* if good judgment requires prompt action on the part of the hotel. Non-security personnel should not attempt to make a citizen's arrest.

There is considerable variation among state laws concerning citizen's arrest, so it is essential that security officers be familiar with their state's statutory arrest authority of private citizens as set forth in the applicable statutes and judicial pronouncements. In New York, for example, a private citizen may make an arrest for a felony only when the suspect has in fact committed it; merely having reasonable grounds for believing the suspect committed a felony is insufficient grounds for making a citizen's arrest. In other states, the felony must be committed in the presence of the citizen making the arrest. Some states do not permit a citizen's arrest for the commission of a misdemeanor of any type, while in other states, such as New York, a citizen's arrest for a misdemeanor is permitted, provided the offense is in fact committed in the presence of the citizen making the arrest. In any event, hotels in all states should check with local counsel before instituting any procedures for detaining persons on their premises.

An arrest made without proper legal authority may constitute false arrest and false imprisonment, and could result in civil and criminal liability on the part of the security officer and civil liability on the part of the lodging property. Except for a felony or misdemeanor arrest when and where permitted under state law, or except as provided for in some areas by state statutes relating very specifically to shoplifting, no other involuntary detention or confinement should be attempted. Moreover, security officers cannot exercise lawful arrest power for any purpose other than to turn the individual arrested over to the proper authorities. Any person who voluntarily consents to being detained must clearly understand that he or she is free to leave at any time.

Even a situation in which sworn police officers make an arrest can lead to a lawsuit against a lodging property. If a guest or patron is arrested without justification as the result of a complaint by a hotel staff member, the property might be faced with a suit for malicious prosecution.

Search. When a security officer makes a legal citizen's arrest for a felony or misdemeanor, the right of self-defense may in some states justify a search for an offensive weapon under certain circumstances. Individual properties, however, should check with local counsel beforehand to determine what circumstances, if any, would justify a search by a private citizen. If a person consents voluntarily to such a search, the consent should be obtained by the security officer in writing if at all possible and should be witnessed by at least one other individual.

Interrogation. There is no prohibition against security officers asking questions. It must be remembered, however, that the person being questioned is under no obligation to answer. Moreover, if a guest is wrongfully accused of criminal activity in the presence of others, even by the form of the questions, the lodging property might be sued for slander. Generally, routine questioning should be conducted quietly in public areas so that there can be no subsequent allegation of false imprisonment or defamation. In-depth interrogation of suspects in private is best conducted by two employees.

There should be no use of physical force or threats of force to coerce answers. Such actions might result in criminal charges being filed against the security officer and a civil suit against the hotel.

Private security officers generally are not required to give prior **Miranda warnings** to persons suspected of crimes (that is, that they have the right to remain silent; that anything said can be used against them in court; that they have the right to an attorney; and that if they cannot afford an attorney, one will be provided). However, police officers who are working as security officers while off duty should give such warnings prior to interrogating a person suspected of a crime.

Use of Force. Generally speaking, a private citizen may only use such force as is reasonably necessary to effect a lawful arrest or to prevent the escape of a person from custody who has been lawfully arrested. If excessive or unreasonable force is used, the security officer may be subject to criminal action by the state, and both he or she and the lodging property may be subject to a civil action for damages by the person against whom force was used.

No employee should use any force calculated to cause death or serious bodily harm unless there is a threat to his or her personal safety or the personal safety of another person. Deadly force may never be used to protect property.

The Team Concept

An important goal of a security training program is to turn an entire staff into a protection team. The development of the team concept may have considerable benefit for a hotel in providing protection to guests, employees, and the property itself. In the team approach, all department heads and supervisors regard security as an aspect of their jobs. While they usually are not directly involved in routine security assignments, they can be invaluable in maintaining the security of the property. Similarly, each employee has a responsibility to assist in a security capacity. It is essential, for example, that room attendants call the security office or the property's management when they notice a suspicious person in the guest-room area or back in the service areas of the property. Such alertness on the part of employees has often been instrumental in the prevention of incidents and in the arrest of criminals on the premises.

In a small property, security is likely to be the responsibility of an assistant manager, a resident manager, or an owner-manager, while a large property will usually have a full-time director of security. In either case, the team concept is still valid. Employees in properties of any size can, for example, be instructed to:

- Be alert to and report any suspicious activities or persons anywhere on the property.

- Avoid confronting a suspicious individual. Instead, the employee should step into a secured area (guestroom, locked linen room, or other space containing a phone), lock the door, and call the office designated to receive such emergency calls.

- Report any drug paraphernalia or other suspicious items that may be exposed to public view when working within a guestroom. (Employees should *never* search through a guest's luggage or property.) In one case, a jewel thief was arrested when a room attendant noticed an open case filled with jewelry. The thief stayed at one hotel while breaking into the other hotels and motels in the community. In another case, a thief left a case of burglar tools open.

- Alert security when rooming guests with large but empty pieces of luggage.

- Check on the proper posting of innkeeper laws, as may be required for the jurisdiction in which the hotel is located.

- Check to make sure that any information cards or tent cards provided for the guest's information on security are in their proper locations.

This list contains only a brief selection from the wide range of activities a security training program can prepare a staff to perform. Every property will be able to construct its own list to deal with its specific security concerns.

The traveling public can also participate in a team approach to security by being alert to their surroundings. To encourage guests to take commonsense precautions against crime, the American Hotel & Lodging Association, in conjunction with the American Automobile Association (AAA), American Association of Retired Persons (AARP), American Society of Travel Agents (ASTA), and the National Crime Prevention Council, produced the "Guest Safety Tips" cards shown in Exhibit 1. There have been instances where crimes have been prevented when guests have followed the campaign's recommendation of calling the front desk to report a suspicious person or incident.

Designing for Security

The security of a hotel begins with the design of the building and the layout of the grounds. Interior security equipment can usually be upgraded or replaced whenever the need arises, but a security vulnerability at the design level may be more difficult to address. As a result, whenever a new hotel is developed, a number of crucial decisions regarding the location and design of the hotel must be made.

A review of the local area's crime statistics should be part of the information collected during the development process (or when the purchase of an existing hotel is being considered). At a minimum, this review will provide hotel personnel with an awareness of the types of crime issues that may be faced during hotel operations. If several development sites or existing hotels are being considered, crime area statistics may have an important influence over which site or hotel is selected.

Exhibit 1   Guest Safety Tips Card

AMERICAN HOTEL & LODGING ASSOCIATION

GUEST SAFETY TIPS

1 Don't answer the door in a hotel or motel room without verifying who it is. If a person claims to be an employee, call the front desk and ask if someone from their staff is supposed to have access to your room and for what purpose.

2 Keep your room key with you at all times and don't needlessly display it in public. Should you misplace it, please notify the front desk immediately.

3 Close the door securely whenever you are in your room and use all of the locking devices provided.

4 Check to see that any sliding glass doors or windows and any connecting room doors are locked.

5 Don't invite strangers to your room.

6 Do not draw attention to yourself by displaying large amounts of cash or expensive jewelry.

7 Place all valuables in the in-room safe or safe deposit box.

8 When returning to your hotel or motel late in the evening, be aware of your surroundings, stay in well-lighted areas, and use the main entrance.

9 Take a few moments and locate the nearest exit that may be used in the event of an emergency.

10 If you see any suspicious activity, notify the hotel operator or a staff member.

© Copyright 2003 The American Hotel & Lodging Association
1201 New York Avenue, NW, #600
Washington, DC 20005-3931
www.ahla.com

American
Hotel & Lodging
Association

COM001727

Source: American Hotel & Lodging Association, Washington, D.C.

Exhibit 2 is a sample security checklist that hotel personnel can use to evaluate their own hotels or those hotels they are thinking of purchasing.

Changes to the area around the hotel may affect security needs. New buildings, changes in traffic patterns, different entertainment venues, and even changes to services offered by the hotel may require adjustments to the security program. Awareness of the interpretation of legal standards of reasonable care in the specific location of the hotel is also required. A hotel's security needs are dynamic and require continued attention, so that, as needs change, modifications can be made to security procedures and equipment.

Many lodging properties are franchise-affiliated. Franchisors will have brand standards regarding various aspects of security and safety that must be followed in order to fulfill franchise requirements. Hotel managers may also wish to incorporate additional security features in their hotels, based on the assessment of the specific needs at their properties. Managers at independent hotels (as well as managers at chain hotels looking for additional input) may hire consultants to assist them with the security aspects of their hotels' design and operation. Compliance with local codes is of course also required.

Lodging developers, owners, and operators should be aware that the National Fire Protection Agency (NFPA) has developed *NFPA 730: Guide for Premises Security*, a publication that addresses a number of building security aspects. While NFPA 730 is not a code, it is likely to be referenced by code authorities and others when building security is discussed, so hotel managers should be aware of it.[3] Four design areas are of particular importance from a security standpoint: a hotel's perimeter barriers, lighting, parking areas, and glass protection.

Perimeter Barriers

It is common that a lodging establishment's perimeter access be restricted by fencing or barriers that separate the property from wooded areas, busy thoroughfares, industrial and commercial complexes, or apartment complexes. Such areas could present security problems or risks to the lodging facility and its guests. Under certain conditions, it may be desirable to restrict perimeter access to a property by planting shrubbery. In such a case, care should be taken to keep the shrubbery from serving as a hiding place for unauthorized persons.

Lighting

Because criminals like to work in the dark, appropriate lighting for the property is a critical aspect of security. It is also one of the least expensive security measures to implement. Efforts may need to be made to eliminate dark areas in the property where someone could hide prior to accosting a guest or employee. Attention should be focused on lighting for entranceways, corridors, steps, walkways, recreational areas, and parking facilities. Outdoor lighting should be reviewed for each specific hotel relative to its special needs. The source of light is very important. Placing the lighting source on a building to illuminate the immediate surroundings may have the advantage of partially blinding an intruder; it may also make the intruder unsure of whether he or she can be observed from the building. However, it may also partially blind those personnel responsible for

Exhibit 2   Sample Security Checklist

Perimeter
1. Will a fence help protect the premises?
2. If there is a fence in place, is the fence too high to climb or protected with barbed wire?
3. Is the fence in good repair?
4. Is the fence designed so no one can crawl under it?
5. Are materials such as trash containers, incinerators, etc., that could be used in scaling the fence placed a safe distance away?
6. Are the gates solid and in good repair?
7. Are the gate hinges in good repair?
8. Are there flammable materials in the receiving area which should be removed?
9. Is there a frequent trash pickup?
10. Is adequate lighting provided for the entire area?

Doors
1. Are all unused doors secured?
2. Are door frames strong and securely in place?
3. Is the glass in back doors and similar locations protected by wire-glass or bars?
4. Are all doors designed so the lock cannot be reached by breaking glass or a light sash panel?
5. Are the hinges designed and located to prevent the pulling or breaking of the pins?
6. Is the lock bolt designed and placed to prevent easy displacement with a "jimmy" or other instrument?
7. Is the lock designed or the door frame placed so the door cannot be pried open by spreading the frame?
8. Is the bolt protected or constructed so it cannot be cut?
9. Is the lock securely mounted so it cannot be pried off?
10. Are the locks on the door in good working order?
11. Are the keys in the possession of trusted personnel and are they secured when employees leave the premises?
12. Are padlock hasps constructed so the screws cannot be removed?
13. Are the hasps heavy enough?
14. Are all doors locked and/or barred during non-operating hours? Is emergency evacuation capability maintained at all times on such doors?
15. In non-operating hours, are access locations properly checked by security staff and/or central station or proprietary protection systems?

Windows
1. Are easily accessible windows protected by gratings, bars, or other access-limiting devices?
2. Are unused windows permanently locked?
3. Are windows which are not protected by bars locked?
4. Are there unneeded windows at lower floors or other areas which could be replaced by glass blocks or other less vulnerable alternatives?
5. Are the windows and locks so designed or located that they cannot be opened by simply breaking the glass?

Other Openings
1. Are unnecessary skylights (which may be subject to hurled objects) protected or have they been eliminated?
2. Are accessible skylights protected with bars, etc.?

(continued)

Exhibit 2 *(continued)*

3. Are roof hatches properly secured?
4. Are the doors to the roof or elevator penthouses in good condition and securely locked?
5. Are laundry and trash chutes provided with locks?
6. Are all ventilator shafts and vent openings protected?
7. Are entrances to sewers and service tunnels protected?
8. Are fire exits and escapes designed to permit easy exit but to limit illegal entry?

Building Construction
1. Are the walls of the building(s) of frame construction and fire-resistive or capable of being made so?
2. Is the roof fire-resistive and secure?

Safes
1. Is the safe fire-resistive?
2. Is the safe fastened securely to the floor or wall, ceiling, and floor, set in concrete, or appropriately alarmed?
3. If a vault is used, are the walls as well as the door secure?
4. Is cash on hand kept to a minimum?

Security Officers
1. Is it feasible to have an in-house security staff? Or, is it more appropriate to employ a contract security service or off-duty police?
2. Do the security officers receive proper screening, training, and supervision, whether they are in-house or contract?
3. If security personnel are armed, are they properly armed and proficient in the use of such arms?
4. If there are full-time security personnel, are they free from "extra duties" so they are able to perform their protective duties fully?
5. If a commercial security service is employed, is the service checked to confirm that it has the ability to provide full services?
6. Would it be beneficial to conduct emergency drills?
7. If available, has complete central station or proprietary supervisory service been considered in addition to standard security services?
8. Has closed-circuit television or a similar monitoring device been investigated as a means of increasing effective surveillance by your security force?

Public Protection
1. Is proper liaison maintained between the hotel or motel and the police and fire departments?
2. Do the police and fire departments have the phone number of key personnel and vice versa?

Electronic Data Processing
1. If there is a computer on the property, have proper steps been taken to ensure computer integrity with proper off-premises backup capability?
2. Is the computer facility in a secure location?
3. Is the computer room protected from the danger of hurled objects, flood, or fire?

Communications Equipment
1. Is the communication center (telephone room, etc.) located in a secure place?
2. Is adequate protection provided for wires and cables, etc.?
3. Has an emergency communications plan been developed?

Exhibit 2 *(continued)*

Other Security Concerns

1. What problems are created by the community in which the property is located?
2. What is the potential for civil disorder, vandalism, or similar security incidents?
3. Does the traffic pattern around the property create special problems?
4. Are there areas or zones for control of traffic when deliveries are being made, bus tours are loading or unloading, guests begin arriving in their own vehicles, cabs, etc.?
5. Are there problems of loitering, begging, or solicitation outside pedestrian entrances to the hotel?
6. Is there easy access to major roadways which could permit a robber to make a quick escape by high-speed roadways?
7. What is the ease of access for police? The fire department? Guests? Employees?
8. Are driveways provided?
9. Do one-way streets adjacent to the property permit easy routing of traffic to and from the location?
10. Are underground access routes available?
11. Is there adequate illumination in all exterior areas including streets, passageways, walkways, alleys, delivery areas, and employee and guest access locations?
12. Is there an adequate supply of water in the event of a fire emergency?
13. Is there auxiliary pumping capacity in the event of failure within the local water system or loss of power on the property?
14. Is there easy access to a water source for the fire department?
15. Is there danger of illegal entry into the property through underground service routes, tunnels, sewers, subways, manholes, and basement areas?
16. Is adequate protection provided for incoming utilities, gas, electric, phone, water service, and sewage disposal lines? Be aware of the special vulnerabilities of these locations. Know all emergency cut-offs for such services.
17. Could there be access from adjacent buildings over the roof or through adjacent windows?
18. Are windows and doors secured between the hotel or motel and adjacent structures?
19. What is the use and occupancy of the adjoining buildings?
20. Is there a fire danger from the neighboring structures?
21. What dangers are present for arriving or departing employees?
22. What transportation facilities are available to employees in addition to private motor vehicles?
23. Are parking facilities adequate and safe for serving the needs of the employees and guests?
24. Is there an adequate guard service, police service, or surveillance system to protect the guests and employees using parking facilities?
25. Are safe employee entrances and receiving areas provided?
26. Are appropriate security personnel and/or systems provided?
27. Are there dangers for guests arriving at the door by taxi or other public transportation?

securing the property. Consequently, care needs to be taken in order to properly place lighting sources.

With regard to energy conservation, many lighting units are available that use minimum energy but provide maximum light. A lighting engineer or specialist may offer guidance about the amount of lighting needed, the best location for lighting, and various other considerations in order to optimize its effectiveness as a security tool.

In addition to the normal lighting system, a standby system of emergency lighting may be provided for backup in the case of a power failure. With the possibility of brownouts and blackouts, the ability to provide backup lighting in critical locations may be important to security management planning.

Another frequently overlooked protection feature is locks for electric switch boxes and control boxes. If an outsider is able to gain access to the switch control for a crowded function room, he or she may gain an important advantage in his or her ability to commit crimes against guests or the property.

Parking Areas

Providing safe parking facilities is another important aspect of lodging establishment security. Whether in a separate structure, attached to the hotel, in a lot surrounding the hotel, or adjacent to the guestrooms, parking facilities should be analyzed to ensure protection for guests, invitees, and employees.

Factors to consider with regard to parking facilities include adequate lighting, proper directional markings to ensure smooth traffic flow, monitored entrances, and other access-limiting systems. Roving vehicle or foot patrols may also be considered. If patrols are warranted, they should be irregularly timed to prevent establishing a patterned routine. Parking security is best handled through cooperative efforts with local police authorities. Whenever possible, arrangements should be made for occasional police car patrols through the parking facility. *Peters* v. *Holiday Inns, Inc.* is a case in which a police patrol played a central role in apprehending four criminals. In this case, four suspicious men were observed and apprehended by a police officer who was routinely patrolling the premises in an unmarked squad car.

Glass Protection

There are a number of glass protection items important to the security of a property. Prior to the 1970s, most glass was single pane that broke easily and caused serious injuries. Today, a common requirement in all jurisdictions is the specification of either tempered safety glass or a glass containing a central plastic element that would reduce the problem of severe injuries from glass shards when a panel is accidentally broken. In order to warn guests that a glass panel is in place, further mandates include precautionary placement of window decals, a planter, or an article of stationary furniture (such as a bench) attached to the floor near the window. These items can help prevent the severe injuries that can occur when a person accidentally walks through an "invisible" glass panel.

Energy conservation programs have also made a difference in the type of glass that is installed in lodging establishments. The introduction of double glazing (using argon gas as an insulator between two panels of glass) provided a tinted glass that made it less likely for a window to be mistaken for an opening to or from a location. Triple-glazed windows (which contain three argon-filled layers) maximize both energy control and protection against accidental breakage by "walk through" incidents.

To help protect against vandalism and violence, enhanced plastic products can provide windows with the strength to withstand anything from a hurled brick to the swing of an axe. The application of special films to existing glass can even make the panels resistant to bullets. However, in considering the use of such protection, evaluate the likelihood of a guest having to escape from an area where breaking through the window may be the only escape path.

Guestroom Security

Guestroom security may be enhanced by the use of security items such as guestroom door locks, safety chains, and similar devices; biometric devices; secondary access-limiting devices on operational windows and on sliding glass, balcony, and connecting room doors; automatic door closers and view ports; guestroom telephones; in-room safes; and decals or notices in guestrooms detailing security information for guests.

Locks

Guestroom locks are a critical aspect of guest protection. Locks and locking systems must lend themselves to the smooth and efficient operation of the property, but must not be easily compromised. If a property uses a master keying system in which one key opens all or many of the property's doors, it should consider the possibility that a master key may be lost or stolen. If this happens, every lock's code or combination (that is, the arrangement of tumblers in the core of the lock) may need to be changed. Depending on the type of locks used, this re-keying can be a relatively quick and inexpensive process or a long and costly one. (One of the best ways to avoid this situation is to follow effective key control procedures.)

There are five basic types of guestroom locks: (1) locks with the key channel in the knob, (2) standard mortise locks, which generally include a face plate with the knob, a separate key channel on the corridor side of the door, and a deadbolt unit on the guestroom side of the door, (3) mortise locks with programmable cylinders for easily changed key combinations, (4) mortise locks with removable cores, and (5) electronic locks with random selection of new key combinations for each guest.

A number of systems have been introduced to add to the re-key and core-change capabilities of guestroom lock sets. Concurrent with this development has been the use by some hotels of mortise locks. A growing number of fire authorities in various states are requiring that the deadbolt be integrated with the knob, so that turning the knob will automatically release the deadbolt as well as the basic latch.

Electronic locks are now in use in over 95 percent of all U.S. hotels (see Exhibit 3). Electronic locks have historically relied on magnetic stripe key cards, which were coded at the time of registration and inserted into the guestroom lock. More recently, access via radio frequency identification (RFID) has been introduced, which allows communication with the lock without the need to insert a card. A key card issued by the front desk is the current method of RFID interface, but other methods are emerging. Cell phone technology is being utilized to provide guests with a "mobile key" allowing their phone to communicate with the RFID system.[4]

Exhibit 3   Percentage of Hotels with Electronic Locks

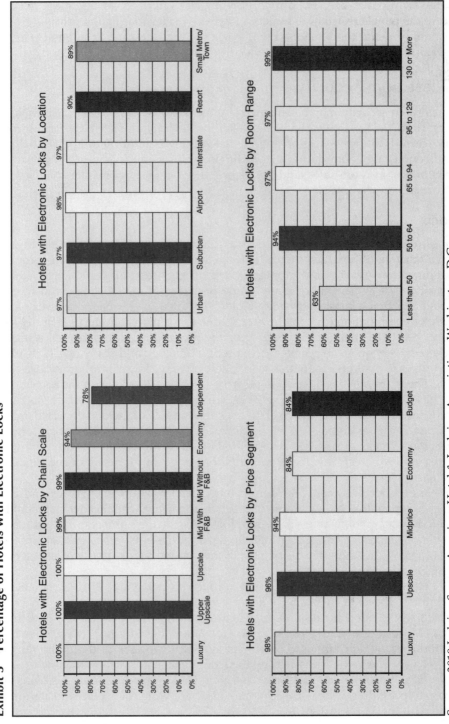

Source: *2010 Lodging Survey*, American Hotel & Lodging Association, Washington, D.C.

Electronic locks are also often installed on doors of meeting rooms. These locks allow users of meeting spaces to secure these spaces during times when they are not in use (such as lunch breaks). Supplying the meeting planner/coordinator with a key providing access to these spaces can help to secure attendee personal items as well as materials used in the meetings themselves.

A variety of electronic systems are available; most include one or more of the following elements:

- A mortise lock integrated with an electronic card reader.

- A key card that either communicates with the front desk computer and permits entry or that is compatible with the permission-level within the microchip in the lockset unit in the guestroom door. This establishes entrance capability either at the time the key card is being produced or upon introduction to the door lock.

- A computer terminal at the front desk or adjacent area that produces the key card and selects the code that will permit entry by a new key card and will reject all prior cards issued for that room.

- A computer capable of providing millions of combinations for entrance to a guestroom.

- A battery source and/or hard-wired system for energizing the lock system.

- A touch-pad system.

- The capability of "timing" the card so that it no longer functions after a set time, such as check-out.

With the use of electronic locking systems, a standby source of emergency power should be considered for the operation of front office equipment. For immediate takeover in the event of a power failure, battery packs may be supported by an auxiliary generating source. That source may be extended to provide emergency lighting and other power use as may be appropriate to a given lodging establishment. Of course, electronic locking systems with a power supply integrated into each lock will not require this backup.

Installing electronic access-control systems for guestroom doors has been helpful for reducing room theft in some hotels. Most systems can keep a record of the number of guest entries, as well as entries made by employees such as room attendants. Not only do sophisticated door control systems deter theft by "outsiders" (unauthorized individuals on the property), it also reduces theft by employees. The employee who may be inclined to remove something from a guestroom no longer has the excuse of claiming that a missing key must have been used by a criminal for illegal entry into the room. Also, with the vast number of possible room-entry combinations in electronic systems, there is very little possibility that a criminal will be able to duplicate a working key card for a given guestroom.

Biometric Devices

Beginning in the early 1990s there was interest in the use of biometric devices in hotel security systems. Biometric devices utilize human characteristics that are unique to a specific individual, such as fingerprints; the retina or iris of an eye; or the size, shape, and print of a hand. Biometric access systems were touted by some as "just around the corner" for use in hotels, with their application being focused on guests. To date, however, biometric access systems for guests have seen limited use in hotels, although there is growing interest in the use of biometrics for other applications. For example, the Venetian Macao-Resort installed fingerprint and 3D face recognition to authenticate its 12,000 employees and control access to restricted areas.[5]

One hospitality firm that has used biometrics in the customer area is Disney. At Walt Disney World, fingerprints of guests are scanned into a biometric reader and linked to their tickets. The result is that a given ticket can only be used by one person. This essentially eliminates the potential for tickets to be shared or for a multi-day pass to be purchased and used by multiple people.[6] The U.S. government also makes extensive use of biometrics in the Department of Homeland Security and other agencies.[7] A more common application of biometrics within the business community is its use in the validation of users of time clocks. Biometric devices can verify the individual clocking in or out and remove the potential for abuse by individuals clocking other people in or out.

Secondary Access-Limiting Devices

Deadbolts are installed in guestroom doors to provide an additional method for guests to secure the room when they are inside. Having a manually activated deadbolt was at one time common, but this caused at least two problems. First, the guest might neglect to activate the deadbolt. Second, if there were more than one guest in the room and a guest left, one of the remaining guests either would have to leave the deadbolt open until the first guest returned or would need to let the first guest back into the room by opening the deadbolt.

Many hotels now use locks that automatically activate the deadbolt when the door is closed. Besides providing additional security, these also eliminate the practice of extending the deadbolt to hold the door open—a security risk as well as a practice that damages the door frame.

Security chains or bars are installed on many guestroom doors to allow the guest to open the door and still restrict room access. These devices may require attachment via screws to the door frame and the door. The screw attachments are a potential weak link in the security equipment and need to be inspected to be sure that the screws provide a strong fastening for the chain/bar.

Connecting doors between guestrooms should be capable of being secured with a deadbolt from either side of the door.

Sliding glass doors are another consideration in establishing the security of a guestroom. A number of secondary access-restricting devices are available and should be examined as possible additions to the single latch provided with each sliding glass door. Hinged bars, metal or wood devices that can be placed in the sliding channel, or additional lock units are sometimes used to add to the security of sliding glass doors. A metal peg may be inserted in a hole drilled through both the sliding door and the frame to prevent the sliding door unit from being lifted out of the channel and removed from the frame.

Windows that open may need secondary latching devices. If local fire codes permit, devices that limit how far windows can be opened may be installed to help prevent intruders from entering through ground floor or balcony windows. These devices can also reduce or eliminate the possibility of children (and even adults) falling out of open windows.

Automatic Door Closers and View Ports

Guests do not always close the door to the guestroom when they enter or leave. Sometimes room attendants fail to close the guestroom door securely behind them after cleaning a room. When such oversights occur, the potential for loss is great.

Guestroom doors equipped with automatic closers can help ensure that the locking hardware engages. In addition, automatic closers help to maintain the separation between the guestroom and the corridor that is needed for fire/smoke protection. Hotels need to be sure that door closers operate properly and that no obstruction (such as loose carpeting) exists that could stop them from acting. Some hotels have switches on the guestroom door to inform the occupant (via a chirping sound) that the door has not closed. Other hotels have systems that inform the front desk of an open guestroom door.

A view port provides the guest with the ability to see someone outside the guestroom door without opening the door. View port locations should comply with provisions in the Americans with Disabilities Act. A wide-angle view port maximizes the view of the corridor adjacent to the guestroom door. If view ports are installed, lighting in the corridors should be arranged to prevent glare and avoid placing faces in the shadows. Hotel security and other personnel should periodically inspect view ports to make sure that they have not been removed or tampered with in an effort to observe roomed guests from outside the room. In light of an incident involving a famous TV personality videotaped in her guestroom through the view port, some hotels have provided interior covers for view ports. Additionally, travelers have been urged to use tape or other methods to block the view port if they are concerned about Peeping Toms attempting to look into the room.[8]

A relatively recent piece of security technology available for hotels is the digital video door viewer. These devices provide guests with a much wider and clearer view of the area outside the guestroom than is afforded by view ports. A camera and video screen provide this view.

Telephones

Most hotels have a telephone in each of their guestrooms. The guestroom telephone can be used by the guest to notify the property of emergencies or suspicious activities, and by the property to notify the guest of emergencies such as fires.

In-Room Safes

In-room safes for the protection of guests' items are becoming increasingly common. Such units may be opened by using a key, key card, digital keypad, or payment card. Ideally, an in-room safe should be capable of holding a standard laptop computer and other electronic guest valuables.

If a hotel does not already have in-room safes, the feasibility of installing them should be reviewed by the hotel's managers and security team. Insurance and legal reviews should also be completed. Postings in the guestrooms should be made in all instances to make it clear to guests that safe-deposit boxes or a safe is provided in the hotel's offices for the storage of guest valuables, and that the hotel is not responsible for valuables not placed there. Otherwise, a state's statutory limits of liability on valuables may not protect the hotel.

In-Room Security Information

In excess of 90 percent of hotels surveyed in the *2010 Lodging Survey* indicated that they provide printed safety information in the guestroom. A sample of this type of material is found in Exhibit 1. Some hotels run videos on TV channels that provide safety and security information as well. Fewer than 10 percent of hotels in the *2010 Lodging Survey* indicated that they provide a safety video in their guestrooms.

Many jurisdictions also require that a floor plan or an information card be provided in each guestroom that indicates the location of the guestroom in relation to the nearest fire stairwell. Such information cards should also review the steps to be taken by guests in the event of a fire emergency.

In addition to fire protection information, management should consider including other safety and security information on the guestroom door. Decals or notices may be posted that:

- Tell guests how to double-lock the guestroom door

- Urge guests not to open the door without first identifying the person seeking entrance

- Explain any special guestroom security devices

- Point out the availability of safe-deposit boxes at the front desk

- Contain any other safety and security information the property's management may decide to include

Other Security Equipment

At any lodging property, choices must be made about which investments will bring the best return. When making decisions about security, management has to decide what sort of balance is desired between personnel and equipment. Some properties opt for elaborate equipment out of a belief that it will better meet their needs than a larger security staff; other properties determine that an investment in personnel better addresses their needs. As with all decisions relating to security, these choices have to be made based on a property's specific requirements.

A property's management should understand the uses and limitations of any given type of security equipment before authorizing its installation. A comprehensive review of need and feasibility should be completed by objective experts to determine whether the system is appropriate for the property (a survey or audit provided at no charge by the representative of a product or system may reflect the seller's natural bias). Even when choosing not to purchase a particular type of equipment, management should be prepared to explain why the equipment would not have significantly improved the security of the property. This is important because many lawsuits filed against lodging properties cite the lack of certain types of security equipment (for example, closed-circuit television) as evidence of negligence. A property that carefully considers all equipment options may be better able to answer such charges of negligence.

Modern technology holds many potential benefits for the lodging industry, but care must be taken to select equipment and systems that are practical and that have proven records of effectiveness within the industry. Before making a purchase, managers should request a list of other lodging properties using that particular item or system to determine whether it is effective for lodging establishments. Managers should also consider the ability of the property's security staff (supplemented by the maintenance staff) to do the necessary preventive maintenance to keep the system working. Finally, a reputable organization with experience substantiated by successful installations should be selected to supply any equipment or systems that are chosen.

This section examines some of the types and uses of security equipment in the lodging industry today, but does not constitute an endorsement of any equipment discussed.

Closed-Circuit Television

Closed-circuit television (CCTV) is now a common surveillance tool used in many aspects of American society. To realize their full value, CCTV systems require appropriate monitoring and follow-up responses to anything observed that requires investigation, but just having a visible CCTV system can help to deter criminals. Some innkeepers have even installed CCTV cameras that were not operational. The rationale for this was that the presence of the cameras would be sufficient to deter criminals who would not realize that they were not actually being observed. Some courts and juries, however, have found the use of such "dummy" cameras to be inappropriate because it implies a degree of protection that is not in fact present. A person being victimized, for example, may base his or her behavior on the belief that the scene is being witnessed by someone in the CCTV control room and that help is on the way.

Communication Systems

In order to respond promptly to a security need, a communication system may be required that facilitates the quick notification of the employee or employees responsible for the security function. When choosing such systems and equipment, a property's management should consider the size and configuration of its property. The communication system should be able to contact all areas of the property where there may be a need for personnel to be reached.

One type of communication equipment sometimes used by lodging properties is a system in which the security officer carries a pager or two-way radio on rounds so that the front desk agent or other appropriate personnel can contact him or her directly at any time. In properties with more than one security officer, the

CCTV to the Rescue

The value of a state-of-the art closed-circuit television (CCTV) system lies in its ability to quickly reveal the source of a security breach. A prime example of the use of a sophisticated system can be found at the Talbott Hotel in Chicago, where general manager Troy Strand had become dissatisfied with the limitations of an outmoded system. In particular, Strand was frustrated by the excessive amount of training time required by the old system and by the need to spend "hours and hours, holding your finger on the mouse, scrolling through video" in order to locate an often inadequate image.

So the Talbott upgraded to a user-friendly intelligent-video management system from 3VR Security, Inc. Within weeks, the new system proved its mettle. When a thief broke into a room and made off with a Neiman Marcus bag and a purse, the 3VR system was quickly able to narrow down video footage based on the hour, the location, and the presence of unusual physical movement. The facial recognition feature then allowed the hotel's security staff to create a video of the incident that included a clear shot of the suspect's face. This evidence was gathered so quickly that it could be presented to police officers soon after they arrived on the scene. Within a matter of hours, the suspect was apprehended and the belongings of the victims were returned.

Douglas Ostrander, director of security at Turning Stone Casino and Resorts in upstate New York, discovered that high-tech crime-solving capability is not the only way in which a CCTV system can demonstrate its worth. The Turning Stone was in the midst of a $308 million expansion project when a security guard discovered an unlocked door on one of the project's secured buildings and notified the police, who launched an investigation. Fortunately, the casino's management had had the foresight at the outset of the project to install CCTV cameras. As a result, the IT department soon was able to pull up the CCTV coverage of the building in question and determine the problem—one of the project's contractors had left an extra key under the building's doormat so that a licensed electrician could get in later. Relieved, Ostrander notified the police that no crime had been committed and the investigation was dropped. Ostrander was also able to show the video clip to the offending contractor and explain the importance of following security protocols.

In both instances, the outcome was all that could be desired. The Talbott Hotel was able to apprehend the thief and return the stolen property to its rightful owners in a rapid and efficient manner. Without the intelligent-video management system, the criminal might well have gotten away, leaving the hotel guests as victims and forcing the hotel staff to worry about when the thief might strike again. The Turning Stone Casino and Resorts was able to rest easy in the knowledge that no crime had been committed and to firm up its security precautions to prevent future problems. Without CCTV technology, casino employees would have been left to wonder about a criminal in their midst while a major security vulnerability would have remained unaddressed. In both cases, CCTV had come to the rescue by providing the peace of mind that all hotel owners and managers seek when making an investment in security technology.

Source: Adapted from Marta Roberts, "CCTV Lowers the Stakes," http://securitymanagement.com/article/cctv-lowers-stakes; and Robert Elliott, "Watching Over Guests," http://securitymanagement.com/article/watching-over-guests.

devices used should also allow security officers, who may be moving about the premises, to communicate with one another.

Some communication systems have been extended to include guests and the public. For example, some properties have installed "duress" systems, which permit the monitoring of a scream or higher decibel sound (indicating a possible call for assistance) at a recording location anywhere throughout a property. Even if it is an "unwanted alarm" activated by screams from children at play, it is better to investigate and determine the cause for the high-decibel alert. In more advanced systems, there is the capability of two-way communication. Such systems are particularly valuable in parking facilities, remote entrances, stairwells, or other locations where protection seems advisable.

Alarm Systems

Alarm systems are increasingly popular for perimeter control around lodging properties and in the entrances and emergency exits found throughout the properties. Access to hotel corridors and guestrooms can be controlled through keys or cards that control admission to both the locked corridor areas and the guestroom. The integrity of the door control system may be enhanced through the use of panic hardware for emergency exits; emergency exit doors may be fitted with an alarm that will sound at a control center if the door is violated. This is critical where a fire door must be secured against illegal entry but still be available for exit.

In some hotels, the telephone room can serve as a control center for all property alarms if it is properly located. Generally, this room should be physically accessible only to authorized persons. It may receive alarm signals from cashiers, safes, or emergency door locations, in addition to being a communications control point.

Basic types of alarm systems include local alarms, contact alarms, remote alarms, and fire alarms.

Local Alarms. **Local alarms** (that is, those not hard-wired to a central monitoring location) can be effective as deterrents. A typical example is the local alarm that is integrated with the panic hardware on a fire exit. When the exit door is opened, the circuit is broken and the alarm sounds.

Contact Alarms. **Contact alarms** (systems which *are* hard-wired to a central point) can be monitored and appropriate action may be taken when the alarm goes off. Silent alarms are always hard-wired to a central point and may be considered for cashier areas, storerooms, and other areas. From such a point, the alarm can be silently transmitted to the telephone room, police department, or private security company; both the police and on-premises security personnel can be alerted. An example of a contact alarm sometimes used in cashier areas that is helpful during robberies involves using a money clip that cannot be removed from a cash register without tripping a silent alarm. Some properties record the serial numbers of the money in this clip, which is usually not used for normal transactions, to make the money easier to trace.

Restaurants, cocktail lounges, ballrooms, and other function rooms attract members of the public who are not registered guests of the hotel. Unfortunately, there is no perfect location for alarms in such facilities. Consequently, protection may include silent alarms at the cashier's locations with security personnel assigned to cover major functions, conventions, or programs that will attract a large number of non-registered individuals.

Remote Alarms. Remote alarm systems typically rely on some sort of transmission—for example, microwaves, radio waves, seismic detection, and photoelectric light and infrared radiation beams.

Microwave detectors—active units that transmit and receive electromagnetic energy—are designed to detect motion. Perimeter protection with microwaves is used in some properties due to: (1) its long-range capabilities; (2) its potential for stability, once adjusted; and (3) its virtually tamper-proof characteristics. This is best used in locations where unwanted movement should be detected.

Radio frequency systems trip an alarm when any intruder breaks the radio waves by moving into a radio frequency field. As with the use of the microwave detectors just mentioned, these systems are of greatest value in locations where there should be no motion. A radio frequency system is best used as an intruder alarm.

A **seismic detector**, which registers pressure, is also used in a perimeter control function. Usually, the device is buried in the ground, thereby escaping detection by even the most sophisticated intruder. Its use is limited within the industry and is generally practical only for highly specialized protection needs, such as in protecting against Peeping Toms.

Another perimeter control system is the **photoelectric light beam system**. In this system, a filtered light beam passes between a sending and receiving unit; as is the case in radio frequency systems, any break in the beam sets off an alarm. This system is generally used for outside perimeter control, especially in resort properties.

Finally, **infrared radiation detection** is another limited-use alarm system that is generally used in areas such as a locked storeroom where only inanimate objects are normally found. Since the system is set to accept a predetermined radiation level, if a person (who always has a higher radiation level than inanimate objects) enters the area, the alarm is triggered. For obvious reasons, such a system is generally used only to resolve a specific problem within a lodging establishment. For example, one large resort uses infrared detection to monitor a rooftop that could provide access to guestroom windows and to protect entryways to the convention center when it is not in use.

Fire Alarms. While the use of safety alarm systems is usually optional, fire alarm systems are generally required by local fire codes. The Occupational Safety and Health Act (OSHA) also requires fire alarms to alert employees to fires or other emergency conditions. Thus, every lodging establishment must have a fire alarm system in operating condition and have it tested at least every two months.

With arson being an ongoing problem within the lodging industry, increasingly sophisticated fire alarm systems are vital. Fire alarms provide an audible alarm in the relevant area; it is important to evaluate the advantage of installing a central console at the front desk or other location where twenty-four-hour coverage is available, thus permitting the prompt notification of local fire authorities when a fire alarm goes off. If a fire alarm can be directly relayed to a fire station in the community, this possibility should be carefully evaluated. In any event, the fire department should always be immediately notified of the alarm. No delays should be made to determine the nature and extent of the fire before calling for professional assistance. OSHA mandates that delays in transmitting alarms should not exceed thirty seconds. In communities that depend upon a volunteer fire service, this may create a major problem and a variance may be necessary. Similarly, in a large city the fire authorities may prefer a verification period in excess of thirty seconds to avoid answering unwanted smoke alarms. An unwanted alarm, as distinguished from a false alarm, may result from the correct functioning of a smoke alarm in reporting a concentration of smoke in, for example, an area of heavy cigarette, cigar, or pipe smoke, even though there is no immediate fire danger.

Choosing an Alarm System. Managers should weigh the following considerations when deciding on any type of alarm system:

- What is the response capability at any time of day for reacting to a local alarm on premises? Would there be an increase in false (unwanted) alarm response by a contract agency or the local police if the alarm is connected to a security service or the police department? Is the sounding of the alarm likely to deter a criminal act?

- Is the contact alarm relayed to an on-site location at which a person is always stationed? What will the delay interval be in calling for the police? How quickly are police officers likely to be able to respond? If the community provides a direct alarm network, would it be feasible for the contact alarms to be directly linked? Where such linkage does not exist, are there contract security services that could receive the initial alarm, relay it to the police, and then proceed as a back-up to the police response?

- A silent alarm, similar to a contact alarm, provides the capability of warning that a crime is in progress. Silent alarms should be used when sounding an audible alarm within the hearing range of a criminal could possibly endanger innocent lives. Managers should ask themselves: In what locations would silent alarms be best utilized? Will the use of silent alarms allow sufficient time for responders to intercept the criminal(s)?

Elevator Security

Hotel elevators may service guestroom floors only or may also provide service to meeting rooms, restaurants, and underground parking areas. It is becoming a more common practice to restrict access to guestroom floors by using a key card system in the elevator. In such systems, guests can only access guestroom floors if they insert a valid key card. Further restriction can also be created for "executive" or "club" floors, with only key cards for guestrooms on these floors able to cause the elevator to stop at these floors. Elevators from parking areas should stop at the lobby level and ideally be within sight of front desk personnel or security staff.

Endnotes

1. www.ahla.com/DHS.

2. For more information on this program, call the American Hotel & Lodging Educational Institute at 1-800-349-0299 and ask to speak with the Professional Certificate Department, or go to this web page: https://www.ahlei.org/Certifications/Hospitality_Skills/ Certified_Lodging_Security_Officer_%28CLSO%29/.

3. http://www.nfpa.org/catalog/product.asp?pid=73011&order%5Fsrc=B484.

4. www.openways.com.

5. http://www.securityinfowatch.com/Gaming+Announcements/venetian-macao-resort-hotel-deploys-bioscrypt-biometric-solutions.

6. http://news21project.org/story/2006/09/01/walt_disney_world_the_governments.

7. http://www.biometrics.gov/ReferenceRoom/FederalPrograms.aspx.

8. http://hotel-online.com/News/PR2009_4th/Oct09_VideoCase.html.

 # Key Terms

citizen's arrest—An arrest made by someone who is not a law enforcement official, or by a law enforcement official who is not working in that capacity. In many—but by no means all—jurisdictions, such arrests are permitted. However, even when permissible, they should only be done when a sworn police officer cannot respond in time and when prompt action is clearly required.

collusion—An activity in which two or more employees secretly interact in an effort to steal from their employer.

contact alarms—Alarm systems hard-wired to a central monitoring point, from which action can be taken when the alarm goes off.

infrared radiation detection—A limited-use alarm system set to accept a predetermined radiation level and trigger an alarm if a person enters the area (since human beings emit a higher level of radiation than do inanimate objects).

local alarms—Alarm systems not hard-wired to a central monitoring location and valuable as deterrents.

microwave detectors—A perimeter control system with long-range capabilities and tamper-proof characteristics that detects motion by transmitting and receiving electromagnetic energy.

Miranda warning—A legally required notification in the United States; people suspected of a crime must be warned before being questioned that they have the right to remain silent, that anything they say can be used against them in court, that they have the right to an attorney, and that if they cannot afford an attorney, one will be provided for them.

photoelectric light beam system—A perimeter control system in which a filtered light beam passes between a sending and receiving unit; any break in the beam sets off an alarm.

proximate cause—The primary or predominating cause from which an injury follows as a natural, direct, and immediate consequence, and without which the injury would not have occurred. Also known as legal cause.

radio frequency system—An alarm system in which radio signals are used to detect motion; the alarm is tripped when an intruder breaks the radio waves by moving into a radio frequency field.

reasonable care—Taking actions that are ordinary or usual to protect against a foreseeable event—the central legal issue being that innkeepers owe a duty of care to all persons on their property. Failure to meet this duty may result in security-related liability.

remote alarm—An alarm system that typically relies on some sort of transmission such as microwaves, radio waves, or photoelectric light beams.

seismic detector—A perimeter control system, usually buried in the ground, which registers pressure; its use is limited within the industry and is generally only for highly specialized protection needs.

tort law—Provides bases for actions permitting one person to remedy a wrong committed against him or her by another. For example, tort law permits an injured party to bring a lawsuit for damages against a security officer and his or her employing property for such unreasonable conduct as false arrest, false imprisonment, malicious prosecution, defamation, and slander.

 Review Questions

1. What are the general areas of concern that should be included in a property's security program?

2. What are the main areas of vulnerability that create security problems for hotels?

3. Why is it important to cultivate a law enforcement liaison?

4. What are the various options for security staffing, and what are the advantages and disadvantages of each?

5. What specific elements should be incorporated into a security training program?

6. What factors should be considered in deciding whether a property's security guards ought to be armed?

7. What activities by a security officer could result in civil liability for a hotel?

8. Why is it important to consider security when designing a hotel?

9. What are some security devices commonly used in guestrooms?

10. What are some of the different types of alarm systems?

Internet Sites

For more information, visit the following Internet sites. Remember that Internet addresses can change without notice. If the site is no longer there, you can use a search engine to look for additional sites.

American Fire Sprinkler Association
www.firesprinkler.org

American Hotel & Lodging
  Association
www.ahla.com

American Hotel & Lodging Educational
  Institute
www.ahlei.org

American National Standards Institute
www.ansi.org

International Code Council
www.iccsafe.org

National Institute of Justice
www.nij.gov

National Safety Council
www.nsc.org

The Police Chief
www.policechiefmagazine.org

SecurityInfoWatch.com
www.securityinfowatch.com

Security Magazine
www.securitymagazine.com

Security Management Online
www.securitymanagement.com

Case Study

Lights ... Camera ... Action?

Ted Kline, COO of Berryworth Inns, greeted the executive committee members as they entered the conference room for their monthly meeting. In attendance were the controller, director of security, and the VPs of operations, engineering, and sales.

"As you may know, this month marks the three-year anniversary of the chain-wide installation of electronic locking systems. After looking over our incident reports and claims for this area, I'm happy to report that the system has been a great success! Besides the number of lock-incident cases dropping to almost none, the cost of the few cases that did occur decreased dramatically—by 30 percent! Since this was a decision agreed on by all present, these statistics are something that we can all be proud of—so give yourselves a hand!"

As the smattering of applause died down, Ted continued, "Since this last investment was so successful, and we have definitely seen the payoff and reaped the benefits, I believe it's time to branch out and implement yet another security feature that can help minimize other security incidents—while reducing expenses, of course. Gerald, why don't you take it from here."

All eyes turned toward their security guru. "Thanks, Ted. Well, as I see it, there are two priorities we can choose to address—actually, they were numbers two and three on our list three years ago when we decided to go with the electronic locking systems, and I believe they are still critical today. I believe our next logical choice would be either updated lighting or a CCTV system. Each of these would help address problems we've been having in the parking lot, corridors, and stairwells."

Frank, the engineer, asked the obvious first question. "Well, what does each actually involve?"

"By lighting we mean both inside and outside lighting," Gerald responded. "We'd be replacing existing fixtures with energy efficient lamps, increasing wattage, and adding additional fixtures wherever necessary—keeping within the aesthetics of the properties, of course—we wouldn't want anything obnoxious."

"What do you mean by inside lighting? Are you talking about brighter corridors and stairwells and such?" asked Frank.

"Yes," Gerald continued. "Who here hasn't stayed at a hotel somewhere where it was just a tad difficult to look through that little peephole and clearly make out who was standing outside your door? Better lighting would make that identification process easier. Anyway, turning to CCTV now. That installation would involve the placement of numerous cameras throughout the property—both inside and out—and some sort of home base or control panel for monitoring."

Alan, the controller, commented, "There's obviously a cost involved for both ideas. What kind of investment are we looking at for each option? I'm sure each is quite hefty."

"Actually, Alan," Ted answered, "it's hard to justify one choice over the other if you look only at the financial aspect. There are many other factors that need to be taken into consideration in order to make the most beneficial decision. But we can start with financial concerns."

Alan continued, "What worries me is the initial purchase price of everything—new lamps and fixtures, along with any increased energy costs to maintain whatever new lighting system or level of lighting that is deemed appropriate—"

"—especially," interrupted Frank, "when before we've just changed the lamps or increased the wattage or cleaned the lenses."

"Those are valid concerns," said Gerald, "but research shows that the new high-tech lighting systems are actually more cost- and energy-efficient and will save money in the long run."

"So does that mean you're in favor of lighting as our next investment?" asked Alan.

"Now, don't go jumping to conclusions. Just because I can validate lighting as a potentially cost-efficient investment doesn't mean I don't have other concerns," answered Gerald.

Ted tried to clarify by asking, "So your choice would be CCTV?"

"Actually, yes," responded Gerald. "Why? Most of all, because it's an excellent deterrent of criminal activity. Chances are, if people see or know that their criminal actions are being caught on tape, they will be less likely to commit their intended act. And if an incident did occur, we'd have a tape recording of it, and the suspect would be much easier to apprehend—something which police officers really like, since they don't need to get a confession and they have immediate evidence."

Frank jumped in, "Well, the same thing can be said for lighting—it's also an excellent deterrent! The brighter it is, and the more lights there are around, the less likely criminals are going to invade that space. They'll move on to another property where it's darker."

Sandy, the VP of sales, finally spoke up. "Gerald, I agree with you—CCTV should be the choice. We can sell that! CCTV is a specific security feature that clients and prospects can immediately understand and see as providing better physical protection for them. On the other hand, it would be really hard for me or our sales staff to make the same point by saying, 'We have lots more lights now.' Lights won't seem to offer the same level of protection or sense of personal security that CCTV does. So, from a sales and marketing aspect, CCTV holds significantly more potential as a salable feature—especially when it comes to repeat customers associating security with our brand image."

Kamron, the VP of operations, finally broke in. "Those are all fine points, too, Sandy, but have you thought about the additional staffing that would be necessary for all those CCTV monitors that would be installed across our thirty properties? In order to be effective, those monitors should be under surveillance twenty-four hours a day, and some of our properties just couldn't handle that."

Gerald, knowing more about security options than the rest of the group, interjected, "Actually, there is a possibility of remote monitoring. It's new but seems to be catching on."

Ted spoke up. "I've never heard of that. What exactly is it—"

"—and how much does it cost? It sounds expensive," Alan finished.

"I'm not sure of the expense," answered Gerald. "The basic premise is that we install the monitors, link them through a satellite to a monitoring office somewhere else—say Texas or Michigan or something—and their staff watches our hotel. Voilà—no additional staff necessary."

"Like I said, that sounds expensive," repeated Alan.

"Look, all I'm saying is that it's something that would need to be investigated—it's another option if we didn't want to add staff," Gerald responded.

Ted broke in again. "Excellent point, Gerald. However, it reminds me of something I read recently—how failure to monitor your CCTV system could actually create additional liability. I mean, what happens if someone is being attacked in full view of a camera and nothing is done about it? That sounds like a budget-breaking lawsuit to me."

Kamron answered, "I agree. But it seems like that would only be a problem in properties that weren't sufficiently staffed. And of course we would take precautions to make sure we definitely weren't understaffed—even if we had to look into that satellite monitoring thing. But, if you think about it, the same negligence lawsuit could happen with lighting, too. You can have the best lighting in the world, but if there's no staff around—security or otherwise—to do anything about an attack, what's the point of increased lighting?"

"Wait a minute," said Alan. "Okay, yes it's true that both CCTV and lighting can be seen as a deterrent to criminal activity. But, lighting makes more financial sense. Although the costs may be about equal up front, the lighting system could pay for itself in a few years, while CCTV would mean a continuous drain on a hotel's labor costs. And what actually may be the most critical point—if our competition has recently increased their lighting systems, we need to do the same thing if we want to stay market competitive."

"You bet—and the same thing could be said about CCTV, too," added Gerald. "Keeping up with the Joneses, as they say."

Sandy shook her head. "Gentlemen, all this talk is well and good, but you're still missing my point. Sales can't use lighting as a selling point. Trust me on this. It would be like asking me to sell romance versus a dozen roses. We all know romance is there, but people can see and touch and feel and smell roses—making for a much easier sell. Sure, additional lighting in the parking lot might make the hotel seem more inviting to transient guests arriving at night, but what about the majority of our business? What about groups and meeting planners? I know for a fact that I can schedule more groups and tours with the added benefit of a CCTV security system. Why? Because I can show them the system. I can't show them lights. They take lights for granted—they might know it was bright, but they wouldn't connect that to increased security. Believe me, in the long run, the increased business brought in by the CCTV system would greatly outweigh the investment cost. "

"Well, people," Ted concluded, "it looks like we have a tough decision on our hands."

Discussion Questions

1. What are the advantages and disadvantages of choosing improved lighting as the security investment?

2. What are the advantages and disadvantages of choosing CCTV as the security investment?

3. Which investment would you recommend and why?

Case Number: 3872CA

The following industry experts helped generate and develop this case: Wendell Couch, ARM, CHA, Director of Technical Services for the Risk Management Department of Bass Hotels & Resorts; and Raymond C. Ellis, Jr., CHE, CHTP, CLSD, Professor, Conrad N. Hilton College, University of Houston, Director, Loss Prevention Management Institute.

Chapter 4 Outline

Key and Key Card Control
    Electronic Access Systems
Surveillance and Access Control
    Procedures
    Patrols
The Presence of Unauthorized Persons
    Individuals Involved with Illegal
      Drugs
Safe-Deposit Box Procedures
    Safe-Deposit Box Keys and Key
      Control
    Access Procedures
    Special or Unusual Access
Lost and Found Procedures
Guest Views of Hotel Security Measures

Competencies

1. Identify various types of key and key card control and their advantages and disadvantages. (pp. 103–109)

2. Explain how effective access control is achieved through surveillance and security patrols. (pp. 109–110)

3. Explain how to deal with the presence of unauthorized or undesirable persons. (pp. 110–112)

4. Summarize effective safe-deposit box security procedures and explain the hotel's liability for safe-deposit boxes. (pp. 112–120)

5. Describe typical hotel lost and found procedures. (p. 121)

6. Discuss some guest views of hotel security measures. (pp. 121–126)

4

Security Procedures Covering Guest Concerns

Every property's management needs to establish procedures for its staff to follow that will help lead to the safe and secure functioning of the operation. All employees, not merely security personnel, should know the appropriate security procedures that will help protect guests and the property from danger and loss at the hands of criminals operating on the premises. Unfortunately, not all losses come at the hands of criminals external to the property; many security procedures are needed to control theft by guests and employees. Other security procedures are needed to address the potential for loss created by or during emergencies, including accidents. Asset protection procedures involve protecting the property from losses arising from any number of sources, both internal and external.

This chapter discusses a number of security procedures that help protect guests and the property from victimization, loss, and liability. We will look at key and key card control, surveillance and access control (including the presence of unauthorized persons), safe-deposit box procedures, and lost and found procedures. The chapter concludes with a look at guest perceptions of various hotel security measures.

Key and Key Card Control

A system of key control is essential to the security of a lodging property. All keys—whether metal for conventional locks or plastic for electronic locks—should be adequately controlled. The best lock in the world can't protect a property or its guests if poor key control allows a criminal to obtain a key to that lock.

Most lodging properties use at least three levels of keying, whether metal keys or plastic key cards. These levels typically include emergency keys, master keys, and guestroom keys. The **emergency key** opens all guestroom doors, even when they are double locked. It can be used, for example, to enter a room when the guest needs aid and is unable to reach or open the door. The emergency key should be highly protected and its use strictly controlled and recorded; it should never leave the property. One procedure for emergency keys is to have them locked in a safe or safe-deposit box and signed out by the individual needing one. The log should be dated and signed by the individual taking the key.

A **master key** opens all guestrooms in a designated area that are not double locked. Types of master keys include section master keys, floor master keys, and grand master keys. As the name suggests, a section master key will open all

103

guestrooms (not double locked) within a certain section of the hotel. A section master key may be issued to a housekeeping supervisor who is providing a quality check on one or more guestrooms cleaned by room attendants in a single section of the hotel. If it is more practical for an entire floor to be supervised by one person, that individual would be provided with a floor master key. Only the executive housekeeper and assistant housekeeper within the housekeeping department would be issued a grand master key, permitting access to any guestroom. Upper management should establish protocols on the use of these levels of master keys for not only housekeeping personnel but also for engineering and maintenance, room service, front office and bell service, and security personnel.

The need for careful control and accounting of all master keys is apparent when one recognizes the numerous reasons for accessing a room while the guest may not be present. The most effective control of a master key is to have it signed in and out each time it is used. Master keys, when not in use on the property, should be retained in a locked case and secured in a designated place of safekeeping—by department in a large property and at the front desk or executive office in a small facility. A master key should only be issued to authorized personnel based on their need to use the key, not simply on their status within the operation. A written record should be maintained that details which employees have received master keys. This record can be made a part of the employee personnel file or it can be a separate file maintained by a representative of management. Employee requests for additional or duplicate master keys should also be in writing. Master keys should be accounted for whenever employees resign, transfer, go on vacation, or leave the property or an area within a property for whatever reason. Just as with emergency keys, master keys should never be removed from the property.

A guestroom key opens a single guestroom if the door is not double locked. Guestroom keys should be controlled by front desk personnel, who should always make sure that the person receiving the key to a guestroom is the guest registered for that room. Appropriate identification should always be requested. An effort should always be made to retrieve keys from guests when they check out. For the convenience of, and as a reminder to, the guest, consider having well-secured key return boxes located in the lobby, at exit points of the hotel, and in courtesy vehicles. In some resort destination areas, such as Hawaii, secured hotel-key receptacles have been placed beyond security screening points in airport terminals. A number of keys are retrieved in this manner as guests awaiting a flight are reminded, when they notice the receptacles, that they had failed to turn in their keys at check-out.

Hotels should consider using keys that do not have the property's name, address, or logo on them. This practice makes it much more difficult for keys that have been lost to be traced to the appropriate property by whoever finds them. (Eliminating any sort of return address also eliminates the expense of return postage.) In a similar vein, most properties do not list the room number on the key. Instead, they code each room or room key to a master list at the front desk. Under this system, the number on the key refers to a number on the list, not a number on the guestroom door. The guest is provided with an identification card, folder, or some other method for identifying the guestroom number. The

AT YOUR RISK

BY ANTHONY MARSHALL

Trade Secrets of a Professional Unwanted Guest

"I think you should go to jail," Harris Rosen, President of Tamar Inns, Inc., suggested to me. "Michael Smith can teach you a lot about locks." Rosen spoke from experience. Michael had visited Tamar's Omni Hotel in Orlando often, but never as a registered guest ....

Michael's story was a fascinating tale of desperation, survival, and smarts. From age sixteen, when he left home, Michael exploited his cunning to live free at various hotels' expense. The secret to his success was easy access to the hotel's keys: guest-room keys, master keys—even safe-deposit keys.

Michael soon learned that stealing a guest's safe-deposit box key from his or her room opened the floodgate to cash, credit cards, and jewelry—all of which could be easily traded for drugs and the other necessities of his life at the time.

Once he had given the correct guest's name and room number to the front desk associate, he often heard the following: "Please sign for the envelope on the signature line." Not once in twenty-two years was he ever asked for personal identification.

Michael learned that front desk associates almost always focus exclusively on getting the signature on the guest's safe-deposit box envelope. That's what they'd been trained to do. Demanding personal identification was never part of their jobs.

Michael earned the equivalent of a master's degree in the hotel industry's history of keys. No lock or security technique could stop him. When Michael started at sixteen, most hotel keys he stole were standard metal keys with the room number stamped right on them. Room identification was a cinch. A few years later, when many hotels began to cross-code guestroom key numbers, he simply broke their codes.

"Most hotel codes were not too difficult to decipher," Michael explained. "They might renumber guestroom 215 to read 512 and that was about it."

Electronic locks eventually entered the market and the hotel industry focused on giving each new registrant a new key code. Security officers breathed a sigh of relief because they assumed key-control problems would vanish. They hoped room burglaries would stop—but that's not what happened.

Michael studied the new electronic locks. He discovered the deadbolt doesn't close on an electric lock when a guest exits the guestroom. Armed only with a 14-inch industrial screwdriver, he could enter a guestroom in two seconds flat. Without a deadbolt, it was easy.

Rosen, like many hoteliers, thought electronic locks were the answer to guest-room security problems. After Michael was arrested, Rosen decided to tackle the problem. Working with his staff and the company that initially installed the locks, they found a solution. Today, all of Rosen's hotels have spring-activated deadbolts. Once guests leave their rooms, a large deadbolt automatically springs into place.

"We've locked out the Michael Smiths," Rosen said, insisting that all Tamar's hotel rooms are now secure. Michael Smith has studied the new system and agrees. In fact, Michael is so impressed with the response to his previous trade secrets, he believes he can help Rosen or other hoteliers even more.

(continued)

At Your Risk *(continued)*

> "I think I'd make a fine security officer with his company," Michael said ....
>
> My interview with Michael provided a great deal of insight into the flaws of hotel security. If some of that information alerts hotels to their vulnerability and promotes improvements in security, then perhaps Michael's true rehabilitation has already begun.

Courtesy of *Hotel & Motel Management,* February 15, 1999. Used with permission.

guest should be reminded to keep the room number identifier separate from the key or key card, or the protection of the unidentified key or key card will be compromised.

Some properties have successfully reduced the number of lost keys by requiring key deposits from guests at the time of registration. This results in a higher number of keys being returned at check-out, since keys must be returned to recover the deposit.

Employees may play an important role in the control of keys and access to guestrooms. Cashiers, door attendants, bellpersons, courtesy vehicle operators, and any other appropriate employees should be instructed to remind guests to return keys at check-out. Whenever a key has been left in a room by a departing guest, it should be secured; it should not be left on the top of a housekeeping cart or in any unsecured area. In order to ensure the security of section master, floor master, and grand master keys, they should be secured by staff members at all times during the work shift and turned in prior to leaving the premises. Many organizations require that keys (from guestroom keys to the grand master) be returned to security and placed in a locked cabinet in a secured area of the hotel. Keys should not be taken from the property by employees, regardless of their responsibilities or position on staff.

Keys issued on a temporary basis should be listed in a log that reflects the reason for the issue, the issue date, the time out, the time in, to whom the key was issued, and by whom it was issued. All keys for which the general manager or other appropriate manager is responsible should be kept in a locked safe-deposit box or other secure area when not in use. For properties that still use metal keys, the management there should determine who will be responsible for room key blanks, control keys, master and submaster blanks, and so forth. These responsibilities are sometimes split up among various personnel such as the controller and the chief engineer. At properties that make their own metal keys, key-making machines should be secured at all times except when actually being used. If it is impossible to secure the key-making machine, the drive belt should be removed and secured instead. All blanks and control keys under the supervision of the key-making function should be locked in a strong, wall-mounted key box.

Whenever there is any known or suspected compromise of any metal keys, a loss or theft, or an unauthorized entry by key, the affected lock(s) should be changed out or rotated to another portion of the property. When master keys or emergency keys are involved, re-keying the locks in all of the property areas affected should be considered.

Electronic Access Systems

The electronic and computer locking systems used by most properties today greatly changed the nature of, and reduced the need for, re-keying. The ability to change the data on an electronic key card permits a level of control that was never attainable with a metal key system. With today's electronic locking systems, the access code to a guestroom lock changes after the departure of every guest, so that lost key cards become a minor problem. Some properties let guests keep their key cards as souvenirs. If a master key card is lost, the process of changing every room's access code is usually fairly easily accomplished, often from a centrally located computer.

There are stand-alone systems that require a computer unit at the front desk or in the front office which contains the ranking of entries for each lockset on the property. The process of ranking ensures issuance of a card that is programmed to block the entry of a person who may have checked out and retained the key card with the intention of re-entering illegally. It further establishes the legal entry of the new guest and protects that entry during the duration of the guest's assigned stay. The lockset, containing a microchip, provides a "smart door" that can read a key card and determine whether admission should be permitted. It also records all entries into the room. Thus, in addition to the entries by the guest, there will be an indication of entries by room service, housekeeping, engineering, and other hotel personnel. The lock may be interrogated as to what cards were used for entry. This capability is invaluable in the event that items come up missing from a guestroom and there is no sign of a break-in; the investigation can be focused on those employees who had access to the room. Many reputations have been restored and many a thankful staff member has been cleared of suspicion due to the capability of electronic lock systems to record guestroom entries. Knowledge of these systems' capabilities may serve as a deterrent to staff members who might otherwise be tempted to steal.[1]

Online electronic systems provide control (changing room access) from a remote center to the guestrooms' locksets through infrared, hard wire, or radio frequency technology. In the instance of a stand-alone system, the key card communicates to the lockset upon insertion or swiping of the key card in the lockset.

During the 1990s, many of the major hotel chains mandated the installation of electronic card access systems for both corporate and franchised properties. This established electronic key card access as "state of the art" and makes it difficult for a property without an electronic lock system to defend itself in a legal case in which key control is a major issue.

Exhibit 1 provides a list of questions concerning key control. Though definitely not exhaustive, it makes a number of points that can help lodging property operators to reduce key control problems.

While electronic locking systems provide a number of advantages over mechanical systems, they are subject to human error. Human error in hotel security has been the subject of a number of exposés by television stations over the years.[2] Some of the key-related security lapses that have been documented in these investigations include the following:

Exhibit 1   Basic Key Control Questions

1. Are key records kept up-to-date by all departments controlling those records?
2. Are keys issued to employees on a basis of need rather than convenience or status?
3. For hotels still using metal guestroom keys, is there a standard policy for rotating all keys and locks at least once a year?
4. For hotels still using metal guestroom keys, are locks replaced promptly when master and emergency keys are lost or found missing?
5. How many master keys are available, and to whom are they issued? Would a system of submaster keys that restricted employees to specific areas be helpful to your property?
6. When did you last spot check to ensure that officials or employees actually had keys that were issued to them? Do your employees turn in their keys at the end of a shift?
7. Are extra keys maintained securely? Do you limit access to extra keys?
8. If you make your own replacement metal keys, what restrictions (if any) do you place on access to this equipment?
9. What restrictions do you make on duplicate keys?
10. How many metal keys leave the premises with guests over a six-month period? What percentage is returned and what is the replacement cost?
11. Do you have a policy requiring employees to inquire about the key at check-out time?

- Issuing guestroom keys to unregistered guests
- Failing to have electronic key cards become inoperable after guest check-out, which allows affected rooms to be entered long after the guest vacates them (until a new key is issued)
- Housekeepers allowing individuals without guestroom keys access to guestrooms without proper identification

Key control procedures are often an issue in lawsuits filed against lodging properties. In *King* v. *Trans-Sterling, Inc.,* the plaintiff charged that she had been attacked and raped in her room at the Stardust Hotel in Las Vegas. The room showed no signs of forced entry and evidence showed that, although the hotel had lost as many as 500 keys a week, the rooms had not been re-keyed since the hotel opened twenty-five years earlier. No records had been kept that would indicate how many master keys had been lost or even which employees had keys to which rooms. The then-owners of the Stardust Hotel were ordered to pay $750,000 in compensatory damages and $2.5 million in punitive damages.

Another case was settled out of court following the visit of the plaintiff's attorney to the defendant hotel in the case. The attorney approached the hotel's front desk and requested the key to the room which his client had been assigned at the time of the incident. The key was given to the attorney without any questions or any request for identification. Upon the attorney's return to court with the key, settlement was arranged in the judge's chambers.

Surveillance and Access Control Procedures

Hotel personnel play a central role in watching for trouble and protecting guests and the hotel from loss and unauthorized access. All employees should be trained to watch for suspicious persons or situations. For example, front desk agents should, when possible, keep an eye on a property's entrances, elevators, and stairways. Surveillance equipment may allow a hotel elevator to be programmed to stop at a certain floor for observation, but it is still up to personnel to actually observe it. Likewise, closed-circuit television is virtually worthless without personnel monitoring it. The point is that even surveillance equipment relies on personnel understanding how to use it most efficiently and effectively to control access to a property. Effective access control calls for the development of procedures that deal with how staff should respond to the information gained through both surveillance equipment and the observations of employees.

Patrols

One aspect of surveillance and access control that is frequently mentioned in lawsuits alleging negligence is the absence or inadequate number of patrolling security officers both inside the property and on the grounds. Obviously, the patrol function is very important. Patrols should follow a varied pattern, in terms of both timing and area. Regularly timed patrols should be avoided, since they establish a consistent pattern which criminals can observe and work around.

The two primary functions of patrolling are to deter and detect security and safety incidents and problems. Security officers who patrol a property should be trained in what to look for. Patrolling is much more than simply walking or driving around a property; it involves being alert to anything unusual and can call on the employee's sight, hearing, smell, and touch. Some properties develop a security patrol checklist which helps ensure that patrolling employees remember to check all areas and aspects of the operation.

Patrolling employees can deter crime in a number of ways. First, their visible presence may deter crime. Second, patrol personnel can note conditions that may result in potential security risks, such as lighting or access control equipment that is not functioning correctly. As part of the patrol function, the employee who discovers such conditions should report the discovery to the appropriate individual or department—immediately, if the situation warrants it. Third, patrol personnel can observe and investigate suspicious persons and situations. Each property develops its own procedures for its security personnel to follow when investigating a suspicious person or situation. Suspicious persons may include drunks and potential prostitutes; non-guests loitering in the lobby, on the grounds or parking lot, and on guestroom floors; and any persons (including employees) who are in areas they should not be in. Suspicious situations may include doors left unlocked or ajar, forced locks, broken windows, and automobiles parked in inappropriate places.

The patrol function allows security officers to move throughout all areas of a property. For this reason, training for patrols should emphasize an awareness of fire and safety in addition to security. A significant contribution may be made to a property's protection through this special training. Fire or smoke and unsafe conditions such as torn rugs, loose handrails, unsafe walking surfaces, missing fire extinguishers, obstructions in stairwells and emergency exits, burned out emergency exit lights, and so forth should be noted and promptly reported by patrolling employees.

Training should inform patrol personnel not only what to look for, but also how to respond to what is seen. Many properties require their patrol personnel to file a report at the end of their shift noting what they have seen, especially if it was unusual or called for some sort of action. In situations calling for immediate action from the employee, the employee needs to know which action his or her property's management considers appropriate or which action is required by applicable laws. When developing guidelines for training patrol personnel, a property's management should consult local counsel.

The Presence of Unauthorized Persons

A lodging facility, although open to the public, is private property. An innkeeper has the responsibility to monitor and, when appropriate, to control the activities of persons on the premises. It is, however, imperative that any activities which limit the freedom of movement of any person or persons in the lodging facility be undertaken by the property's staff with the utmost discretion. Such actions should always be reasonable and appropriate. Recall that the authority of security officers may be limited, that the unauthorized restraint of an individual may cause the employee and the property to be liable for false arrest, and that some activities are best handled by local law enforcement officials if time permits.

Unauthorized or undesirable persons (as determined by management for each particular property) should be discouraged from visiting the property, but, again, extreme discretion and tact should be used. When deciding whether to evict persons from the premises, great care should be taken to react to what they actually *do* as opposed to who they are or seem to be. For example, persons suspected of being prostitutes should be evicted with great care. It can be a costly and embarrassing error to question the character or reputation of an individual. Such questioning, if unfounded, can serve as a basis of legal action for slander. The eviction of persons from public space (such as the lobby and any restaurants) is governed by laws applicable to places of public accommodation. Management should review the statutes applicable to its location.

On the other hand, guestrooms and guest corridors are not deemed open to the public. No one other than guests, legitimate visitors of guests, and the property's employees should be in these areas. The normal laws of trespass apply in these areas and should be consulted. If employees see a suspicious person on a floor or in an elevator, they have the right to ask if he or she is a guest or a visitor. They can also ask to see the person's room key or accompany the person to the room he or she intends to visit. Unauthorized persons may be asked to leave the property and warned not to return. Such action should be documented and, if the person returns, the police should be notified.

The problem of prostitution is of particular concern to the security department (in large properties) or the individual responsible for security on the premises (in small properties). In a number of cities, prostitution is also connected with theft and assault. The presence of prostitutes eventually affects the reputation of the property and can seriously affect future occupancy rates. Consequently, it is a problem that may involve the security staff, the local police, the property's management, and legal counsel. Managers should determine what legal recourse exists within the community by consulting with legal counsel to determine if protection may be found under laws covering trespass, pandering, soliciting, loitering, or other local rulings on prostitution. This is a problem that requires close liaison with legal counsel and local police authorities and the commitment of management to prosecute. The security staff must also be aware of the possibility of organized prostitution activity on the property. In some cases, employees working in collusion with the front desk or even with security staff members have provided prostitutes to guests.

Unfortunately, legitimate guests sometimes invite undesirable persons (such as prostitutes) to their rooms. When this occurs, the property may be unable to keep such a person out. The property may, however, closely watch the guestroom involved so the undesirable person can be escorted off the premises as soon as he or she emerges. If this precaution is not taken and the undesirable person assaults another guest before leaving the premises, the property may be found negligent, since it knew of the presence of the person yet failed to take adequate action. After escorting an undesirable person off the premises, the security officer should record the circumstances. If the facts seem to warrant it, management should consider informing the police.

Individuals Involved with Illegal Drugs

Sometimes a property has to deal with undesirable persons who are guests. One such type that deserves special mention is the drug dealer, smuggler, or manufacturer. Smugglers sometimes stay at hotels while waiting for drug shipments to arrive. Because of the unusual nature of their business, their behavior may be atypical of the property's regular guests. A property's employees can be trained to watch for certain suggestive signs. For example, drug smugglers often pay cash for everything. One person may register and pay with cash for several people. Because of the uncertainty involved in when an illegal drug shipment will arrive, smugglers may stay at the property for an indeterminate time, paying day by day. They may drive expensive late-model cars, or arrive in trucks, vans, campers, or recreational vehicles (in other words, anything with a large storage capacity). Drug dealers or smugglers may, at registration, incorrectly or falsely report their vehicles' license plate numbers. They may make and/or receive many long-distance or room-to-room telephone calls.

Of course, many guests who are not drug dealers or smugglers may meet one or even a few of these conditions. And even if a guest meets several of these conditions, that is not proof that the person is involved with illegal drugs. Still, when several of these signs and/or any other unusual behavior arouse the suspicions of hotel staff, management should consider contacting a local law enforcement agency.

During the closing decades of the twentieth century, the problem of illegal drug labs began to involve hotels and motels on a large scale, as drug labs were set up in guestrooms to illegally manufacture methamphetamines, a drug known on the street as *speed* or *crank*. The introduction of highly toxic and explosive chemicals used in the manufacture of meth creates major health hazards and often leads to damage to the property. One authority notes that the fumes from the cooking process smell like dirty diapers; these fumes may have a long-term effect on the lungs and liver. The greatest danger is the residue left from the manufacturing process. It can cost a property anywhere from $2,000 to $20,000 to clean a guestroom that has been used to house a meth lab.[3]

When an offensive odor that may indicate a drug lab is detected by the staff when passing an occupied room, special care should be taken at the time of room cleaning to determine whether the room has been used for drug production. If there is obvious residue and other evidence that a room may have been used for manufacturing drugs, the room should immediately be sealed and the authorities called. Guests in adjoining rooms should be moved, with the explanation that a guest spilled chemicals and so all nearby guests are being moved for their convenience and comfort; no further explanation should be given. The authorities responding to the incident should include the Department of Drug Enforcement Administration (DEA), the local office in the community that handles drug spills and removal of toxic wastes, and the local police and fire authorities.

It is interesting to note that even though the end product may be an illegal drug, the chemicals used in concocting the drug often present the most serious problem for the hotel, hence the possibility of the Occupational Safety & Health Administration (OSHA) becoming involved to protect hotel personnel participating in the cleanup. To help ensure everyone's safety and that proper procedures are followed, all matters associated with the discovery of a drug lab on the property should be reviewed with the agencies just mentioned in order to follow a process that will maximize the safety of hotel guests and staff. Guestrooms that have housed drug labs should not be returned to inventory for assignment to other guests until approval has been given by the appropriate authorities.

The U. S. Environmental Protection Agency has prepared a document outlining voluntary cleanup guidelines for meth lab remediation.[4] A brief review of this document shows the extensive procedures that may be necessary in order to remediate a guestroom and a hotel that has been used as a site to make illegal drugs. The Educational Institute of the American Hotel & Lodging Association has a video, *Methamphetamines: Too Dangerous to Ignore*, that includes topics such as how to spot potential problems, security tips to prevent problems, and what to do if a lab is discovered.[5]

Safe-Deposit Box Procedures

In most states, there is a limit to a property's liability for the loss of a guest's valuables if the property has safe-deposit boxes or a safe for the storage of the guest's valuables and the guest is notified of the availability of the safe or safe-deposit boxes.[6] The notice given to guests of such safekeeping facilities usually takes the form of public postings. The appendix to this chapter includes sample room postings from two states. By law, these postings typically must appear at several conspicuous places on the premises, often within the guestroom itself. Since the laws in this regard vary from state to state, legal counsel should be contacted to ensure that a property is in compliance with the applicable state laws concerning safes, safe-deposit boxes, and the posting of notices. Properties should verify from time to time if there have been any amendments to a specific state's requirements.

A number of states require that a receipt be issued when items are placed in a safe-deposit box. This creates a number of potential problems that senior management should review with legal counsel. For example, if a hotel issues a receipt for $100,000 in cash or jewelry, has it now abrogated its state limitation on liability protection? Has the property encountered a privacy issue, since the guest must divulge the items and values if a receipt is to be issued?

The innkeeper's limited liability laws often also apply when a guest's property is lost or stolen from a safe-deposit box, unless the property is lost or stolen through the negligence of the lodging operation. If a guest files suit over property missing from his or her safe-deposit box, a court may inquire into the degree of care exercised in the safe-deposit operation. Failure to use the degree of care which the law requires can result in liability on the part of the hotel. Even in cases in which the hotel is negligent, however, some states place limits on the innkeeper's liability. Some lawsuits have begun challenging the validity of such laws.[7]

It is the responsibility of management to develop and monitor safe-deposit procedures for its property. Due to the variety of properties using a variety of safe-deposit facilities, a uniform procedure for all properties cannot be established. The following discussion presents general guidelines that may be used by managers to develop specific procedures for their properties. This discussion does not, however, examine every situation that may arise concerning the use of safe-deposit boxes.

All employees with safe-deposit responsibilities should be thoroughly trained in proper safe-deposit procedures and be aware of the reasons for the various rules. Supervisors should impress upon safe-deposit attendants the importance and seriousness of this responsibility, ask for an immediate report of any unusual incident, and require accurate, up-to-date records and complete compliance with procedures.

Safe-deposit boxes should be located in an area to which there is limited access. Unauthorized persons, whether guests or employees, should not be permitted in the area. Such a location may be in the vicinity of the front desk, where the box may be secured while still visible to the guests.

Safe-Deposit Box Keys and Key Control

One of the fundamentals of sound safe-deposit box protection is the control of unissued keys to prevent any unauthorized persons from having access to them. Strict control should apply to the storage, issuance, and receipt of keys.

AT YOUR RISK

BY ANTHONY MARSHALL

Liability Notices: More Than Just Part of Guestroom Décor

It's attached to the back of most hotel guestroom doors, almost always in an inexpensive frame. The small print necessitates a magnifying glass for anyone who wishes to read it. As a room furnishing, it's unattractive. That's probably why hoteliers who don't understand the law often put the hotel's limited liability notice in such inconspicuous places.

I recently surveyed several local housekeepers as to the importance of having the posted notice in guestrooms. None of them knew much about it, other than that their supervisor had told them it belonged there.

In my opinion, if housekeepers are responsible to see that the notice is posted, management should take the time to explain it to them. Educated employees always do a better job.

Every state has some sort of limited liability statute, though the titles often vary. These statutes modify the old Common Law rule that held innkeepers liable for the loss of guests' valuables. Strict compliance with the statute's specific requirements reward hoteliers with a legal windfall: limited liability for the loss of guests' valuables—very limited.

Most hotel interior decorators squirm at the ugliness of the limited liability signs posted in hotels. That's why they often conceal them or dispose of them during renovations. The signs vanish—and with them goes the hotel's most important protection in liability claims.

I have never understood why something so important can be treated so frivolously. In one hotel, during a recent stay, I found the liability notice attached to the back wall of a dark closet. In another, I located it inside a chest of drawers.

These errant designers need only read their state's innkeepers limited liability statutes to understand the disservice they are doing to their clients. Concealing what the law requires to be conspicuous can needlessly expose the hotel to substantial liability.

States provide protection

State legislatures have provided hotels with an out in case of a loss of guests' valuables, but they can only do so if the hotel informs their guests properly. Therefore, should the notification not be in compliance with the statutory requirements, the hotel is left defenseless against any liability claims.

In New York state, for example, the business law limits the hotel's liability to $1,500, but the hotel is required to provide a safe for guests to use and to prominently notify guests of its availability. If a hotel is in full compliance with a statute, it cannot be held liable for a sum in excess of $1,500 unless otherwise agreed upon by the parties in writing.

As with so many other hotel-related issues, there is a training component to hotel liability. Don't allow an overzealous safe-deposit box attendant who, in an ill-conceived attempt to please the guest, erroneously commits the hotel to insuring the guests' valuables. Attendants should be properly trained to accept—or reject— the guests' valuables.

At Your Risk *(continued)*

I asked Bruce M. Young, the hotel liability expert with Kanterman & Taub in New York, if guests actually sue a hotel for $1,500.

Young hesitated a moment, judiciously weighing his answer.

"Yes, they do," he said. "But the guest is not after a mere $1,500!"

He explained that the guest's lawyer has to sue for $1,500 to get the case into court. Once he's there, though, he wants to recover the full value of the loss. To do this, the plaintiff must prove that the postings of the notice were insufficient or that the hotel agreed to insure the valuables.

As it is unlikely that any hotel manager agreed to insure the valuables, that leaves the posting of the notices to attack. A hotel that had not bothered to post the notices would obviously lose the battle.

Young said that hoteliers should review their state's limited liability statute to determine if they are in compliance. In New York state, the statute requires "posting a notice ... in a public and conspicuous place in the office and public rooms, and in the public parlors of such hotel, motel or inn...." The law here is simple: no notice, no benefits.

Don't display the hotel's limited liability notices in portable picture frames. That runs contrary to the most famous Marshall's Law: Don't screw it up by not screwing it down. Securely attach the notices to the walls, because if they're carried off and aren't replaced, the hotel's liability blooms.

Portable frames also tempt the wicked. As Young said, "Where portable, home-style picture frames are used, it's a great motivation to steal."

In other words, why make the presence or absence of the notice a question in a jury's mind for the price of a few screws you could buy at a hardware store for ten cents?

Notices do not have to be in multiple languages, but Young said hotels that exclusively book persons speaking a common language other than English might consider it. Why leave open any possibility for a lawsuit? Do whatever it takes.

Hoteliers have been blessed by their various state legislatures with limits to their liabilities in cases where guests lose valuables.

As hoteliers can't afford to lose these blessings, the "amen" of this story is to encourage full compliance with the requirements of the innkeepers' limited liability laws.

Courtesy of *Hotel & Motel Management*, June 16, 1997. Used with permission.

Keys to unused boxes should be stored in a place not accessible to unauthorized employees or to guests; there should be no access to the unissued keys except by employees responsible for this function. When such employees receive the key to a surrendered box, they should immediately secure the key. Spare locks and locks out for repair should also be carefully controlled. An adequate record should be maintained of all losses of keys, all changes of locks and safe-deposit boxes, and all forcings of safe-deposit box doors.

Two keys should be required to open any safe-deposit box. The control or **guard key**, which must be used in conjunction with the guest's key to open the box, should always be secured. Great caution should be exercised in the use of the control key. Only those persons authorized to grant access to boxes should ever have possession and control of this key. It should never be taken from the safe deposit area or left where it is accessible to guests or to unauthorized employees. It should be accounted for at each change of shift.

There should be only one guest key for each safe-deposit box, even when more than one guest is using the same box. Under normal circumstances (that is, when one box is being used by one guest), the guest receives this key to his or her box. Under no circumstances should there be any duplicate keys for a guest's safe-deposit box. If a key is lost, the box should be drilled open in the presence of a witness, the guest (or the guest's legally authorized agent), and someone from the property. Because no extra keys are kept, the safe-deposit agreement signed by the guest should make it clear that the guest will be billed for all drilling and replacement costs that arise from the loss of the guest's key.

Access Procedures

Clearly, the primary goal in using effective safe-deposit procedures is to prevent unauthorized access. Access control is the most vital of all safe-deposit responsibilities. It is imperative that the identity of the guest be established before access is granted. One way of doing this is to require the guest to sign his or her name on a form requesting access. This signature is then compared with that on the agreement signed by the guest when the box was first issued. Some properties ask guests to include some other piece of information about themselves (such as a mother's maiden name) on the agreement, so that if there is doubt regarding the guest's signature during a request for access, the employee can ask for this other information.

Whatever procedure is used at a property, it should be followed for every access, regardless of the frequency and regardless of how well the attendant knows the guest. A wife or other family member or the box holder's representative, regardless of how well known, should not be granted access to the box unless that person's signature is on the initial agreement. No exceptions should be made to this procedure.

After a guest's identity has been verified, the safe-deposit attendant should accompany the guest to the safe-deposit area and, in the clear sight of the guest, use the control key and the guest's key to open the box, always being careful that the guest sees his or her key and box. The attendant should give the box to the guest. Some properties then require their employee to step out of the area until the guest is finished, in order to provide the guest with privacy. Other properties require their employee to remain in the area, but without handling the contents of the box or taking notice of the amount or type of valuables in the box. In any event, the employee should *not* place items into or remove items from a guest's box; only the guest should do so. Also, the guest should be with the employee at all times while the box is being opened or locked. The employee should never be alone with a guest's valuables. When the guest is finished, the attendant should re-lock the box and return the guest's key, making sure that the guest always has the opportunity to see the key and box while in the attendant's possession. Upon final release of the box and return of the guest's key, the guest and employee should sign the release notice, which should then be filed.

Because space considerations often preclude maintaining a safe-deposit box for every room on a property, the demand for such boxes may sometimes exceed the supply. When this happens, alternative procedures may be needed. One method of dealing with excess demand is to allow guests the opportunity to place their belongings in a larger safe-deposit box that contains the belongings of more than one guest. If the guest declines, some properties explore with the guest the possibility of using boxes at a nearby bank, sometimes at no cost to the guest.

If the guest agrees to share a larger box, his or her property needs to be placed in some sort of sealable container (such as an envelope) to keep it separate from the other guests' property. When the guest desires access, the attendant verifies the guest's identity and then gives the guest the appropriate container(s).

The key to a large safe-deposit box used to hold sealed containers containing the property of more than one guest should be maintained in a secure place together with a log. Each time the key is used to open the box, the entry should be recorded in the log. Some properties require this key to be kept by a member of management when not in use.

Special or Unusual Access

Safe-deposit boxes are sometimes the subject of court orders. When court orders are received, they should be referred to the property's management. All right of access should be suspended until the property's rights and obligations are determined. Management should consult with legal counsel prior to granting box access, unless the property already has specific legal instructions in effect regarding compliance with this type of access.

Under no circumstances should access to a safe-deposit box be allowed based solely on telephone, e-mail, or fax authorization. A letter requesting access should not be recognized unless it is a proper legal authorization.

If a guest leaves a lodging property without properly surrendering a box and then mails the key to the property, the property should secure the key and ask the guest to sign a release form. The box should not be opened until this form is received. If, when the box is opened, it contains property, the box should be re-locked, the key secured, and a notice sent to the guest requesting him or her to personally remove the contents and surrender the box, or to forward a power of attorney for the guest's representative to do so.

If a departed guest returns a key by messenger, the messenger should be requested to return the key to the guest and request that the guest come in person. If the guest cannot do so, he or she should sign a release form if the box is empty or forward a power of attorney if the box contains property.

When a guest does not surrender a box upon check-out, the property should send the guest a registered letter requesting surrender of the box. If the guest does not respond within the appropriate legal time limit, the hotel should dispose of the contents of the box in accordance with state law and the advice of counsel. This same procedure is sometimes followed in cases in which the key is returned by a guest who will not follow the prescribed surrender procedures. Exhibit 2 lists a sample outline for safe-deposit box procedures that could be adopted by an establishment.

Exhibit 2   Sample Safe-Deposit Box Procedures

A.   Purpose
The following procedures will ensure that all properties are in compliance with state Innkeeper's Statutes as they relate to the use of safe-deposit boxes by registered guests (boxes are not to be issued to non-registered individuals). Failure to comply with state requirements can result in the forfeiture of protection offered by these statutes. Any departure from these procedures must be reviewed by management.

B.   Responsibility
The hotel manager is responsible for procedure implementation and training of front desk personnel. Periodic, documented audits of critical elements of the program are also required.

C.   Safe-Deposit Box Location
A protected area should be provided for guest activity with his/her box. If the area is enclosed, the door should be kept shut at all times. Entry should be by means of a key- or code-activated locking device. If the area is not enclosed, a location should be used that provides adequate security for this activity (i.e., back office, business center). Closed-circuit TV is recommended for enclosed rooms in order to detect someone who is not supposed to be there.

D.   Limits of Liability
Each state's Innkeeper's Statute defines specific limits for monetary liability of a registered guest's property. Limits of liability for safe-deposit boxes should be (1) in writing on the *Safe-Deposit Box Agreement* card (along with the state statute reference number), (2) posted over the safe-deposit boxes, and (3) placed on the inside lid of the safe-deposit box tray. The dollar amount stated must be the same as the state statute.

E.   Safe-Deposit Box Agreement Card
See sample on next page. *Note: The information provided on the card is the minimum allowable. Never delete or change information without review by management.*

F.   Safe-Deposit Box Keys
Guest keys for boxes are to be kept in a locked key cabinet until issued. The key to this cabinet is to be on the MOD/designate key ring *at all times.* The property's control key is not to be kept (1) in a drawer, (2) in the door of an empty box, or (3) on a hook/ring behind the front desk. *Note: There is to be only one guest key for each box and one control key in existence.*

G.   Procedures—Sign Up and Initial Use
1.   The registered guest completes the *Safe-Deposit Box Agreement.*
2.   The front desk agent checks the card for completeness, fills in time and date of box issuance, and signs the card. The card is filed by box/key number.
3.   The agent hands the box key to the guest and informs him/her about the "one-key policy" and the fee for drilling if a key is lost.
4.   The guest is escorted to the safe-deposit box area.
5.   The agent unlocks the box by inserting the guest key and control key.
6.   The box tray is removed by the agent and given to the guest along with his/her key. The guest places his/her property into the tray.
7.   The guest returns the tray to the agent, along with his/her box key. After locking the box,the agent returns the guest key and secures the control key.

H.   Procedures—Accessing the Box
When a guest wishes to access his/her box, the following procedures must be followed.
1.   The guest shows his/her key and requests access. The front desk agent asks for the guest's name. The agent does not take the guest's key at this time.
2.   The agent pulls the *Agreement* card and verifies the information to confirm the guest's identity. This includes room number, home address, and other information given on the card.

(continued)

Exhibit 2   *(continued)*

No	SAFE-DEPOSIT BOX AGREEMENT

AM/PM

Key No.   Date Issued   Time

Front Desk Agent   Check-Out Date

As a condition of the receipt of such articles deposited by me in this safe-deposit box, I hereby agree that access to this safe-deposit box will be obtainable only through this signature and upon the presentation of this key in person, and for any failure to present this key in person the HOTEL shall not be liable for any loss occasioned by such failure to personally present such key. And I hereby agree that, in the event I should not personally surrender this key and remove the contents of this box within ten (10) days after I shall cease to be a guest of the hotel, the HOTEL may force entrance to said safe-deposit box and remove the contents thereof, and while retaining the said contents, the HOTEL shall not be liable for any loss occasioned by my failure to remove such contents, and in any such event or in the event that the key is lost while in my custody, I hereby agree to pay the HOTEL for the cost of opening the safe-deposit box and replacing the key.

PLACE YOUR STATE'S "INNKEEPERS STATUTE"
REFERENCE CODE NAME, NUMBER, AND
DOLLAR ($) LIMIT OF LIABILITY HERE

Signature

Guest Name (Please Print)   Room No.

Home Address

City

State   Zip Code

Mother's Maiden Name

DETACH STUB BELOW AND GIVE TO THE DEPOSITOR AS THEIR RECEIPT

- -

DEPOSITOR'S RECEIPT   No

Name _____

          Cashier to print clearly

Room No. _____ Key No. _____ Date Issued _____

The safe-deposit key must be turned in to the Front Desk before or at the time of departure.

Exhibit 2 *(continued)*

3. Upon confirmation of the guest's ID, the agent has the guest sign a *Safe-Deposit Box Access* slip. The signature is checked against the original on the *Agreement* card.

4. If the signature is the same, the agent signs and dates the *Access* slip and staples it to the *Agreement* card. All subsequent *Access* slips are stapled to the card.

5. The process continues from "Sign Up and Initial Use" procedures, Step 4.

I. Procedures—Surrendering Box

The following procedures are to be followed whenever a guest wishes to surrender his/her box.

1. Follow the same procedures for box access up to and including the handing of the tray and guest key to the guest, Step 6.

2. After the guest empties the tray and returns it to the agent, the agent asks if the tray is empty. If the guest says "Yes," the agent visually checks the tray.

3. The agent places the tray back into the box, inserts both keys, locks it, and removes the control key.

4. The guest signs and dates the line on the back of the *Agreement* card for surrendering the box. The agent confirms this and signs and dates the card. The card is filed with the hotel registration card.

J. Procedures—Guest Leaves without Surrendering Box

The following procedures must be followed whenever a guest checks out of the hotel without emptying his/her box.

1. The guest must send a notarized letter indicating:
   - his/her request that the box be opened
   - the box's contents and value
   - how the contents are to be returned to the guest
   - if the guest will have a representative present when the box is opened

2. The MOD and one front desk agent must be present when the box is opened.

3. The guest's letter is signed and dated by the MOD and agent, indicating that the written instructions were followed.

K. Procedures—A Warrant Is Presented for Box Contents

Whenever a law enforcement officer presents a warrant for the contents of a safe-deposit box, the following procedures must be followed:

1. The property retains a copy of the warrant.

2. The MOD is present when the box is opened and contents are inventoried.

3. The warrant is signed and dated by the MOD, indicating that the box was opened and all contents were delivered to the officer.

L. Procedures—Abandoned Box

The determination of whether property in a safe-deposit box has been "abandoned" must be considered carefully in accordance with local laws. The process must involve the hotel manager, and complete documentation of all actions must be maintained.

M. Procedures—Special Requirements

1. Guest loses key—The property has the box drilled by a qualified locksmith or facilities engineer. This procedure is witnessed by the MOD, and proper documentation is maintained. The guest is charged for drilling according to the property's policy.

2. Property loses control key—To maintain the integrity of the safe-deposit box system, a new control key must be made for all control locks replaced.

3. Record retention—Safe-deposit box records (cards, guest letters, warrants, etc.) must be retained for seven (7) years.

4. Audits—Keys, cards, and boxes should be audited nightly by the night auditor. The hotel manager should conduct an audit of the safe-deposit box program at least quarterly. All audits are to be documented.

Lost and Found Procedures

Clear procedures should be developed to deal with lost and found items. The personnel in charge of the lost and found function need to be aware of their state's laws concerning lost and found items so they can ensure that the property avoids any liability with respect to the disposition of such items. The management at various properties can assign the lost and found function to any number of departments. The selection of the department, however, does not affect the nature of the job.

All found items should be turned over to the lost and found function. Some properties require the employee finding the item to fill out a form stating where the item was found, a description of the item, the date, and the employee's name. Other properties have the lost and found personnel fill out such a form.

Some states require that an effort be made to return lost items to their owners. Articles found in guestrooms or those with addresses on them obviously make it easier to find the owner. When such items are turned in, a letter should be sent requesting the guest to contact the property for proper identification and return of the item.

If a guest calls the property either to ask questions about a letter he or she has received concerning a found item or to report a lost item, the call should be directed to lost and found personnel. This helps to avoid giving conflicting information to the caller—it can greatly upset a guest if one employee says a lost item has been found when it in fact has not, especially if the guest has returned to the property to claim his or her item based on the erroneous information. The employee who takes a call reporting a lost item should ask for all pertinent information, including a description of the item, the area in which it was lost (if known), the date it was lost (if known), and the guest's name and address. Some properties keep an inquiry log for this information.

Upon receipt of a found item, lost and found personnel should log, bag, tag, and store the item. When the item is valuable, it should be secured. Some properties place wallets, jewelry, money, payment cards, and other valuables in a safe-deposit box.

When an article is claimed, this fact should be recorded in the log. If the article was mailed to the owner, the date of the mailing should be noted.

Guest Views of Hotel Security Measures

Hospitality security professionals invest their careers in the design and management of secure hotels. These professionals identify and evaluate advances in hotel security products and procedures, such as enhancements to electronic lock systems, and implement new products and procedures when appropriate and feasible. When security incidents occur, security professionals reevaluate their security designs and procedures in light of these incidents. Given the highly guest-focused nature of hospitality, it is also important that guest perceptions of various security options be known and considered before security actions are taken. This section summarizes research articles concerning guest perceptions of various aspects of hotel security. Readers are encouraged to refer to the original articles (see the endnotes in this section) for more in-depth information as well as a list of further references.

AT YOUR RISK

BY ANTHONY MARSHALL

Finders Keepers, Losers Weepers—After Ninety Days

When is the next flight to Miami? I asked the reservationist at the other end of the line. An hour? A glance at the clock in my guestroom convinced me I could make it.

"Book me!" I said.

I threw my clothing into my suitcase, used express check-out, and raced to grab a cab at the front entrance. I barely made my flight home.

A couple of days later, I discovered that my favorite blue blazer was missing. It wasn't in the laundry or hanging in my closet. Could I have left my favorite jacket at the hotel? Inconceivable—I am not a careless person.

The next day, I went to Burn's clothing store. I told Mike, the proprietor, that my treasured blue blazer was missing. After selling me another one, Mike suggested that I call the hotel. Why not, I thought. If the hotel had it, I'd simply be the proud owner of two identical blazers.

I called the hotel and asked to be connected with the lost-and-found department. The operator told me there were two—one was for items left in guestrooms, the other for items left in public space. The housekeeping department was in charge of the former and the security department oversaw the latter.

"Where did you lose the jacket?" the telephone operator asked, anxious to connect me with the correct lost-and-found.

I maintained my composure and politely told her that I was sorry, but I did not know where I had lost my jacket.

Mislaid, legally speaking

Putting my legal hat on I realized that I had misspoken. I had not "lost" my jacket; to the law, I had "mislaid" it. Property is mislaid when its owner voluntarily puts it aside and forgets where it is. It's not lost, because the owner knows that it's missing. For property to be lost, the owner must have unintentionally parted with and forgotten about it. I never forgot about my blue blazer—I was sick about it.

Unfortunately, neither of the lost-and-found departments had my blazer. But I'm a good sport—I hope whoever is wearing my jacket enjoys it as much as I did.

According to the law, if I had "abandoned" my jacket, it would immediately belong to the finder. Legally, to abandon property the owner must voluntarily discard it with no intention of reclaiming it. I didn't do that. For abandonment to occur, I would have had to throw my jacket into the wastebasket with no intention of reclaiming it, like I've done with old shirts.

When does the finder of lost property get to keep it? It varies according to state law, but ninety days is common. In other words, many states have passed statutes that reward the finder for turning over lost property to the police. If it is not claimed by the owner in ninety days, it belongs to the finder. These laws are intended to encourage the return of found property to the proper authorities.

Hoteliers who require employees to turn over to the hotel any property found in the hotel, and to waive all rights to possession of it, don't get very much found property from their employees.

At Your Risk *(continued)*

I called some local hotelier friends of mine to find out what treasures have turned up in their lost-and-found departments. Usually, it's the same old stuff: eyeglasses, old clothing, keys, junk jewelry. But a few hotels had some real treasures.

Paul Breslin, executive assistant manager of Fountainbleau Hilton Resort & Towers in Miami Beach, had a $50,000 diamond ring turned over to him by a room attendant. It was returned to its owner; the attendant was given a reward.

Tom Soule, director of security at the Omni Colonade Hotel in Coral Gables, said his hotel has found several sets of dentures. (Wouldn't you think people would want to have their teeth back?)

Rich Hancock, GM of the Biscayne Bay Marriott in Miami, said his hotel's lost-and-found has lots of bathing suits, sunglasses, and one set of new handcuffs. Maybe the police had a training session at his hotel.

What treasures does your lost-and-found harbor? Take a look—those treasures might be yours. Legally.

Courtesy of *Hotel & Motel Management*, October 2, 1995. Used with permission.

One group of researchers[8] asked tourists in Central Florida to evaluate the impact of twenty physical and behavioral measures on their overall sense of safety and security while visiting sixteen Central Florida hotels and motels. A total of 166 responses were received out of a distribution of 640 questionnaires (representing a 26 percent response rate).

Using a five-point scale (1 = very little impact, to 5 = a great impact), respondents' rankings of physical safety devices' impacts were as follows, giving an indication of how important each of these devices were to the surveyed guests:

Physical Safety Devices	Mean Ranking (rounded)
Deadbolt locks	4.46
Closed-circuit TV cameras	4.46
Door view ports	4.45
Hotel security employee patrols	4.39
Alarms on emergency exit doors	4.27
Additional door locks such as latch bars or door chains	4.23
Electronic door locks	4.14
Brightly lit parking lots	4.10
Fences or shrubs around the hotel's perimeter	3.91
Locks on low floor windows or sliding glass doors	3.21

Using a similar five-point scale, respondents' rankings of behavioral safety impacts were as follows:

Behavioral Safety Devices	Mean Ranking (rounded)
Telephone operator asks for guest's name before connecting caller	4.53
Side entrances into the hotel locked at night	4.38
Routine visits to the hotel by law enforcement officers	4.31

Hotel employs highly visible security officers   4.25
Hotel employee is available to escort guests to remote areas   4.10
Room numbers are not printed on hotel keys   4.06
Room number written down rather than announced at check-in   3.96
Availability of brochures or other information describing
   recommended guest safety precautions   3.82
Requiring guest identification before replacing lost or
   missing room keys   3.51

In looking at the "Physical Safety Devices" rankings, we can see that most items have high scores. It would be interesting to see if security professionals would agree with these rankings. If security professionals were surveyed, one might expect that some items on the list would drop in importance (perhaps "Alarms on emergency exit doors"), while others would rise ("Locks on low floor windows or sliding glass doors"). And, while most security professionals would not have a problem with fences around a hotel's perimeter, shrubs is another matter, since shrubs can serve as hiding places.

Items in the list of "Behavioral Safety Devices" also have generally high scores. Probably the most surprising is the relatively low score given to "Requiring guest identification before replacing lost or missing room keys." This practice would probably receive a very high score from security professionals and has been a major focus of television exposés of hotel security.

Another team of researchers[9] surveyed meeting planners on the relative importance of hotel safety and security attributes in influencing their decision to choose a hotel for their meetings. The survey was distributed at two different meetings-industry conferences; a total of 100 completed surveys were collected.

The following shows the meeting planners' responses regarding their current decision-making practices ("Neutral" responses were removed):

	Strongly Agree/ Agree	Strongly Disagree/ Disagree
Safety is an important factor when I select a hotel for a meeting	79	6
I routinely ask about hotel safety and security attributes during site inspections	56	21
Hotel safety and security attributes play a significant role in my decision to choose a hotel for a meeting	47	20
I routinely ask about hotel safety and security attributes in RFPs	34	36

Meeting planners were also asked to indicate the importance they placed on various hotel safety and security attributes when they were choosing hotels. The survey used a five-point scale (1 = Strongly Disagree to 5 = Strongly Agree); the results of the survey were as follows:

Attribute	Importance (rounded)	
Hotel located in a low-crime area	4.44	Security
Smoke detectors	4.17	Fire
Well-lit and marked emergency exits	4.17	Fire
24-hour security staff	4.14	Security
Sprinkler system	4.13	Fire
Audible and visual fire alarms on guest floors	4.05	Fire
Electronic key cards for guestrooms	4.03	Security
Audible and visual fire alarms in public areas	4.01	Fire
Guestroom located along interior corridors	3.97	Security
Controlled after-hours access to hotel	3.95	Security
Staff training in CPR, first aid	3.92	Process
Training for staff action in crises	3.92	Process
Security cameras in public areas	3.79	Security
In-room safety materials for guests	3.76	Process
Written policies for assisting disabled guests in emergencies	3.71	Health/Life
Written security plans	3.65	Health/Life
Automated external defibrillator (AED) on site	3.57	Health/Life
Back-up electrical generator	3.54	Health/Life
Parking facility connected to hotel building	3.50	Security
Safety videos playing on in-room guest televisions	2.92	Process

As you can see, a hotel's location in a low-crime area ranked first in importance for these meeting planners, and attributes concerning fire safety were all ranked very high.

A third group of researchers[10] surveyed 930 hotel guests from a range of hotel properties regarding how acceptable certain hotel security features would be to them. This study covered some different security features than those mentioned in the two studies we just discussed and included metal detectors, video surveillance, photo identification of guests at check-in, armed security guards, a check of guest IDs against law enforcement records, and first aid kits in guestrooms.

Most of the respondents disagreed with or were ambivalent (neutral) about the idea of having armed security guards at hotels; most security professionals would agree with these guests that armed security guards are generally not a good idea for hospitality properties. Metal detectors received a slightly positive response, which is surprising, given the negative reaction most people have to metal detector screening in airports. More guests than not thought that checking law enforcement records would be an acceptable practice at hotels, but the researchers pointed out in their report that such a practice is potentially very time-consuming, and a hotel would need a contingency plan for staff action should a guest have a serious criminal record. Providing first aid kits in guestrooms is clearly a security and safety practice that is of interest to most guests, with over 70 percent of respondents indicating they would welcome this practice.

It should be noted that this survey was conducted just one year after the 9/11 terrorist attacks and was undertaken to provide some insight into how guests might react if hotels instituted enhanced security measures. For hoteliers, the good news in the survey was that respondents said they would be willing to pay, on average, 10 percent more for increased hotel security measures.

Endnotes

1. Elizabeth Lauer, "The Evolving Electronic Lock," *The Hotel & Restaurant Technology Update*, Spring 1999.

2. One example is Dateline 6/4/2004 http://www.msnbc.msn.com/id/5114121/.

3. AH&LA Statement on Methamphetamine Labs, http://www.ahla.com/PressRoom.aspx?id=15680.

4. U.S. Environmental Protection Agency (2009), *Voluntary Guidelines for Methamphetamine Laboratory Cleanup*, http://www.epa.gov/oem/meth_lab_guide lines.pdf.

5. http://shop.ahlei.org/Methamphetamines-Too-Dangerous-to-Ignore-DVD_p_2681.html.

6. For more information about safe-deposit box procedures, see Jack P. Jefferies and Banks Brown, *Understanding Hospitality Law*, Fifth Edition (Lansing, Mich.: American Hotel & Lodging Educational Institute, 2010), chapters 11 and 13.

7. For more information concerning innkeeper's laws and challenges to their validity, see Jack P. Jefferies and Banks Brown, *Understanding Hospitality Law*, Fifth Edition (Lansing, Mich.: American Hotel & Lodging Educational Institute, 2010), Chapter 8.

8. A. Milman, F. Jones, and S. Bach, "The Impact of Security Devices on Tourists' Perceived Safety: The Central Florida Example." *Journal of Hospitality & Tourism Research*, 1999; 23; 371–386.

9. T. W. Hilliard and S. Baloglu, "Safety and Security as Part of the Hotel Servicescape for Meeting Planners," *Journal of Convention and Event Tourism*, 2008, 9(1), pp. 15–34.

10. J. Feickert, R. Verma, G. Plaschka, and C. S. Dev, "Safeguarding Your Customers: The Guest's View of Hotel Security," *Cornell Hotel and Restaurant Administration Quarterly*, 2006; 47; 224–244.

Key Terms

emergency key—Opens all guestroom doors, even when they are double locked. An emergency key should be highly protected and its use strictly controlled and recorded; it should never leave the property.

guard key—One of two keys required to open any safe-deposit box, it must be used in conjunction with the guest's key to open the box; this key should always be secured.

master key—Opens all guestrooms within a designated area that are not double locked. A master key should be highly protected and its use strictly controlled and recorded; it should never leave the property.

Review Questions

1. What are the three levels of keying that most properties use?

2. Why is key/key card control essential to the security of a lodging property?

3. How do electronic and computer locking systems change the nature of key control? How do these systems reduce the need for re-keying?

4. What are the primary functions of patrolling? Why is patrolling an important part of surveillance?

5. Who might a hotel deem as unauthorized persons? Why should great care be taken when deciding whether to evict them from the premises?

6. What problems can occur with the manufacture of illegal drugs in guestrooms?

7. Why might the issuance of a safe-deposit box receipt create problems?

8. What key control and access procedures are typically used for safe-deposit boxes?

9. Why is it important to have the lost and found function assigned to only one department?

10. What are some guest views concerning hotel security measures?

 ## Internet Sites

For more information, visit the following Internet sites. Remember that Internet addresses can change without notice. If the site is no longer there, you can use a search engine to look for additional sites.

Associated Locksmiths of America
www.aloa.org

Loc International
www.loc-international.com

Drug Enforcement Administration
www.justice.gov/dea

PLI
www.plicards.com

Guest Access International
www.guestaccess.com

Securitron
www.securitron.com

Kaba
www.kaba-ilco.com

 ## Case Study

The Safe-Deposit Box That Wasn't

Amanda Muldinado stood behind the front desk of the Metropolitan, a 376-room upscale hotel, and tried to ignore the butterflies in her stomach. It was just her second day on the job, and there was so much to remember! She glanced over at Ron, standing at the other end of the counter. It was comforting to have him working the shift with her—he had worked for the Metropolitan for two years and had been a big help yesterday whenever she got flustered or confused. Her first day was extremely busy because everybody was checking in for the annual aluminum siding trade show and convention that started today. In a way, it was good that her first day was so busy, because she hadn't had time to be nervous. But today, most of the hotel's guests were off attending the show at the convention center downtown and the Metropolitan was relatively quiet.

Amanda gazed across the opulent lobby at the bank of house phones. A middle-aged woman in a tight, leopard-print jumpsuit was speaking angrily into one of the telephones, her free arm, festooned with gold and black bracelets, waving in the air as she pounded home her points to the unfortunate soul on the other end of the line. At this distance Amanda could faintly hear the clicking of the bracelets but could not make out what the woman was saying. Finally the woman slammed the receiver down in its cradle and started looking frantically around the lobby. When her eyes settled on Amanda, the woman grabbed the gold vinyl suitcase at her feet and strode purposefully toward the front desk. Oh, please, thought Amanda, don't come over here, go talk to Ron!

But the woman stayed on course, and Amanda had plenty of time to take in the big hair, the heavy makeup, and the wounded, self-righteous expression before the woman stopped in front of her and said: "There's something wrong with your phones!"

"Ma'am?"

"I can't get through to my husband's room. I kept dialing '326,' but I couldn't get through."

Ron stepped in smoothly. "Our house phones no longer connect directly to the guestrooms."

"Yeah, yeah, that's what the operator said. That's not very convenient, you know," the woman responded.

"We changed our system in order to provide more privacy and security for our guests," Ron continued. "Did the operator reach your husband for you?"

"No, she started explaining why dialing '326' wasn't working and I told her what I thought of her new system before I hung up on her."

From her training, Amanda remembered that you were never to put callers through to guestrooms if they only asked to be put through to a certain room number. You always had to ask whom the person was calling, so you could confirm that the person knew the guest and was not simply calling rooms at random. Thieves, for example, had been known to call room after room until they found one that was unoccupied, then go ransack the room.

"What's your husband's name?" Amanda asked. "We can try to connect you here at the front desk."

"Virgil Jones," the woman responded.

Amanda moved to the computer and called up Virgil's reservations record. Yes, a Virgil H. Jones was registered in Room 326. "Mr. Jones checked in to Room 326 yesterday—let me try to reach him for you."

Amanda picked up the front desk telephone, dialed, and listened to the phone ring ten times. "Sorry, there's no answer."

"That's okay—just give me a key to the room then," ordered the woman.

Immediately a red flag went up for Amanda. New as she was, she was well aware that key control was an extremely important issue at the Metropolitan.

"I'm sorry, ma'am, but it's against our policy to give out keys to people who are not registered guests. Mr. Jones is the only person registered for that room."

"But I'm his wife! Look," the woman rummaged through her handbag and came up with her driver's license, "here's my ID. I'm Sheila Jones. See? That's me there."

"I'm sorry, Ms. Jones," Amanda said. "Had your husband told us you were coming, we would have noted it in the reservations record and there'd be no problem. But we're not allowed to let unregistered guests into rooms." She glanced at Ron.

"That's right, Ms. Jones," Ron said. "We'd do the same thing for you. It's actually against the law to admit an unregistered guest to a room."

"My husband doesn't know I'm coming. I didn't think I would get off work, but my boss finally gave in." Sheila Jones put on an ingratiating smile. "Can't you break the rules just this once? I really want to surprise Virgil."

"I'm sorry," Amanda said. "We really can't." She looked at Ron again for support, and he nodded in agreement.

"Is your husband here for the big convention?" Amanda asked.

Sheila nodded sulkily.

"Then he's probably at the Grandthorpe right now—that's the big convention hotel downtown. That's where the trade show is."

"I'll never find him there," Sheila fumed.

"You're welcome to look around in our restaurant and lounge to make sure he's not still here."

"It would be a lot easier if you'd just let me in the room," Sheila grumbled. "I'm tired—it was a long drive to get here."

Amanda tried to give Sheila her best empathetic smile. "I'm sorry. I'll tell you what—if you can't find him, let us know and we'll put you in another guestroom temporarily so you can freshen up."

"I suppose that'll have to do," Sheila said wearily. "I'm not gonna bother looking for him. I'm tired, and if he's not in his room he's probably at the convention like you said. Just give me a room."

After Sheila collected a key to Room 287 and left in a huff, Ron congratulated Amanda for a job well done. "You did the right thing. Her ID proves she's Sheila Jones, but it doesn't prove she's Virgil's wife. She probably really is his wife, and ninety-nine times out of a hundred probably nothing bad would happen if we let a wife or a husband or a brother or somebody like that into a room. But it's not worth taking a chance on violating the privacy or compromising the safety of our guests. It's that one time in a hundred that can lead to serious trouble."

Thankfully, Sheila did not make another appearance and the rest of the morning passed uneventfully. Just after Amanda returned to the front desk after lunch, a short, balding fellow in a shiny blue suit approached the desk and gave her a big smile. "Hi, I'm Virgil Jones, Room 326. Any messages or mail for me?"

"No, Mr. Jones, but someone was asking about you. A Ms. Sheila Jones was here. She said she was your wife and wanted to wait for you in your room, but we had to turn her down."

Virgil looked startled rather than pleased. "Where is she now?"

"We put her in another room so she could freshen up. Let me call her and let her know you're here." Amanda called Room 287 and in a few minutes Sheila appeared in the lobby.

"Hi, baby!" Virgil called out when he saw her, rushing up and giving her a bear hug.

Sheila looked at Amanda over Virgil's shoulder and tried to pull away. "That's enough, honey." She extracted herself and approached the front desk. "Thanks for the room," she said to Amanda. "I feel so much better after my shower."

"You're welcome."

"I forgot to bring my room key down with me. Can I return it later, or do you want it right away? I'll be moving over to Virgil's room now."

"Just leave it in the room, that's fine," Amanda said. "Do you need any help with moving your luggage? I can send a bellperson up."

Virgil shook his head. "We can handle it, thanks."

•   •   •

The next day Amanda experienced her first time alone at the front desk. Ron had an early dental appointment and wouldn't be in until 11:00. Even though the front desk manager assured Amanda that he would be available in case things got busy, Amanda crossed her fingers and hoped for an uneventful morning.

It was just before nine o'clock when Sheila appeared in the lobby again, dressed slightly more conservatively in a tight purple jumpsuit. She smiled at Amanda and held up a safe-deposit box key. "Good morning. I'd like to get into our safe-deposit box, please."

Thank goodness I don't have to say no to her again, Amanda thought gratefully. "Yes, Ms. Jones, right this way, please." Quickly, Amanda mentally reviewed her training in how to handle safe-deposit box requests as she led Sheila into the small safe-deposit box room just to the right of the front desk. One side wall contained the bank of safe-deposit boxes; the master key to all the boxes hung by a chain secured to the wall. Pushed against the opposite wall was a narrow table with a file box on it.

Let's see, Amanda mused, I'm supposed to ask for identification, pull the card, get the card signed, initial the card—okay, I can do this. "Can I see some identification, please?"

Sheila groaned. "Not this again," she grumbled. She opened her handbag and came up with her driver's license again.

"Thank you," Amanda said, and looked under the "J's" in the file box for the right card. There it was: Box 116, signed out by Mr. Virgil H. Jones. There were no other names on the card.

"Will you sign the card, please? And I'll initial your signature." Amanda gave Sheila the card and a pen and indicated the narrow table. Sheila signed the card and gave the pen to Amanda; Amanda initialed the card and recorded the date and time.

"Thank you." Amanda put the card back in the file box. "Now I'll put my key in the box and turn it." Amanda found Box 116 and turned the master key in the appropriate lock. "And now your key."

Sheila stepped forward and turned her key in the second lock. Amanda swung the box door open, pulled the long, narrow drawer from the box, and handed the drawer to Sheila. "I'll be right outside—just let me know when you're finished."

"That won't be necessary," Sheila said—somewhat grimly, Amanda thought. "This will only take a second."

Amanda turned her back discreetly while Sheila placed the drawer on the table. Amanda heard the metallic creak of the lid lifting, then a sharp intake of breath from Sheila, and then something like a sob. Amanda resisted the impulse to turn around. *It's none of our business, it's rude, and it might get us into trouble,* she remembered Ron telling her, *so never watch guests get into their safe-deposit boxes.* Amanda was thinking of quietly leaving the room when she heard the lid close and Sheila said, "Okay, I'm done, thank you."

Amanda turned around and took the box from Sheila. The lighting in the room made it hard to tell, but Amanda thought Sheila's eyes were redder and puffier than before. Amanda returned the drawer to its box, swung the box door shut, and turned both keys in their locks. She returned the master key to its chain and handed the guest key back to Sheila. "Is there anything else I can do for you?"

"No, thanks," Sheila sniffed with a sad smile. "You've done quite enough."

•　　•　　•

The next day was Amanda's day off. Ron was at the front desk with another guest service representative named Dennis when Virgil Jones approached just after 8 A.M., looking puzzled. "This is going to sound like a strange question," he said, "but—have you seen my wife?"

"No, sir, not this morning," Ron replied.

"I didn't hear her get up, and her suitcase is gone." Virgil rubbed his chin for a moment, then shrugged. "I'm sure she'll turn up," he said as he turned to go. "Like a bad penny," he muttered under his breath as he walked away.

About twenty minutes later, Virgil was back at the front desk, looking considerably more anxious than before. "I can't find my safe-deposit box key!" he exclaimed to Ron. "Do you have a spare? I need to check on something right away."

Ron shook his head. "I'm sorry, sir, but, for security reasons, we don't have spare keys to any of our boxes."

"What do we do now? I gotta get into that box!"

"Well, you have two options," Ron said. "One, we can call a locksmith. The firm we use is good about coming out right away. They're usually here between a half hour and an hour after we call—and I believe the last time they came out for this they charged around $80. Whatever the charge is, we will add it to your room bill. Or, two, I can call our maintenance department and have one of the staff 'punch' the lock for us. He can probably be up here in just a few minutes, but if you choose this option there's a $100 charge because we'll have to replace the lock."

"Call the maintenance guy!" Virgil said quickly. "I'm not waiting no hour."

"Very well." Ron moved to the front desk phone, dialed, and spoke a few words into it before returning to Virgil. "He'll be up right away. Do you remember your safe-deposit box number?"

Virgil was churning his fingers through his hair, a worried expression on his face. "No," he said. "Maybe 110, 218? I don't know."

"Well, we can look it up in our files. Excuse me for a moment please." Dennis was busy with another guest, so Ron answered the front desk telephone.

When Ron hung up, he smiled and waved to a young man just getting off one of the lobby elevators. "Ah, here's Ted already." Ted was in a gray maintenance uniform and carrying a box of tools. "Come with me, please," Ron said to Ted, and then, "Mr. Jones, right this way."

The three men entered the safe-deposit box room. Ron opened the file box and turned to Virgil. "Can I see some ID, please?"

Virgil pulled out a fat wallet and gave Ron his driver's license.

"Thank you." Ron put the license on the table and flipped quickly to the "J's" in the file box. There was the card: Box 116, signed out by Virgil H. Jones. Ron compared the signature on the license to the signature on the card, nodded, and gave the license back to Virgil. Ron noticed that Virgil had not gotten into the box since he had first opened it up, but that Sheila Jones had signed for it yesterday. Ron looked at the initials alongside the signature: "A.M."—Amanda Muldinado—and shook his head. Rookies, he thought.

"It looks like you reserved box 116, Mr. Jones," Ron said. "Sign here, please, and we'll get it open for you right away." Ron pushed the card over to Virgil before turning to put the master key in the master-key lock for box 116 and turning it.

Virgil started to sign the card but stopped. "I see my wife's signature here. She got into the box yesterday?"

"Looks like it," Ron said. Behind them Ted set down his box of tools. After a couple of sharp blows, Ted said, "All set."

Ron pulled the long drawer out of box 116 and handed it to Virgil. "We'll leave you alone now, Mr. Jones," Ron said quickly, and motioned for Ted to exit. Ron was hardly back at the front desk before Virgil reappeared.

"Is everything all right, Mr. Jones?"

"No, everything is not all right," Virgil said in measured tones. "Something's missing."

Ron's heart started to pound. "Oh, no! What's missing? Can you describe it?"

"There was a solid gold ID bracelet in there with the name 'Mitzy' engraved on it," Virgil said angrily. "Now it's gone."

"Oh, no!" Ron said again.

"And now my wife is gone," Virgil continued. "I hope this hotel makes a lot of money," he said with quiet fury, "because the Metropolitan's going to pay for my divorce."

Discussion Questions

1. Why does Virgil Jones think that he might have grounds to compel the Metropolitan to "pay for his divorce"? Or, to put it another way, did Amanda, Ron, or any other hotel staff member make any serious mistakes in dealing with Virgil or Sheila? If so, what were they?

2. Generally speaking, what are the essential security precautions hotel staff members should take when checking a guest into a hotel room?

3. Generally speaking, what are the essential security precautions hotel staff members should take when allowing guests access to safe-deposit boxes?

Case Number: 3873CA

The following industry experts helped generate and develop this case: Wendell Couch, ARM, CHA, Director of Technical Services for the Risk Management Department of Bass Hotels & Resorts; and Raymond C. Ellis, Jr., CHE, CHTP, CLSD, Professor, Conrad N. Hilton College, University of Houston, Director, Loss Prevention Management Institute.

Chapter Appendix

Sample Room Notices

The following sample room notices are typical of most states' notices in that each contains information regarding its state's limited liability laws—sometimes including the wording of the actual law. Some of them also post room rates. The laws of these two states suggest the similarities and differences that can be found in such laws from state to state.

TEXAS

LIMITED LIABILITY LAW
BE IT ENACTED BY THE LEGISLATURE OF
THE STATE OF TEXAS

Article 4592—Liability for Valuables. Any hotel, apartment hotel or boarding house keeper, who constantly has in his hotel, apartment hotel or boarding house a metal safe or vault in good order and fit for the custody of money, jewelry, articles of gold or silver manufacture, precious stones, personal ornaments, or documents of any kind, and who keeps on the doors of sleeping rooms used by guests suitable locks or bolts and proper fastening on the transom and window of said room, shall not be liable for the loss or injury suffered by any guest on account of the loss of said valuables in excess of the sum of fifty dollars, which could reasonably be kept in the safe or vault of the hotel, unless said guest has offered to deliver such valuables to said hotel, apartment hotel or boarding house keeper for custody in such metal safe or vault, and said hotel, apartment hotel or boarding hotel or boarding house keeper has omitted or refused to deposit said valuables in such safe or vault and issue a receipt therefore; provided such loss or injury does not occur through the negligence or wrong doing of said hotel, apartment hotel or boarding house keeper, his servants, or employees and that a printed copy of this law is posted on the door of the sleeping room of such guest.

RATE POSTING
ROOM NO. _____

    This room will accommodate _____ people during a capacity period and when the exclusive use of the room by one or more guests is demanded to the exclusion of other guests desiring accommodations, the full charge of $_____ will be made per day for such room.

    During a period when it is necessary to utilize this room to its full capacity, the same will be assigned to one or more guests at the following rates:

1 guest, $ _____	3 guests, $ _____
2 guests, $ _____	4 guests, $ _____
Posted _____ day of _____ 20 _____	

NEW YORK

NOTICE TO GUESTS

A Safe is Provided in the Office for the Safekeeping of Money, Jewels, Ornaments, Bank Notes, Bonds, Negotiable, Securities, and Precious Stones Belonging to Guests.

DAILY RATE FOR ROOMS*

Single from	$_____	to $_____
Double from	$_____	to $_____
Extra Persons (each) from	$_____	to $_____

* * *

Charge for this Rental Unit:
Single $_____ Double $_____

MEALS*

Table d'hote Breakfast from	$_____	to $_____
Table d'hote Luncheon from	$_____	to $_____
Table d'hote Dinner from	$_____	to $_____

A la Carte as per menu

*SUBJECT TO APPLICABLE TAXES
GENERAL BUSINESS LAW—SECTIONS 200, 201, 203-a, 203-b, 206, 206-d

SECTION 200. SAFES; LIMITED LIABILITY. Whenever the proprietor or manager of any hotel, motel, inn, or steamboat shall provide a safe or safe-deposit boxes in the office of such hotel, motel or steamboat, or other convenient place for the safe keeping of any money, jewels, ornaments, bank notes, bonds, negotiable securities, or precious stones, belonging to the guests of or travelers in such hotel, motel, inn or steamboat, and shall notify the guests or travelers thereof by posting a notice stating the fact that such safe or safe-deposit boxes are provided, in which such property may be deposited, in a public and conspicuous place and manner in the office and public rooms, and in the public parlors of such hotel, motel, or inn, or saloon of such steamboat; and if such guest or traveler shall neglect to deliver such property to the person in charge of such office for deposit in such safe or safe-deposit boxes, the proprietor or manager of such hotel, motel, or steamboat shall not be liable for any loss of such property, sustained by such guest or traveler by theft or otherwise; but no hotel, motel, or steamboat proprietor, manager or lessee shall be obliged to receive property on deposit for safe keeping, exceeding one thousand five hundred dollars in value; and if such guest or traveler shall deliver such property, to the person in charge of such office for deposit in such safe or safe-deposit boxes, said proprietor, manager or lessee shall not be liable for any loss thereof, sustained by such guest or traveler by theft or otherwise, in any sum exceeding the sum of one thousand five hundred dollars unless by special agreement in writing with such proprietor, manager or lessee.

SECTION 201. LIABILITY FOR LOSS OF CLOTHING AND OTHER PERSONAL PROPERTY LIMITED. 1. No hotel or motel keeper except as provided in the forgoing section shall be liable for damage to or loss of wearing apparel or other personal property in the lobby, hallways or in the room or rooms assigned to a guest for any sum exceeding the sum of five hundred dollars, unless it shall appear that such loss occurred through the fault or negligence of such keeper, nor shall he be liable in any sum exceeding the sum of one hundred dollars for the loss of or damage to any such property when delivered to such keeper for storage or safe keeping in the store room, baggage room or other place elsewhere than in the room or rooms assigned to such guest, unless at the time of delivering the same for storage or safe keeping such value in excess of one hundred dollars shall be stated and a written receipt, stating such value, shall be issued by such keeper, but in no event shall such keeper be liable beyond five hundred dollars, unless it shall appear that such loss occurred through his fault or negligence, and such keeper may make a reasonable charge for storing or keeping such property, nor shall he be liable for the loss of or damage to any merchandise samples or merchandise for sale, unless the guest shall have given such keeper prior written notice of having the same in his possession, together with the value thereof, the receipt of which notice the hotel or motel keeper shall acknowledge in writing over the signature of himself or his agent, but in no event shall such keeper be liable beyond five hundred dollars, unless it shall appear that such loss or damage occurred through his fault or negligence; as to property deposited by guests or patrons in the parcel or checkroom of any hotel, motel or restaurant, the delivery of which is evidenced by a check or receipt therefore and for which no fee or charge is exacted, the proprietor shall not be liable beyond two hundred dollars, unless such value in excess of two hundred dollars shall be stated upon delivery and a written receipt, stating such value, shall be issued, but he shall in no event be liable beyond three hundred dollars, unless such loss occurs through his fault or negligence. Notwithstanding anything hereinabove contained, no hotel or motel keeper shall be liable for damage to or loss of such property by fire, when it shall appear that such fire was occasioned without his fault or negligence.

2. A printed copy of this section shall be posted in a conspicuous place and manner in the office or public room and in the public parlors of such hotel or motel. No hotel, motel or restaurant proprietor shall post a notice disclaiming or misrepresenting his liability under this section.

SECTION 203-A. HOTEL AND MOTEL KEEPER'S LIABILITY FOR PROPERTY IN TRANSPORT. No hotel or motel keeper shall be liable in any sum exceeding the sum of two hundred and fifty dollars for the loss of or damage to property of a guest delivered to such keeper, his agent or employee, for transport to or from the hotel or motel, unless at the time of delivering the same such value in excess of two hundred and fifty dollars shall be stated by such guest and a written receipt stating such value shall be issued by such keeper; provided, however, that where such written receipt is issued the keeper shall not be liable beyond five hundred dollars unless it shall appear that such loss or damage occurred through his fault or negligence.

SECTION 203-B. POSTING OF STATUTE. Every keeper of a hotel or motel or inn shall post in a public and conspicuous place and manner in the registration office and in the public rooms of such hotel or motel or inn a printed copy of this section and section two hundred three-a.

SECTION 206. RATES TO BE POSTED; PENALTY FOR VIOLATION. Every keeper of a hotel or inn shall post in a public and conspicuous place and manner in the office or public room, and in the public parlors of such hotel or inn, a printed copy of this section and sections two hundred and two hundred and one, and a statement of the charges or rate of charges by the day and for meals furnished and for lodging. No charge or sum shall be collected or received by any such hotel keeper or inn keeper for any service not actually rendered or for a longer time than the person so charged actually remained at such hotel or inn, nor for a higher rate of charge for the use of such room or board, lodging or meals than is specified in the rate of charges required to be posted by the last preceding sentence; provided such guest shall have given such hotel keeper or inn keeper notice at the office of his departure. For any violation of this section the offender shall forfeit to the injured party three times the amount so charged, and shall not be entitled to receive any money for meals, services or time charged.

SECTION 206-D. POSTING OF RATES OF VARIOUS TYPE ACCOMMODATIONS. In addition to other provisions in this article relating to posting of rates, every keeper of a hotel, motel or inn shall post publicly and conspicuously at the place maintained for the registration of guests so that it can be easily and readily seen and read by guests registering, a statement of the charges or rate of charges by the day indicating the standard rates for rooms or suites of different accommodations, and for meals furnished. The standard rates shall be that schedule of rates available to guests who do not qualify for special discounts or rate reductions.

Check-Out Time _____

Chapter 5 Outline

Competencies

1. Identify slip, trip, and fall risks posed on hotel premises, and explain what hotels can do to minimize them. (pp. 139–143)

2. Describe fire safety risks in hotels and the various measures and equipment hotels use to address these risks. (pp. 143–152)

3. Explain safety risks and concerns pertaining to hotel water systems, including water potability, hot water temperatures, and *Legionella* bacteria. (pp. 152–155)

4. Identify safety risks and concerns that hospitality operators and managers potentially face in regard to power outages and emergency power, indoor air quality, foodborne illness, and bed bugs. (pp. 155–161)

5

Lodging Safety

WHEN EVALUATING THE RISKS that lodging operations face, it can be easy to focus on sensational, headline-grabbing security incidents and any large lawsuits that were subsequently filed. However, security- and crime-related incidents make up just a portion of the risk management issues that may affect hotels and their guests. Lodging safety issues are much more common and can affect both guests and hotel staff. This chapter addresses the following safety topics: slips, trips, and falls; fire safety; water system safety issues; emergency power; indoor air quality; foodborne illness and travelers' health; and bed bugs.

Slips, Trips, and Falls

In a study by the Institute of Real Estate Management, 57 percent of respondents ranked slips and falls as the single leading cause of current disputes, and 64 percent ranked such accidents as among the top three management issues they and their colleagues face.

Premises liability is the legal responsibility of a property owner or manager of real property for injuries caused to others or their property due to conditions or activities on the real property. Slips and falls in public places are far and away the leading cause of premises liability injuries.[1]

As this quote indicates, safety issues involving slips, trips, and falls are very common.[2] They cause millions of injuries and thousands of deaths each year in the United States. Hotels are also affected by these problems, which can involve both guests and employees. Guests in hotels may find themselves in unfamiliar surroundings, may be juggling luggage and personal items, may be distracted as they navigate their way through the hotel, and may also be under the influence of alcohol. Such factors increase the chance that guests might slip, trip, or fall.[3] The hotel must be sure that its design and maintenance procedures lower the risk of these incidents.

Exhibit 1 features recommendations from a Continental Casualty Company (CNA) risk control report addressing slips, trips, and falls in public buildings. Hotel administrators should review these recommendations in light of the hotel's design and operating procedures, and then implement appropriate action. (On occasion, CNA offers a webinar that provides information about trends in slip-and-fall events, liability, and intervention strategies.)

Parking areas and walkways certainly can pose safety problems. Adequate lighting will help users see areas of transition and potential obstacles. Maintaining these surfaces and repairing them as necessary will also help ensure visitor safety.

Exhibit 1   Recommendations for Lowering the Risk for Slip and Fall Incidents

These recommendations are based on results from a study conducted by CNA Risk Control and reported in *InControl / Slips, Trips and Falls for the Real Estate Industry: New Techniques to Control Slips and Falls in Public Places.* Hospitality industry owners and managers are encouraged to use these recommendations to help decrease the risk of slip-and-fall incidents on their properties.

1. **Select high-traction, slip-resistant flooring materials when building, expanding, or remodeling facilities.** Installation of such materials with proven high-traction characteristics on the front end is one of the most cost-effective ways to avoid slip-and-fall issues. To a great degree, texture determines a floor's slip resistance. Smooth floors made of glazed ceramic tile or terrazzo can be dangerously slippery under typical footwear when wet. Other floors with abrasives in their surface or specially textured metal plates can be quite slip resistant, even when wet or contaminated.

   The best chance of reducing slip-and-fall accidents is during a facility's design phase when choosing floor materials. Some problem floors can be made safer by surface treatments, but others may need to be replaced or carpeted over, if possible. A good place to start is with flooring materials certified by the National Floor Safety Institute (www.nfsi.org).

2. **Know what the "out-of-the-box" slip resistance is on the floor materials in a facility.** These numbers provide a baseline when considering changes to cleaning and floor maintenance practices. Have flooring COF-audited after installation to confirm slip resistance. Use the NFSI/ANSI B101.1-2009 *Test Method for Measuring Wet SCOF of Common Hard-Surface Floor Materials* as the test method.

3. **Select floor treatment, cleaning, and maintenance products with proven slip-resistance characteristics that are compatible with the particular flooring surfaces in a facility.** A good place to start is with products certified by the National Floor Safety Institute.

4. **Be alert for workers substituting cleaning materials or supplies.** Ensure that sufficient cleaning supplies are available.

5. **Ensure that floor cleaning and maintenance products are applied in accordance with the manufacturer's recommendations.**

6. **Verify with cleaning personnel that they are familiar with and are using the correct cleaning and maintenance product application procedures.** There must be a continuing effort to orient new employees to proper procedures and ensure they have the right skills to perform the job. If there is a change in personnel or contractor, monitor application to verify that manufacturers' recommendations continue to be adhered to.

7. **Remove any unauthorized or incompatible cleaning and maintenance products and educate staff on the potentially dangerous consequences that using the wrong products can have on the slip resistance of flooring surfaces.**

Exhibit 1 *(continued)*

8. **Separate cleaning and maintenance materials and equipment between the heavily soiled areas, such as food service areas, restrooms, and breakrooms, from other areas to reduce the likelihood of transporting a problem from one area to another.** Color-coding materials and equipment can provide instant recognition for personnel using them and can prevent usage of the wrong materials or equipment in an area of the facility.

9. **Ensure that permanently installed features like carpet runners and mats are included in the maintenance and housekeeping program.** These materials need to be regularly inspected for the buildup of contaminants and for deterioration that could lead to the creation of slip, trip, or fall hazards. Keep in mind that while mats reduce the likelihood of producing slips, improperly maintained mats can create trip hazards.

10. **Implement a good mat program.** One of the surest ways to prevent the transmission of dirt, water, and other materials from the outdoors to the interior of a facility is to implement a good mat program. Ensure that mats are frequently inspected and are checked regularly for wear and the build-up of contaminants. A poorly managed and maintained mat program can significantly increase the likelihood of reducing the slip resistance of flooring surfaces.

    In warm weather, place an abrasive mat outside and an absorptive mat inside. In cold weather, put an absorptive mat just inside the door, followed by an abrasive mat. When mats get dirty or saturated, they must be exchanged for clean ones. Offer plastic bags at the entrance for umbrella storage when it's raining, so visitors don't shake out water from their umbrellas far into the building.

11. **Limit the difference in height between flooring surfaces and mats to no more than ¼" to ½", while frequently inspecting mats to ensure they have not buckled or curled.** Ensure that mats are firmly secured to prevent migration and that the floor beneath the mat is clean and dry. Evaluate these changes in height regularly, since they can deteriorate and create trip hazards.

12. **Make sure each area has good lighting.** Good visibility is essential for the prevention of slips, trips, and falls. Evaluate the facility and grounds during different times of the day and seasons of the year to determine whether lighting is adequate. Consider the earliest and latest times when visitors, pedestrians, or employees are on the premises. Provide additional lighting for walking surfaces, as needed. Don't forget to include parking areas, stairways, and loading docks. Promptly replace any burnt-out bulbs.

13. **Regularly review all slip-and-fall incident reports associated with a facility and understand the critical factors associated with them.** Look for trends in location, time of day, etc., and focus staff training on cleaning procedures for these factors. Train workers on how to properly respond to slip-and-fall incidents. All incidents should be promptly investigated. Consult with legal counsel on the best way to document investigation results.

(continued)

Exhibit 1 *(continued)*

14. **Ensure that staff is well-trained in spill prevention and response programs.** They must know where clean-up materials are located and how to properly use them in the event of an emergency. Instruct staff on the importance of reporting incidents and conditions that could result in incidents, even if none have actually occurred. Such reports will be the first indication of a potential issue that should be addressed.

15. **A walkway auditing program can help identify trends within a facility that can result in reduced slip resistance of flooring surfaces.** To be effective, the testing should be completed in a consistent manner, including more than a single set of measurements and following the NFSI/ANSI B101.1-2009 established floor-auditing protocols.

16. **Maintaining open and clear communication between staff, cleaning personnel, and the walkway floor auditor is crucial to the identification of trends and the elimination of factors that could reduce the slip resistance of floor surfaces.**

17. **Make sure stairs comply with local building codes and that nosings are easy to see—even for a visually impaired person.** Stairs need to have very uniform rise and run, and handrails that are firmly mounted and easy to grip. Avoid having confusing carpet patterns on stairs or steps that make it hard to tell where each step's nose ends. On hard surfaces, abrasive tapes can help. Outdoor stairs must be slip-resistant when wet and should have stripes on each tread.

18. **Institute a program to regularly inspect all walkways, parking areas, stairs, and indoor walking surfaces for condition and maintenance.** Repair any unstable surfaces, such as loose tiles or torn carpet. Secure any mats, rugs, or carpets that don't lie flat. Provide adequate clearances for doors, walkways, and aisles. Keep floors clean and dry, and remove any obstructions or tripping hazards. Conduct routine monitoring of any walking surface that is periodically wet or icy, such as sidewalks, building entrances, or walk-in food coolers.

19. **Maintain surveillance of potentially slippery areas and clean up spills before anyone falls.** Instruct maintenance personnel to use "Wet Floor" signs to mark contaminated areas until the contaminant can be cleaned up.

Most surfaces used for parking and walkways are inherently slip resistant, but this quality decreases or disappears entirely if ice or snow covers the surface. Therefore, removal of ice and snow and use of salt and/or sand is necessary.

The design of hotel parking areas and walkways is of the utmost importance. For example, consider a hotel at which, after a snowfall, employees use snow removal equipment to clear the parking lot surface of snow and pile it at one end of the lot. Unfortunately, that end of the parking lot is higher than the other end, and the lot's only drain is at the lower end. Snow melting during the day lays a sheet of water over the parking lot's surface. The water then freezes at night, creating a thin sheet of ice that is very difficult to see. This hazard results in plenty of slipping and falling. During the initial planning and building stages of this hotel and its premises, administrators would have been wise to consider the snow removal issue and install a drain to intercept the runoff.

Guests entering a hotel located in a cold winter climate may in the wintertime inadvertently carry inside with them water, snow, and de-icing materials on their footwear. Therefore, hotels in such areas should choose flooring that is slip resistant when wet as well as when dry. Providing track-off mats inside hotel entrances will help keep floors dry and reduce potential damage to floors, and will also decrease the staff's need to frequently clean floors of moisture and dirt.

Hotels in all areas often cover public floor areas with carpeting, which reduces the potential for slips and falls and also cushions the floor surface. However, carpeting that has become worn can create a tripping hazard.

Power cords can pose a tripping hazard as well. Hotels should minimize the use of extension cords when possible. When extension cords are in use, the hotel should secure them to the floor to reduce tripping hazards.

Many hotels carpet guestroom floors as well as floors in public areas. However, hotels in tropical and international locations may instead install hard floor surfaces in each guestroom, and place area rugs in some spots in the room. The hard surface should be evaluated when dry and when wet for slip resistance, as should any area rugs. The design of the hotel building itself should also be reviewed for potential hazards. For example, one Caribbean hotel was designed in such a way that warm, humid outside air entered guestrooms and came in contact with a floor surface chilled by air conditioning. This caused condensation to form on the floor during the night, which resulted in a floor surface that was as slick as ice, a fact that unsuspecting guests discovered only upon getting out of bed in the morning.

Or consider the experience of one family staying overnight at a hotel that was part of a major franchise chain. The property had an indoor pool that appealed to young kids, which is why the family chose to stay there. The flooring surrounding the pool had a soft, pebbled surface that felt pleasant to walk on. Unfortunately, when the floor got wet—as of course it did every time swimmers splashed water or exited the pool—it became an extremely slippery surface. Almost every user of the pool slipped on the floor to some degree, and some actually fell.

These examples go to show that hotel designers and managers must consider the slip-resistant properties of floors in all foreseeable conditions.

Fire Safety

One rather universal safety risk associated with hotels is the risk of fire. Fires can and do occur in all types of buildings. The vast majority of fires begin accidentally rather than willfully as an act of arson. Whatever the cause, building occupants must be alerted when a fire occurs and provided with a safe means of exit; the building itself, as well as its contents, must be protected from the spread of fire and the damage it could cause. Generally, hotel guests are staying in an environment unfamiliar to them, spend a large part of their time in the hotel sleeping, and the hotel itself may consist of a high-rise structure that is difficult to evacuate quickly. As a result, fire safety in hotels takes on added dimensions that fire safety in other buildings does not.[4]

Statistics for the United States regarding hotel fires show a significant reduction in the risk of fire as a result of improved safety code standards and operational practices. A number of independent studies have illustrated the success of efforts to reduce fire risk in hotels.[5] Free-standing restaurants have also seen improvements in fire safety.[6]

From a guest (and employee) perspective, fire protection equipment is very important. But, as with security, fire protection really begins with the design of the building itself, including its layout, the materials the building is made of, and the various types of equipment inside the building. Fire protection also involves following maintenance and operational procedures developed to ensure that original design features are not compromised and that fire risk is not inadvertently heightened through routine operational activity.

The National Fire Prevention Association (NFPA) offers publications and resources that address fire safety and protection. Exhibit 2 shows the major areas of fire safety as covered in *NFPA 101: Life Safety Code,* which forms the basis for the fire codes in many states. In the aftermath of major hotel fires such as the MGM Grand Hotel fire in 1980, fire codes were substantially changed. which contributed greatly to the fact that, in recent decades, hotel fires in the United States in particular have been much less frequent and deadly than in the past.[7] Lessons learned from major hotel fires have also influenced the design of new hotels and casinos throughout the world.[8]

Means of Egress

Means of egress (such as corridors, exit stairwells, and exit doors)[9] are established during the design process of the hotel and approved by local code authorities. It is the responsibility of the hotel's managers to make sure that means of egress are maintained during hotel operations. This means, among other things, that stairwells and corridors must not be blocked by items stored or placed there, even temporarily. In addition, exit doors must not be chained closed. Chained exit doors have been cited in several fires in clubs and entertainment venues in the past few decades (in the Philippines, Argentina, Russia, and in Chicago in the United States). Historically, the 1942 fire at the Cocoanut Grove nightclub in Boston, which resulted in the deaths of 492 people,[10] revealed severe problems with means of egress, as did the tragic Triangle Shirtwaist fire in 1911.[11]

The U.S. Occupational Safety & Health Administration's "OSHA Standard 1910 Subpart E" addresses means of egress.[12] The major items covered in this standard are the following:

OSHA Standard 1910 Subpart E—Means of Egress

- 1910 Subpart E App—Exit Routes, Emergency Action Plans, and Fire Prevention Plans
- 1910.33—Table of contents

Exhibit 2   Major Fire Safety Issues Covered by the *Life Safety Code*

- **Means of Egress.** Adequate, protected exits must be available in a fire or other emergency. Number of exits, exit width, exit placement, emergency lighting, exit signs, and maximum travel distance to an exit are all covered.

- **Protection Against Fire Spread.** The construction of a building should help prevent the spread of smoke and fire. Floor/ceiling assemblies, stairwells, and building service shafts are all required to be fire-rated to help contain smoke and fire to its floor of origin. Stairwell doors should be self-closing.

- **Protection of Hazardous Areas.** Areas of the hotel with a significantly higher chance of fire or explosion than the rest of the hotel should be separated from the rest of the building with fire-rated walls and self-closing doors, and be protected with a sprinkler system.

- **Floor, Wall, and Ceiling Finish Flammability.** Because of the high flammability and smoke toxicity of some fabrics and finishes, acceptable flame spread and toxicity ratings allowed in various parts of the hotel are regulated. Improper materials could greatly speed fire or produce highly toxic smoke.

- **Fire Detection and Alarm Systems.** A building fire alarm system is required in all hotels and motels except existing buildings up to three stories high with exterior access in all rooms. Components include smoke or heat detectors and automatic sprinkler systems.

- **Fire Hose Standpipe Systems.** Building codes generally require fire protection standpipe systems in hotels above specific heights. The type required is determined by the applicable code, building height, and the presence or absence of sprinklers.

- **Fire Sprinkler Systems.** Sprinkler systems are required on all existing high-rise hotels except those with exterior exits for all guestrooms. The system design depends on the occupancy classification.

- **Room and Corridor Isolation.** Because a simple closed door can contain smoke and fire to the room of their origin—leaving the corridor usable for exiting—twenty-minute rated doors with self closers are required for all new and existing guestrooms. Walls between corridors and guestrooms are also required to be fire-rated.

Source: William J. Beasland, "Fire Safe Hospitality," *The Construction Specifier,* December 1993.

- 1910.34—Coverage and definitions
- 1910.35—Compliance with alternate exit-route codes
- 1910.36—Design and construction requirements for exit routes
- 1910.37—Maintenance, safeguards, and operational features for exit routes
- 1910.38—Emergency action plans
- 1910.39—Fire prevention plans

Hotel designers, managers, and others should be aware of these standards and make sure that their facilities are in compliance.

Protection Against Fire Spread and Protection of Hazardous Areas

Many design features have addressed protection against fire spread by including fire stops in plumbing risers, automatic closers on doors, and fire-resistive construction materials. It is management's responsibility to see that these features are never compromised, such as when maintenance work is performed, or during the course of normal daily operations. For example, when maintenance work is done on plumbing risers, any affected fire protection, such as installed fire stops, must be replaced after the work is completed. Proper maintenance and inspection of fire dampers and fusible links in ductwork are also key safety considerations.

An illustration of how important it is to control the spread of fire and smoke is the MGM Grand Hotel fire of 1980. The building design of the MGM Grand allowed fire and smoke to spread extensively (including vertically) throughout the building, resulting in deaths and injuries far from where the fire actually originated. Modern building practices call for a number of items to be installed to contain the spread of fire and smoke. Maintenance and testing of these items is an ongoing management responsibility.

Protection of hazardous areas within hotels is most likely to involve mechanical spaces as well as areas where paint and chemicals are stored. For example, hotels commonly store paint and chemicals in fire-rated storage cabinets. Fuel for equipment used for lawn maintenance or snow removal should not be stored within the hotel. Hotel managers should refer to *NFPA 30: Flammable and Combustible Liquids Code*, as well as local codes, for proper procedures.

Floor, Wall, and Ceiling Finish Flammability

Floor, wall, and ceiling finish flammability has become a matter of increasing study in the aftermath of several hotel and restaurant fires.[13] The actual potential fuel that these materials can contribute is of concern, as are the gases and smoke the materials give off when they burn. Materials selected for use in new construction should have smoke and flammability characteristics consistent with *NFPA 101* standards. All other materials introduced into a hotel or restaurant should also be evaluated. Any renovations made to a hospitality operation must conform to code standards as well.

Fire Detection and Alarm Systems

Fire detection and alarm systems are installed in virtually all hotels and other hospitality operations.[14] Smoke and/or heat detection units are located throughout the typical hospitality property. In some instances, smoke and heat detectors may consist solely of single-station devices powered by battery or connected to an electrical source. Single-station devices sound an alarm only at the device itself. Because of this limitation, multiple-station detectors are installed more commonly. These communicate with a central control panel to transmit information regarding the location of the fire alarm that sounded, and to activate building alarm and evacuation alerts. Many modern fire alarm systems also feature a speaker system to allow for voice communication of evacuation instructions and other information.

Hotels must meet requirements for ongoing maintenance and replacement of fire detection and alarm systems.[15] The NFPA offers a number of publications and resources that address fire detection and alarm system maintenance issues. Among these publications is *Fire Protection Systems Inspection, Test and Maintenance Manual*, Third Edition, by Wayne G. Carson and Richard L. Klinker.[16] In addition, lodging operations with installed fire sprinklers should be aware of *NFPA 25: Water-Based Fire Protection Systems Handbook.*[17]

Fire detection and alarm systems must be tested on a regular basis. Local code and fire authorities establish minimum test frequency and required procedures, which generally focus on evacuation.

Carbon Monoxide Detectors

Twenty-five states have mandated the installation of carbon monoxide (CO) detectors in certain residential properties, while a few states (six as of this writing) require CO detectors in some hotels as well.[18] Hotels have experienced instances of CO poisoning resulting in serious injuries and deaths due to a variety of problems, including a lack of adequate venting of combustion gases when using oil or gas space heaters in interior areas as well as maintenance issues (cracks in combustion gas venting or blocked venting on furnace equipment). Since CO is odorless and invisible, hotels operating fossil-fuel heaters must be particularly vigilant. CO poisoning has been caused by faulty operation of indoor pool heaters, space-heating equipment, and water heaters, and also can be caused by faulty installations and modifications made during building maintenance.

Fire Sprinkler Systems

Many U.S. and overseas hotels currently have fire sprinkler systems[19] installed throughout the premises. In the United States, building codes requiring fire sprinklers were passed after several major hotel fires in the 1980s (including the MGM Grand Hotel previously mentioned, the Las Vegas Hilton, Stouffer's Inn of

---

American Hotel & Lodging Association
Statement on Carbon Monoxide

The safety of its guests is the highest priority of the lodging industry. Carbon monoxide (CO) is a colorless, practically odorless, and tasteless gas. It has multiple industrial uses. Trace amounts of it occur naturally and are part of the atmosphere. Nevertheless, in high enough concentrations, it can be deadly and the risks of exposure to abnormal levels of CO are well-known and well-publicized. Although there are no federal rules on CO detection, nor is AH&LA empowered to set standards and policies, we urge our members to continue their CO monitoring and prevention policies.

Source: www.ahla.com/PressRoom.aspx?id=15654.

Westchester, and the DuPont Plaza Hotel). In addition, the U.S. federal government passed the Hotel and Motel Fire Safety Act of 1990, which required (for listing as approved for federal employee travel), among other things, sprinklers in properties having three or more stories.[20] This, together with the pressure of potential litigation brought by hotel guests and increasing meeting-planner insistence on more stringent hotel safety standards, resulted in further expansion of sprinkler installations. The standards of many hotel chains today require sprinkler installations in most or all company properties.

Fire sprinklers installed in most areas of hotels are wet sprinklers, which use water to suppress fire. These sprinklers have a fusible link that melts in the heat of a fire, thus activating the sprinklers. Wet sprinklers systems always have water in them.

Dry sprinkler systems should be installed in hotel areas that are subject to freezing temperatures, such as outdoor parking structures or a hotel's porte cochere. The dry system is pressurized with air, and water is introduced into the system only when a sprinkler head activates through the melting of a fusible link. This releases air from the pipes and replaces the air with water, which then flows from the sprinkler heads. Dry systems carry a risk of corrosion in the systems as well as the potential for moisture to be trapped in the systems and freeze. Hotels should refer to *NFPA 13* and supplier/installer information for maintenance instructions for dry sprinkler systems.

Restaurants are required to install fire-suppression equipment over many cooking appliances.[21] Restaurant fire-suppression equipment has shifted from the dry-chemical systems of yesteryear to wet-agent fire-suppression designs. Wet-agent systems generally provide quicker flame knockdown and faster fire suppression than dry-chemical systems. Wet-agent systems also make for far easier cleanup following discharge.

Fire sprinklers in areas in the **back of the house** might potentially be blocked if hotel employees store inventory or other materials nearby. Therefore, an element of maintenance of fire sprinkler systems involves inspection of back-of-the-house spaces to be sure that sprinklers are not blocked. *NFPA 25* addresses additional maintenance aspects.

A unique aspect of fire protection involves protection for computer facilities. For more information, see *NFPA 75: Standard for the Protection of Information Technology Equipment*. Some suppression equipment used in computer facilities is toxic, so special procedures are required when the suppression equipment is activated.

Lodging operations should be sure to stock a supply of replacement sprinkler heads for use when sprinklers have been activated or broken. Following a fire and subsequent sprinkler activation in a hotel, fire departments would probably not allow the hotel to be re-occupied until the sprinkler system is once again fully operational.

Portable Fire Extinguishers

OSHA and building codes require that portable fire extinguishers be installed in most hospitability buildings to provide a means of suppression of incipient (early stage) fires.[22] The appropriate type of extinguisher depends on the fire's location within the building and the type of fire that may occur there.[23, 24] (Exhibit 3 provides information about portable fire extinguishers and the types of fires they are designed to fight.) In the United States, building codes and OSHA regulations have established requirements that apply to portable fire extinguisher selection, mounting, maintenance, and employee training in properly operating fire extinguishers. Exhibit 4 summarizes OSHA provisions regarding portable fire extinguishers.

OSHA Provisions Regarding Fire Protection

OSHA Standard 1910 Subpart L, comprising provisions 1910.155 through 1910.165, addresses items pertaining to other elements of fire protection. U.S. lodging operations must comply with OSHA provisions, as well as with any local or state rules and regulations. In some cases, some hotel chain standards may exceed some of these provisions.

"OSHA 1910 Subpart L—Fire Protection" provisions include the following subject areas:[25]

1910 Subpart L—Fire Protection

- 1910.155—Scope, application and definitions applicable to this subpart
- 1910.156—Fire brigades
- 1910.157—Portable fire extinguishers
- 1910.158—Standpipe and hose systems
- 1910.159—Automatic sprinkler systems
- 1910.160—Fixed extinguishing systems, general
- 1910.161—Fixed extinguishing systems, dry chemical
- 1910.162—Fixed extinguishing systems, gaseous agent
- 1910.163—Fixed extinguishing systems, water spray and foam
- 1910.164—Fire detection systems
- 1910.165—Employee alarm systems
- 1910 Subpart L App A—Fire Protection
- 1910 Subpart L App B—National Consensus Standards
- 1910 Subpart L App C—Fire protection references for further information
- 1910 Subpart L App D—Availability of publications incorporated by reference in section 1910.156 fire brigades
- 1910 Subpart L App E—Test methods for protective clothing

Again, hotel designers, managers, and others should be aware of these standards and make sure that their facilities are in compliance.

Fire Protection: Emerging Issues

Fire protection in hotels is influenced by general issues that affect the fire protection community and the broader safety and security community (and vice versa,

Exhibit 3   Types of Portable Fire Extinguishers

There are five different types of portable fire extinguishers, each type with its own unique extinguishing agent. Most fire extinguishers display symbols to show the kind of fire on which they are to be used.

Types of Fire Extinguishers

 Class A extinguishers put out fires in ordinary combustible materials such as cloth, wood, rubber, paper, and many plastics.

Ordinary Combustibles

 Class B extinguishers are used on fires involving flammable liquids, such as grease, gasoline, oil, and oil-based paints.

Flammable Liquids

 Class C extinguishers are suitable for use on fires involving appliances, tools, or other equipment that is electrically energized or plugged in.

Electrical Equipment

 Class D extinguishers are designed for use on flammable metals and are often specific for the type of metal in question. These are typically found only in factories working with these metals.

Combustible Metals

 Class K fire extinguishers are intended for use on fires that involve vegetable oils, animal oils, or fats in cooking appliances. These extinguishers are generally found in commercial kitchens, such as those found in restaurants, cafeterias, and caterers. Class K extinguishers are now finding their way into the residential market for use in kitchens.

K
Combustible Cooking

There are also multi-purpose fire extinguishers—such as those labeled "B-C" or "A-B-C"—that can be used on two or more of the above types of fires.

Source: U.S. Fire Administration, http://www.usfa.dhs.gov/citizens/home_fire_prev/extinguishers.shtm.

as major hotel fires of the 1980s influenced codes for many commercial buildings). This section addresses a few issues that currently affect hotels or that may emerge in the future.

Exhibit 4   Summary of OSHA Provisions Regarding Portable Fire Extinguishers

Some jurisdictions will permit the elimination of fire extinguishers in a fully sprinklered facility. This section [of the Occupational Safety and Health Act, Subpart L— Fire Protection (1910.155–1910.165)] permits the omission of extinguishers where a standpipe and fire-extinguishing suppression system is properly installed and maintained. However, consideration should still be given to the use of extinguishers, as this would permit the fighting of incipient fires rather than waiting for a fire to generate enough heat to activate an automatic sprinkler head.

The employer has the responsibility of:

- Providing portable fire extinguishers mounted, located, and identified so as to be readily available to employees.

- Ensuring that the extinguishers are approved by a reputable national testing organization.

- Ensuring that the extinguishers are maintained in a fully charged and operable condition.

- Providing fire extinguishers for employee use based upon the classes of anticipated workplace fires and on the size and degree of hazard which would affect their use.

- Placing extinguishers for Class A (wood, cloth, paper) fires so that the greatest distance for access by an employee is 75 feet or less.

- Placing fire extinguishers for Class B (flammable liquids, gases, oils, greases) fires so that the greatest distance for access by an employee is 50 feet or less.

- Placing fire extinguishers for Class C (electrical) fires on the basis of the appropriate pattern for the existing Class A or Class B hazards, at electrical cabinets and rooms and at intervals appropriate to the size of the property, not to exceed 75 feet, preferably less.

- Inspecting, maintaining, and testing all portable fire extinguishers in the workplace.

- Providing an annual maintenance check of all portable fire extinguishers and hydrostatic testing of the canisters as required under the law. This should be contracted with a reputable fire service company in the community, since there are technical aspects that are better handled by professionals. If the decision is made to handle this maintenance in-house, reference should be made to *29 Code of Federal Regulations,* Ch. XVII (7-1-94 Edition), Section 1910.157.

- Training employees in the correct and effective use of fire extinguishers in extinguishing incipient fires. It is recommended that consideration be given to training *all* employees, so that time is not lost while awaiting the arrival of a fire emergency team. Of course, the fire department should be immediately notified, plus notice given to the property's emergency response group. The Act permits special training of a fire emergency team, but training all employees is still a good idea.

Source: Adapted from Raymond C. Ellis, Jr., *A Guide to Occupational Safety and Health Standards Compliance for the Lodging Industry.* Used with permission.

Means of egress discussions in recent years have been influenced by the attacks on the World Trade Center towers on September 11, 2011, and the evacuations of other high-rise structures. The long-standing practice of not using elevators for evacuation in fires (and other emergencies) is being reevaluated, as is the use of areas of refuge. Other egress issues may yet emerge.[26]

Protection against fire spread is likely to draw further attention in light of studies conducted and recommendations set forth by such groups as the National Institute of Standards and Technology (NIST). NFPA fire codes as well as International Code Council (ICC) building and fire codes have been changed to be consistent with recommendations set forth in NIST's WTC Towers investigation. During the investigation of the effect the terrorist attacks had on the Twin Towers, a number of concerns were raised about high-rise building construction, some of which may apply to hotels. For example, one issue identified is the large amount of fuel stored on site for emergency generators and the possibility that the stored fuel may feed fires that occur in the building.[27]

Notification systems for fire have evolved from alarm-only systems to systems that provide voice communication. A discussion of some emerging issues associated with emergency communication in high-rise structures is available at the listed reference.[28]

International travelers may notice different design standards and fire equipment in use in hotels in other countries. Some of these differences are due to variations in code standards throughout the world (and within countries themselves, since it is not unusual to have differences in codes within a country) as well as possible variations in the enforcement of the codes. In some countries, for example, hotels have exit stairwells that open to each floor in the building, allowing the stairways to fill with smoke in the instance of a fire. This would not be allowed under existing U.S. codes.

Hotels outside the United States may supply fire evacuation equipment that is not available in the United States. Among the more interesting are evacuation harnesses and smoke hoods in use in some Korean hotels. The evacuation harnesses are connected to a coil of cable that is affixed to the wall next to a window. Guests would use the harness to evacuate the hotel by leaving the building via the window, and lowering themselves down the outside wall of the building. Usage instructions are posted on the wall next to the attachment point.

A piece of equipment available in several hotels in China is a respirator/smoke hood, which a guest wears over his or her head during evacuation from a fire. The hood allows the wearer to avoid breathing toxic fumes and smoke, and keeps the fumes and smoke from interfering with the wearer's vision.

Safety Issues Involving Water Systems

Hotel water systems may be affected by safety problems pertaining to water potability, the temperature of hot water provided to guests, and *Legionella* bacteria.

Water Potability

Hotel guests expect the water they use in hotels to be safe. In many locations, the hotel simply purchases **potable water** from a local water utility and, with appropriate plumbing practices, the water should remain safe for guest consumption. However, a hotel in a rural or remote area may have to operate its own potable water system. In this case, the hotel must ensure that the water provided by its treatment system is in fact potable.[29]

Even if the hotel's water is provided by a reliable and safe local utility, it is possible it can become contaminated. This may happen in conditions such as flooding or when the water treatment system fails. Water utilities may issue "boil water" advisories under such circumstances. Hotels may find it necessary to take actions to inform guests to treat water supplied within the hotel as non-potable, and to provide bottled water to guests and hotel staff until the water utility notifies the hotel otherwise. A hotel may also have to engage in flushing and purifying the building's water system in the aftermath of contamination.

In some locations around the globe, potable water is not available, and hotels must clearly inform guests of that fact and tell them to use bottled water only. This information should be prominently displayed at each tap and probably in the shower as well. One would think that under such circumstances the hotel would provide bottled water to guests free of charge, but this is not always the case. One hotel in an Asian country, part of a major hotel brand, provides bottled water to guests for a very expensive price, a price not disclosed up front. In addition, at least two other hotels in the same area—where the consensus is that the tap water is not potable—do not post signs indicating that fact.

Hot Water Temperatures

Probably the second most common safety problem associated with hotel water systems involves the temperature at which hot water is supplied to guestrooms (or, more specifically, the temperature at which the hot water leaves the showerhead or tap). Some hotels provide hot water for guest use far in excess of the safe level of 115°F (46°C).

A hotel shower safety study published in 2007 reported the results of a survey of 350 guestrooms in 101 individual hotels representing 52 different hotel chains. The study found about 88 percent of these hotels had showers that delivered water in excess of 115°F, 53 percent in excess of 125°F, and 12 percent in excess of 140°F. The highest recorded shower temperature was 171.5°F![30] A further illustration of the widespread existence of scalding hot water in hotels is available to anyone using one of the online travel satisfaction sites (such as TripAdvisor®) and entering "scalding" in the search field. The number and severity of the results is quite sobering.

When conducting a water conservation and energy audit some years ago, one hospitality industry consultant encountered a roadside motel (carrying the flag of a well-known limited-service franchise) that supplied water to the guestroom at 175°F (79°C)! When the hot water tap was opened, it released a stream of excessively hot water that felt almost as hot as steam pouring from an opened steam line. Why was the water so hot? It turned out that this motel was heating water electrically. The motel had two water heaters. The owner was concerned about his high electric bill, specifically the demand charge. Therefore, to ensure a sufficient amount of hot water but only one water heater contributing to the demand charge, the owner had disconnected the electric supply to one heater and used it only as a storage tank for the 175°F water produced by the other heater. Saving money on the electric bill while increasing the potential for a large, costly lawsuit resulting from a burn case is not good business.

Setting the hot water temperature via the thermostat on a water heater will not meet code, does not provide adequate control, and can be dangerous.[31] Plumbing codes may require the installation of **anti-scald valves** to control the delivered temperature of water, and require that these valves be adjusted to limit maximum water temperatures to safe levels. Anti-scald valves come in the following types: balanced pressure, thermostatic, and a type that combines balanced pressure and thermostatic. Hotels are more likely to install balanced pressure anti-scald valves than thermostatic valves or balanced pressure/thermostatic valves. Balanced pressure anti-scald devices must be set properly upon installation and may need to be adjusted over time. As with many safety devices, ongoing maintenance is essential for proper operation.[32]

Legionellosis

A third safety concern associated with water systems is that of **legionellosis,** an infectious disease caused by *Legionella* bacteria. **Legionnaires' disease,** the more serious of two forms of legionellosis, first appeared when an outbreak occurred among people attending an American Legion convention at the Bellevue-Stratford Hotel in Philadelphia in 1976. The outbreak sickened 221 people, of which 34 died. It was subsequently discovered that the bacteria were fairly widespread and could be found in many other locales and buildings throughout the country. The serious infection caused by the bacteria at the Bellevue-Stratford Hotel resulted from a combination of factors. Legionellosis has since been identified with a number of building types and contributing factors.

The potential for legionellosis continues to exist in hotels and other buildings around the world. *Legionella* bacteria occur naturally in the environment, usually in water, and grow especially well in warm water. Investigations of the first outbreak identified the bacteria source as the humid air discharged from the hotel's cooling tower and introduced into the hotel by the air-handling system. Subsequent outbreaks have been traced to a variety of other sources, including whirlpool spas, hot tubs, indoor water fountains, large plumbing systems, and hot water heaters. Common to all of these sources is that they create a mist or vapor that can contain the bacteria and can be inhaled by individuals. The bacteria are not spread from person to person. Those especially susceptible to the bacteria include the elderly and people with depressed immune systems.

European studies of *Legionella* infections identified 900–1,000 travel-related cases per year during the period 2005–2007.[33] Approximately 3 percent of these cases were fatal. Travel-related legionellosis makes up 15–20 percent of the total cases in Europe. Governments in Europe and elsewhere have recognized the growing risk of *Legionella* bacteria and have formed agencies to monitor the risk and suggest solutions and treatment.[34]

The steps hotels can take to prevent and treat an outbreak of legionellosis vary depending on the specific building system or possible source being treated. One challenge is the common recommendation that hot water systems be operated in excess of 140°F (60°C). This, however, creates a safety concern related to scalding temperatures. The fact that equipment and systems can rather quickly become re-infected presents further challenges. Various guidelines have been prepared to help building operators deal with *Legionella*.[35] Strict attention to these guidelines can help reduce the possibility of disease outbreaks.

While *Legionella*-related illness is rare, it can create nightmares for hotels. As of this writing, a recently opened Las Vegas hotel is being sued for more than $300 million by guests claiming *Legionella* exposure.[36] A Dubai hotel, part of a major lodging chain, is being sued for $16.7 million.[37] While the underlying validity and outcomes of these lawsuits are yet to be determined, such lawsuits illustrate a hotel's potential liability. Some recent legal decisions involving *Legionella* have awarded almost $500,000 for a case involving a water system (which contributed to the affected hotel's bankruptcy),[38] and $307,000 for a case involving a hotel hot tub.[39] It appears that none of these cases involved a loss of life.

Emergency Power

Modern hotels require electrical power for their operation. A loss of electrical power can put hotels at risk of the following conditions:

- Life safety systems that do not operate, or that are limited by battery life

- An increased likelihood that guests will become trapped in elevators or who must negotiate building stairwells to leave the building or access their rooms

- Computer equipment that crashes or otherwise becomes inoperable

- Refrigerated or frozen food that spoils

- Damage to other components of the building

Emergency power can be provided by batteries, emergency generators, or both. Batteries are generally used to power a dedicated emergency lighting system capable of operating for a relatively short time (1–2 hours) for the purpose of building evacuation. Batteries may also be used to supply backup power for computer operation (referred to as an uninterruptible power supply, or UPS). Hotels should carefully determine which of their computer equipment pieces need to be part of the UPS system. For example, installing a computer on the UPS system but powering that computer's monitor off the normal building power would mean that the computer could operate during a power outage—but the monitor could not.

Hotels and other public buildings may be required by code to install emergency generators on the premises. Emergency lighting can be powered by batteries, but building fire alarm systems, smoke control systems, fire pumps, and elevators intended for use in emergencies cannot be battery powered. And, although likely not required to do so by code, hotels may want to connect computer and refrigeration equipment to an emergency power supply as well.

Testing and properly maintaining emergency generators is required by most building codes. Many such requirements are based on *NFPA 110: Standard for Emergency and Standby Power Systems*.[40] While codes may require that enough fuel be on hand for a limited time of operation (two hours is common), hotels should consider the potential for longer-term emergency power needs, which requires attention to the question of fuel supply.

The need for emergency power during an extended outage became apparent during the August 14, 2003, power outage that affected large areas of the northeastern United States. Hotels in the affected geographic area had no electricity for sixteen hours, on average; some hotels were forced to function without power for days. Fortunately, no one was seriously injured, nor was property seriously damaged, in part because the outage occurred on a warm summer day. If the outage had happened on a subfreezing, snowy winter day, the results might well have been more serious for many properties. As it was, hotel guests and employees could comfortably evacuate outdoors without fear of freezing, and buildings suffered no risk of frozen pipes due to lack of heat. The performance of hotels during the blackout clearly indicated gaps in their ability to function during a power outage, as automatic doors, refrigerators and freezers, elevators, cooking systems, computers, guestroom lights, and air conditioning systems were all affected.

In the aftermath of Hurricane Irene, the American Hotel & Lodging Association (AH&LA) polled its members affected by the hurricane for recommendations and tips they would like to pass on to other hoteliers who might face hurricanes in the future. One of the recommendations was that hotel managers make sure their hotels have emergency power generators.

Indoor Air Quality

Carbon monoxide poisoning and *Legionella* are part of a potentially larger area of concern related to indoor air quality (IAQ) in commercial buildings. IAQ has become a subject of increasing attention in the lodging industry in the last few decades, perhaps beginning when hotel operators recognized the need to provide no-smoking guestrooms. Today, for instance, entire hotels have been designated no-smoking buildings, and IAQ issues now include mold and mildew, as well as **volatile organic compounds** in newly installed indoor finishes and furniture. In addition, hotels seeking certification from organizations such as LEED will need to address IAQ considerations.[41]

Mold and mildew issues in the lodging industry have long existed in a limited form in areas such as guest bathrooms. Mold and mildew issues throughout the hotel can derive from problems with building design, construction, and operation. Design and construction issues can range quite widely, from the location of air intake ducts and cooling towers, to excess amounts of humid outside air, to the protection of construction materials from moisture. Operational issues include proper maintenance of heating, ventilation, and air conditioning (HVAC) equipment, attention to levels of humidity in the supplied air, and general employee education.

Government and professional organizations have developed publications and resources to assist in the identification, management, and prevention of IAQ problems. Examples of these are the *Building Air Quality Action Plan* from the U.S. Environmental Protection Agency, and *The Indoor Air Quality Guide: Best Practices for Design, Construction and Commissioning,* from ASHRAE.[42]

The potential severity of mold and mildew problems is illustrated by what happened in 2002 to the Hilton Kalia Tower in Hawaii. This 453-room hotel closed in July of that year and did not reopen until August 2003—more than one year later—due to a mold infestation. The cost of remediation and lost revenue was estimated at $55 million.[43] Discussions of the causes of the Kalia Tower outbreak centered on design issues associated with the building's HVAC system, structural air leaks, and wet building materials. Severe problems such as this illustrate one aspect of potential loss that hotels are exposed to involving building construction.

Because of the wide-ranging nature of, and wide-ranging human responses to, IAQ components, hotels need to be aware of a variety of possible variables affecting IAQ. Cleaning supplies and volatile organic compounds from paints, adhesives, carpets, and other interior finishes and furniture are all potential sources of chemicals that may adversely affect guests. To this list of IAQ components we could add allergens—those substances that cause allergic reactions. Hotels have identified technologies to install in guestrooms to help remove allergy-triggering materials such as dust and pollen. The resulting hypoallergenic rooms have proven popular with guests, so much so that hotels have found that they can generate room rate premiums of up to $30 per night. The potential market for these rooms appears to be substantial, considering the increasing number of individuals who have allergies.[44]

In regard to IAQ and smoking, anti-smoking organizations have argued that employers may be legally liable for exposing employees to smoke in the workplace and that provisions of the Americans with Disabilities Act of 1990 may apply.[45] Many locales have passed legislation prohibiting smoking in, and even near, public buildings. As a result of these and other factors, many hotels have initiated no-smoking rules that have included penalizing guests who violate the rules with substantial additional charges. Most hotels and restaurants have discovered that business has not been negatively affected by smoking prohibitions and that the change has brought actual benefits to the business as well as employees and guests.[46, 47]

Foodborne Illness and Travelers' Health

Serving safe food to the public is a major responsibility of food service owners and staff members. Food establishments that do not have effective food safety programs run the risk of initiating an outbreak of foodborne illness—one that could have dire consequences for the business as well as its guests, staff members, and owners.[48]

Many hotels provide food for the traveling public and for the benefit of individuals in the community. Outbreaks of foodborne illness in hotels are fortunately very rare, due in large part to the diligence of various regulatory agencies in the United States as well as hotel management's own diligence. In terms of the latter, food safety risk management involves paying serious attention to the principles of the Hazard Analysis Critical Control Point (HACCP) approach to identifying, evaluating, and controlling food safety hazards.[49]

Health department officials periodically inspect hotel food service operations. It is vital for hotel managers to take seriously the results of these inspections and take prompt corrective action if defects are noted. Cleanliness in food service operations is certainly essential, and represents one of the ten steps addressed in the HACCP approach to food safety.

Manager and employee training in food and alcohol safety is available through the National Restaurant Association Educational Foundation's ServSafe® training program. ServSafe® provides other resources pertaining to food and alcohol safety as well.[50] The National Restaurant Association provides additional valuable information and resources concerning food safety.[51]

While foodborne illness cases in U.S. lodging operations are rare, U.S. citizens traveling internationally may become ill due to factors such as foodborne and waterborne contamination, ingestion of unfamiliar foods and drinks, and contact with pathogens and diseases naturally occurring in the travel destination's general environment. The U.S. Centers for Disease Control and Prevention[52] and the World Health Organization[53] recognize that travelers encounter risks that differ from those they encounter at home. Hotel operators should not only address issues such as foodborne illness and diseases that might arise in their hotels, but should also take a proactive stance within the community to reduce such risks to travelers, hotel employees, and the population at large.

Exhibit 5 is a list of steps a hotel might take, should a guest or guests make a foodborne illness complaint.

Bed Bugs

The issue of bed bugs has received a significant amount of attention in recent years. Bed bugs have been discovered in a number of settings, including hotels.

American Hotel & Lodging Association
Statement on Bed Bugs

Although the National Pest Management Association (NPMA) estimates there has been an increase in bed bugs in America over the last several years, the increase has had a minimal impact on the vast majority of hotels.*

Bed bugs are brought into hotels by guests; it is not a hotel sanitation issue. Education, awareness, and vigilance are critical. A trained and knowledgeable housekeeping staff is one of the best lines of defense, along with having regular pest control inspections.

Typically, the bites produce redness, swelling, and itching. It is important to note bed bug bites do not transmit any human diseases.

Although not empowered to set standards for the lodging industry, the Association offers additional resourceful tips, information, and products for hoteliers through its Educational Institute, based in Orlando, Florida.

*Information provided by Ecolab Pest Elimination and the National Pest Management Association, Inc. For further information, please contact Ecolab and NPMA.

Source: www.ahla.com/PressRoom.aspx?id=15650andterms=bed+bugs.

Exhibit 5   Handling a Foodborne Illness Complaint

The following eleven-step procedure for handling guest foodborne illness complaints should prove valuable to hotel managers in their risk management programs.

1. **Just one person in the operation, usually a manager, should be responsible for the investigation of a foodborne illness complaint.** It is important that the manager keep accurate, detailed records, since these records may be beneficial during a health department investigation.

2. **Listen to the complaint.** As the guest relays the complaint, the manager should be courteous and avoid arguing with the guest.

3. **Get the facts.** The manager should keep a supply of complaint forms on hand; by using a standard form, the manager is more likely to get all of the essential information.

4. **Promptly and properly evaluate the guest complaint.** After hearing the guest's complaint and promising to get to the bottom of it, the manager should contact the people who dined with the complaining guest (if any) to determine whether they have experienced similar symptoms.

5. **Promptly notify the health department if the complaint appears to be valid.** It is the obligation of the health department to investigate foodborne illness outbreaks (an outbreak being a situation in which more than one person becomes ill from eating a particular food).

6. **Isolate the suspected food products, if samples are still available.** The manager should promptly take possibly contaminated ingredients or batches of finished menu items out of circulation, placing them in clean, sanitized containers that are clearly labeled "DO NOT USE—SUSPECTED SOURCE OF FOODBORNE ILLNESS."

7. **Cooperate with the health department.** The manager should tell health department officials everything related to the incident, accurately and quickly; cooperation is essential.

8. **Take corrective action to reduce future risks.** The manager should evaluate the operation's staff member training, its system of food handling, and its overall food safety risk management program. Corrective action should address the four resources under the manager's control: human (staff), product, equipment, and facilities.

9. **Close the complaint with the guest.** When the investigation is completed, it is time to contact the guest(s) involved and apologize; some operations have a policy of offering to each guest involved in the incident a gift, a free meal, a coupon, or a small check.

(continued)

Exhibit 5   *(continued)*

---

10. **Index all complaints.** The manager should maintain a file of guest complaints. Such a file can be useful in future investigations and may help the hotel discover a pattern or underlying cause of guest complaints.

11. **Follow up to ensure that corrective action has been taken.** The hotel is responsible for preventing a recurrence of the foodborne illness outbreak. Therefore, the manager who headed the initial investigation should conduct an in-house follow-up inspection, documenting the results in the complaint file. The manager should also periodically spot-check the critical areas associated with the foodborne illness outbreak, to make sure they are under control and a similar outbreak is not likely to occur.

Source: Adapted from Ronald F. Cichy, *Food Safety: Managing with the HACCP System*, Second Edition (Lansing, Mich.: American Hotel & Lodging Educational Institute, 2008), pp. 48–50.

AH&LA has worked to identify resources to help the hospitality industry deal with bed bug infestations. Since these infestations generally arise from locations outside the hotel, it is challenging for hotels to stop the infestations from happening. Therefore, hotel staff must keep a close watch for infestations and must take appropriate actions to eliminate them when they occur.

AH&LA provides a number of resources on its member website that deal with the issue of bed bugs. (Exhibit 6 features a sample of the information provided by AH&LA and its industry partners.) Hotels are most likely to rely on trained and licensed pest management firms to treat bed bug infestations. However, the detection of the presence of bed bugs is likely to be done at the property level. AH&LA's Educational Institute has prepared a DVD (*Bed Bugs: Facts and Prevention*) to help hotel staff members perform the important tasks of spotting bed bugs when they first appear, and responding appropriately before a major infestation results.[54]

Besides the obvious individual guest satisfaction issues associated with bed bugs and the irritation caused by their bites, hotels also face a possible public relations issue. Some Internet sites have been developed to identify outbreaks of bed bugs in hotels and other locations.[55] These sites, as well as other media sources, can direct a significant amount of media and public attention to existing and potential infestations.

This chapter has discussed a wide range of safety issues that guests and employees may encounter in hotels. For the most part, these issues originate within the hotel itself, and can potentially be largely controlled by management. However, the list of issues covered in this chapter is not exhaustive. Clearly, other safety (and security) issues exist, and others that are unknown today may emerge in the years ahead.

Exhibit 6   Bed Bug Prevention

Guidelines for Guests:

- Thoroughly inspect the entire guestroom before unpacking; check your bed sheets for tell-tale blood spots.
- Do not put your luggage on the bed.
- Wrap luggage in a large plastic bag when traveling, or spray suitcases with an insect repellent.
- If you discover or suspect bed bug activity in your guestroom, contact the front desk immediately. The room will be put out of service until a pest elimination expert certifies it to be pest-free.
- When returning from a trip, check your luggage and clothing.
- Vacuum suitcases after returning from a vacation.
- Immediately launder any item from your travels.
- If you are bitten, apply anti-itching cream.

Guidelines for Hotel Staff:

A free digital toolkit produced by AHLEI and Ecolab, available at www.bedbugtool-kit.com, features downloadable materials on how to train staff to detect bed bugs early and what to do if an infestation is suspected. Also included are a fact sheet, poster, instructional video, and convenient pocket card for housekeeping staff. To effectively treat a one-bedroom space, pest elimination company charges range from $800 to $1,200.

The following guidelines provide an overview of what hotel staff members should do, from detection to protection:

- Create a formal policy on how to handle a bed bug outbreak or complaints.
- The best prevention is daily inspection. Employees should check guestrooms for bed bug activity every day by thoroughly inspecting the following:
    - Guestroom linens
    - Mattress and box spring seams
    - Headboards
    - Bedding
- Staff should look for live insects, and also for cast skins or speckles of dried blood or excrement on furniture or in places where bed bugs hide.

Hotel staff members should pay close attention to cleaning guestrooms by doing the following:

- Vacuuming rooms and accessories daily.
- Inspecting incoming furniture and wall hangings that may have been stored or warehoused.
- Inspecting and repairing loose wallpaper and cracks in baseboards to reduce areas where bed bugs can settle.

Source: www.ahla.com/MembersOnly/Content.aspx?id=24326.

Endnotes

1. *InControl / Slips, Trips and Falls for the Real Estate Industry: New Techniques to Control Slips and Falls in Public Places* (Chicago: CNA Risk Control, 2011); http://www.nfsi.org/pdfs/CNA_RC-071_InControlSTF_r1b.pdf.

2. The National Floor Safety Institute is a good source for information on this topic; NFSI's website can be found at www.nfsi.org.

3. AH&LA's Educational Institute sells a DVD called *Avoid Slips, Trips and Falls* at http://shop.ahlei.org/Simpsons-Safety-Training-Supplement_p_2272.html#.

4. An excellent overview of hotel fire history is available at www.iklimnet.com/hotelfires/hotelfiresmain.html.

5. Jennifer D. Flynn, *U.S. Hotel and Motel Structure Fires* (Quincy, Mass.: NFPA Fire Analysis and Research, 2010); www.nfpa.org/assets/files//PDF/OS.Hotels.pdf.

6. Jennifer Flynn, *U.S. Structure Fires in Eating and Drinking Establishments* (Quincy, Mass.: NFPA Fire Analysis and Research, 2007); www.ansul.com/en/Products/kitchen_sys/Ansul_Restaurant_Interactive/Documents/EatingandDrinkingEstablishments.pdf.

7. For further discussion of state and local fire legislation as well as the impact of major hotel fires on codes, see Jack P. Jefferies and Banks Brown, *Understanding Hospitality Law*, Fifth Edition (Lansing, Mich.: American Hotel & Lodging Educational Institute, 2010), Chapter 34.

8. For an example, refer to this article discussing the design of fire protection for a casino and hotel in Macau, China: http://magazine.sfpe.org/fire-protection-design/retail-and-restaurant-fire-protection-challenges-venetian-macau-resort-hotel-.

9. For a further discussion of egress issues, including some that are specific to hospitality operations, see Carl Baldassarra, "Means of Egress: Lessons Learned," *Fire Protection Engineering*, April 1, 2011; http://magazine.sfpe.org/occupants-and-egress/means-egress-lessons-learned.

10. "Cocoanut Grove fire"; http://en.wikipedia.org/wiki/Cocoanut_Grove_fire.

11. "Triangle Shirtwaist Factory fire"; http://en.wikipedia.org/wiki/Triangle_Shirtwaist_Factory_fire.

12. www.osha.gov/pls/oshaweb/owadisp.show_document?p_table=STANDARDS&p_id=12885.

13. For a perspective on issues involving floor, wall, and ceiling flammability with several hospitality references, see Robert Brady Williamson and Frederick W. Mowrer, "The Role of Interior Finish in Fire Development: A review of past fires where interior finish contributed, and new ideas for evaluating flammability characteristics of combustible interior finishes," *Fire Protection Engineering*, September 30, 2004, at http://magazine.sfpe.org/special-hazards/role-interior-finish-fire-development; and Doug Evans, "Unique Interiors on the Las Vegas Strip: How fire protection engineers approach design in some of the most diverse buildings in the world," *Fire Protection Engineering*, September 30, 2004, at http://magazine.sfpe.org/special-hazards/unique-interiors-las-vegas-strip.

14. For a perspective on the development of *NFPA 72: National Fire Alarm Code*, see NEMA, "It's Not Your Father's Fire Alarm Code Anymore: In fact, it's not just a fire alarm code," *Fire Protection Engineering*, September 30, 2007; http://magazine.sfpe.org/fire-detection-and-alarm/its-not-your-fathers-fire-alarm-code-anymore.

15. For a good article concerning maintenance and inspection of fire protection systems, see Stacy N. Welch, "Marriott's Inspection Program: How Marriott Runs Its Fire Protection Inspection Program," *Fire Protection Engineering,* October 1, 2010; http://magazine.sfpe.org/professional-practice/marriotts-inspection-program.

16. See www.nfpa.org/catalog/product.asp?pid=FPS00&cookie%5Ftest=1.

17. See www.nfpa.org/aboutthecodes/AboutTheCodes.asp?DocNum=25.

18. "Carbon Monoxide Detectors State Statutes," National Conference of State Legislatures, updated December 2012; www.ncsl.org/issues-research/env-res/carbon-monoxide-detectors-state-statutes.aspx.

19. Fire sprinkler systems are covered in the NFPA 13 series of documents, while fire hose standpipe systems are covered in NFPA 14.

20. American Hotel & Lodging Association, "Hotel & Motel Fire Safety Act"; www.ahla.com/issuebrief.aspx?id=20300.

21. For a rather extensive look at restaurant fire suppression equipment available from one supplier, see www.ansul.com/en/Products/kitchen_sys/Ansul_Restaurant_Interactive/index.html.

22. AH&LA's Educational Institute offers a DVD entitled *Hospitality Fire Prevention* (2007); see http://shop.ahlei.org/Hospitality-Fire-Prevention-DVD_p_2679.html#.

23. For further background on the various types of portable extinguishers and some international perspectives on extinguisher labeling and applications, see http://en.wikipedia.org/wiki/Fire_extinguisher.

24. A brief video about portable fire extinguishers, produced by FEMA, is available at www.youtube.com/watch?v=BLjoWjCrDqg.

25. www.osha.gov/pls/oshaweb/owasrch.search_form?p_doc_type=STANDARDS&p_toc_level=1&p_keyvalue=1910.

26. David A. DeVries, "Emerging Issues in High-Rise Building Egress: Traditional high-rise evacuation strategies that have been incorporated into model codes in the U.S. have been based on defend-in-place and/or partial evacuation and relocation," *Fire Protection Engineering,* June 30, 2006, http://magazine.sfpe.org/occupants-and-egress/emerging-issues-high-rise-building-egress; and James K. Lathrop and Clay Aler, "Means of Egress: Interesting and controversial means of egress changes over the last decade," *Fire Protection Engineering,* March 31, 2011, http://magazine.sfpe.org/occupants-and-egress/means-egress.

27. A list of reports and other publications addressing the attacks on the World Trade Center on September 11, 2001, and the World Trade Center bombing in 1993, is available at www.nist.gov/el/disasterstudies/wtc/wtc_publications.cfm.

28. "It's Not Your Father's Fire Alarm Code Anymore: Continuation of a two-part series," *Fire Protection Engineering,* September 30, 2007; http://magazine.sfpe.org/fire-detection-and-alarm/its-not-your-fathers-fire-alarm-code-anymorecontinuation-two-part-series.

29. Potability is defined by local government authorities. In the absence of such authorities, hotels should refer to the World Health Organization, *Guidelines for Drinking-water Quality, Vol. 1, 3rd Edition, Incorporating 1st and 2nd Addenda,* 2006; www.who.int/water_sanitation_health/dwq/gdwq3rev/en/.

30. *Hotel Shower Safety Study* (Powers, a Division of Watts Water Technologies Worldwide, 2007); http://media.wattswater.com/07-POW-714_safety_survey_v2.pdf.

31. For more information on issues involving control of hot water temperatures, see Ron George, "What Are Safe Hot Water Temperatures?" *Plumbing Engineer*, August 2009; http://plumbingengineer.com/aug_09/code.php.

32. Ron George, "Warning! Anti-scald shower valves can scald you! (Part I)," *Plumbing Engineer*, March 2012, http://plumbingengineer.com/march_12/code.php; and "Warning! Anti-scald shower valves can scald you! (Part II)," *Plumbing Engineer*, April 2012, http://plumbingengineer.com/april_12/code.php.

33. C. A. Joseph, R. Yadav, and K. D. Ricketts, "Travel-associated Legionnaires' Disease in Europe in 2007," *Eurosurveillance* 14 (18), May 7, 2009; www.eurosurveillance.org/ViewArticle.aspx?ArticleId=19196.

34. One such group is the European Centre for Disease Prevention and Control (ECDC) and its ELDSNet activity; http://ecdc.europa.eu/EN/ACTIVITIES/SURVEILLANCE/ELDSNET/Pages/Description_of_the_network.aspx.

35. For example, see *European Guidelines for Control and Prevention of Travel Associated Legionnaires' Disease*, European Surveillance Scheme for Travel Associated Legionnaires' Disease (EWGLINET) and the European Working Group for *Legionella* Infections (EWGLI), January 2005; www.legionellaonline.it/linee-guidaEWGLI_gen2005.pdf.

36. Kitty Bean Yancey, "Former guests at Aria Las Vegas resort sue over Legionnaire's disease," *USA TODAY*, August 25, 2011; http://travel.usatoday.com/destinations/dispatches/post/2011/08/former-guests-at-aria-las-vegas-resort-sue-over-legionnaires-disease/416618/1.

37. "Dubai hotel faces $16.7m lawsuit over legionnaires," *ArabianBusiness.com*, April 12, 2011; www.arabianbusiness.com/dubai-hotel-faces-16-7m-lawsuit-over-legionnaires-393411.html.

38. "Jury awards woman nearly $500,000 in Cortina Inn Legionnaires' disease case," *Rutland (Vermont) Herald*, January 8, 2010; www.rutlandherald.com/article/20100108/THISJUSTIN/100109944.

39. "Hotel guest contracts Legionnaire's disease from a hot tub: Records indicate bromine content poor, allowing for Legionella spore to thrive," *Michigan Lawyers Weekly*, March 11, 2011; http://milawyersweekly.com/news/2011/03/11/hotel-guest-contracts-legionnaires-disease-from-a-hot-tub/.

40. List of NFPA Codes & Standards (Quincy, Mass.: National Fire Protection Association); www.nfpa.org/aboutthecodes/AboutTheCodes.asp?DocNum=110andcookie%5Ftest=1.

41. John J. Lembo, "Hotel Indoor-Air Quality: Balancing Comfort, Health, Efficiency," *HPAC Engineering* (Cleveland, Ohio: July 1, 2008); http://hpac.com/ventilation-iaq/hotel_indoorair_quality/.

42. U.S. Environmental Protection Agency, *Building Air Quality Action Plan*, June 1998, www.epa.gov/iaq/largebldgs/pdf_files/baqactionplan.pdf; and ASHRAE, *Indoor Air Quality Guide: Best Practices for Design, Construction and Commissioning* (Ashland, Ga.: American Society of Heating, Refrigerating and Air-Conditioning Engineers, Inc., 2009), www.ashrae.org/resources--publications/bookstore/indoor-air-quality-guide.

43. Dan Nakaso, "Kalia Tower, rid of mold, opens Monday," *The Honolulu Advertiser*, August 30, 2003; http://the.honoluluadvertiser.com/article/2003/Aug/30/bz/bz02a.html.

44. AllerPassMD provides "unbiased information for allergic travelers" at www.aller-passmd.com.

45. Americans for Nonsmokers' Rights, "Legal Requirements to Protect Nonsmokers" (Berkeley, Calif.: October 15, 1998; updated 2005). www.no-smoke.org/search.php?q=l egal+requirements+to+protect+nonsmokers.

46. "Hospitality Industry Guest and Employee Health: Studies of 'Smoke-Free' Law in Wisconsin Show 'No Adverse Economic Effects.'" *Hospitality Risk Solutions*, January 31, 2011; http://hospitalityrisksolutions.com/2011/01/31/hospitality-industry-guest-health-studies-of-smoke-free-law-in-wisconsin-show-no-adverse-economic-effects/.

47. World Bank. *Smoke-Free Workplaces* (Washington, D.C., 2002); https://openknowledge.worldbank.org/handle/10986/9764.

48. Ronald F. Cichy, *Food Safety: Managing the HACCP Process* (Lansing, Mich.: American Hotel & Lodging Educational Institute, 2004), p. 3.

49. For a discussion of HACCP and the hospitality industry, see Ronald F. Cichy, *Food Safety: Managing with the HACCP System*, Second Edition (Lansing, Mich.: American Hotel & Lodging Educational Institute, 2008).

50. www.servsafe.com.

51. www.restaurant.org.

52. For information on travelers' health, see wwwnc.cdc.gov/travel/.

53. World Health Organization, *International Travel and Health* (Geneva, Switzerland: WHO Press, 2012 edition); www.who.int/ith/en/.

54. http://shop.ahlei.org/Bed-Bugs-Facts-Prevention-DVD_p_2496.html.

55. Such sites include www.bedbugregistry.com and www.raveable.com/bed-bugs-in-hotels.

🔑 Key Terms

anti-scald valves—Plumbing devices that automatically control the flow of hot water from taps to prevent burn injuries.

back of the house—Areas of a hospitality operation that have very little direct guest contact, including the engineering, accounting, and human resources departments.

Legionella—Bacteria that grow in warm water, in such sources as cooling towers, air conditioning systems, whirlpool spas, hot tubs, plumbing systems, indoor water fountains, and water heaters. Individuals especially susceptible to the bacteria include the elderly and those with depressed immune systems.

legionellosis—An infectious, potentially very serious disease caused by *Legionella* bacteria.

Legionnaires' disease—The more serious of two forms of legionellosis, an infectious disease caused by *Legionella* bacteria. The disease first appeared when an outbreak occurred among people attending an American Legion convention at the Bellevue-Stratford Hotel in Philadelphia in 1976. The outbreak sickened 221 people, of which 34 died.

means of egress—An unobstructed path from a point in a building to the outside of the building.

potable water—Water that is safe for humans to consume.

volatile organic compounds—Any toxic carbon-based compounds that have a strong smell and readily evaporate, such as paint and lacquer thinners, dry-cleaning fluids, degreasers, acetone, and rubbing alcohol.

 Review Questions

1. What is typically involved in a hotel's fire protection program?

2. What does *means of egress* mean? What is a hotel's responsibility regarding means of egress?

3. What are the differences between wet sprinkler systems and dry sprinkler systems?

4. What are the five types of portable fire extinguishers? What kind(s) of fire does each type fight?

5. How have fire alarm notification systems evolved since the 1980s?

6. What fire protection issues have emerged since the major hotel fires in the 1980s and the terrorist attacks on New York City's World Trade Center in 2001?

7. What can hotels do to care for and protect staff and guests in power outages?

8. How prevalent is the problem of scalding-hot water in hotels? What can hotels do to prevent scalding incidents in their facilities?

9. How do legionellosis outbreaks occur? What steps can hotels take to prevent outbreaks?

10. What indoor air quality issues are of concern to hotels?

11. What steps should management take when handling a foodborne illness complaint?

 Internet Sites

For more information, visit the following Internet sites. Remember that Internet addresses can change without notice. If the site is no longer there, you can use a search engine to look for additional sites.

ASHRAE
www.ashrae.org/

European Working Group for Legionella Infections (EWGLI)
www.ewgli.org

HVAC
www.epa.gov/iaq/schooldesign/hvac.html

LEED (Leadership in Energy and Environmental Design)
http://new.usgbc.org/leed

National Floor Safety Institute
www.nfsi.org/

National Institute for Occupational Safety and Health
www.cdc.gov/niosh

U.S. Environmental Protection Agency Indoor Air Quality Home Page
www.epa.gov/iaq

Chapter 6 Outline

Losses Affecting All Departments
    Responding to Employee Theft
The Human Resources Department
    Exit Interviews
    Violence in the Workplace
    Alcohol and Drugs—Use and Abuse
The Engineering Department
    Key Control and Guestroom
        Maintenance
    Renovations
    Water Treatment Plants
    Control Issues
The Rooms Division
    The Front Office
    The Housekeeping Department
Purchasing and Receiving
Storage and Issuing
The Food and Beverage Department
    Spoilage and Pilferage
    Alcohol Storage, Issuing, and Service
    Point-of-Sale (POS) Systems
The Recreation Department
    Swimming Pools
    Health Clubs and Jogging Trails
Casino and Gaming Security
Report Writing and Recordkeeping
Special Guests and Events
    Guests with Disabilities
    VIP Guests
    Youth Groups
    Conventions, Meetings, and Exhibits

Competencies

1. Discuss losses that affect all departments, including losses due to employee theft, and describe security considerations faced by the human resources department. (pp. 169–180)

2. Discuss security issues within the engineering department and the rooms division. (pp. 180–189)

3. Describe security issues within the purchasing and receiving, storage and issuing, and food and beverage areas of a hotel. (pp. 190–197)

4. Describe common security and safety issues within a hotel's recreation department, and summarize casino and gaming security issues. (pp. 197–204)

5. Identify the general types and uses of security reports and records. (pp. 205–207)

6. State the security concerns involved in serving guests with disabilities, VIP guests, and youth groups. (pp. 207–210)

7. Explain the safety and security considerations for handling conventions, meetings, and exhibits. (pp. 211–213)

6

Departmental Responsibilities in Guest and Asset Protection

L ODGING PROPERTIES may need to protect their guests and premises from a variety of risks and dangers. Every hotel and motel has assets it must protect as well. In order to meet these goals, security and asset protection should be a priority of every employee. At the same time, the specific security responsibilities of employees may differ greatly from department to department.

Despite the importance of asset protection, there is a tendency in many properties to concentrate on security incidents relating to guests and the public on the premises. Little or no attention may be paid to internal security problems that can significantly erode profitability. Internal theft, for example, is a problem in many American businesses, and, unfortunately, the lodging industry has not been spared. Indeed, it is particularly susceptible to internal theft since hotel and motel services and materials can often be readily exchanged in the community for cash or other services or used directly by the thief. High employee turnover and the vast expanse of many lodging establishments limit the ability of hotels and motels to effectively secure their operations against internal theft. As a result, there is a need for a concerted effort on the part of the management team to involve the security staff in controlling internal theft on a department-by-department basis. There must be strong management commitment to this aspect of the security program or it will not succeed.

Management should be aware of the security considerations involved in the operation of every department of its lodging establishment. Whether the property is a fully staffed, 1,000-room hotel or a sixty-room motel operated by an owner/manager, there should be a continuing audit of the functions in each department in order to protect the profitability of the property.

Losses Affecting All Departments

Asset protection is a crucial aspect of security for lodging establishments. Each property should examine the layout of its premises to determine how to more adequately protect the cashier location, receiving operations, and employee entrances, as well as other entrances not in the direct view of an observation center. Wherever there is a work process involving the assets of the property, attention should be given to protecting that function.

169

Before considering specific departments and their internal theft problems, we will review some losses that affect all departments. For example, losses may grow as the effectiveness of a property's system of accounting for its employees' time declines. How well do time clocks or sign-out sheets keep track of employee hours? Is a security staff member assigned to this function? Is the assignment rotated to prevent **collusion**? Does management insist that each employee sign out or clock out individually? There may be a major security problem if one employee is permitted to sign out or clock out for another individual or a group.

Hotels that have a large number of part-time personnel may need to regularly verify that checks issued by the property are received by the employees to whom they are addressed. In one case, a department head carried a number of part-timers "on the books" who no longer worked for the hotel. In this instance, the collusion extended beyond the hotel and involved a teller at the bank who allowed a number of the former employees to cash checks made out to them.

Another loss issue occurs when a hotel's managers and supervisors ask the hotel's gardeners, painters, and maintenance personnel to provide personal services on company time. Not only is this wrong, but word of this activity will spread and other staff members will expect similar treatment.

Hotel companies should reconsider policies that allow executives and/or key staff members to receive free services from the dry cleaning and laundry departments. Who defines "executive" or "key staff member"? Who monitors the exceptions? To avoid misunderstandings and possible abuses of the system, it may be best for hotels to simply require all staff members to pay for dry cleaning and laundry services.

Another service with high theft potential is the long-distance phone call. When reviewing bills, managers should check and verify repeat numbers, looking especially for numbers with a 900 prefix, which are typically entertainment-oriented numbers that include costly per-minute charges. Also, managers should check unaccounted-for calls, such as off-hour calls made from executive and administrative offices.

A no-exception policy on employee meals is another vital element in an internal control system. Some properties spot-check food facilities at times when meals are not normally provided to certain employees or categories of employees within the hotel. Regular monitoring may be necessary in instances where union contracts, or non-union agreements made at the time of employment, provide that certain classes of employees are not entitled to meals. A security person may monitor on an occasional basis to prevent collusion between food service personnel and other employees.

There may be advantages to monitoring the arrival and departure of a property's employees. Monitoring employees tends to discourage the unauthorized removal of the property's and guests' assets. If the design of a property permits, management may designate an employee entrance and exit. When separate employee entrances are feasible, they should be well lit, adequately secured, and provided with round-the-clock security. The employee entrance may include a security staff office from which arriving and departing employees may be monitored.

Properties with large staffs may consider using some sort of employee identification to ensure that anyone attempting to use the employee entrance is in fact

For Some Employees, Crime *Does* Pay

Studies conducted by the Department of Commerce, American Management Association, Joint Economic Committee of Congress, universities, and trade associations all conclude that losses from employee theft have a dramatic effect on the financial stability, profit level, and survival of most businesses.

Several studies estimate that employee theft and dishonesty cost U.S. businesses billions of dollars every year, not including the billions spent on protecting against theft (guards, security systems, etc.). Most security experts agree that nearly every type and size of business is likely to experience some form(s) of employee theft and not realize the existence or extent of it. In fact, small and medium businesses are often more vulnerable to employee theft due to less of a separation of duties, less supervision/more autonomy, lack of controls/procedures/audits, and blind loyalty.

Consider the following:

- Opportunity to steal—not need—is the primary cause of employee theft.

- A majority of employee theft goes undetected by management.

- Employee theft is often committed in reaction to favoritism, unreasonable discipline, inconsistency, and other acts of poor or abusive supervision.

- A majority of honest employees look the other way regarding employee theft and fail to report it.

- Dishonest employees steal to the degree the system allows and don't stop until they are caught.

- There is a direct correlation between drug abuse and employee theft.

Source: John Case & Associates.

an employee. Some properties provide name and/or photo identification badges to the staff. Some organizations color-code identification by department. This allows for rapid identification of employees, not only when they are arriving and departing, but also when they are (perhaps inappropriately) in areas outside of their departments. This means of quick identification can be very helpful to patrolling security officers as well as to any employee monitoring the entrance.

If possible, there should be a package room in which employees' packages may be checked and stored. Ideally, the time clock or time sheets would be kept at this location under the control of a security officer. In smaller properties where this is not feasible, an effort should be made to have employees pass a control point, such as the supervisor's or department head's office, to sign in and out.

Employees should be informed about what items they may bring onto or remove from the premises. To enforce this policy, management may establish a claim checking system for bringing items onto the premises and a parcel (or package) pass system for taking items off the premises. Employees bringing parcels onto the premises may be required to leave the parcels with a designated employee—for example, a security officer, department head, or entrance monitor—until they depart the premises. A parcel pass system includes a list of supervisors and managers who are authorized to issue passes for removing parcels from the premises. Such a pass system is helpful when employees purchase items from surplus or salvage. A parcel pass system should also include a list of the actual signatures of these authorized personnel for comparison. An employee wishing to leave the premises with any parcel (other than one brought onto the premises by that employee) should be required to present a parcel pass to the security officer or other appropriate employee. The pass should state the date, employee's name, parcel contents, and the signature of the employee's supervisor or department head. In cases in which the property being removed is not that normally found in the department for which the employee works (for example, a desk clerk removing cooking utensils), the signatures of the employee, his or her supervisor or department head, and the department head of the second department involved should be required. Employees should be informed of parcel control procedures when they are hired.

Restricting employee parking to a carefully selected area may also help control losses. The employee parking area should not be so close to the building that it allows employees to easily and quickly transfer stolen property to their cars. If possible, it should not be too near the food and beverage area or any unsecured doors with access to unsecured assets. From another perspective, it also should not take the best parking places away from guests. On the other hand, employee safety should also be a consideration—the employee parking area should not be located in an overly remote or essentially unprotected area.

With the expansion of concealed weapons laws in many jurisdictions, it is increasingly necessary for every property to enforce company rules that may prohibit concealed weapons on the premises. Of course, any policies that restrict concealed weapons among employees, guests, or the general public should be reviewed thoroughly with legal counsel. Issues of liability involving firearms may be far-reaching and confusing. For example, an operation that does not allow guests to carry concealed weapons might be held liable if the guest leaves a gun in a vehicle that is subsequently stolen and the weapon is used in a fatal shooting. Special consideration must be given to the responsibility of the lodging operation if guns are to be received and stored on the premises.

Responding to Employee Theft

A variety of different responses are available to management in dealing with assets lost through employee theft. Many properties state during the hiring interview or in the employee handbook that theft will be considered grounds for dismissal. A property's management may also decide to prosecute. Depending on the seriousness of the offense, prosecution may result in high fines and/or imprisonment for former employees.

Whatever the decision, all employees should be treated equally under the rules. Making exceptions dilutes the effectiveness of the effort. Management should realize that if it allows a department head or supervisor to resign after being caught in criminal activity, other employees will almost certainly hear of it, no matter how confidential the incident was intended to be. Such a decision may

Guests Take Things from Hotels, Too

Not only is employee theft a problem that affects every hotel department; theft by guests is also a problem, as the following article points out.

Hotel Guests Believe in Taking It with Them

Washcloths, towels, and even duvet covers? Nothing unusual about hotel guests walking off with those relatively inexpensive items, says Karen Lampert, general manager of the upscale Whitelaw Hotel in fashionable South Beach in Miami, Florida. "That happens all the time, but they usually don't take a 42-inch plasma TV. They just walked out with it, which was shocking to me," she says. Surveillance cameras caught the culprit, who eventually reimbursed the hotel at least part of the $1,000 cost of the TV, which had recently been installed.

But hotel thefts, sometimes of outrageous items, are nothing new. Hotel guests steal up to $100 million worth of goods a year, according to the American Hotel & Lodging Association. And no hotels are immune: stealing happens in the big chains, roadside hotels, boutique outlets, and even luxury resorts.

Televisions have been reported stolen more than once, even in broad daylight. Hotel manager Marcus Roberts remembers watching a man walk out the front door of his hotel carrying a television set. "We didn't stop him at the time. But pretty soon we realized, 'Hey, that TV belongs to us!'" he says. In this case, the man was arrested and charged with theft.

A study of British hoteliers found that women are more likely to steal from hotels than men. Two out of three women confessed they had walked out with usually inexpensive items; only 59 percent of the men said the same. Sometimes guests have creative ways of stealing, at least when it comes to smaller items. A majority of the women in the survey who admitted to stealing said they would refill mini-bar liquor bottles with tea or water to make them look untouched. That same survey of 1,000 hoteliers found that towels were the most commonly stolen item; bathrobes were in second place. Toilet paper is not worth much but it is also popular with pilferers.

The Sagamore—The Art Hotel, also in Miami's South Beach, is very popular with bachelor parties. But here, where guests are typically paying $900 a night, thefts are also not unheard of. "We sometimes have DVD players missing, or clock radios," says Henry Schaeffer, general manager. He says the hotel's policy is always to have guests reimburse the hotel, though the hotel apparently winks at small items, such as missing towels.

The general manager at a Holiday Inn told Peter Greenberg, the *Today* show's travel detective, that one time a couple requested a guestroom near the hotel's parking lot because they were moving and wanted their U-haul to be close to their room. The next day, when housekeepers went to clean the room, every single item in the room was missing. The couple had loaded up their U-haul with furniture and other guestroom items, then disappeared. Their home is presumably decorated in all–Holiday Inn style. Greenberg reported that another man made off with an entire marble fireplace from the Four Seasons Beverly Wilshire Hotel in California.

(continued)

(continued)

Other hoteliers report thefts of everything from koi fish to heavy statues:

- Perennially popular with rock 'n' roll bands, the Phoenix Hotel in San Francisco will not be checking in one reggae singer again, who took one of the hotel's koi fish from the courtyard fishpond. Not only did he take the fish, but hotel personnel, noticing a strange odor, found that the guest had cooked the fish on a hot plate in his room.

- A thief at the Benson Hotel in Portland, Oregon, chiseled out and stole a statue built into the wall of a suite. Guests are usually associated with stolen items from guestrooms, but in this case a former assistant manager was found to be the culprit. He admitted it took close to an hour to chisel out the statue.

- One of two 250-pound iron statues resembling greyhound dogs who kept watch in the garden of The Broadmoor in Colorado Springs "took a walk" with an unknown guest. The missing statue was later found in an unbooked hotel room, apparently because the thief could not complete the job.

- Another guest in the same hotel once stripped an entire room. The guest took a television, artwork, even a mini-bar by using an exit stairway.

The most popular item for guests to steal is far more mundane: washcloths. Holiday Inn loses about 100,000 a year. Guests can also take items that turn out to be useless. Guests were so persistently stealing the remote controls at the Grand Hyatt in Dallas that the hotel started selling them for $14. The only problem: the remotes only worked in the hotel.

What can hotels do about thefts? Typically, hotel managers attempt to get reimbursement for expensive items and often just write off inexpensive amenities such as washcloths. In most cases, hotels do little or nothing, because the smaller items are not worth the trouble. Some hotel managers also point out that Holiday Inn towels or Marriott drinking glasses with the hotel's name on them are a form of free advertising. At least one unnamed chain prepares for thefts by factoring them into its operating budgets.

Some hotels have tried to turn something negative into a positive. The Holiday Inn chain in 2003, for example, declared a "Towel Amnesty Day," saying that it "did not want to hear your towel's story," but simply wanted a returned, distinctively green-striped Holiday Inn towel. The Doral Golf Resort & Spa celebrated its 45th anniversary last year by searching for what it called "Pieces of the Past." The hotel asked former guests to turn in hotel items such as room keys, menus, towels, and anything else that might have followed them home. Those who returned items to the hotel received 15 percent discounts for their next stay.

Roger Gerard, who teaches at Shasta College and writes often about hospitality issues, says that all these thefts add up to substantial sums and lead to higher hotel prices. "Having worked in hotels over the years, I've often been told by my supervisors that the high rate of theft by guests leads directly to higher room prices," he says.

Karen Lampert at the Whitelaw, where rooms are in the $200–$300 range, also manages the Metropole Hotel Miami, which is even more upscale; suites there

(continued)

can push the $1,000 mark. "The most curious part of stealing is that it happens in even higher-priced hotels," she says.

But not televisions, at least not at the Metropole, where they have been so solidly bolted to the wall that potential TV thieves would have to take part of the room's structure with them.

"I've learned my lesson," says Lampert.

Source: Adapted from David Wilkening, "Hotel Guests Believe in Taking It with Them: You Won't Believe What Hotel Guests Try to Steal," Hotel Interactive, Inc., February 2008; www.hotelinteractive.com/article.aspx?articleid=9891.

lead other employees to conclude that the theft of time, materials, or services will not be severely punished. If lower-level employees are in fact severely punished while higher-level employees are not, the uneven treatment will be obvious. Care should be taken in applying disciplinary policies uniformly in order to avoid a claim of discrimination or an assertion of bad faith and unfair dealing. In some cases, collective bargaining agreements may govern disciplinary proceedings.

The Human Resources Department

The human resources function (often handled by a full-fledged human resources department in larger properties) faces security considerations even before an employee is hired. Since a property may be responsible for the acts of its employees, care should be taken to adequately screen job applicants. A failure to do so can be disastrous. In August 1984, an Arizona jury awarded $1 million in compensatory damages and $5 million in punitive damages to the husband of a woman who was murdered by a motel employee. The defendant was held liable because it hired the murderer three days before the crime without performing any background check. The plaintiff claimed that if the motel had taken the time to check the applicant's personal references or past employers, it would have learned that the applicant had a long history of violence and arrests for aggravated assault and attempted rape. Instead, he was hired and put to work immediately following his interview.

Whatever the size of a lodging property, job application forms and hiring procedures should be developed with the advice of legal counsel. In this way, properties can guard against making pre-employment inquiries that would leave them vulnerable to charges of discrimination by a rejected applicant and employment practices that might subject them to civil and criminal liability. If not prohibited by federal, state, and local regulations, the following screening methods may be considered:

- Criminal conviction check.

- Background check through professional investigators.

- Possible fingerprinting with submission to the appropriate law enforcement agency.

- Polygraph (lie detector) testing. Note, however, that the Employee Polygraph Protection Act of 1988 prohibits nearly all private employers from using polygraph tests as pre-employment or screening tools. One exception is for those job candidates applying for security officer positions. Consult legal counsel before using such a device.

- **"Honesty exams"**—tests prepared by outside organizations, administered at the lodging property, and returned to the source organization for evaluation.

- Credit check, particularly for any employee handling cash.

- **Bonding**—that is, taking out an insurance policy for protection from employee theft. Bonding allows for a more thorough background investigation. Bonding is usually provided through a blanket bond that specifies job classifications rather than individuals. For an additional premium, the policy may be endorsed to cover theft by and/or excess fidelity coverage (sometimes called "dishonesty insurance") on specific employees. This may be desirable for employees with significant access to the operation's assets.

- Department of Motor Vehicles check, particularly for employees involved in valet parking or in the operation of courtesy vehicles.

- An authorization form signed by the job applicant allowing access to job performance data from former employers. This will permit the source to provide full information without fear of violating privacy rights as established under federal, state, or local guidelines. Information asked of former employers may include the nature of the applicant's duties, his or her attendance and tardiness record, a performance rating, the reason the employee resigned or was terminated, whether the employee is eligible for rehiring, an appraisal of the applicant's character, and other job-related information. (Note that Title VII of the Civil Rights Act of 1964, as amended by the 1972 Equal Employment Opportunity Act, applies to hiring practices. In addition, discrimination based on age or disability is covered under the Age Discrimination in Employment Act of 1967, the Rehabilitation Act of 1973, and the Americans with Disabilities Act of 1990. However, none of these laws prohibits the use of appropriate background investigations to screen applicants.)

Every application form should include a statement warning that any false information entered upon the form may result in immediate discharge. This is an important statement to include and is acceptable in most jurisdictions. (Managers should be sure to check with local legal counsel.)

In addition, there are several jurisdictions where state gambling commissions or local union organizations establish requirements for applicants and provide applicant certification.

Generally, the educational records of a job applicant are not pertinent unless the applicant is being considered for a supervisory or management training program. In that case, a form signed by the applicant authorizing access to school records is usually required. Schools usually charge a fee for providing such data.

In small properties, where such a comprehensive screening process may not be possible, having an applicant fill out a formal application form and following up on the information provided is important. When someone interviews the applicant, the application form can be used to guide the interview. For example, when significant gaps in an applicant's employment record are revealed on the form, the interviewer should be sure to ask the applicant about those gaps before the applicant is considered for the job, since they may indicate prior employment or criminal problems. Interviewers should avoid making derogatory notes on an applicant's application form, but they should document the reason(s) they have for not hiring the applicant and file this documentation with the application.

After a new employee is hired, the property should (when not prohibited by law) ask for appropriate identification to ensure that the applicant is in fact who he or she claims to be. Identification should be requested only *after* notification of hire to avoid the possibility of being accused of age discrimination by rejected applicants.

The human resources department plays many roles, though these can vary from property to property. Some properties use the department to train or help train new employees. The security department or employees in charge of the security function may assist in the training process of a new employee in order to emphasize the employee's role as an adjunct to the security staff. The employee should be instructed to promptly call the security office or another designated office or individual whenever a suspicious person, action, or condition is observed. Such vigilance can be invaluable in extending the security presence throughout the hotel.

Employee discipline is another issue that sometimes affects the human resources department. A property may need to discipline an employee for several reasons. Some of these reasons may be security-related, such as theft or some other infraction of the property's security rules. The human resources department itself generally will not discipline employees; such actions are usually left to the employee's department head or supervisor. It can, however, assist in developing discipline programs that help to ensure that all employees are disciplined fairly and equally. The human resources department is sometimes asked to maintain records detailing why an employee was disciplined or terminated. If an employee or ex-employee challenges a disciplinary action, such records may be produced to justify the action taken.

Lodging properties should consult with counsel to determine termination procedures that will reduce or minimize subsequent claims by the terminated employee. When a union employee is involved, that employee may have rights under a collective bargaining agreement in addition to his or her rights under federal and state law.

The human resources department is also often responsible for keeping records listing any keys, equipment, uniforms, and other property of the hotel issued to employees. The department compiles these records from information submitted by the appropriate management throughout the operation. When employees leave the organization for any reason, they should be required to return all keys, equipment, uniforms, identification cards, lockers, and so forth. Personnel records should be consulted to ensure that the departing employee has accounted for everything that the property issued to him or her.

Exit Interviews

Departing employees sometimes have things of interest to say. In addition, **exit interviews** can provide information relating to illegal activity on the property. The human resources director, security director, or general manager should conduct such interviews. The session should be informal and should be held on the final day of work. Allow sufficient time to obtain in-depth information. The executive should be ready to listen to complaints, indicate appreciation for the employee's time with the organization, and seek suggestions concerning how the employee's department might be improved. Subtle interviewing can lead to a discussion of problems in the department, including loss of services, time, and materials. Unfortunately, there are many functions within the hotel for which employees are the best or only sources of information. If the employee is being dismissed, there is still value in a full discussion of the factors leading to the dismissal. If it appears that any elements in the dismissal could be adjudicated, such an interview may permit a delay of the dismissal for further investigation and review.

Violence in the Workplace

Violence in the workplace received considerable attention in the 1990s, a decade that saw many high-profile incidents of workplace violence.[1] In response, many organizations assembled resources to study and address the issue, and corporations of all sizes took action. The result was a dramatic decline in violent incidents at work. From 1993 to 2002, the rate of nonfatal workplace violence declined by 62 percent; from 2002 to 2009, the rate experienced a further decline of 35 percent. Overall, the rate declined by 75 percent between 1993 and 2009.[2] Not only did this lead to lower financial costs for all involved, but also a substantially reduced human cost for the victims of the violence and their families.

In light of the human and financial costs, many companies are taking a closer look at ways of identifying and screening out applicants with violent inclinations. If the local jurisdiction permits the use of psychological testing in the hands of competent administrators, this should be reviewed as an option by senior management. The use of a waiver on the part of the job applicant will also permit some questions that might uncover problems of a violent nature in a prior work assignment.

Some hoteliers enlist the services of outside firms to aid the screening process. According to Ben R. Furman, a former FBI agent and current president of Charlotte, North Carolina–based Rexus Corporation, conducting employee background checks has become a substantial part of his company's security business.

In addition to making such checks a standard element in the hiring process, Furman recommends establishing an in-house violence-prevention team that can work to develop policies and train supervisors and staff in risk management. Such a team might also identify specific jobs that involve a high risk of violence—for example, jobs involving direct contact with guests, access to weapons or other dangerous items, or minimal supervision. "Don't ignore an employee's history of confrontations, threats, or violence," Furman notes. "Liability and the risk of injury are greatest in those companies that bury their head in the sand."

It is most important that an organization establish that it will not tolerate behavior or activities that might lead to workplace violence. That focus must include situations that typically are mandated by federal or state law but which may be overlooked or "winked at" in the actual workplace. These areas include fair treatment without discrimination, sexual harassment, substance abuse or alcoholism, and the possession of firearms on the property at any time (unless required by some special assignments or local requirements).

Employee Assistance Programs. Every property, regardless of its size, should have an employee assistance program in place to deal effectively with violent incidents. Smaller properties likely will rely on off-site services, while larger properties may choose to offer on-premises resources as well. Consultants and other agencies within the community may assist in:

- Identifying problems and assessing risks before they result in violence
- Resolving employee-supervisor conflicts
- Providing stress management training
- Developing a written policy for handling workplace violence

Alcohol and Drugs—Use and Abuse

Of critical concern to the security of a lodging establishment is the use and abuse of drugs and alcohol by employees while on the premises. While employee effectiveness may be affected by the use of controlled substances away from the premises, the major concern is when the problem occurs on the premises of the hotel.

Management should have a written policy clearly indicating specific actions to follow when it finds that employees are using or dealing in drugs on the premises. Providing for medical and psychological assistance is one possible policy. If drug use or drug dealing by employees will be considered a cause for legal action, that should be thoroughly explained to all employees.

Evidence of illegal drug activities may be discovered through locker inspections or by observing drug use or transactions. However, properties should consult with legal counsel to determine their rights and liabilities in connection with the inspection of employees' lockers. Inspections, if permitted by law, should always involve more than one person and should be supervised by the human resources director. If the employee whose locker is being inspected is represented by a union, a union steward or other representative should accompany the management representative during the inspection process. If drugs are discovered, management should call the police and request that they take the appropriate actions (which will require securing a search warrant).

As is the case for many industries, the lodging industry may also face the problem of alcohol abuse among its employees. After reviewing the problem with legal counsel, management must decide whether to treat the problem by providing medical and psychological help or to take punitive actions such as dismissing the employee.

If assistance will be provided to employees, contact the various drug and alcohol programs within the community. Key staff members from the human resources and security departments should take any training available through these agencies to assist them in dealing with the problem effectively. Supervisors should also be involved, since they will probably be the first to notice their employees' drug- or alcohol-related problems. The security staff or other key staff members may provide in-house training sessions for supervisors. Review with legal counsel how support may be provided to the employee involved with drug or alcohol abuse, if that is management policy.

One cautionary note regarding dealing with an intoxicated employee deserves mention. In the case of *Otis Engineering Corp.* v. *Clark* (1983), an employer in Texas sent home an employee who had become intoxicated while working a night shift. En route, the employee was involved in a two-car collision that took his own life and those of two women in the other car. The Supreme Court of Texas held that an employer who exercises control over an intoxicated employee has a duty to act in a reasonably prudent manner to prevent such an employee from causing an unreasonable risk of harm to others. Review with legal counsel how to best handle a situation of this kind. The related topic of liquor liability is discussed in more detail later in the chapter.

The Engineering Department

The engineering department plays an important role in the security of a property. In coordination with the security function, engineering maintains the security devices and systems on the property. For example, regular elevator inspections and maintenance must be performed for continued licensed operation. Fire alarms and sprinklers will also require periodic testing, and portable extinguishers will require recharging. Engineering should give high priority to any security or life-safety system or device in need of repair, maintenance, or replacement. In establishments where work orders are issued, the overprint "SECURITY PRIORITY" in red ink or security work orders printed on colored paper can be used to highlight urgency. Whenever a failure in the security systems or devices is detected, a work order form should be completed and immediately sent to the proper person for authorization and action. A copy of the work order form should also be provided to the security office for follow-up.

Engineering personnel may be called upon to react to various emergencies endangering the safety or security of a property's guests or employees. For this reason, some properties that use radio communications on the premises put the engineering and security functions on the same frequency for at least certain periods of the day. When an emergency arises, this technique saves valuable time by allowing the dispatcher to notify security and engineering personnel with a single transmission.

Key Control and Guestroom Maintenance

Engineering personnel may play a crucial role in key control procedures. While many hotels now use electronic locks in guestroom and public space areas, locks requiring metal keys continue to be used for back-of-house spaces, and there are many small lodging properties that still use metal keys for all of their locks.

Depending on the size of the property, the engineering department may have the key-making machine and key blanks under its direct responsibility; if so, the equipment, key blanks, and reserve keys should be kept secured. Only authorized engineering staff members should have access to the machine, the blanks, and the reserve keys.

At properties still using metal keys, managers should decide how many keys will be stored in the key rack and in reserve for any given guestroom. An audit and inventory of these room keys may also be helpful. No new keys should be issued without a formal requisition signed by an authorized person. Some organizations require authorization by the rooms manager, while others assign this responsibility to the security director, a resident manager, or another management employee. Whichever employee is designated, his or her signature should be required before the engineering department produces a key or purchases one from a contract locksmith. The engineering department should retain all requisitions for keys and should prepare and file a record of all keys duplicated.

There are a number of security-related responsibilities of the engineering department that go beyond keys. Maintenance of guestroom door hardware is one of these. Making sure that guestroom door closers are operating properly should be part of the preventive maintenance inspections done in hotel guestrooms. Windows and sliding glass doors should also be inspected to be sure that devices designed to limit secondary access are in place. View ports on guestroom doors should be inspected for tampering. Security-related lighting should be inspected on a regular basis for burnt-out lamps or other maintenance problems.

Engineering personnel need to visit guestrooms on a regular basis. They should check the physical condition of guestroom furniture, fixtures, and equipment (and other elements) when doing guestroom preventive maintenance checks or making repairs. (Housekeeping personnel should also do this when cleaning rooms.) While most problems will be cosmetic in nature, staff members must keep a keen eye out for potential safety issues. If serious issues are identified, the room should be designated "out of order" and taken out of inventory until the issues are resolved.

Renovations

Engineering may be given safety responsibilities when a property is being renovated. Property renovations are particularly risky times for a number of reasons. Contractors are operating within the building using equipment and supplies that can compromise property safety—for example, they may need to use open flames. In addition, some of the existing building life-safety systems (such as elements of the fire protection system) may have to be shut down, or some design features of the structure (such as fire and smoke barriers) may be altered while the work is being done.

As an illustration of renovation risks, in 1995 the Palace Hotel in New York City was undergoing a renovation when construction workers on the fifth floor, working on the air conditioning and electrical systems, pierced and shorted an electrical cable. Smoke permeated the hotel, causing a building evacuation. Much of the electrical system of the hotel was destroyed, and the smoke damage was extensive. Guests had to be relocated to other hotels, and the Palace, which had been trying to do the renovation while remaining open, was forced to close for a number of months to repair the electrical system. Thankfully there were no serious injuries or deaths, but there was a huge disruption to the hotel's operations and some extensive litigation in the aftermath.

In another renovation nightmare, the daughter of a hotel guest was taking a bath when the bathroom mirror fell and broke over the child. When her parents rushed to the bathroom, they found her bleeding profusely, with fragments of the mirror in her hair and surrounding her on the floor. She received a number of severe cuts likely to result in visible scarring. An investigation revealed that the hotel had recently been renovated and new bathroom fixtures and vanities had been installed, but the old bathroom mirrors had not been replaced. The new vanities were slightly taller than the ones they replaced, and they placed pressure on the old mirrors, causing them to separate from the wall. To make matters worse, the mirror that fell on the child was not the first mirror to come off a bathroom wall after the renovation! Although other mirrors had previously fallen (fortunately without a guest in the bathroom at the time), the hotel was in the middle of negotiating with the renovation contractor regarding needed remedial action when the child was injured. Needless to say, guest safety should have been the first priority.

Water Treatment Plants

Some hotel properties located in remote areas may operate their own water treatment plants, providing not only potable water but also wastewater treatment. In many instances, the engineering staff in such properties oversees these water treatment plants and must be aware of any regulations regarding water safety. Within the United States, the Environmental Protection Agency has established National Primary Drinking Water Regulations that set forward maximum permissible levels of contaminants in water systems. Private water systems are subject to these regulations, as well as other regulations imposed by local health authorities. Around the world, national and local governments are likely to have their own standards for water quality. Many of these are based on the standards of the World Health Organization (WHO).[3]

Control Issues

Since hotel maintenance requires equipment and materials that may also be used in homes or resold, it is important for the engineering department to institute strict controls over tools and materials. Tools should be issued only when they are signed out in a log or on an equipment check-out sheet. Similarly, a requisition should be drawn up for the materials required for a repair or maintenance job. Some properties require that the damaged or worn parts be returned upon completion of assignments. Unless a property is unusually large, tool storage cribs and tool crib clerks are rare. The supervisor or the chief engineer often controls the issue of tools. That person is responsible for making sure that tools are returned at the completion of a job.

In some properties the engineering staff is used for repair and maintenance functions off the premises for members of the management staff. This is legitimate only when the manager in question is also the owner of the lodging property (and therefore pays the engineering staff) or when owner or corporate approval has been given. Otherwise, the engineering department may be involved in the misappropriation of the organization's time, materials, and monies. If an employee is doing an off-the-job assignment on his or her own, the chief engineer should ensure that no materials are taken from the hotel without proper authorization. There may be an agreement for the use of special tools, but these should be checked in and out through the regular tool log control. Purchase orders from the engineering department are usually authorized by the chief engineer and approved by the general manager or controller. In addition, the chief engineer or supervisor should determine which materials are necessary for an engineering or maintenance activity and then authorize the job requisition.

Unscheduled inventories should be conducted from time to time. Whenever practical, the accounting staff should arrange for such an inventory to be accomplished without the involvement of engineering personnel. Inventories and audits may uncover problems such as engineering and maintenance materials that are paid for but never ordered or received. For example, a fraudulent company using a post office box may bill a property $200 for light bulbs. Unless adequate controls and follow-up procedures are in place, the accounting office may pay the bill without verifying the purchase order or checking with engineering to ensure that the bulbs were in fact ordered and received. Coordination between the engineering, purchasing, and accounting functions can prevent this type of loss.

The Rooms Division

The Front Office

Front office personnel are important allies of the security staff. Door attendants, bellstaff, valet parking attendants, and front desk staff continually observe everyone who enters or leaves the premises. Any suspicious activities or circumstances that they observe should be promptly reported to security or another designated staff person.

Front desk personnel play a crucial role in key control, for example. Front desk clerks should never simply give room keys or key cards to anyone who asks for them. Some sort of identification should be checked to ensure that the person requesting the key or key card is the guest registered for that room. For the protection of arriving guests, the desk clerk should announce the guest's room number quietly and privately. In addition, when the layout of the lobby permits, the front desk may become the control center for the elevators and the entrance to the property. In a smaller property where there may be few or no uniformed service personnel, the front desk person may be the only staff member on the premises during the night hours. Under such circumstances, some properties limit access to the lobby and reception area. The decision of whether to admit someone is generally assigned to the front desk clerk. Access is sometimes controlled through the use of locks at the main entrance that may be released by remote control from the front desk.

The front desk may also serve as the command center in the event of an emergency such as a fire or flood. In many hotels and motels, there is always someone at the front desk and there is usually access to telephone service. In an emergency, on-premises security staff and/or the local police may be summoned as determined by established procedures or by management. An alternate location should be predetermined in the event that the front desk is disabled during the crisis.

Some (generally larger) hotels and motels find it desirable to locate the command center elsewhere, often in the telecommunications or PBX (private branch exchange) area. Some properties have designated a special extension number (for example, 66) for guests and staff members to use in an emergency. This number is monitored by the PBX operator and possibly also by security. This system may improve response capability in an emergency.

An aspect of emergency response is the capability for the guest to call 911 directly from the guestroom. Some properties have considered intercepting such calls and routing them through the hotel's switchboard. However, legal counsel usually will advise against such an action; should there be a delay in relaying an intercepted 911 message, the liability would be considerable. Rather, it is recommended that an effective liaison be developed between the establishment and the police, fire, and emergency medical service units in the community. In such a relationship, the emergency response unit would make a point of contacting the front desk en route to the room from which the 911 call had been made. Where such liaison has not existed, there have been embarrassing discrepancies between the management's listing of police calls and those of the police department itself. If a hotel employee testifies in court that there were only ten emergency calls during a given year, but the police then report that they had actually made twenty-five emergency calls, it may appear to the court and the jury that management really doesn't know what is going on—and apparently does not have an effective or coherent security program in place.

The guest may be further protected by procedures that prohibit staff members from giving the room numbers of guests or any other guest information to any callers. People calling from off the property may be connected to the appropriate guestroom without being told which room it is. Anyone inquiring in person about a guest can be asked to use the house phone to place the call to the guestroom.

It is also a good idea to remind guests of simple safety precautions. For example, when a guest arrives in his or her own vehicle, valet parking attendants or front desk staff (or, for that matter, appropriate signage or posted notices) may recommend that the guest take any removable units (laptops, DVD players, cell phones, and other electronic devices) and lock them in the trunk. They may suggest that valuable articles be removed from the floor, seats, or window shelf and locked away. When valet service is provided, the valet should remove the key from the vehicle and secure it so that the vehicle cannot be removed by anyone except an employee. This is especially important when the vehicle is left at the front of the property before it is moved to the parking facility by the car valet. There have been incidents in which unattended vehicles have been stolen because the keys were available.

When luggage and other articles are received by the door attendant, a receipt should be given and the items should be moved to a secured area. Guests may then recover their belongings by presenting luggage receipt stubs at registration. If such a system of control is not feasible, other methods for ensuring the safety and security of guests' luggage should be examined.

When the bellperson picks up the luggage from the secured area and joins the guest, usually at the room, he or she generally provides instructions on the lighting, radio, and television, and checks the ventilation. In addition to this standard information, the hotel's management may consider having the bellperson review with the guest the use of all access control devices on the guestroom doors, connecting doors, sliding glass doors, and windows. The bellperson may also inform the guest of pertinent security information (such as the availability of safe deposit boxes and the telephone number to call during an emergency), point out or distribute the Guest Safety Tips card (available from the American Hotel & Lodging Association), point out the presence of any decals or notices posted in the room relating to guest security and the property's limited liability, and explain procedures for emergency evacuation.

Front office personnel also play a particularly important role in asset protection. The failure to collect payment for the products and services received by guests is usually a more significant source of loss than the theft of towels or similar items. Management should establish procedures that ensure that all charges made on the premises are promptly included on the guest's folio for proper billing. The use of computers and POS (point-of-sale) terminals can help the front office keep guest folios accurate. POS terminals immediately record any charge made by any guest anywhere on the property to his or her folio; lag time in updating the folio, which could allow the guest to check out without paying for all products and services received, is eliminated.

Also, by following the procedures established by management and the accounting department with respect to handling cash, checks, and credit requests, the front office can help keep the property from incurring losses through bad debts.

The Housekeeping Department

The housekeeping department also has a special responsibility for security, since its employees have direct access to the guestrooms and the guests' belongings. Consequently, careful screening of housekeeping personnel should be done during the hiring process.

Housekeeping personnel should receive instructions from the security department or the director of security regarding their role in the security of the property. Housekeeping staff should be instructed to promptly inform security personnel or another designated person when guests or visitors are in unauthorized areas or are acting in an unusual or suspicious manner. The employee should not attempt to confront or detain such people. Instead, he or she should get to a phone—preferably behind a locked door—to notify security or the management office, which will take appropriate action. A policy on this procedure should be established following consultation with the appropriate department heads.

Housekeeping personnel are also an important element in a property's key control program. Management should consider issuing section master keys—whether metal keys or electronic key cards—to the housekeeping staff that limit the staff's access to only those rooms for which they are responsible. Some properties establish a policy requiring that all master keys be issued and retrieved daily. Security personnel may verify that all keys are secured in a locked cabinet in the housekeeping area. Electronic key cards provide a valuable security advantage, since many systems record whose card was used to enter a room, as well as the time of entry.

Management should instruct room attendants to secure any key left in a guestroom after checkout. Such keys should never be placed on top of a housekeeping cart or anywhere else that may leave them vulnerable to theft. Some properties use housekeeping carts that have locked metal boxes to hold found keys. Other properties instruct their room attendants to carry found keys on their person. Room attendants finding keys should be instructed to turn them in in a timely manner.

Individuals who ask a room attendant to unlock a guestroom door for them (often stating that they have forgotten or lost their key) should be referred to the front desk. Legitimate guests may initially object to this response, but once they see that it is part of a property's organized security effort, they likely will appreciate such vigilance.

Guestroom access by the guest while the room is being serviced by the room attendant involves a critical decision as to whether the room is to be cleaned with the door open—and the housekeeping cart serving as a barrier to entrance—or with the door closed and locked. (A third alternative would be a team of two attendants cleaning the room with the door either open or closed.) Several investigative journalists with national broadcast media have focused on the ease with which an intruder could gain access to a guestroom while the room is being cleaned. To help guard both the employees' safety and the guests' belongings, many properties now instruct their housekeepers to clean guestrooms with the doors closed and locked. A sign can be placed on the door that informs the guest that the housekeepers would be happy to return later if the guest wishes to enter the room using a key. This helps properties avoid the problem of requiring the room attendant to serve as a security guard.

Housekeeping staff have opportunities to check security equipment to see that it is functioning properly. (See Exhibit 1 for a sample security checklist for housekeepers.) Inoperative access control devices such as locks, deadbolts, window latches, and so forth should be reported immediately. If the security of a room is being compromised by equipment failure, the engineering department should be informed so that it can repair or replace the defective equipment. The front office may also need to be notified that the room is not secure, so that it will know not to rent the room until the problem has been corrected. Many properties have room attendants ensure that security decals or notices and other room postings are present as well. In the case of *Courtney* v. *Remler* (1983), a property's policy of having room attendants check for the presence of a security decal played an important part in establishing that the property had exercised reasonable care.

Staff should also take the time to check the room's furnishings for signs of wear and breakage—all with guests' safety in mind. Chairs with loose screws or broken springs should be noted and repaired or replaced before they can cause a guest injury. Torn or loose carpeting, which might cause a trip-and-fall accident, should

Exhibit 1   Security Checklist for Housekeeping Staff

Here are some common security features in guestrooms that housekeeping staff should make sure are functioning properly:

- Deadbolt on corridor door and connecting room door
- Security chain on guestroom door
- Security bar and/or metal pin on glass sliding doors
- Stop devices on windows to limit access from outside the room, where windows may be opened
- View port (peephole), to verify that the unit has not been reversed so individuals in the corridor can look into the guestroom
- Telephone
- In-room safe, secure and with no evidence of tampering

be repaired. Interior door locks and door chain assemblies should be checked to make sure that they are firmly attached and are not missing any parts.

Finally, inspection of those items that are not a regular part of a guestroom but might appear in guestrooms, depending on guest needs, should not be neglected. For example, a few years ago U.S. hotels were in the national spotlight over the condition of cribs used in hotel guestrooms. The design of some of the cribs in use did not meet current safety standards, the maintenance of the cribs was poor, and the materials used for bedding were problematic. As a result, the U.S. Consumer Product Safety Commission developed the checklist shown in Exhibit 2. Room attendants and others who deal with the hotel's cribs should use this or a similar checklist to make sure that cribs are in good working order and do not pose a hazard.

Unfortunately, methamphetamine ("meth") labs have become a problem that many hotels are dealing with today. Because manufacturing meth is dangerous, many people choose to set up meth labs in hotels rather than in their own homes. Highly toxic gases are produced during the manufacture of meth, and it can cost a property anywhere from $2,000 to $20,000 to clean up a guestroom used as a meth lab. Room attendants should therefore be on the lookout for warning signs that a guestroom is being used to manufacture this illegal drug. Strong odors, chemical-stained fixtures in the bathroom, excessive trash that includes items such as drain cleaner, antifreeze, denatured alcohol, and bottles or jars with glass tubing—all are signs of a possible meth lab and should be reported to management.

Linen rooms should have self-closing and self-locking doors, and the locks should be changed periodically. Storerooms and equipment rooms should have locks that are keyed differently from any other locks on the property. The availability of the keys should be strictly controlled. Room attendants' closets and all utility access doors should be locked at all times.

Since many items used in lodging properties have home-use or resale value, they may be stolen by both guests and employees. Such items include bath towels,

Exhibit 2   Safety Checklist for Cribs Used in Hotels and Motels

US Consumer Product Safety Commission

▶ Consumer Safety   ▶ About CPSC   ▶ Library - FOIA   ▶ Business

CPSC Home > Publications > Current

Hotel and Motel Crib and Play Yard Safety Checklist

Cribs

Crib brand name and model # _____

<u>Check the crib for the following safety hazards</u>:

	Yes	No
1. Crib has been recalled (check on <u>CPSC's web site</u>).	___Yes	___No
2. Crib slats are more than $2^{3/8}$ inches (60 mm) apart.	___Yes	___No
3. Slats are loose, missing, or cracked.	___Yes	___No
4. Mattress is too loose -- more than two finger-widths between the edge of the mattress and the crib side.	___Yes	___No
5. Corner posts are higher than $1/16^{th}$ inch ($1^{1/2}$ mm).	___Yes	___No
6. There are cutouts in the headboard or foot board.	___Yes	___No
7. Drop-side latches could be easily released by baby.	___Yes	___No
8. Screws or bolts that secure crib components are loose.	___Yes	___No
9. Mattress support is not securely attached to head/foot board.	___Yes	___No
10. Crib is provided with a normal sheet instead of a crib sheet.	___Yes	___No
11. Crib is provided with a pillow, comforter, or soft bedding.	___Yes	___No

Additional comments or concerns:

_____

_____

_____

Note: If any item receives a "yes" response, the crib should be removed from service until it is repaired or replaced.

Source: http://www.cpsc.gov/cpscpub/pubs/5136.html.

tableware, china, glassware, sheets, pillowcases, blankets, bedspreads, and table linens. Linens often disappear through room service, while other items may be taken either during regular table or banquet service. Prompt removal of room service trays and equipment can help to control these losses. In addition, management should consider providing guests with two courtesy items to reduce the loss of towels. In properties with swimming pools, towel losses may be reduced by providing plastic bags for use with wet swimsuits. Instead of wrapping the wet suits in towels to protect dry clothing in the suitcase, departing guests may place them in plastic bags provided by the property. In facilities where vehicles may be parked adjacent to the guestroom, towels are sometimes used by guests to wipe condensation from the windows of the vehicle. Frequently, the towels are then thrown into the trunk for future use. Some properties have overcome this problem by providing specifically designed and marked paper or cloth towels as a courtesy item for wiping vehicle windows.

Asset control for the housekeeping department can be improved through an effective inventory program. It may even reveal that thefts by guests are not always as common as may be claimed. One hotel was suffering a sizable loss of sheets, pillow cases, and blankets. Room attendants claimed that guests were responsible for the thefts. Management questioned this assertion and changed the locks on the linen rooms. New key controls were also established requiring housekeepers entering the linen rooms for supplies to sign for a key and to return it immediately. Surprise inventories were taken several times a month. Losses eventually dropped by 80 percent. Consider weekly inventories of floor supplies and room set-ups,

Housekeeping: Invasion of Privacy

Guests have a reasonable expectation of privacy in guestrooms, and that privacy should be protected. Consider the following case:

A couple stayed in the honeymoon suite of the Canterbury Inn in Coralville, Iowa, on their engagement night in the summer of 1988. During the night, the couple heard noises behind the wall and thought it strange since there were no guestrooms near them, said their attorney, Nestor Lobodiak.

The noises emanated from behind the guestroom mirror. When the couple decided to investigate, they found that a section of drywall behind the mirror, approximately 8 x 8 inches, had been removed, and that they could see through the mirror from the back side—that it was, in fact, a two-way mirror.

Lobodiak says the hole led to an adjoining attic space that was easily reachable from a housekeeping storage room below. The carts were stored there at night and all one had to do, he says, was "step up onto a cart, remove the cover, and pull up" into the attic space. While the existence of the mirror situation and the means for gaining access to the attic space were apparently well-known to the employees, the inn claimed that because its management was unaware, it could not be liable for damages.

The case went to trial in July 1992. The jury found that the housekeeping supervisor was aware of the secret viewing area, and further found that because of her responsibilities, she should be considered in a management position. (There is also apparently a rule in Iowa that punitive damages may be awarded against a corporation only if there was knowledge of the wrong by someone at a management level.)

The verdicts were a combined $300,000 in compensatory damages and $2 million each in punitive damages, for a total verdict of $4.3 million.

Source: *Hospitality Law,* LRP Publications. Used with permission.

monthly departmental inventories, and quarterly accounting department inventories of the housekeeping department.

Laundry and Dry Cleaning. As noted earlier, it is usually advantageous for management to follow a policy of allowing no personal cleaning or laundry services for employees. Written policies should make it clear that cleaning and laundry services are provided only for uniforms required for the job assignment. Any violation of this policy may be considered theft of the property's services. Some organizations with large cleaning facilities may wish to institute a cleaning service for employees at a special rate; however, such services should be controlled and allow no exceptions to the established employee charges. Any policies regarding the use of laundry services should be uniformly applied.

Protection of the establishment's and guests' laundry items may be accomplished through the use of a careful receipt and identification system; a secured area for holding guest cleaning; thorough inventories of supplies; a control system for linens, uniforms, towels, and other company items; and an employee parcel pass program. These procedures will help ensure that employees do not remove items from the property except when they are authorized to do so.

Purchasing and Receiving

Lodging properties must purchase a wide variety of products, supplies, and services in the course of daily operations. In small properties where the owner/manager is responsible for the purchasing function, there is less concern about theft. As properties get larger and more people become involved in purchasing, however, the chances of theft increase. Purchasing is one of the most difficult functions for security to monitor. Unless information on kickbacks or other forms of collusion between the purchasing agent and the vendor is available, it is difficult to prove that such an illegal relationship exists.

Theft can occur during the purchasing process in a number of ways—kickbacks, the use of fictitious companies, processing thefts, credit memo problems, intentional delivery invoice errors, quality substitutions, and more. Each of these problems can be prevented, or its incidence reduced, by using effective purchasing and payment procedures. Exhibit 3 offers strategies for asset protection.

Kickbacks occur when the purchaser works in collusion with someone from the supplier's company. One type of kickback involves purchasing products at higher prices than normal with the added amount being split by the purchaser and the supplier's employee. To control this type of theft, management should regularly review invoices. If a seemingly inordinate number of products is being purchased from a single supplier, management may wish to investigate the situation. Management should also consider soliciting price quotations randomly to ensure that the prices it pays are competitive.

Dishonest purchasers may create fictitious companies that "sell" products to an operation and then bill the operation for the nonexistent goods. The checks for such products are usually sent to a post office box. To help combat this form of theft, management or appropriate accounting function employees should periodically review the company checks sent to suppliers. Unless the management is familiar with the supplier, it may wish to consider establishing a policy of not sending checks to companies with only post office box addresses.

Exhibit 3   Points for Asset Protection

- Maintain a division of duties.
- Fix responsibility in one individual.
- Limit the number of employees with access to assets.
- Keep cash banks and stores to a minimum.
- Have third-party employees perform surprise counts.
- Bond employees with access to cash, records, or stores.
- Schedule mandatory vacations and rotate employees.
- Conduct frequent external audits.
- Use cost-benefit analysis.

Division of Duties

Division of duties, also referred to as separation of duties and segregation of duties, is the most important principle of internal control.

It is a simple but powerful concept. Here's how it works: No one individual should have total control over any transaction. If there are two or more people involved with each transaction, it would take collusion (i.e., a conspiracy) between those two (or more) persons in order to falsify or otherwise change that transaction.

One important way to implement the principle of division of duties would be to keep the custody of assets separate from the recordkeeping or accountability for those assets. In a hotel, cash handling is kept separate from bookkeeping. Front office cashiers, for example, have constant custody of large sums of cash. Why can't they simply take a handful? Because in a well-controlled operation, they have custody of the cash, but they do not have access to or control over the accountability for that cash. Their original bank, or float, is issued by another person who records the amount and shift time of that issue. The individual banks are also recorded in the general ledger by yet another person. The transactions that change the cashier's bank during the shift—such as revenue collections—may be posted by the cashier, but are likewise not under his or her total control. So, a cashier has custody and access, but cannot control the accountability. An income auditor may have access to the audit trail and accountability, but should not have access to the cash. As transactions get more complicated, more people are involved, making collusion more difficult.

The essential preventive role that division of duties plays is that when several people are involved in a transaction (that is, no one person has complete control), collusion becomes a necessary condition to fraud or embezzlement. Collusion is a difficult and fragile process to achieve. When two or more people must collude to perpetrate a fraud, the probability of that fraud coming to fruition is far smaller than if one of the individuals had complete control.

Division of duties, by itself, is not sufficient to prevent internal control problems. The division must be an effective one. If a hotel gives two relatives (or two lifelong friends) control over parts of a transaction, the separation may not be effective. Division of duties also can be expensive, and adding staff strictly for the sake of accomplishing it is generally not recommended.

When operations are small, and effective division of duties may be difficult to cost-justify, management must assume more of the duties. If duties must be combined, such combinations should involve management personnel.

Finally, division of duties should be combined with other principles to yield effective internal controls.

Processing thefts occur when suppliers request payment for an invoice more than once. The hotel needs an effective internal control system to verify whether an invoice has already been paid or not. Likewise, the property must protect itself from delivery invoice errors—intentional or not—such as problems with arithmetic or short counts or weights.

Dealing with delivery invoice errors brings up an important point. A number of potential purchasing losses or thefts can be detected during receiving. For this reason, many properties choose to separate the purchasing and receiving functions. If a dishonest purchaser is allowed to receive products, he or she will find it much easier to hide any thefts.

The general manager may find it helpful to maintain a roster of sources for purchases made through the purchasing office. Occasionally reviewing that list with the purchasing director and the director of the department for which the purchases are made is also helpful. The general manager, chef, and food and beverage manager should also meet occasionally to review the price and quality of products purchased. Another element of control over certain purchases can be obtained by requiring multiple price quotations. For large purchases, management can insist on sealed bids and should participate in the bid opening and evaluation.

In properties that separate the purchasing and receiving functions, an effective system is needed to ensure that the employees receiving products know what the purchaser actually ordered. If receiving employees lack this information, they have no way of knowing whether everything that was ordered has been received. This may lead to various problems. For example, credit memo problems occur when receiving personnel sign delivery invoices for items not received. When products are not received in the required amount or number or are not received at all, a "request for credit memo" should be issued to reduce the original delivery invoice by the value of the items not delivered. If effective communication does not exist between the purchasing and receiving functions, credit memo problems may result. They may also arise through collusion with a supplier's employee.

Quality substitutions are another problem that can be controlled during receiving. Quality substitutions occur when a price is quoted for the proper quality item, but a lower quality product is delivered. Receiving personnel should be qualified or trained to verify the quality of incoming products so as to ensure that the operation does not pay a high price for a low-quality item. Quality substitutions do not necessarily lead a property to spend more than it had planned to spend, but they may lead to long-term losses due to guest dissatisfaction with the product. Dissatisfied guests tend not to return.

Relatively few lodging properties have a formal receiving area that includes a dock, receiving office, and holding area for temporary storage. However, every property should designate an area for receiving materials in order to protect its assets. It is also helpful, regardless of the size of the property, to establish times for receiving goods and materials. This permits the supervisor to schedule an adequate number of staff members to receive, verify, and store the items. All materials should be weighed in and verified by count while the delivery person is still present so that delivery documents may be corrected if a discrepancy is found. If it is impossible to weigh or count the items when they are received, management should consider using a conditional receipt stamp, which allows for a verification period. The receiving clerk should also check for damage or spoilage. This is of particular concern when foodstuffs are received.

In properties that do have a formal receiving platform, the platform should have a metal or other appropriate-strength door that can be securely locked. That door should in turn be supplemented by an adjacent door for emergency exit. The emergency door may be alarmed and provided with panic hardware. The frames and doors in the receiving area should be metal, with concealed hinges and anti-shim protection at the lockset. Adequate lighting should be provided at all times. CCTV might also be used to monitor the receiving area.

Storage and Issuing

After items are received and verified, they should be immediately moved to locked storage. The hotel's employees should move the items. If the receiving personnel are not available to move the items, the appropriate storage room supervisor should move the materials into storage. The supplier's delivery person should not be allowed to enter the property's storage areas. A copy of the receiving document should be given to the storeroom staff for further verification before the items are stored.

Storerooms may contain several thousand dollars' worth of a property's assets. Clearly, they must be secured. There are a number of security procedures which, when implemented, help to protect stored assets. For example, the locking system for storage areas should be different from that used for guestrooms and public areas. This keeps employees who use master or section master keys in their normal duties (for example, room attendants) from having access to storerooms that they are not authorized to enter. A policy of limited access allows only authorized personnel to enter storage areas, which should be locked when not in use.

An important element in storeroom control is the use of effective inventory procedures. A **perpetual inventory** (which involves writing down all items as they are received for storage and issued from storage) could be kept for high value items. A **physical inventory** (which involves actually counting the items in a storage area) should be conducted from time to time. The perpetual inventory will reveal what *should* be in the storeroom. The physical inventory will reveal what actually *is* in the storeroom. Discrepancies may indicate a security problem.

In addition to departmental inventories, the accounting department should also conduct inventories at a frequency determined by management. Such inventories may vary from a weekly inventory of floor supplies and room setups in housekeeping to an annual inventory of furniture and equipment. These inventories should be conducted by a team of personnel from accounting or by a department other than the one being inventoried.

Nothing should be issued from storage without a requisition bearing an authorized signature. After-hour entrance to a storeroom should require a manager, supervisor, or security officer to accompany the employee needing to enter the locked storage facility. The key should be obtained from the front desk and should be logged. The names of the people entering the storage area and the reason for entry should also be logged. An authorized requisition for the materials taken should be completed and left at the desk of the storeroom manager.

The Food and Beverage Department

Numerous technological developments have been adopted by the hospitality industry to improve or change existing control systems. In most instances, basic control processes have not been altered. Instead, technology has enhanced the accuracy, depth, and effectiveness of these processes, while reducing the labor involved.[4]

Spoilage and Pilferage

Adequate checks in the receiving portion of the food service cycle can help stem loss due to spoilage and pilferage. Implementing a Hazard Analysis Critical Control Point (HACCP) program, which identifies critical points in the food-production cycle as they relate to food safety, will reveal points at which loss prevention controls may be most effective.

In addition to the HACCP system, there should be a continual review of spoilage. If frequent and excessive spoilage is reported, those responsible for the receiving process should evaluate product quality when it is delivered by the vendor; if substandard foods are arriving, receiving personnel should be empowered to refuse shipments or accept partial shipments. If the situation is chronic, a change in vendors may be warranted. In addition, storage equipment should be checked regularly for proper maintenance and temperature control. Many establishments maintain written temperature logs; electronic monitoring and control systems also are available that provide running temperature logs for refrigeration equipment. Other possible causes of spoilage include the following:

- An inordinate delay may have occurred during the transport of product from the receiving area to the storage area.

- Food may have been over-purchased, causing inventory levels to be too large.

- Staff members may be taking food and covering their tracks with a spoilage report.

Automated Purchasing Systems. Automated purchasing and inventory management systems allow for greater ease in auditing these aspects of the food service cycle and are a deterrent to theft and collusion. Some systems use electronic scanners to control the flow of product in and out of the receiving and storage areas of the hotel. The collected data is linked directly to inventory databases that track the flow of product through designated control points and prompt for reordering, comparing the amount of product available with preset par stock levels. Additionally, these systems assist in controlling product quality and food costs by issuing product based on production forecasts generated through the system by management.

By automating the receiving and requisition process, auditing may be performed in greater depth and with greater ease. By utilizing the data maintained by these systems and comparing theoretical cost information with actual data produced through physical inventories, proper control is maintained. The increased control and accuracy provided by such systems creates a higher level of confidence for management and a greater deterrent against pilferage.

Even an automated requisition system does not eliminate the need for signed requisitions and human oversight. On the contrary, no food product should ever leave a storage area without proper authorization. However, in an automated system, signatures often can be obtained through the system itself. For example, product requisitions initiated in the system by the executive chef will carry with them his or her user identification code; the system will not accept a requisition from an unauthorized user.

Such systems may allow for electronic interface with suppliers for the transmission of data related to the bidding process and order placement. These systems may also use data from the inventory management database to ensure proper product specifications and order amounts. In this process, the system compares vendor prices and suggests a vendor based on that comparison. This use of technology adds additional barriers to collusion between the purchasing staff and vendors. Collusion, once established, compromises the control system as well as profits and product quality, eventually leading to loss of food and beverage sales and profits. With this in mind, it is imperative that periodic audits of the purchasing process be conducted by management to enhance the control offered by these advanced systems.

Alcohol Storage, Issuing, and Service

Storing and Issuing Alcoholic Beverages. Alcoholic beverage storing and issuing demand extensive control. The food and beverage manager and hotel controller are often assigned the responsibility for ordering, receiving, storing, and issuing liquor as required.

Liquor requisitioned for a cash bar or hospitality bar in a suite or meeting room should be carefully monitored. Since the patron is eventually billed, food and beverage management must be able to provide an exact accounting for liquor consumed during the event. Technological developments in the area of beverage control allow for greater ease of monitoring this count. Some systems allow bartenders to control and count drinks poured through the use of electronically controlled spouts mounted on the liquor bottles themselves. Other systems, primarily used in large properties, dispense and monitor liquor served from a single central location. These systems use a network of tubing to deliver the liquor to set locations within the property.

A supervisor or manager should also monitor the service at cash bars on the property. When a cash bar is used for a function, it is preferable for cashiers to sell tickets that are then exchanged for drinks. This makes verification of the drink sale easier than in a situation where the bartender must also collect payment and issue change. In the hotel lounge, however, the bartender is often responsible for all of these processes. In these instances, electronic control over liquor dispensing is often mandatory. Overpouring, underringing, brand switching, and nonringing of drink sales all threaten a good beverage control system. Many dishonest bartenders will go to great lengths to subvert the effectiveness of even the best control system. The key to eliminating such pilferage is to monitor all fluctuations in cash and bank reconciliation reports filed by bar staff and to watch very carefully the activities surrounding the sale of beverages in the hotel bar. This may be done by surveillance cameras. Another, more effective, method is to use a **spotter.** The spotter may be a contracted employee of the hotel or restaurant, or a "shopper" or spotter from an outside contract organization, who visits the bar, poses as a guest, and watches the activities of the bar staff. Spotters may be used when a problem is suspected or as a routine aspect of a good beverage control system.

Alcohol Service. Legislation in many states has created **dram shop acts** that generally create a *statutory*, as distinguished from common law, cause of action in favor of "[a]ny person who shall be injured in person, property, means of support or otherwise by any intoxicated person, by reason of the intoxication of any person" against "any person who shall, by unlawful selling to or unlawfully assisting in procuring liquor for such intoxicated person, have caused or contributed to such intoxication."[5]

Under many dram shop acts, a plaintiff must prove the following four elements of the statutory cause of action: (1) an unlawful sale (2) of liquor or other alcoholic beverages (that is, beer or wine) (3) to an intoxicated person which (4) causes injury to another party. Under New York law, for example, "unlawful sale" refers to the law prohibiting the sale to minors, known habitual drunkards, or to intoxicated persons actually or apparently under the influence of alcoholic beverages.

Management should review this matter with legal counsel to determine the best course of action for: monitoring the amount of liquor served to a patron; suggesting that a patron who appears to be intoxicated go home in a cab or remain at the premises overnight if he or she is not a registered guest in the hotel; and handling the patron who insists he or she is not intoxicated and can drink more and/or drive without any difficulty. In these instances, it may be best to contact the local police. Management must also carefully monitor the drinking age as mandated by the various states and request appropriate identification in those instances when there is any question about the age of the patron. Food and beverage serving staff should be regularly reminded of their responsibilities under the state's alcoholic beverage control laws and related dram shop act.[6]

This is an area of liability that has seen a tremendous increase in the number of suits filed. Under a state's dram shop act, the potential liability of taverns, restaurants, and hotels and motels that serve alcoholic beverages is usually very large. The owners may be directly liable to the injured or deceased party or parties for various damages including medical expenses, property damages, damages for pain and suffering, support for spouse and dependents, lost wages, funeral expenses, and perhaps punitive damages.

Three examples will illustrate the potential exposure for liability under state dram shop statutes. A Minnesota restaurant was held liable for $207,097 in damages after it was found (despite its claims to the contrary) to have served alcohol to an intoxicated man who, after leaving, ran a stop sign and collided with the plaintiff's car, breaking her neck and causing permanent damage. In a Washington state case, a tavern was held liable for $450,000 in damages for allegedly serving approximately nineteen drinks to a driver who then crashed into and killed someone. Finally, a Colorado bar was held liable for $15.4 million in damages after it served alcohol to an intoxicated, underage youth who then caused a car wreck that paralyzed a two-year-old boy.[7]

Point-of-Sale (POS) Systems

Point-of-sale (POS) systems have replaced traditional cash registers in all major hotel operations. These computer-based systems allow for a very high level of control for a reasonable price in all areas where guest transactions are processed. The food and beverage department has gained the greatest benefit from this control.

Restaurant POS systems have eliminated the need for the cumbersome check control systems of the past. Checks no longer need to be issued to servers at the beginning of each shift. Control numbers no longer need to be recorded on lengthy and time-consuming check logs. The POS system maintains open guest checks in a database and assigns a check number based on the transaction number and the server's identification code. Management may then report on all transactions performed by a specific server for any given period of time. Other POS functions, such as open drawer alarms and keys that can be programmed for specific menu items or functions, give management more flexibility and greater reporting capabilities to track sales and control losses.

POS systems can interface with inventory management systems to trigger reorders of specific items by tracking the number sold over a specific period of time. For example, the system might be set up to track strip steak sales and inventory; once the system recognizes that the number sold has reached the predetermined reorder point, strip steaks are added to the requisition for the following day. This enhances production control, as the physical inventory level should match the POS report at the end of each shift or business day.

Transaction processing is the final area of technology that has seen marked improvement. Restaurant POS systems, as well as hotel property management systems (PMS), now have transaction processing and credit card approval as integrated features. At each transaction, the credit card is swiped through a reader that is attached to the POS or PMS. The system then obtains approval from the credit card company through a modem connected to the system's main computer. This integration of approval processing allows for a more efficient work flow as well as better integrated and more extensive reporting capabilities than were previously available.

The single caveat for hotel managers when addressing control through technology is to establish and review policy constantly. Technology certainly is helpful, but it is the policy and physical systems that determine how effective control functions will be in any operation. Extensive planning and research should be done before automating any system. It should also be remembered that sometimes a system is more effective in its manual state than it would be if automated.

The Recreation Department

Swimming Pools

Many guests find a property's swimming pool to be one of its more attractive features. Properties with swimming pools should, however, realize the potential safety hazards and liability associated with pools. Adhering to responsible pool practices will reduce the possibility of tragic accidents.

A property should be aware of all local and state laws and codes relating to such things as fencing off swimming areas, posting clear and concise pool instructions for pool users, employing lifeguards, following appropriate pool construction and maintenance procedures, keeping rescue equipment visible and readily available, posting accurate depth markings, and more. Consult legal counsel. Lawsuits filed against pool owners often cite one or more of the following issues: no fencing, inadequate fencing, unlocked gates, lack of safety equipment (such as a shepherd's hook or life ring), inadequate and/or inaccurate depth markings, poor pool maintenance, inadequate supervision, poor construction practices, and more. See Exhibit 4 for a comprehensive swimming pool safety checklist.

Be sure that all electrical lighting, connections, and equipment are protected by a ground fault circuit interrupter (GFCI), as this can prevent electrocution should there be a short or other electrical malfunction. (This is an OSHA mandate. Employees must be protected by a GFCI in any moist atmosphere where the employee might be in danger of shock or electrocution.) Ensure that lighting is adequate for persons approaching or leaving the pool area.

OSHA requires that an employee trained in first aid be present on each work shift. Have such an employee on call for any pool area incidents requiring immediate attention prior to the arrival of emergency medical personnel. Similarly, consideration should be given to having staff with knowledge of water rescue and cardiopulmonary resuscitation (CPR) on the premises and on call during pool operating hours. Of course, where the local jurisdiction mandates an attendant or lifeguard, that person must have all of the necessary certifications.

The employee treating the pool with chemicals should be thoroughly trained to perform such functions by the Association of Pool & Spa Professionals (APSP). The APSP regularly conducts training sessions on the basics of water chemistry and maintenance. Close the pool for daily cleaning; never permit guests in the vicinity of the pool during chemical treatment.

Install slip-resistant surfaces around the pool area—especially on the pool deck. Treat slippery tiles with an anti-slip coating, or install tiles containing slip-proof materials. Check with professionals for such treatments or materials.

Secure all pool ladders. Monitor the weather and clear the pool when threatening weather approaches. This is critically important when there is the threat of an electrical storm with the danger of lightning strikes in the open pool area.

Pool drains can pose dangers, especially if they are not properly maintained. In one incident, a swimmer's hair became caught in a malfunctioning drain and drowned despite strenuous rescue efforts. In another incident, a 16-year-old New Jersey girl was held underwater by drain suction in a hot tub and drowned. These and many similar incidents led to the passage in December 2007 of the Virginia Graeme Baker Pool and Spa Safety Act, which required that all existing public pools and spas be retrofitted with drain covers that met federal safety standards. Some of the new drain covers proved to be problematic, and in May 2011 a number of manufacturers recalled their pool drain products, creating a challenge for compliance with the federal law. As of this writing, these product concerns have not been resolved.[8] In any event, drain covers should be inspected regularly as part of the property's preventive maintenance program.

Even when not required by law in a particular property's jurisdiction, certain procedures may increase pool safety and reduce the likelihood of an accident that could result in the injury or death of a guest and liability on the part of the property. For example, the fencing around a pool should be of a sufficient height to make it difficult for small children to climb over it. In the pool itself, some

Exhibit 4   Swimming Pool Safety Checklist

This checklist may seem extreme, but the source for each item is a real case in which the subject matter was the basis for liability on the part of the hotel.

Regulations

- Make sure your pool complies with all safety regulations for public pools.
- Be aware of all applicable state, county, and municipal regulations concerning the operation of your pool.
- Know whether a lifeguard is required. Even if a lifeguard isn't required by law, it's the surest step innkeepers can take to prevent tragedy and its enormous expense.
- If you use lifeguards part time, use them during the hours of greatest pool use.

Employees

- Instruct employees that when they enforce any pool rule, they must document it. That is tangible evidence you can take to court to defuse the usual arguments that pool areas are largely ignored by hotel employees.
- Have employees monitor the weather and clear the pool when threatening weather approaches.
- Be sure your employees prohibit alcohol-impaired guests from using the pool. This may be a difficult situation to handle, but it is essential; just like intoxicated drivers, intoxicated swimmers are far more prone to accidents.
- Instruct your employees to stop any rough-housing. Not only will this prevent accidents, but it's good public relations, since other pool users will be grateful.
- Have employees watch to make sure only registered guests use the pool. Also have them watch for prohibited material in the pool area.
- Police the pool area even when it is closed. Assume guests will try to use it outside of normal hours.
- Increase pool safety awareness during times of increased use.

Training

- Be certain that all lifeguards and pool attendants are certified and trained.
- Always have an employee who is trained in emergency first aid on duty when the pool is open.
- Provide an illustrated description of artificial respiration procedures with instructions that resuscitation should continue until help arrives.
- Make safety equipment immediately available. Have items that are required in your jurisdiction: life poles, ropes, life preservers, and so on.

Physical Checks

- Remove all diving boards and water slides.
- If you do retain a water slide, regularly check the water depth near the slide's release.

(continued)

Exhibit 4   *(continued)*

- Make the division between shallow and deep ends obvious by means of ropes, floats, or coloring on the pool floor. A common source of trouble is when adults remove the rope dividing the shallow end from the deep end to swim laps. That rope rarely gets replaced, resulting in a dangerous situation.

- If appropriate, fence in the pool area to control access. Have self-closing and self-locking gates.

- Provide a pool telephone with clearly posted emergency numbers. This should be an outside line, not one to the front desk.

- Check to see whether the pool is adequately lit and whether the underwater lights work. Most hotel pools are open after dark, and underwater visibility has been a factor in many lawsuits.

- Make sure the lighting in the pool area is sufficient for passage. Many guests become relaxed around the pool and may not be safety-conscious.

- Install slip-resistant surfaces around the pool area.

- Test the water temperature. There have been cases of guests jumping into freezing cold water, resulting in shock and cardiac complications.

- Secure all pool ladders.

- Equip all wading pools for children with firmly attached drains, and inspect them regularly.

- Repair and clean the pool regularly.

Signs

- If you do not employ lifeguards, place a sign in a conspicuous spot informing all guests of that fact. The sign should also tell guests that they swim at their own risk.

- Display signs prohibiting all diving. Even if you don't have a diving board, the sign will prohibit diving from all sides of the pool. Be sure the signs have letters at least five inches high and that they are placed throughout the pool area.

- If you retain a water slide, post signs prohibiting head-first sliding.

- Correctly mark water depths in feet or meters.

- Display signs prohibiting glass or hard plastic containers in the pool area and enforce this rule.

- Display a sign prohibiting children from using the pool without adult supervision.

- Post and enforce pool hours.

- Post a notice requiring all swimmers to shower before using the pool.

- If your property has many international guests, write signs and markings in appropriate foreign languages, as well as in English.

Source: *Hospitality Law,* LRP Publications. Used with permission.

properties use float lines to separate the shallow and deep ends. (Such lines can also provide helpful handholds for swimmers who find themselves in distress.) Pool depth markings can appear on both the deck and the side of the pool above the water level in clearly visible characters. Properties may wish to mark pool depth in both feet and meters, especially if they have a large number of international guests. Depth markings should be accurate—many diving accidents occur in water that is shallower than marked.

Swimming pool signage should be posted around the pool area and written in letters large enough to be easily read. The signage might point out any number of instructions for pool users, though the instructions should be concise; guests might not read instructions that are too lengthy. Signage may point out, among other items determined by the property and the laws of its jurisdiction, the hours the pool is open; that the pool is for the use of registered guests only (if this is the case); that children should be accompanied by an adult; that users swim at their own risk; that running, horseplay, and diving (if appropriate) are prohibited; and either that the property has no lifeguard or (in properties that do have lifeguards) that swimming is not allowed unless a lifeguard is on duty (if this is the case).

Some properties do not serve alcohol at poolside and do not allow visibly intoxicated guests to use the pool. In addition, many properties keep glass out of the pool area.

Some properties inform guests who check in with children that children are not allowed to use the pool without parental supervision. Guests may be asked to sign a form indicating that they have read and understood the policy.

Police the pool area even when closed, and enforce the pool's posted hours of operation. Assume guests will try to use the facility other than during the pool hours. Increase pool safety vigilance during times of increased use.

Special groups, such as disabled persons, may require special assistance. The Americans with Disabilities Act (ADA) requires that there be special devices to assist guests with disabilities in using the pool. Seek professional advice in installing devices that will be effective and acceptable to the disabled community.

Special occasions, such as athletic competitions, prom nights, or other social events where out-of-town teams and visitors may be staying at the property, may also require special attention.

A concern of a different nature involves developing procedures for issuing and retrieving towels. Properties with pools (or, for that matter, with beach facilities) may lose a large number of towels if effective towel service procedures are not in place. Some properties have pool or beach attendants list all towels issued by guest name and room number; towel returns are then checked against this list.

Health Clubs and Jogging Trails

Health clubs and jogging trails are becoming increasingly popular. Many properties have installed or are installing exercise equipment for guest use. Properties that offer these services can take steps to reduce both the possibility of injuries to guests and the property's potential liability for such injuries.[9]

Many properties with health clubs post a disclaimer and/or have guests sign a release stating that the guest is using the facilities at his or her own risk. Some jurisdictions, however, do not recognize such exculpatory agreements. Consult legal counsel.

In addition to containing a disclaimer stating that the guest is exercising at his or her own risk, signs in an exercise room may make a number of points:

- Guests should consult their physicians before exercising and follow their advice. Guests should not over-exercise.

- The improper use of exercise equipment can result in injury. Equipment should be used carefully and only for its intended purpose.

- If the room is not supervised, guests should not exercise alone.

- If the manufacturer of the equipment provides written instructions for its use, they should be posted and guests should be directed to read them.

- If the property has a minimum age requirement for the use of the exercise facilities, this requirement should be posted.

Guests sometimes do not know their limits. If the property has an exercise room attendant, guests may ask the attendant for advice concerning an appropriate exercise program. Professional advice in a fitness program should only be given by a qualified person; guests should be urged to consult their physicians to determine whether they are able to meet the regimen of a particular exercise program. An attendant should not be permitted to test a guest's heart rate and blood pressure and then recommend a program of physical exercise. If a guest suffers a heart attack while following the program, a property could face liability for the injury or death because the attendant was not medically qualified to assess the victim's overall health in recommending a physical fitness program.

If the property decides to offer aerobics classes, similar care for the guests' welfare should be taken. The instructor should be qualified to teach. He or she should not give any medical advice; participants should be advised to consult their personal physicians. Ideally, perhaps, the instructor will be an outside, independent contractor willing to insure against personal injury claims. Often, however, lodging properties allow employees to teach aerobics classes. Since an employer may be held liable for the acts of an employee acting within the scope of his or her employment, care should be taken to ensure that the employee is indeed qualified to teach such a class.

The lodging property is responsible for maintaining any equipment in the health club. The attendant (or other designated employee in properties that do not use an attendant) should check the equipment frequently to make sure that it is working properly and is safe for guest use. Properties that do not use an attendant sometimes place a telephone in the exercise room and post a number to call for assistance.

Properties offering saunas and hot tub whirlpools should post instructions for the use of these items. For example, guests with heart disease, high or low blood pressure, diabetes, or who are pregnant or under medication should be instructed not to use a whirlpool without a doctor's permission. People who fatigue easily should be requested not to use a sauna. Sauna and whirlpool companies or physicians may inform the property that users should not exceed a certain length of time of continuous use. If so, this time limit should be posted for the guests' information. These sources can also indicate an appropriate temperature for saunas and whirlpools; if so, those guidelines should be followed.

Other instructions might include directing guests to shower before entering a whirlpool. No pets should be allowed in the sauna or whirlpool. There should be no jumping or diving into a whirlpool. If children need to be accompanied by an adult, this should be noted.

It is critical that the unit and its water be maintained in a sanitary condition. Bacteria, viruses, or skin diseases may flourish in hot water if special cleaning and sanitizing are not provided on an ongoing basis.

Jogging trails present a different potential problem. Many jogging trails leave the hotel premises to wind their way through any number of areas not under the control of the property. Even trails that stay on hotel property cannot always be perfectly maintained or protected from all possible hazards. For this reason, some properties choose not to post "recommended" or "approved" jogging trails for their guests. A property that does suggest jogging trails should tell its guests that it cannot guarantee the safety of anyone using the trail in any respect and that the guest assumes all risk. If rules and warnings are posted, guests should be told to heed them. If the property becomes aware of any specific dangers associated with a jogging trail (such as traffic problems, construction, or assaults), it should warn the guests of these known dangers. Failure to do so may result in liability.

Casino and Gaming Security

Casino and gaming facilities present additional challenges for protecting guests and employees. Many of these facilities are integrated with a large hotel, which may have as many as 5,000 or more rooms.[10]

Many gaming operations are overseen by special state gaming commissions. Because of the commissions' requirements, gaming operations often are required to implement rigorous hiring procedures. This is a definite benefit for establishments that deal so openly with guest and operation assets. In addition, state gaming commissions typically require that there be armed, plainclothes state police officers on the casino floor. (It should be noted that 95 percent of a casino's own security officers are unarmed.)

The security function includes the casino as well as any guestrooms; meeting rooms; banquet, restaurant, and other food and beverage services; theme parks and attractions; and special amenities for "high rollers," which may include penthouse apartments, separate garden units, or other elaborate and sequestered accommodations.

A variety of crimes must be considered and planned for. What level of protection should be provided for big winners? What cooperative initiatives should be employed when the **casino bank** (cash cage or cash call window) becomes the target of gangs from neighboring metropolitan areas or when known criminals attempt to make the rounds of the local establishments? Larceny and pickpockets are continuing problems. Prostitution may be a problem. Parking-lot altercations, assaults, and the use of weapons are further concerns.

In coping with these potential incidents, the regulatory commissions are invaluable sources of information. They also can provide oversight for coordinating strategies. For example, when one gang took action against a casino bank, a cooperative venture involving the commission and casinos was able to overcome the gang's numerical superiority—the result was multiple arrests and a resolution of the problem. It also led to construction requirements that included bars as part of the casino bank.

It is common practice to rotate security staff between the casino and hotel or other units. This protects against criminal collusion between the security staff and other staff members of the organization.

Surveillance capability and continuous monitoring are the hallmarks of gaming security. Contact between the surveillance facility and the "floor" should be uninterrupted, with security personnel watching the games for the rate of play and the amount played. They must also be alert to a dealer who may be compromised or tempted to collude with a player or players.

Surveillance is one of only two departments that typically does not report directly to the president/CEO of the property. The other department is internal audit. Both departments report to the audit committee of the board of directors in order to prevent white-collar and executive-level crime.

The advances in technology have become a double-edged sword. Counterfeiters have become so proficient at duplicating tokens that it has become difficult for the "house" to distinguish counterfeit from legitimate tokens. The metal content, and the exact size, shape, indentations, weight, and so on are all readily achieved with the high-tech equipment and systems available to anyone willing to pay the purchase price.

The development of "family" attractions to supplement the casino and gaming facilities has involved the investment of hundreds of millions of dollars. This results in an increased number of minors in a property that includes both a large casino and a family attraction. The security officers must be trained to effectively handle this security challenge.

Underage gambling is illegal and can compromise the gaming license for a casino. Any person who might be underage must be requested to provide a valid proof of age. Senior management must consider alternative action for ensuring the safety and security of any underage person who has been directed to leave the casino floor but has not been registered for any family program that may be available at the casino.

Finally, casino and gaming security personnel should be trained in CPR and basic first aid. In the late 1990s, the casino and gaming industry introduced the use of automatic external defibrillators (AEDs) for the treatment of sudden cardiac arrest. At properties equipped with such devices, security staff should be thoroughly trained in their use. "Good Samaritan" legislation has been enacted in several states and is under review in others to protect against litigation aimed at a person who was properly trained and used the AED correctly but was unable to resuscitate the victim.

Report Writing and Recordkeeping

While the physical presence of security personnel may serve as a deterrent to some crime, the properly recorded findings and observations of the personnel on patrol are the most effective way to enhance security. For example, such reports may alert security and management officials to such security issues as burned-out lights, broken locks, or safety hazards. The departments responsible for dealing with these problems can then take appropriate steps.

Another value of an effective recordkeeping system is that it may help a property to discover that a certain type of security incident is occurring with disproportionate frequency. If this is the case, the property can focus attention on that particular problem and a plan for action can be developed. In addition, such records may be a great asset if a security incident results in a lawsuit.

Because of the importance of report writing, many properties require their security personnel to possess good writing skills. The importance of neat, clear, concise, objective reports should be explained to security officers, who need to be aware that their reports may be used in the future by security investigators, law enforcement agencies, and management.

Of course, writing skills alone do not produce good reports. Security personnel need to be trained in how to file appropriate reports. They need to know the types of information to collect and report concerning the various situations they may face. They need to know the appropriate format in which to present the information and who should receive the information.

The most common type of report filed by a security officer is the **daily report** (or shift report). This report details a security officer's patrols for the day or shift, noting anything out of the ordinary or anything calling for action of some kind. When a security incident occurs on the premises, an **incident report** (or special report) is called for (see Exhibit 5). Such reports may be filed for criminal acts such as assault, theft, robbery, embezzlement, fraud, and anything that has resulted in an arrest, and for problems such as guest or employee injuries or deaths, fires, and other safety incidents. Any incident involving the following circumstances should be thoroughly documented:

- A loss or injury to a guest, employee, or other person

- Damage to or destruction of a facility asset

- Any other situation or incident that management feels may be appropriate to document

A security incident report generally contains at least the following information:

- The time and date of the occurrence

- A narrative of the incident—what occurred, when, why, where, and by whom. Identify each person involved and list all witnesses and their addresses. In short, provide all the relevant facts that would assist another person in an investigation. Do not surmise or add subjective comments.

- The nature and amount of the loss, if any

Exhibit 5 Incident/Loss Report

INCIDENT/LOSS REPORT

Time_____	
Guest_____	Room_____
Employee_____	Dept._____
Other_____	

(Please type or print)

Type of Incident/Loss (Fire, Theft, Disturbance, Etc.)

_____

Person Reporting Incident/Loss (Victim)

Name_____Phone #_____

Address_____

City/State/Zip_____

Place of Employment_____Phone #_____

Date & Time of Incident/Loss Date_____ Time_____

Date & Time Hotel Notified Date_____ Time_____

Description of Incident (Who, What, Where, When, Why)_____

_____

_____

_____

_____

_____

Stolen Vehicle_____|_____|_____|_____|_____|_____

                Year   Make   Model   Color   Serial#   License#

Witness to Incident_____ Phone #_____

Value of Property_____

Were Police Notified?_____ By_____

Police Officer's Name & Badge No._____ Report #_____

Action Taken

General Manager Notified   ☐ Yes   ☐ No

Security Notified   ☐ Yes   ☐ No

_____Notified   ☐ Yes   ☐ No

Person Taking Report_____

Position/Department_____

Home Phone #_____

- The time the police were notified, if the incident involves the violation of a law

- The date of the report and its author's signature

Certain security records are confidential and should not be released to anyone. Generally speaking, guest and employee records are confidential by law, and as such should only be released, following review by a property's legal counsel, to an authorized person with a proper court order.

Developing a recordkeeping system that meets the needs of the organization may be of value in the event of litigation. A property may wish to acquire all police reports relating to the incident, along with the incident report. Appropriate file and backup storage capabilities are also important. Records, including records of daily security officer rounds and special logs, should be held for the length of time recommended by a property's local counsel. Such time intervals may vary from two to seven years.

The expanded use of computers within the lodging industry may be helpful in developing recordkeeping systems for security departments. Careful consideration should be given, however, to the possible security implications of using computers for this purpose. Security protocols should be in place to keep unauthorized individuals from viewing or altering restricted files. This is especially critical if the computer's information is accessible by another computer via either an internal intranet or an external connection to the Internet.

Special Guests and Events

Lodging properties often go out of their way to attract special guests and events. Events such as conventions, meetings, and exhibits are sought for the prestige and profits associated with them; in addition, properties may seek to attract various specialized categories of guests and groups. Unfortunately, such special guests and events may also increase the potential for security incidents on the premises.

When a guest or a group needs or requests additional security, many properties include a clause in the contract stating that the guest or group will be charged for the additional cost. For example, the growth of terrorism may be a factor to consider when booking guests who might attract terrorist actions. The property should also evaluate its security preparedness when accepting any group that may entail special security risks. Appropriate agencies should be contacted, especially if those involved are at a level that would involve the U.S. State Department.

The advice of legal counsel should be sought when establishing security measures for special functions or events. In addition, the following precautions may be worth considering:

- Identify potential problems.

- Accomplish reference checks for groups. Check with prior hotels or convention centers where the group has held functions.

- Determine how to manage a problem group and its functions.

The prevention and containment suggestions for working with problem groups in Exhibit 6 may appear to be less-than-hospitable approaches to handling what could be quite profitable group business. Bear in mind, however, that these suggestions only apply to groups that are known for making trouble. They should not be used when dealing with a respectable and reputable business association or corporation—although various steps could be implemented if incidents warrant them.

Exhibit 6   Working with Problem Groups

PREVENT:

- Restrict rooms availability.
    1. Do not allow single-night stays.
    2. Charge maximum rates (or time-limited group rates).
    3. Require a significant damage deposit.
    4. Where history and references will support it, deny room rental to some parties under authority of the Innkeepers' Law, which permits denial of occupancy based upon an innkeeper's concern that the presence of the denied individual would not be in the best interest of the property and its guests.
    5. Require credit cards.
    6. Require picture identification.
    7. Have the catering department handle all aspects of ballroom packages.
- Restrict access to hotel guests only.
- Make sure security/police officers maintain a strong, visible presence.
- React quickly when problems occur.

CONTAIN:

- Ask function leader/parents to sign a damage waiver.
- Require managers to be on duty.
- Restrict hotel access to guests only.
- Restrict guestroom floor access; limit the number of persons allowed in guestrooms.
- Have scheduled group functions/events.
- Require groups to police themselves by having their own security. Provide a roster of approved security contract organizations in the community—organizations with which you have a working relationship and whose management and staff may be trusted.
- Require photo identification wherever alcohol is served.
- Allow no outside liquor on the premises.
- Set "quiet hours" in advance and enforce them.
- React to potential problems swiftly and with authority.
- Restrict parking lot access.
- Explain to guests at check-in that eviction may occur if complaints are received.

Some categories of guests have been recognized as having special characteristics that a lodging property may wish to address. Three of these special categories are guests with disabilities, VIP guests, and youth groups.

Guests with Disabilities

In 1990, the Americans with Disabilities Act (ADA) became law, changing the way in which U.S. businesses employ and serve people with disabilities. There are five titles to the law, but two are critical to the hospitality industry. Title I refers to employment issues and is administered by the Equal Employment Opportunity Commission. Title III addresses facility accommodations that affect all employees, guests, and the general public; this section is administered by the U.S. Department of Justice. (It should be noted that Title II—Public Services covers public transportation and includes courtesy van service that may be provided by a lodging facility. For example, all courtesy vans with seating for 17—16 passengers and a driver—must be wheelchair accessible. Additional requirements may apply as well; consult legal counsel.) ADA legislation includes a potential for litigation and fines. Title III permits action through civil suits when a disabled person encounters a barrier to ready access. Should a civil penalty be awarded, it must not exceed $50,000 for the first violation or $100,000 for each subsequent violation.

According to the law, "readily achievable" changes must be made to "reasonably accommodate" guests before their arrival. "Readily achievable" has been interpreted as meaning that the change is easy to accomplish and can be made without too much difficulty or expense. Consequently, a change deemed to be "readily achievable" for a major chain might not be expected of an independent property of smaller size and lesser financial resources. Similarly, "reasonable accommodations" must be provided unless they create a significant difficulty or expense.

When constructing a new lodging establishment, architects should consult the U.S. Department of Justice, Civil Rights Division, for the current requirements. Government sources or knowledgeable consultants on disability accommodation should be involved whenever changes are considered within existing structures. For example, specific requirements for the minimum number of handicapped-accessible spaces in the parking lot, wheelchair-accessible rooms, rooms with roll-in showers, and hearing-impaired rooms should be verified.

As a result of ADA legislation, many properties now have rooms designed specifically for guests with disabilities. Such rooms should include switches, handles, and view ports that are at the correct height for wheelchair users, TDD (Telecommunications Device for the Deaf) equipment for guests with hearing and speech impairments, closed-captioned television, etc.

Emergency evacuation of people with disabilities is a primary concern for security personnel. This is a matter that must be reviewed with local fire authorities. In the event of fire, the fire department may prefer that they be met by a staff member with a full list of disabled persons on the property and their locations. In addition, fire alarms must provide a strobe light to alert those with impaired hearing. A public address system that includes guestrooms permits notice and instructions for guests with visual impairments.

Properties should consult with legal counsel to determine whether there are any additional state or local laws that apply to serving guests with disabilities.

The Importance of Folio Information. Many properties develop methods by which the folios of disabled guests may be readily identified to ensure that prompt assistance is provided during an emergency. If an emergency leads to an evacuation of the property, employees may be sent to the rooms of disabled guests to offer assistance. All staff should be prepared to assist local fire and police with the evacuation of guests with wheelchairs, walkers, Seeing Eye dogs, and so on.

If the nature of the handicap is listed on the folio, employees will be better prepared to deal with situations that may arise. For example, if the guest is deaf, the employee will not presume that the room is empty simply because no one responds to knocking at the door. The employee may know to deliver written rather than verbal instruction. Similarly, an employee may offer an arm to a blind person. Some properties choose to give an appropriate key to employees going to assist disabled guests, just in case the guest cannot get to or open the door on his or her own.

VIP Guests

Special cooperation and liaison between all departments is critical when VIP guests are at a property. In particular, coordination between front desk, food service, sales, housekeeping, security, and executive office personnel is essential.

VIP guests may require additional security personnel. Well-known figures often wish to keep a very low profile, and all staff should be instructed on how to appropriately respond to inquiring media and the general public. If the guest has a personal security staff, armed or otherwise, arrangements and accommodations may need to be made by the property and the local police. If the guest is controversial, the property may wish to request the assistance of the local police, the FBI, or some other authority. Properties expecting the arrival of a controversial guest may also want to review emergency evacuation and bomb threat procedures with their employees before the guest arrives.

Youth Groups

Depending upon the supervision provided by the adult leadership of a youth group, such a group may present a problem with vandalism and/or excessive noise that may disturb other guests. The security staff should develop a plan of action that will be of benefit to all parties—the group, the property, and the other guests. Planning and a close liaison with the adult leaders of the youth group will make a controlled group experience more likely. Properties may consider whether they wish to add an insurance premium or some other method of reimbursement to the guest group's contract to cover any property damaged through vandalism or pranks. However, properties should first consult with legal counsel to ensure that such conditions do not constitute age discrimination in jurisdictions where it is prohibited.

Conventions, Meetings, and Exhibits

Conventions, meetings, and exhibits are major functions that require close cooperation among all departments and careful administrative attention. Assembling a large number of guests, exhibitors, and members of the general public also involves a number of special security considerations. The nature and number of guests and exhibits and the degree of public involvement may make it necessary to supplement the security staff. The sales department—which usually will be informed of any special group needs when the event is booked—can play an important initial role in disseminating the information that every other department will need to know in order to plan the most efficient and secure method of handling the event.

Analyzing the nature of the group may also help in forecasting potential problems. Is the group controversial? Does the group include guests with special needs? Will there be a potential problem with alcohol consumption? If a school group is coming on tour, what is the ratio of adults to students? Have there been prior experiences with the group?

If exhibits are involved, the hotel should determine its liability for them. Protection may be provided by the group or the property (depending on the stipulations of the contract and applicable law) from the time the exhibits arrive until they are dismantled and leave the premises. When special valuables are involved, such as an exhibition of jewelry, it may be advisable to require the exhibitors to provide additional contract security and to coordinate security with the local police. Properties doing this might consider obtaining a named insured agreement and a certificate of insurance. The contracts with exhibitors may also specifically note the exhibitors' responsibility for the receipt and shipment of their own materials.

An exhibit area should be secured when exhibitors and viewers are not present. It may be advisable to supervise cleaning personnel. Closed-circuit television (which is most useful in areas where there should be no motion) can, where available, be used to supplement the security effort when the exhibit area is closed.

Experience indicates that the heaviest loss of exhibits and exhibit materials occurs during shipment prior to installation at the assigned area and during the breakdown and shipment of exhibits to their next destination. A spot-check of empty containers and cartons as they are removed from the exhibit area during setup may deter or discover the attempted theft of exhibits. It may be wise for the contract with exhibit planners to include provisions for extra funds for securing exhibits during these critical periods.

Some properties suggest to exhibitors that they use some sort of badge system. Since a great number of extra personnel may be present, it may be difficult to distinguish between people who have a legitimate right to be on the premises and those who do not. If the hotel has contracted to provide some of the extra personnel, the property may choose to use a badge system as a matter of policy.

One exit should be established for the control of hand-carried items removed by exhibitors from the exhibit area. The exhibit or convention manager may choose to place at this control point a list containing the signatures of persons qualified to remove hand-carried materials. A pass system under the control of the organization conducting the exhibition may also help increase security, even when the hotel is directly involved in the setup, breakdown, and general security of the exhibits and the exhibit area.

When a convention or exhibit comes to a property, the convention or exhibit area is not the only area that may experience greater security problems. Perimeter, parking area, and guestroom incidents may also increase. Security personnel should be alert to people found in guestroom areas who seem to be loitering or to be present without a legitimate reason. (Remember that an unregistered person, unless accompanied by a registered guest, is a trespasser.) If a person is a legitimate guest in need of helpful directions, a security officer can offer assistance; if the person is not a guest, he or she should be asked to provide identification and then escorted from the area.

Sometimes, meetings take place at lodging properties that require special security considerations. Such meetings, whether political or business, may call for lock changes just prior to the group's arrival, special identification for the attendees, and steps to help ensure that the business conducted in the meeting room cannot be overheard. Some meeting planners may ask that rooms next to the meeting room be left unoccupied; they may even choose to rent them simply for that purpose. Such groups may bring their own security personnel and equipment. When this happens, there should be clear communication beforehand between the group and the property about who is responsible for what. The local police may even become involved, depending on the importance and sensitivity of the meeting. "Sweeps" to debug the meeting room may be provided, along with other high-tech security measures.

Special Safety Considerations. Another aspect of convention, meeting, and exhibit management involves safety. The added construction and equipment used for some of these events may present a number of potential safety hazards.

Electrical outlets should be adequate for the power demands being made on them. Sufficient power and proper fuses should be used. Potential trip-and-fall hazards (such as electric wires and cables that run along the floor and platform areas, torn carpeting, and loose tiles) should be avoided. When it is impossible to provide overhead connections, wires can be placed in channels under carpeted areas in a manner that minimizes the height of the ridge formed. If wires are placed under carpeting, something should protect them from the damage that could be caused by people walking on them or by wheeled equipment moving over them.

Assembling platforms, daises, and podiums may also pose problems. Units that fit together to create a raised platform should form a rigid and interlocked surface. If steps are required to reach the platform level, the steps should be secured to the side of the platform. It may also be wise to provide a sturdy handrail. The Americans with Disabilities Act states that the platform or dais must be accessible by a ramp or lift. The ramp or lift should not block access to an aisle or the emergency exit.

Platform units should be constructed with adequate space requirements in mind. Platforms should have enough room to allow food servers (when appropriate) and meeting attendees to pass behind those seated without danger of falling from the platform or bumping the chairs of those seated.

A property may wish to perform periodic inspections of any chairs, tables, platforms, easels, and other equipment used for meetings. Since these items are constantly moved from room to room throughout the property, there may be an increased possibility for broken parts, slivers, and rough edges to develop. Water glasses should be inspected for chips or cracks; broken and chipped glasses should be discarded.

A property should provide adequate, well-lit exits that are properly marked and kept clear at all times. Platforms and exhibits should not block access to an exit. Draperies or decorations should not obscure the exit sign or exit access.

If any special flags or banners are used by a visiting group, they should be securely fastened. Employees should have access to safe ladders when installing these flags and banners. If the decorations are extensive and require an outside contractor who must use scaffolding, management should consider obtaining a special insurance certificate from the contractor that provides named insured protection, in the event of injuries to the contractor's employees, the property's employees or guests, or the public through the negligence of the contractor or his or her employees.

A property should ensure that adequate and appropriate fire extinguishing equipment is readily available. It should also consider reviewing the property's emergency evacuation plan for a convention or exhibit area with the management of the convention or exhibition. The potential for injury is likely to be reduced when all parties know in advance what to do and whose directions to follow in an emergency evacuation.

Endnotes

1. The Occupational Safety and Health Administration has a number of resources on this topic on its website at http://www.osha.gov/SLTC/workplaceviolence/index.html.

2. "Special Report: Workplace Violence, 1993–2009." U.S. Department of Justice, NCJ 233231 March 2011; http://bjs.ojp.usdoj.gov/content/pub/pdf/wv09.pdf.

3. EPA information can be found at http://www.epa.gov/safewater/; WHO information is available at http://www.who.int/water_sanitation_health/en/.

4. For more information about food safety, see Ronald F. Cichy, *Food Safety: Managing with the HACCP System,* Second Edition (Lansing, Mich.: American Hotel & Lodging Educational Institute, 2008).

5. New York Gen. Oblig. Law SS 11-101.

6. For a detailed examination of the responsible service of alcohol, see *Controlling Alcohol Risks Effectively* (Lansing, Mich.: American Hotel & Lodging Educational Institute, 1993).

7. For more information about how alcoholic beverages can be served responsibly, see the CARE (Controlling Alcohol Risks Effectively) program created by the American Hotel & Lodging Educational Institute.

8. *Eight Manufacturers Recall Pool and In-Ground Spa Drain Covers Due to Incorrect Ratings: Covers Pose Possible Entrapment Hazard to Swimmers;* http://www.cpsc.gov/cpscpub/prerel/prhtml11/11230.html.

9. *Risk Management for Spas,* an online course developed by the International SPA Association, the ISPA Foundation, and the Resort Hotel Association (and available through AH&LA's Educational Institute) contains risk management information that might be of interest to hotel managers with health clubs, spas, and/or other exercise facilities on their hotels' premises.

10. Casino and gaming security is a vast and complex subject that can only be touched on in this section. Those readers desiring more information should see Derk J. Boss and Alan W. Zajic, *Casino Security and Gaming Surveillance* (Boca Raton, Fla.: Taylor & Francis Group, LCC, 2010).

Key Terms

bonding—Insuring for protection from employee theft, usually provided through a blanket bond that specifies job classifications rather than individuals. For an additional premium, the policy may be endorsed to cover theft by and/or excess fidelity coverage on specific employees. This may be desirable for employees with significant access to the operation's assets.

casino bank — The cash cage or cash call window of a casino.

collusion—An activity in which two or more employees secretly interact in an effort to steal from their employer.

daily report—Details a security officer's patrols for the day or shift, noting anything out of the ordinary or anything calling for action of some kind. Also referred to as a shift report.

dram shop acts—Legislation establishing third-party liability for accidents involving intoxicated drivers. Such laws often hold that bartenders, servers, and owners can be jointly held liable if they unlawfully sell alcoholic beverages to a minor or an intoxicated person who then causes injury to others.

exit interviews—Meetings conducted between the employer and an employee leaving the organization that attempt to identify the factors that have led to the employee's decision to leave.

honesty exams—Tests prepared by outside organizations, administered at a lodging property, and returned to the source organization for evaluation.

incident report—Written when a security incident occurs on the premises. Also referred to as a special report.

kickbacks—Money or services paid to unethical employees who work in collusion with someone from a supplier's company. For example, higher-than-necessary prices may be charged by the supplier and approved by the hotel employee. Once the supplier is paid, the hotel employee and his or her contact in the supplier's company split the remaining money.

perpetual inventory—Keeping a list of all items as they are received for storage and issued from storage. This inventory will reveal what *should* be in the storeroom.

physical inventory—Counting all items in a storage area. This inventory will reveal what actually *is* in the storeroom.

processing thefts—Occur when suppliers request payment for an invoice more than once. A hotel needs an effective internal control system to verify whether an invoice has already been paid or not.

spotter—A contracted employee of the hotel or restaurant or someone from an outside contract organization who visits a bar, poses as a guest, and watches the activities of the bar staff.

Review Questions

1. What are some of the losses likely to affect a hospitality operation?

2. How can hotels respond to employee theft?

3. What can the human resources department do to screen potential employees?

4. What is an exit interview? How can it be useful?

5. Should guests be able to make direct 911 calls from the guestroom? Why or why not?

6. What security procedures should housekeeping staff follow when cleaning a guestroom?

7. Why is "division of duties" considered the most important principle of internal control?

8. What steps can hotels take to make swimming pool areas more safe?

9. Why are accurate reports and records important to an operation's overall security/safety program?

10. What actions can a hotel take in response to a problem group that is already on-site?

Internet Sites

For more information, visit the following Internet sites. Remember that Internet addresses can change without notice. If the site is no longer there, you can use a search engine to look for additional sites.

ADA Requirements—Architecture/
new construction
www.usdoj.gov/crt/ada/adahom1.htm

Association of Pool & Spa
Professionals
www.apsp.org

Equal Employment Opportunity
Commission
www.eeoc.gov

IMI Data Search, Inc. (Employee Background Checks)
www.imidatasearch.com

Workplace Violence Research Institute
http://noworkviolence.com

Case Study

Soccer and Spice and Everything Chaotic

Michael Shepherd, the front desk manager at The Greenwood Hotel & Suites, caught up with Emily Gresch, the food and beverage manager, as they walked to the weekly staff meeting. They had both started at the 500-room full-service hotel on the same day six years ago. They'd remained friends, building a network of communication that helped their departments work together in new ways.

"So, Emily," Michael grinned, "which one of us do you think is in trouble—they've got the director of security in on this week's meeting."

"No kidding?" she asked. "I don't think I've seen Hannah at a meeting in the five years she's worked here. Maybe they're finally going to expand the electronic locking system to the employee areas and she's going to train us on it."

"If it's new equipment, it better be an upgrade to the point-of-sale system so we don't keep losing so much revenue on guests who don't tell our front desk agents that they ate at our $40 Sunday brunch buffet before checking out."

Michael held the door open for Emily as they arrived at the meeting room. They took their seats and after a few minutes of small talk, Jacob Kerr, the general manager, stood up and started the meeting. This was Jacob's second month at the property; he'd been transferred to The Greenwood from a similar sized property in a smaller town. He reviewed the sales and financial reports of the past week, then turned the meeting over to Samantha Zimmerman, the director of sales.

"I've got some good news and some bad news," Samantha began. Emily and Michael covertly exchanged amused glances—the sales director invariably tried to cushion any announcements of hardships on other departments with a glowing report of what wonderful work she'd done to increase the hotel's revenue.

"I've managed to bring back a group that is going to book 420 of our 500 rooms. They'll be here for two nights during our slow time and will be using our banquet services for at least one dinner. I was also able to sell them on a group rate that was only $30 off our rack rate, so our RevPAR will still be good."

"That sounds fantastic," Michael said.

"What's the bad news?" asked Emily.

The GM's lips twitched into a quirky smile, "The group is National Youth Soccer League and they're here for a rock concert, the Spice Girls, being held at the arena down the street."

Nearly every department head who had been with the hotel for longer than a year groaned. "Those are the folks that trashed the rooms last year," Ashley, the chief engineer, complained. "It took us almost a week to get all of our rooms back into rentable condition."

"We had to write off several rooms because they were signed for by teenagers who decided they weren't going to pay," said Matthew, the controller. "We never should have allowed a minor to register for a room—it's against our corporate policy. Minors can't be legally held to a contract."

"They also made a mess of the lobby," Michael said. "On Sunday morning they dropped all their luggage in the lobby and took off for breakfast. Our regular guests could barely get through to the check-out desk. Then one of the kids got angry when his bag was stolen."

"I seem to remember one of my room attendants telling me about this group," Brandon said. Brandon had assumed the position of executive housekeeper two months after the soccer group had last stayed at the hotel. "She told me that she found evidence of more than a dozen people staying in one room."

Samantha stood, bringing her fist down on the table. "Well, they weren't too thrilled with us either. I had to work really hard to get them to come back. It's a great piece of business, but we'll never get it again if we don't fix the problems that happened last time. Here's a list of the problems that the meeting planner said we needed to fix." Samantha walked around the table, giving everyone a sheet of paper. The list read:

- Several guests had items stolen from their rooms.

- The hotel was overcrowded.

- There was no parking in the hotel lot.

- The swimming pool was dirty.

- There was too much noise at night and the response from the front desk was unacceptable.

- There were too many kids that weren't a part of our group.

- There were funny smells coming from some of the rooms. We don't want our kids exposed to drugs.

"Of course the pool was dirty," muttered Ashley, the chief engineer. "Every kid and his ten closest friends were using it. We should have shut it down or not let so many kids use it."

Hannah, who had been quietly taking notes throughout the meeting, stood up as the other department managers began to grumble. "I'm here at Jacob's request. Last year, the security staff did have to respond to a lot of problems with this group. But by the time we got involved things were out of control. This year, we are going to coordinate the security efforts among the departments to ensure that this group is taken care of and that The Greenwood continues to live up to its reputation as the place where guests get service that astounds."

"We're going to make sure our mistakes of last year are not repeated," Jacob said. "Which means that each of you will take responsibility for the security issues in your department. Hannah is going to assign responsibility and we'll evaluate the effectiveness of everyone's security plan after the event is over."

Hannah chewed on her lower lip, wishing Jacob hadn't taken the hard-line approach so early. "All of our departments can contribute to making sure that both our guests and the property are safe. We all have some great ideas on how to maintain security. Let's take a quick look at some of these issues and we can brainstorm ways to handle each of them. Then as each department develops its plan, I'll work with you to coordinate with other departments. Let's start with the room theft."

"Austin, the group's president, said that three different soccer players had items taken from their rooms," Samantha said. "As I remember, one of those incidents involved a room attendant getting shoved against her cart while some punk grabbed a leather jacket in the closet and ran off with it. I think one of the other thefts also occurred while the room was being cleaned."

"There's an area with an easy solution," Ashley said. "Just have the room attendants close the door while they clean. I've never understood why the doors are left open anyway. We certainly don't have maintenance staff leave the door open when they work on the room."

"That's because you don't have to worry as much about your maintenance staff getting assaulted," Brandon said. "If you close the door, there's no way to tell if a room attendant is in trouble. Right now, a closed door with a room attendant cart in front of it is a warning sign."

"Perhaps you should adopt a team-based paradigm," suggested Madison, the human resources director.

"Come on, Madison," Brandon said. "You've interviewed these folks. If I put two of them in the same room, they'll be chattering the whole time. And with the door shut, they'll probably have the TV on the whole time so they don't miss their soaps."

Hannah raised her eyebrows, wondering if this attitude contributed to the high turnover among room attendants. "Does it really matter if they talk or watch TV?" she asked. "Just give them their room assignments and make sure they meet their quota of rooms and that the rooms are up to standard. Let them talk while they're cleaning."

"It is more productive to focus on outcome rather than process," Madison encouraged.

Brandon sighed, "I suppose I could test it for a week before the group checks in."

"So housekeeping will keep room doors shut," Hannah said. "That's a good start. Are there any other issues that we need to add to the list that Samantha passed out?"

"We need some sort of crowd control procedures," Michael said. "Last year we must have had a thousand people in the hotel, and they were all as rowdy as the crowd in Times Square on the eve of the millennium."

"We could put wrist bands on registered guests," suggested Megan. "If the only way they can get into the hotel is with a wrist band, that should control access to the property."

"We did use wrist bands last year," Emily said. "It didn't work."

"Actually, I think it could work," Michael said. "The problem was that we were giving away too many wrist bands. There was no control over how many wrist bands were issued. One of the valets told me that he saw some kids tossing them out the window to their friends—they must have found some way to slip them off their wrists—or they simply didn't go out into the lobby again once they were in the hotel."

"Let's order wrist bands that can be removed only if they're broken," Madison suggested.

"That's going to go over real well with my regulars," Michael said. "I've got three executives that come stay with us one night a week—they brought in

$100,000 last year. I'm supposed to tell the CEO of a Fortune 500 company that she's got to wear a toe tag?"

"Here's another issue for you," Emily said. "Last year we must have had every pizza joint in the city delivering to our hotel. Not only did that hurt our food and beverage revenue, but we had delivery kids wandering the hotel. It can't be good security to have people wandering the halls when we have no way of keeping track of them."

"So let's just send them to the front desk, and have a front desk agent call the room and have someone come and pick the meal up," Megan said.

"That's a nice idea," Michael responded. "Except the guests usually will give their room number to the delivery people and they'll go right up to the room."

"Ah, but they won't be able to get in without wrist bands," Hannah said. "We'll just have the security people at the doors direct any delivery people to the front desk."

"Better make that the bell stand," Michael said. "They have a courtesy phone and can take care of it without disrupting check-ins. Besides, if the guest doesn't want to come down to the lobby, we could always have a bell attendant deliver it instead of the outside vendor."

"Good idea," Hannah said. "What other issues are there?"

"We've got to be more careful about minors abusing alcohol in their rooms," Emily said. "I can make sure my staff doesn't sell alcohol to minors, but last year they were bringing their own in."

"Anyone checking in with a cooler is going to be trouble," Ashley said. "I could tell there were a few drunken parties going on by the number of curtains that got used as bed sheets."

"We also need to limit the number of false alarms," Matthew said. "We got fined by the fire department last year because they had to respond to four false fire alarms that some kids decided to set off at all hours of the night."

"Why don't we just turn the alarms off during the event?" Brandon suggested.

"Perhaps because it would violate federal, state, *and* local law," Ashley shot back.

"Speaking of alarms," Hannah spoke up quickly. "We need to make sure that all of our emergency procedures are in place. Everyone needs to be clear on evacuation plans and how to handle medical emergencies. Madison, could you make sure there is a training checklist for all employees on our emergency response plans? Perhaps we could plan a drill for the week before the event."

By the end of the meeting, each department head had made an appointment with Hannah to set up security plans for the upcoming event. Samantha left to assure the meeting planner that the event would be the best ever.

Discussion Questions

1. What are the issues that each department's security plan needs to address?

2. What would be some of the responses to those issues?

Case Number: 3874CA

The following industry experts helped generate and develop this case: Wendell Couch, ARM, CHA, Director of Technical Services for the Risk Management Department of Bass Hotels & Resorts; and Raymond C. Ellis, Jr., CHE, CHTP, CLSD, Professor, Conrad N. Hilton College, University of Houston, Director, Loss Prevention Management Institute.

Case Study

Is It Getting Hot in Here?

Scenario #1: Why Train?

Rudy Jamison is the general manager of the newly remodeled Briarwood Inn. He is looking through the upcoming training schedule and sees that a fire extinguisher session is planned for the following month. Since the renovation brought the hotel up to current fire codes with the installation of a fully automated sprinkler system, Rudy doesn't see the need for any additional expenses, like fire-related training sessions. When he announces at the weekly management meeting that he is canceling the session, everyone is shocked. The security manager tries to convince him that the training session is critical, but Rudy seems set in his ways and doesn't seem about to change his mind.

Scenario #2: Flaming Dessert

Lucas Romalin, a soon-to-be graduate of a local culinary arts program, was hired as a part-time server in the dining room of the Lancelot Lodge. When one of his tables ordered Bananas Foster, he was in his glory—he just loved the tableside flambé. He was a showman at heart, and enjoyed the reactions of guests when the flames leapt from the dessert cart. This particular table seemed to be in a partying mood, so Lucas doubled the amount of rum (he had also discovered the better the show, the bigger the tip!). However, this time, when he lit the match, the overabundance of alcohol and fumes caused the flame to burst upwards about three feet. Taken completely by surprise, Lucas stood momentarily stupefied as the drapes caught on fire. Then, in the ensuing commotion, Lucas tipped the burning dessert plate onto a guest's lap.

Scenario #3: Fire in the Guestroom

Julie, a seasoned front desk agent, is taking a breather in what otherwise has been a hectic morning. Then, this frantic call comes in from a guestroom: "There's a fire in my room—I dropped a cigarette into the wastebasket and it just caught on fire. Oh no! Now it's spreading to the drapes! What do I do?"

Scenario #4: Rags to Ruin

Gerrett Miller and Ronnie Jenkins still can't believe the hotel's entire laundry facility had been gutted from a fire the previous day.

"What do you think could have possibly caused this?" asks Ronnie.

"Well, my first instinct is always the lint traps. Those little devils will get you when you're not paying attention."

"No, it can't be that—we clean them between each load."

Gerrett paused, his mind searching for any plausible idea. Then it hit him. "What was the last load washed? It wasn't kitchen rags, by chance, was it?"

"As a matter of fact, it was. But I don't think that could be the reason. I mean, I did the same thing I always do—I put the rags straight into the washer and then the dryer. Then I set the timer and left. Nothing unusual there."

"I'm not so sure about that, Ronnie. I think we've found the problem."

Discussion Questions

1. *Scenario #1: Why Train?*
   How should the security manager go about convincing the GM to reinstate the fire extinguisher training session?

2. *Scenario #2: Flaming Dessert*
   What are the property's options for future flambés?

3. *Scenario #3: Fire in the Guestroom*
   What immediate instructions should Julie give the guest and what further action should Julie take?

4. *Scenario #4: Rags to Ruin*
   What was wrong with the laundering process Ronnie used and what needs to be changed?

Case Number: 3874CB

The following industry experts helped generate and develop this case: Wendell Couch, ARM, CHA, Director of Technical Services for the Risk Management Department of Bass Hotels & Resorts; and Raymond C. Ellis, Jr., CHE, CHTP, CLSD, Professor, Conrad N. Hilton College, University of Houston, Director, Loss Prevention Management Institute.

Chapter 7 Outline

Competencies

1. Summarize the business case for employee safety. (pp. 223–229)

2. Cite some employee safety statistics. (pp. 229–230)

3. Discuss strategies for managing employee safety, and explain how a hotel can establish a safety committee. (pp. 230–236)

4. Describe some emerging issues concerning employee safety. (pp. 237–239)

7

Employee Safety

The profit thief may be an unusual title for a dissertation on safety, but safety is an unusual topic. We all advocate safety. It's like the flag, motherhood, and apple pie. Yet few managements do anything about it. Of course, we're all "safe." We don't have accidents — accidents happen to the other guy.

As management you have a moral obligation to your employees to do all you can to prevent accidents while they are at work. This is a moral obligation to the people who look to you for leadership and direction to prevent human pain and suffering. Accidents are caused. Therefore, most can be prevented.[1]

THE PRECEDING WORDS were written in 1972, not long after the passage of the Occupational Safety and Health Act. Their author was the Corporate Risk Manager and Director of Safety for the I.T.T.–Canteen Corporation, the parent company of Sheraton Hotels at the time. As we will see in this chapter, management's awareness of safety in the hospitality workplace has improved substantially since 1972. The moral obligation continues and has expanded into other elements, including employee lifestyle issues.

As a service industry, the hospitality industry is especially concerned about the safety and security of its guests and patrons; sometimes hospitality managers pay less attention to safety and security issues involving their employees. For many hospitality businesses, however, the actual dollar cost of employee-related safety and security facilities and procedures exceeds that of guest-related costs.

When a lost-time accident occurs, it results in direct, quantifiable costs such as overtime pay to cover an injured employee's duties, the expenses associated with paying an insurance claim, and, perhaps, increased insurance premiums. Such an accident also results in indirect costs, including the costs associated with recruiting, hiring, and training a replacement employee, the time lost by supervisors investigating the accident, the medical care required, and the quality issues that result from having a new, inexperienced employee take over the job. In many cases, these harder-to-quantify indirect expenses can exceed the direct costs. Morale can also suffer, especially if employees begin to question the safety of their workplace. For all of these reasons, farsighted managers devote attention to employee safety issues as well as guest safety issues in their operations.

What follows is a discussion of the business case for employee safety. Afterward, we will take a look at some statistics regarding employee safety in the industry. The chapter then examines methods for managing employee safety and establishing a safety committee, before concluding with a look at some emerging issues in employee safety.

223

The Business Case for Employee Safety

These six elements (see Exhibit 1) are part of the business case for employee safety:

- Legal repercussions
- Protection of human assets
- Operational benefits
- Financial costs
- Customer expectations
- Social responsibility

The following sections briefly cover each of these elements. Hotel managers are encouraged to refer to resources from their corporate office and their insurance provider for additional information on employee safety and the business case that can be made for it.

Exhibit 1   The Business Case for Employee Safety

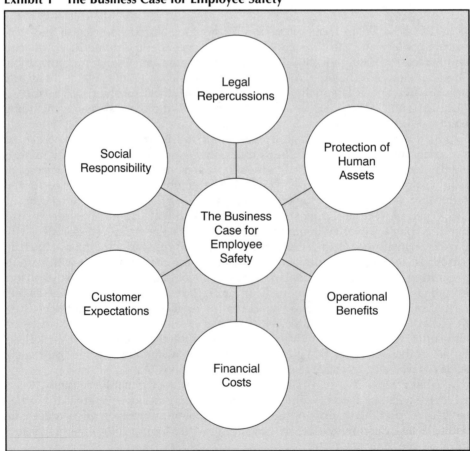

Legal Repercussions

Governmental regulation of employee safety in the United States is handled by the Occupational Safety & Health Administration (OSHA), which came into being as a result of the Occupational Safety and Health Act of 1971.[2] That act has many provisions, with the following ones being of particular relevance to hotels:[3]

- State Plans (Part 1902)
- Inspections, Citation and Proposed Penalties (Part 1903)
- Recording and Reporting Occupational Injuries and Illnesses (Part 1904)
- Rules of Practice for Variances, Limitations, Variations, Tolerance, and Exemptions Under OSHA (Part 1905)
- Consultation Agreements (Part 1908)
- Occupational Safety and Health Standards (Part 1910)

The chapter appendix, "Occupational Safety and Health Act," provides some further background information about the Act that is of particular relevance to hotels.

When an employee is injured during the course of employment, the punishments faced by the employer are generally limited to the penalties imposed by OSHA, along with workers' compensation benefits. OSHA liability is generally in the form of fines, with criminal penalties being very rare. OSHA fines are generally not unduly burdensome for most businesses, so motivation for employee safety is not strongly driven by the potential cost of OSHA fines. More information about OSHA penalties and fines can be found at the OSHA website at www.osha.gov.

Protection of Human Assets

Using a term such as "human assets" has a rather cold sound to it when applied to employees, but then again (some would argue) so does "human resources." But the word "asset" certainly does apply to hotel employees, as hotels have a lot invested in their employees. In turn, good employees acquire a wealth of knowledge about the hotel and become very difficult to replace. Hotel employees often become part of the hotel "family" by building friendly relationships with frequent guests. When such an employee is injured and misses work, the loss of this "asset" has guest service implications as well as job productivity implications. Protecting employees from injury is not only the right thing to do from a moral or human standpoint, it is also important for many business reasons and provides a clear financial benefit to the hotel.

Operational Benefits

The operational benefits of employee safety are best appreciated by considering all of the things that happen when an employee is injured severely enough that medical care is required. Other employees may stop work or their work time may include delays while they talk about what happened. Someone may have to call for medical transport or provide transport. A member of management should accompany the employee to the medical treatment facility, leaving the business even more short-staffed. Treatment will not be immediate and the employee then

---

Ergonomics

Many workplace injury and illness problems in hotels could be addressed using the application of ergonomics, particularly the field of ergonomics known as physical ergonomics. Ergonomics is the scientific discipline that applies theoretical principles, data, and methods to design in order to optimize human well-being and overall system efficiency. Practitioners of ergonomics—ergonomists—contribute to the planning, design, and evaluation of tasks, jobs, products, organizations, environments, and systems in order to make them compatible with the needs, abilities, and limitations of users.

An Internet search of the terms "hotel workplace injuries" and "ergonomics" indicates that there has been growing interest in applying ergonomic methods to various areas of lodging properties, particularly in the housekeeping area. Further developments and additional data can be expected in the years ahead.

Certainly there is room for improvement. To cite a simple example, consider the case of a very large urban hotel in which the soiled guestroom linens arrive for cleaning via a linen chute and land on the basement floor. Hotel employees have to bend over to pick up the linen from the floor to sort it into waist-high bins for movement to the laundry operation. There are more than 1,200 rooms in the hotel, so you can imagine how many sheets, pillowcases, towels, etc., must be picked up from the floor in the course of a year.

---

needs to get home. Meanwhile, back at the hotel, other employees must pick up the work that the employee would have done, and the manager's work must either be done by others as well or will have to wait until the manager's return.

What happens if the employee does not return to work the following day, and is absent for many days and even weeks? Work schedules will need to be changed—either someone else will have to be called in to replace the injured employee or shifts will have to be extended. If the missing employee was a solid performer, productivity and quality may well suffer. In addition, there is now the uncertainty as to the return of the employee and whether the employee's performance when he or she returns will somehow be affected by the injury. Since an injury this severe is a recordable case and workers' compensation is involved, there is paperwork and documentation that will be required. Clearly, there is a long list of operational benefits to keeping employees safe.

Financial Costs

An injured employee will probably incur medical costs. An on-the-job injury is covered by workers' compensation, which means that all medical costs will be charged to the hotel's workers' compensation coverage. This may be an external insurance company or it may be an internal "self-insurance" fund created by the hotel company. Workers' compensation costs within service industries average between 1 and 3 percent of wages.[4] The worse the safety record for a given business, the higher these costs will be. A poor safety record that raises workers' compensation costs by 0.5 percent of wages could cost even a medium-sized business $10,000 or more per year.

Depending on the nature of the injury, there may be other direct costs. If a server slips and falls, he or she might drop food, beverages, and dishes in the process. This results in a financial loss that might be compounded by needing to comp a meal or pay for the cleaning of a customer's clothing. If kitchen employees cut themselves, food product coming into contact with blood must be thrown out. A shuttle bus driver who has an accident may damage the property's shuttle bus, which could force it out of service as needed repairs are made. If guests riding the bus are injured, there could be additional costs, including the potential for lawsuits.

Indirect Financial Costs. The literature on employee injuries often uses words such as "hidden," "invisible" or "indirect" when discussing the additional costs of employee injuries. The "iceberg effect" is another phrase that is used. All of these terms refer to the same thing—the hard-to-fully-quantify financial (and other) costs that result when employees are injured. The discussion in the popular literature on these topics often doesn't cite sources and cannot be considered authoritative, so at times the terms are a little misleading. For example, the term "iceberg effect" might cause one to assume that only 10 percent of the financial costs are direct and 90 percent are indirect. In fact, one major research study performed on this topic indicated that the indirect costs were probably 1.6 times that of the direct costs, with these estimates "likely to be low, because they ignore costs associated with pain and suffering as well as those of within-home care provided by family members, and because the numbers of occupational injuries and illnesses are likely to be undercounted."[5] Other organizations have come up with higher multipliers, sometimes much higher multipliers (up to ten times the direct costs, for example). Taking everything into consideration, it is likely that any direct measure of the cost of employee injuries should be multiplied by at least 2.5 to get the total cost.[6] This would mean that direct costs are 40 percent of the total true costs of employee injuries, indirect costs 60 percent. Exhibit 2 outlines some of the indirect costs of employee injuries.

Customer Expectations

It is not easy to determine exactly what customer expectations are with regard to employee safety. As one researcher wrote in the *Journal of Safety Research*, discussing some recently introduced amenities in hotels: "Does the public know and understand the impact of these luxuries [high-end sheets, pillows, marble surfaces, etc.] on the health of those who clean their rooms, and will they be willing to pay more for them as a consequence?"[7]

One development that may give some indication of customer interest is the discussion of sustainability and **triple bottom line** issues taking place around the globe. Besides the ubiquitous "green" elements of these discussions, workplace safety issues are included in the information collected and are also part of sustainability evaluations. The occupational safety and health elements of the Global Reporting Initiative (a non-profit organization that works toward a sustainable global economy by providing sustainability reporting guidance) illustrate this coming together of sustainability and safety.[8] Thus it appears that employee safety is of concern to at least some percentage of customers.

Exhibit 2   The Indirect Costs of Employee Injuries

The true financial cost of a workers' compensation incident includes a lot of indirect or hidden costs; when an employee is injured, the actual total cost to the lodging property is much higher than the insurance premiums or medical benefits paid. According to a study by OSHA, the indirect costs of a workers' compensation claim are 4.5 times the direct cost. These indirect costs can include the following:

1. Time lost and the productivity lost by the accident response and providing immediate aid, by both the employee's supervisor and co-workers.
2. Time lost by co-workers' distraction—watching the emergency response and/or standing around discussing the accident after the employee is transported to the medical provider.
3. Time lost for the remainder of the workday by the injured employee, which is normally paid by the employer.
4. Reduction in morale as co-workers realize and think about the risk related to the job.
5. Damage to equipment, tools, machinery, or vehicles being used by the employee at the time of the accident.
6. Missed sales if the injured employee is a salesperson and is off work for an extended period of time.
7. Continuation of the employee's benefits while the employee is off work due to the accident.
8. Time spent handling the accident investigation and reports.
9. Time spent handling the worker's comp claim.
10. Loss of production from the injured employee.
11. Expense of rescheduling the work the employee would have performed.
12. Cost of overtime pay to other employees to do the work of the injured employee, or
13. Cost of hiring and training a temporary or permanent employee to replace the injured employee.
14. Lower productivity of the replacement employee until the replacement employee is up to speed or the injured employee returns to work.
15. Potential OSHA or state-imposed penalties and/or fines.
16. Potential legal expenses.

Source: Adapted from "The Hidden Cost of Workers' Compensation," Amaxx Risk Solutions, August 31, 2012; http://reduceyourworkerscomp.com/hidden-cost-of-workers-comp/.

Social Responsibility

The previous discussion has largely focused on legal liability and the direct and indirect financial aspects of employee safety. The argument for paying close attention to workplace safety based on these items alone is compelling. The social responsibility component is less obvious because it is more difficult to measure, but it should not be overlooked.

The issue of corporate social responsibility (CSR) has received a great deal of attention in recent years. This interest takes many forms, ranging from philanthropic efforts to enhanced employee benefits. Some argue that corporate social responsibility can help to improve employee morale and retention by enhancing the reputation of the company with its employees. Some investment funds have used measures of CSR to help guide their investment philosophy. In addition, many corporations include employee safety when reporting their corporate social responsibility initiatives.

Another way to look at the social responsibility question is by considering the toll that a workplace injury takes on the employee's family. In addition to the potential lost income, an injured parent may not be able to help care for children or elderly family members. Instead, the injured person may need additional help from family members who are already overburdened.

A few years ago, a group called UNITE HERE drew attention to the issue of housekeeper safety.[9] UNITE HERE presented information suggesting that housekeepers were experiencing injuries due to—among other things—changes in the design and amenities in hotel guestrooms. A rather large amount of press coverage resulted, but the long-term ramifications of the attention brought to this issue are difficult to predict.

Similarly, the consequences of a failure to demonstrate social responsibility are hard to quantify, yet that does not mean that the losses that can result from failing in this area are not very real. Taken in conjunction with all of the other reasons for placing an emphasis on employee safety, there clearly is a very strong business case for hospitality industry managers to make employee safety a top priority.

Employee Safety: Some Statistics

The U.S. Bureau of Labor Statistics (BLS) publishes annual reports containing workplace injury statistics. As shown in Exhibit 3, the BLS data shows that between 1994 and 2009 the lodging industry saw about a 50 percent reduction in the rate of employee injuries/illnesses. (For simplicity, "injuries" rather than "injuries/illnesses" will be used for this category for the balance of this discussion.) "Lost Workday Cases," a measure of potentially more severe injuries, dropped by 45 percent over this period. During this same period, employee injuries in all private industry (including hotels) dropped by 57 percent and the rate

Exhibit 3   Injuries and Illnesses Within the Lodging Industry

Year	1994	2009
Total Cases of Injury and Illness	10.1*	5.0
Total Lost Workday Cases	4.7	2.6
Total Cases Without Lost Workdays	5.3	2.4

*Data per 100 full-time-equivalent workers.

of lost workday cases was reduced by 53 percent. Despite this dramatic improvement in hotel employee safety, there is still room for further improvement

Bureau of Labor Statistics data provide some further insight into the more serious and costly injuries that involve days away from work. Almost 24 percent of lodging injuries involved 31 or more days away from work. As shown in Exhibit 4, the most common injuries to lodging employees were "Sprains & strains" (35.5 percent), followed by "Soreness pain" (13.2 percent) and "Bruises/contusions" (9.4 percent). The three most common sources of injury for hotel workers were "Floor ground surfaces" (27.5 percent), "Worker motion or position" (15.5 percent), and "Containers" (11.6 percent). The top three causes of lodging employee injury were falls (two fall categories combined for 21.7 percent), "Contact with object/equipment" (17.8 percent), and "Overexertion" (14.9 percent).

The lodging industry does have a rate of recordable injury and illness higher than private industry (5.0 versus 3.6 per 100 full-time-equivalent workers). The lodging industry rate for cases with days away from work is also higher (1.4 versus 1.1). Fortunately, all of these values have shown a pretty consistent decline over recent years. These values should be compared with actual property or corporate safety statistics over time to help identify improvement opportunities.

The Bureau of Labor Statistics has a number of other statistics on its website that could prove useful as well. The site can be queried for a vast array of data on other aspects of workplace injury for hotels and other hospitality business sectors. Workplace injury statistics are available for many countries and regions.[10]

Managing Employee Safety

The reduction in employee injuries in recent years within the lodging industry did not "just happen." It is the result of hotel managers and employees taking actions to identify and reduce safety hazards in the workplace. Exhibit 5 provides some insight into how one hospitality corporation was able to reduce its injury rates during this period.

To cite another example, the Marriott chain has "safety designers" whose job it is to analyze and design Marriott hotels with worker safety in mind. Job-safety training at Marriott helps employees keep safety uppermost in their minds, as do regular safety discussions during staff meetings. In addition, Marriott developed an innovative and award-winning workers' compensation program to achieve two objectives: (1) to promptly respond to workplace injuries with quality medical care, and (2) to return staff members to work as quickly and safely as possible. As part of the program, Marriott made it possible for employees to report injuries twenty-four hours a day via a toll-free hotline or the Internet. The system prompts claims adjusters and nurses to contact injured employees quickly; cases are then assigned to nurse advocates who help manage the employees' care. Over a five-year period, the program helped reduce Marriott's workers' compensation claims by 15 percent and claims costs by 15 percent.[11]

Other large hotel companies have made similar strides in the area of employee safety and have resources available for managers at the property level to assist them in meeting safety goals. For smaller companies, their insurance providers can assist them with developing and managing effective safety programs.

Exhibit 4   BLS Data-2010 Accommodation Occupational Injuries and Illnesses
Involving Days Away from Work

Nature of injury/ illness:	%	Source of injury/ illness:	%	Event or exposure:	%
Sprains & strains	35.5%	Chemicals/chemical products	1.9%	Contact with object/equipment	17.8%
Fractures	6.2%	Containers	11.6%	Struck by object	8.9%
Cuts/lacerations/ punctures	8.8%	Furniture fixtures	11.3%	Struck against object	6.1%
Bruises/contusions	9.4%	Machinery	4.8%	Caught in object/ equipment/material	1.7%
Heat burns	2.2%	Parts and materials	2.2%	Fall to lower level	4.5%
Chemical burns	0.8%	Worker motion or position	15.5%	Fall on same level	17.2%
Amputations	0.2%	Floor ground surfaces	27.5%	Slips/trips	3.9%
Carpal tunnel syndrome	0.5%	Hand tools	3.6%	Overexertion	14.9%
Tendinitis	0.3%	Vehicles	5.4%	Overexertion in lifting	7.3%
Multiple injuries	3.7%	All other	16.0%	Repetitive motion	1.0%
with fractures	0.3%			Exposed to harmful substance	4.1%
with sprains	2.0%			Transportation accidents	1.1%
Soreness pain	13.2%			Fires/explosions	0.1%
Back pain	3.3%			Assault/violent act	1.2%
All other	13.4%			by person	0.9%
				by other	0.3%
				All other	8.8%

Source: Occupational Injuries and Illnesses and Fatal Injuries Profiles, U.S. Bureau of Labor Statistics; http://www.bls.gov/iif/oshsum.htm#09Summary%20Tables. BLS changed from the Standard Industry Classification (SIC) system to the North American Industrial Classification System between 1994 and 2009. The effect on these statistics is expected to be small but should be noted.

Exhibit 5   Reducing Workplace Injury Rates at Harrah's

Putting safety first at both the corporate and individual-property level can pay big dividends for hotel companies and their employees. A few years ago, Harrah's introduced a company-wide safety program with the following elements:

- Management involvement

- Safety meetings

- Safety inspections

- Accident investigations

- Policy of reporting all injuries

- Continual employee contact regarding safety

- A company-developed Risk Control Profile Summary to measure each hotel's safety efforts

When the program was begun at Harrah's, the company was experiencing OSHA-recordable injuries at a rate of 7.9 per 100 full-time-equivalent employees. After six years of the program, the OSHA recordable rate was 3.4—a drop of almost 60 percent!

Other hospitality firms have found similar success with their own safety initiatives. New safety programs and a greater focus on safety issues are major factors in the reduction of both overall injury rates and serious injury rates within the industry in recent years.

Source: Adapted from J. LaChapelle, "A New Approach to Safety"—a presentation at the Fifth Annual Hospitality Law Conference, Houston, Texas, 2007.

Each property is going to exhibit a somewhat different mix of workplace injuries and will need to tailor its workplace safety programs accordingly. For example, an examination of an "outbreak" of knee and lower back injuries at one hotel revealed that the freight elevator was out of service and that management, as a cost-cutting move, did not repair the elevator but instead instructed employees to carry materials up and down the stairs! The result was a lot of workers' compensation costs—probably far in excess of what it would have cost to repair the freight elevator. Needless to say, such shortsighted thinking must be avoided.

The American Hotel & Lodging Educational Institute (EI) has resources to assist hotel managers in the identification and reduction of safety hazards in the workplace. EI recognizes that housekeepers represent a large percentage of hospitality employees and that their daily work may involve equipment and strenuous physical activity—both of which can increase the risk of accident and injury. EI's housekeeping text, *Managing Housekeeping Operations*, has an extensive chapter devoted to safety and security.[12]

Establishing a Safety Committee

Establishing an on-site safety committee is one way for lodging properties to help ensure the effectiveness of their safety programs. In addition, because employees serve on the committee and assist in establishing safety policies, reviewing accidents, recommending corrective action, and participating in safety inspections and other related safety functions, a safety committee can be a valuable means for creating employee acceptance of safety programs.

The Value of Communication

One of the purposes of a safety committee is to bring managers and employees together in a cooperative effort to improve the safety and health of everyone at the property. Managers and employees on the committee can discuss their unique and common concerns regarding safety. The safety committee thereby becomes a forum for achieving solutions that make sense to both management and staff.

A safety committee will succeed only if management actively participates. Yet, at the same time, it is important that the safety committee not be dominated by the managers that are on it—or by any other individuals. To help avoid such a situation, it is worth devoting some meeting time to establishing ground rules and techniques for decision-making that promote consensus.

Management representatives and the committee chair will be the primary conduits of communication between the safety committee and the hotel's upper management. Employees on the committee will be the primary communicators with the hotel's other employees. For everyone to feel well-represented and appropriately informed, it is important that communication occur in both directions.

Many properties find it helpful to establish a written operating policy prior to creating a safety committee. Such a policy establishes the committee's mission, guidelines for membership, member duties, and general procedures for handling a variety of safety issues. Exhibit 6 is an example of a generic policy that may be adapted to suit a property's specific needs.

The Roles of the Safety Committee

Ideally, the safety committee is a genial and open forum for managers and employees to communicate safety-related concerns. The benefits of such communication may be substantial. Every hazard the committee identifies and helps to eliminate means significant potential savings in accident costs, not to mention the considerable value in the avoidance of human suffering. The safety committee can serve as a valuable problem-solving group that addresses workplace conditions, morale, and quality. By developing solutions, the safety committee improves the company's competitive advantage.

The committee also provides an excellent arena for employees to improve their professional skills in communications, human relations, problem-solving, meeting management, and analysis. Since supervisors and managers should be well-informed about occupational safety and health, the safety committee is a natural "school" of preparation for those employees interested in becoming managers someday. In fact, some companies make safety committee involvement a prerequisite for managerial advancement.

Exhibit 6   Sample Safety Committee Policy

Introduction

[Hotel Name] is committed to accident prevention in order to protect the safety and health of every employee. Injury and illness losses due to hazards often are needless, costly, and preventable. To prevent these losses, a joint management/staff safety committee will be established. Employee involvement in accident prevention and support of safety committee members and activities is necessary to ensure a safe and healthful workplace.

Purpose

The purpose of our safety committee is to bring staff and management together in a nonadversarial, cooperative effort to help our operation promote and maintain a safe and healthful workplace.

Organization

There will be at least two management representatives on the safety committee. One employee representative from each department will also be selected or encouraged to volunteer as a safety committee member. Managers and employees are encouraged to volunteer as members of the committee.

Safety committee members will serve a continuous term of at least one year. Length of membership will be staggered so that at least one experienced member is always serving on the committee.

Membership in the committee will be considered professional development and added to each participant's performance appraisal.

Responsibility

The safety committee has the following responsibilities:

1. Meet regularly to discuss safety and health
2. Communicate with employees and the employer
3. Identify hazardous conditions and unsafe work practices
4. Recommend strategies to eliminate hazards

Recommendations

Written recommendations concerning potential hazards will be submitted by the safety committee to management. Management will respond to recommendations according to the following schedule:

Identified Hazard	Severity of Injury	Response
Fatal	Fatality	Immediate
Serious	Serious physical harm	Immediate
Minor	Minor injury	14 days
Administrative	Not applicable	30 days

Exhibit 6   *(continued)*

Procedures

The committee's plan of action requires procedures by which the committee may successfully fulfill its role. Procedures developed should include:

- Meeting date, time, and location
- Election of chairperson and recorder
- Order of business
- Records

Duties of each member should include:

- Reporting unsafe conditions and practices
- Attending all safety and health meetings
- Reviewing all accidents and near-accidents
- Recommending ideas for improving safety and health
- Setting an example by working safely
- Completing assignments
- Effectively representing employee safety interests

Summary

Only the planning and effective leadership of management and the safety committee can build a program that lasts. The safety committee should be an effective problem-solving team, providing guidance and leadership in safety and health matters.

Safety Committee Duties

Safety committee meetings should be scheduled regularly, with a consistent meeting time established. Postponements should be avoided, as they tend to reduce the effectiveness of the committee and employee involvement. A set agenda should be followed (a sample is provided in Exhibit 7) and minutes of the meetings should be kept. A chairperson and recorder should be chosen from the committee membership.

Chairperson. Typically, a chairperson's responsibilities are to:

- Prepare agendas for meetings.
- Arrange for the meeting room.
- Notify members of scheduled meetings.
- Distribute the agendas.
- Delegate responsibilities.

Exhibit 7   Sample Safety Committee Meeting Agenda

1. Call to order/roll call.
2. Review minutes of last committee meeting.
3. Review results of periodic workplace safety inspections.
4. Review accident investigations. When appropriate, submit suggestions to management for the prevention of future incidents.
5. Review reports of alleged hazardous conditions.
6. Submit recommendations to assist in the evaluation of employee suggestions.
7. Agree on a time and place for next committee meeting.

- Make assignments.
- Preside over and conduct the meetings.
- Enforce committee ground rules.
- Communicate with hotel management.
- Report the status of recommendations.

Safety Committee Recorder. Typically, a recorder's responsibilities are to:

- Assist the chairperson with meeting agendas.
- Record minutes of the meetings.
- Distribute and post the minutes.
- Assume the chairperson's duties if necessary.

Safety Committee Members. Safety committee members should expect to:

- Attend all safety committee meetings.
- Receive suggestions, concerns, and reports from other staff members.
- Present staff suggestions, concerns, and reports to the committee.
- Report back to staff members about how the committee is dealing with their suggestions, concerns, and reports.
- Receive training on safety and health subjects.
- Review injury and illness reports.
- Monitor safety and health programs and systems.
- Set a good example by working safely.
- Conduct safety inspections.
- Make recommendations for corrective action.
- Assist in communicating committee activities to all employees.

Employee Safety: Some Emerging Issues

As we have seen, the lodging industry has made important strides toward providing a safer workplace in recent years. To ensure that this improvement continues, the National Occupational Research Agenda (NORA) of the Centers for Disease Control and Prevention has identified some key occupational physical and psychological stressors for hotel and motel employees.[13] NORA goals for addressing those stressors are listed in Exhibit 8.

The NORA report also identified employee safety issues likely to face the lodging industry in the future. The following factors were cited as being likely to lead to worker skin disorders, respiratory disease, or stress-related disorders:

- Cleaning compounds

- Pesticides

- Environmental tobacco smoke

- Heat

Concern over cleaning compounds also includes the issue of whether increased physical exertion is needed to obtain acceptable levels of cleanliness when using environmentally friendly cleaning compounds. As the lodging industry adopts "green" practices, housekeepers will need to be trained on how to use new chemicals. There may also be a need to provide education (and even research) on the benefits of these new chemicals to the well-being of the housekeeping staff and others.

Pesticide use concerns may increase as the industry responds to bedbugs and other pests. Pesticide application is generally done by outside contractors; careful supervision of these contractors when they are on-site may be warranted. Continuing education of managers and employees regarding the use of pesticides will probably also be needed.

The NORA report also identified the need to address "musculoskeletal disorders to reduce exposure or to otherwise improve work practices." It can be expected that UNITE HERE will closely monitor this issue and other issues that affect the health and well-being of housekeepers.

While these issues are emerging, environmental tobacco smoke is becoming less of a concern because an increasing number of hotel chains and local community health codes prohibit smoking in hotels. The benefits of smoke-free hotels include a reduced risk of fire—smoking was once one of the most common causes of hotel fires, but the frequency of such fires has declined dramatically.[14] Employers are likely to see improved worker health and reduced absenteeism when employees enjoy no-smoking environments.[15] In addition, a facility that does not permit smoking can expect a reduction in damage and cleaning costs.

However, as long as smoking is permitted at some lodging establishments, it will remain a health issue for employees at those properties. In particular, casinos have been reluctant to ban smoking, despite a Centers for Disease Control and Prevention report that states: "We recommend eliminating tobacco from casinos and implementing a smoking cessation program. The casinos should also eliminate smoking near building entrances and air intakes to protect employees from

Exhibit 8   NORA Goals Related to Hotels and Motels

HOTELS AND MOTELS

The number of workers employed in the U.S. hotel industry is estimated to be 1.8 million. This industry employs a variety of workers, including many immigrants and young, first-time job holders who may be employed part-time or on a seasonal basis. Hotel and motel workers are potentially exposed to several occupational physical and psychological stressors. Nearly all hotels and motels have continuous operations, which necessitates shift work. Hotel room cleaners are at high risk of dermatitis and respiratory diseases due to exposure to cleaning agents and microbial agents in water-damaged buildings. They are also at high risk of musculoskeletal disorders due to frequent bending and lifting of heavy beds, linen, and carts, and awkward postures. Heavy workloads may increase the risks for injuries.

Strategic Goal 5: By 2015, reduce the incidence and severity of occupational injuries by 20% as measured in lost work days among hotel and motel workers.

Surveillance Goal 5.1: Establish programs for collection and analysis of illness and injury event information, including standard elements for severity, in order to identify trends, emerging issues, and intervention needs among hotel and motel employees through collaboration among employers, employees, workers' compensation insurance carriers, labor, academic, and government agencies.

Intermediate Goal 5.2: Develop guidelines and training materials for effective injury interventions for hotel and motel workers through collaborative efforts of management, labor, workers, and other stakeholders in the hotel and motel industry.

Strategic Goal 6: Reduce by 20% the incidence and severity of occupational illness and morbidity that result in lost work days among hotel and motel workers by 2015.

Intermediate Goal 6.1: Create and disseminate information to reduce risk for skin disorders, respiratory disease, stress-related disorders, adverse reproductive health outcomes, and musculoskeletal disorders associated with working conditions in hotels and motels through collaboration of management, labor, workers, manufacturers, government agencies, and research and community-based organizations.

Strategic Goal 7: Eliminate health disparities for priority population workers in the hotel and motel industry by 2015.

Intermediate Goal 7.1: Develop training materials for supervisors and workers that address environmental, organizational, and behavioral factors associated with health disparities, if any are found to exist, among hotel and motel workers through collaboration of employers, employees, labor unions, and community-based organizations.

Source: http://www.cdc.gov/niosh/nora/comment/agendas/services/pdfs/ServApr2009.pdf.

involuntary exposure to ETS [environmental tobacco smoke]. A physician should evaluate employees with respiratory symptoma, especially symtoma related to asthma that are associated with workplace exposures."[16]

Hotel managers are becoming increasingly aware that concerns about workplace safety are part of the broader issue of the general health and well-being of employees and their families. Employee wellness programs are becoming increasingly popular, in part as a response to rising insurance costs.

Endnotes

1. A. J. Saret, "Accidents — The Profit Thief." *Cornell Quarterly*, May 1972.

2. For a similar discussion from a European perspective, refer to "Business Aspects of OSH," European Agency for Safety and Health at Work, at: http://osha.europa.eu/en/topics/business-aspects-of-osh.

3. The parts of the Act cited here do not list all the aspects that apply to hotels but rather those elements of the Act that are applicable to most hotels. A complete listing of all the regulations can be found at: http://osha.gov/pls/oshaweb/owasrch.search_form?p_doc_type=STANDARDS&p_toc_level=0.

4. Employer Costs for Employee Compensation—June 2011. BLS News Release; http://www.bls.gov/news.release/pdf/ecec.pdf.

5. J. P. Leigh, et al., "Occupational Injury and Illness in the United States: Estimates of Costs, Morbidity, and Mortality," *Archives of Internal Medicine* 157 no. 14, July 28, 1997.

6. In his paper "Valuing the Economic Consequences of Work Injury and Illness" (*American Journal of Industrial Medicine*, 40 [2001]: 418-437), David Weill discusses the challenges of determining indirect costs of workplace injuries and illnesses with an interesting review of the literature and a conclusion that we probably "understate the true economic costs."

7. J. V. Johnson, "Rapporteur's Report Services Sector," *Journal of Safety Research* 39 (2008): 191–194.

8. http://www.globalreporting.org/NR/rdonlyres/D8B503A9-070C-43DB-AD0F-5C4AC-B1EBF39/0/G31RefSheet.pdf; L. Walter, "Safety 2011: Incorporating Safety Into Sustainability," *EHS Today*, June 15, 2011; http://ehstoday.com/environment/news/incorporating-safety-sustainability-0615/.

9. UNITE HERE, "Hotel Housekeepers Are Getting Hurt," http://www.hotelworkersrising.org/media/fact_sheet_housekeepers_are_getting_hurt.pdf; and *Creating Luxury, Enduring Pain: How Hotel Work is Hurting Housekeepers* (UNITE HERE, April 2006), http://www.hotelworkersrising.org/media/Injury_Paper.pdf.

10. As an example, workplace safety information for British Columbia, Canada, can be found at http://worksafebc.com/publications/reports/statistics_reports/assets/pdf/stats2011.pdf.

11. "Putting Employees First," ONE.Aon.com, Q3 2008; http://one.aon.com/sites/default/files/putting_employees_first.pdf.

12. See Chapter 7, "Safety and Security," in Aleta A. Nitschke and William D. Frye, *Managing Housekeeping Operations*, Revised Third Edition (Lansing, Mich.: American Hotel & Lodging Educational Institute, 2008), pp. 247–316.

13. National Occupational Research Agenda (NORA). Nora Services Sector Council. Centers for Disease Control 2009; http://www.cdc.gov/niosh/nora/comment/agendas/services/pdfs/ServApr2009.pdf.

14. Hotel and Motel Fires. Topical Fire Report Series. 10, no 4., January 2010; http://www.usfa.fema.gov/downloads/pdf/tfrs/v10i4.pdf.

15. http://www.surgeongeneral.gov/library/secondhandsmoke/factsheets/factsheet6.html.

16. http://www.cdc.gov/niosh/hhe/reports/pdfs/2005-0201-3080.pdf.

Key Terms

ergonomics—The scientific discipline that applies theoretical principles, data, and methods to design in order to optimize human well-being and overall system efficiency.

triple bottom line—An accounting framework that incorporates three dimensions of a business's performance: social, environmental, and financial (often referred to as "people, planet, and profits"). This differs from traditional measures of business success, in that the triple bottom line includes environmental and social measures, not just financial ones.

Review Questions

1. What are the elements of the business case for employee safety?

2. What are some of the operational benefits to employee safety?

3. What are some of the financial aspects to employee safety?

4. What are some of the social responsibility aspects to employee safety?

5. How can a safety committee benefit a hotel?

6. What are some of the typical duties of a hotel safety committee?

7. What are some emerging issues in employee safety?

Internet Sites

For more information, visit the following Internet sites. Remember that Internet addresses can change without notice. If the site is no longer there, you can use a search engine to look for additional sites.

European Agency for Safety and
  Health at Work
https://osha.europa.eu/en

U.S. Bureau of Labor Statistics
www.bls.gov

Occupational Safety & Health
  Administration
www.osha.gov

Appendix

Occupational Safety and Health Act

The Occupational Safety and Health Act of 1970[1] created the Occupational Safety and Health Administration (OSHA) of the U.S. Department of Labor to administer and carry out the purpose of the legislation. The purpose of the Act and of OSHA is "to assure so far as possible every working man and woman in the Nation safe and healthful working conditions and to preserve our human resources...."[2] The Act further states the duty of each employer to furnish to each of his or her employees a "place of employment which is free from recognized hazards that are causing or are likely to cause death or serious physical harm to his [or her] employees."[3]

To fulfill this purpose, OSHA establishes standards to protect employees from safety and health hazards, conducts inspections of workplaces to check compliance with safety standards, requires that certain records of work-related injuries be kept, and enforces its regulations with citations and fines for violations.

OSHA has jurisdiction over any employer of one or more employees engaged in a business "affecting commerce." Hotels are clearly within the broad coverage of the Act, and, therefore, must comply with all of the applicable standards and procedures established by regulations promulgated by OSHA. This appendix gives hotel and motel operators a general overview of how OSHA operates. For specific details of health and safety requirements, consult your attorney or contact the regional or area offices of OSHA.

A hotel has certain responsibilities under the Act and OSHA regulations. Hotel managers must become familiar with and comply with all occupational safety and health standards promulgated by OSHA.

The safety and health standards set forth by OSHA are extensive, and include such subjects as safeguards for walking and working surfaces, stairs, doors, and exits; personal protective equipment and clothing; laundry equipment; maintenance shops and equipment; machine and fan guards; the use of appliances and electrical equipment; hazardous and flammable materials; environmental safeguards (ventilation, noise, etc.); storage conditions and materials-handling rules; parking garages; rodent and vermin controls; drinking water safety; restrooms; bloodborne pathogens; medical and first aid requirements; etc.[4] Management must inspect the hotel premises to ensure compliance with OSHA regulations and to alleviate any hazardous condition that may develop. If any potential hazards to employees exist, posters, labels, or signs must warn them of this potential danger. Employers must establish or update any procedure required by OSHA, and must also communicate this to employees.

Reporting and Recordkeeping Requirements

OSHA regulations require an employer of eleven or more employees to maintain an annual record of work-related employee injuries and illnesses.[5] This information must be maintained in the employer's establishment on an OSHA Form 300 (see Figure 1) or an equivalent form. The employer may maintain the log at a place

Exhibit 1 OSHA's Form 300

OSHA's Form 300 (Rev. 01/2004)

Log of Work-Related Injuries and Illnesses

Attention: This form contains information relating to employee health and must be used in a manner that protects the confidentiality of employees to the extent possible while the information is being used for occupational safety and health purposes.

Year 20___

U.S. Department of Labor
Occupational Safety and Health Administration

Form approved OMB no. 1218-0176

You must record information about every work-related death and about every work-related injury or illness that involves loss of consciousness, restricted work activity or job transfer, days away from work, or medical treatment beyond first aid. You must also record significant work-related injuries and illnesses that are diagnosed by a physician or licensed health care professional. You must also record work-related injuries and illnesses that meet any of the specific recording criteria listed in 29 CFR Part 1904.8 through 1904.12. Feel free to use two lines for a single case if you need to. You must complete an Injury and Illness Incident Report (OSHA Form 301) or equivalent form for each injury or illness recorded on this form. If you're not sure whether a case is recordable, call your local OSHA office for help.

Establishment name _____

City _____ State _____

Identify the person

(A) Case no.	(B) Employee's name	(C) Job title (e.g., Welder)

Describe the case

(D) Date of injury or onset of illness	(E) Where the event occurred (e.g., Loading dock north end)	(F) Describe injury or illness, parts of body affected, and object/substance that directly injured or made person ill (e.g., Second degree burns on right forearm from acetylene torch)
___/___ month/day		
___/___ month/day		
___/___ month/day		
___/___ month/day		
___/___ month/day		
___/___ month/day		
___/___ month/day		
___/___ month/day		
___/___ month/day		
___/___ month/day		
___/___ month/day		
___/___ month/day		
___/___ month/day		

Classify the case

CHECK ONLY ONE box for each case based on the most serious outcome for that case:

Death (G)	Days away from work (H)	Remained at Work — Job transfer or restriction (I)	Remained at Work — Other recordable cases (J)

Enter the number of days the injured or ill worker was:

Away from work (K)	On job transfer or restriction (L)
___ days	___ days
___ days	___ days
___ days	___ days
___ days	___ days
___ days	___ days
___ days	___ days
___ days	___ days
___ days	___ days
___ days	___ days
___ days	___ days
___ days	___ days
___ days	___ days
___ days	___ days

Check the "Injury" column or choose one type of illness:

(M)

(1) Injury	(2) Skin disorder	(3) Respiratory condition	(4) Poisoning	(5) Hearing loss	(6) All other illnesses

Page totals ▶

Be sure to transfer these totals to the Summary page (Form 300A) before you post it.

Page ___ of ___

Public reporting burden for this collection of information is estimated to average 14 minutes per response, including time to review the instructions, search and gather the data needed, and complete and review the collection of information. Persons are not required to respond to the collection of information unless it displays a currently valid OMB control number. If you have any comments about these estimates or any other aspects of this data collection, contact: US Department of Labor, OSHA Office of Statistical Analysis, Room N-3644, 200 Constitution Avenue, NW, Washington, DC 20210. Do not send the completed forms to this office.

other than the business establishment or by means of data processing equipment (or both), if (1) at this "other" place there is sufficient information to complete the log to a date within seven working days of a reportable accident or illness (as is required for logs maintained on the premises), and (2) the employer can provide employees with a copy of the log within one business day and can provide a government investigator with such a copy within four hours.[6]

Even if a hotel has no employee work-related injuries or illnesses during the year, it may be in the hotel's best interests to maintain an OSHA Form 300 for that year indicating "no recordable work-related injuries or illnesses." This may help matters in a non-incident year if the hotel is subject to an inspection by an OSHA compliance officer.

Furthermore, the regulations require that, by February 1 of the calendar year, the employer shall conspicuously post in places where employee notices are generally posted an annual summary of the prior year's totals from the OSHA Form 300. A separate OSHA Form 300A must be used to present this summary information.

Employers must retain these records (the OSHA Form 300 and annual summary) for five years following the end of the year to which each relates.[7] Other regulations requiring the maintenance of medical records for thirty years for work-related employee injuries or illnesses stemming from the use of or exposure to certain hazardous chemicals[8] might apply to hotels. For example, certain hotel employees may work with or be exposed to pesticides, fungicides, cleansing or bleaching chemical agents, or water purification chemicals (e.g., chlorine used in swimming pools) in the course of their work. Should a work-related injury occur in connection with the use of or exposure to such chemicals, hotels should consult their attorney or safety consultant with respect to the hotel's obligation as to recordkeeping and reporting.

The regulations also require employers to carefully guard the privacy of their employees by, for example, establishing procedures for access to records and by requiring that names be withheld in certain cases.[9]

Separate reports of any accidents that result in a fatality or the hospitalization of three or more employees must be made to the nearest Office of the Area Director of OSHA *within eight hours after the occurrence.*[10] This report may be made in person or by telephone and "shall relate the circumstances of the accident, the number of fatalities, and the extent of any injuries."[11]

Posting Requirements

Hotels must post a notice furnished by OSHA that informs employees of their rights and obligations under the Act (see Figure 2). The notice must be posted in a conspicuous place or in places where notices to employees are usually posted. Hotel management is responsible for maintaining this poster and ensuring that it is not altered, defaced, or covered in any way. OSHA notices should be permanently posted under glass. In addition, employers must post any citation for violation of an OSHA safety and health standard at or near the place of the alleged violation referred to in the citation. If this is impractical, the citation may be posted where employees report to work each day.

Figure 2   Occupational Safety and Health Act Notice

Job Safety and Health
It's the law!

OSHA
Occupational Safety
and Health Administration
U.S. Department of Labor

EMPLOYEES:

* You have the right to notify your employer or OSHA about workplace hazards. You may ask OSHA to keep your name confidential.

* You have the right to request an OSHA inspection if you believe that there are unsafe and unhealthful conditions in your workplace. You or your representative may participate in that inspection.

* You can file a complaint with OSHA within 30 days of retaliation or discrimination by your employer for making safety and health complaints or for exercising your rights under the *OSH Act.*

* You have the right to see OSHA citations issued to your employer. Your employer must post the citations at or near the place of the alleged violations.

* Your employer must correct workplace hazards by the date indicated on the citation and must certify that these hazards have been reduced or eliminated.

* You have the right to copies of your medical records and records of your exposures to toxic and harmful substances or conditions.

* Your employer must post this notice in your workplace.

* You must comply with all occupational safety and health standards issued under the *OSH Act* that apply to your own actions and conduct on the job.

EMPLOYERS:

* You must furnish your employees a place of employment free from recognized hazards.

* You must comply with the occupational safety and health standards issued under the *OSH Act.*

This free poster available from OSHA –
The Best Resource for Safety and Health

Free assistance in identifying and correcting hazards or complying with standards is available to employers, without citation or penalty, through OSHA-supported consultation programs in each state.

1-800-321-OSHA
www.osha.gov

OSHA 3165-12-06R

Inspections: Employers' and Employees' Rights and Remedies

OSHA inspectors may visit the hotel premises at any time without delay during regular working hours and walk around with a selected employee to check compliance with OSHA regulations. Advance notice of inspections may be provided only in the event of a reported dangerous condition requiring immediate attention. Pursuant to a U.S. Supreme Court decision, *Marshall* v. *Barlow's, Inc.,*[12] an employer may demand that the inspector have a search warrant before being required to allow the inspector access to non-public work premises. A search warrant authorizing an OSHA inspection may be issued by a court on the showing of probable cause, based on specific evidence of an existing violation or on showing that reasonable legislative or administrative standards for conducting an inspection are satisfied with respect to the hotel. Employers have the right to request proper identification from any OSHA inspector prior to an inspection and to be advised of the reason for the inspection. It is recommended that employers avoid taking a confrontational attitude toward OSHA inspectors.

During an OSHA inspection of a hotel, the compliance officer is entitled to take environmental samples; take relevant photographs; question privately any employer, owner, operator, agent, or employee of the hotel; and use other reasonable and necessary investigative techniques. Hotel management has the right to accompany the inspector on the inspection of the workplace and is further entitled to confer with the inspecting compliance officer at the conclusion of the inspection. At this time, the compliance officer may informally advise management of any apparent safety or health violations, and management may respond with any pertinent information regarding conditions of workplaces in the hotel.

The hotel operator may file a notice of contest with the nearest OSHA assistant regional director within fifteen days of receipt of a citation for an alleged violation and notice of penalty. Also, within fifteen days the hotel may file a written notice with the area director alleging that the period of time fixed in the citation for alleviating the violation is unreasonable. The regional administrator may also hold an informal conference at the request of the hotel operator to discuss any issues raised by the inspection. When a citation is issued, the hotel should contact its attorneys to protect its rights under the Act.

Employees can request that an OSHA area director conduct an inspection of the hotel. This employee request must be in writing and must specify the hazard believed to violate OSHA standards. The name of the employee making such a request is never given to hotel management.

The Act prohibits an employer from discriminating against any employee who exercises his or her rights under the Act. For example, in *Whirlpool Corporation* v. *Marshall,*[13] the U.S. Supreme Court held that an employee may refuse to perform a task that he or she reasonably believes may result in serious physical injury or death. The employer may not then discriminate against the employee who refuses such a dangerous task; that is, the employer may not treat this employee less favorably than he or she treats other employees similarly situated.

(The OSHA regulations, however, do not require employers to pay workers who refuse to perform assigned tasks.)

United States v. *Cusack*[14] established for the first time that the government can in some cases prosecute a corporate officer, as an "employer," for OSHA violations. On February 22, 1993, the U.S. District Court (Dist. New Jersey) sentenced John Cusack, president of Qualified Steel, Inc., to three years' probation, six months of home confinement, 200 hours of community service, and a $2,500 fine. The court held that an officer or director who exercises pervasive and complete control over the corporation can be held liable as an employer under the criminal provisions of OSHA.[15] An employer who willfully violates an OSHA standard rule, resulting in the death of an employee, may be criminally prosecuted under 29 U.S.C. § 666(e).

The extensive OSHA regulations have been criticized in recent years because of the high cost of administering the standards and the burden upon employers to fulfill the recordkeeping requirements. If a hotel has any questions concerning OSHA standards or procedures, it should consult legal counsel. An additional source of information is the OSHA regional or area office.

State Workplace Safety and Health Programs Under OSHA

OSHA provides that state jurisdictions may enact and administer their own occupational safety and health programs, provided that such programs are "at least as effective" as the federal OSHA program. Such state programs must be approved by OSHA, and, if approved, OSHA will provide funding for 50 percent of the costs of the state programs. States and territories with approved plans (so-called "Little OSHAs") include Alaska, Arizona, California, Connecticut,* Hawaii, Indiana, Iowa, Kentucky, Maryland, Michigan, Minnesota, Nevada, New Jersey, New Mexico, New York,* North Carolina, Oregon, Puerto Rico, South Carolina, Tennessee, Utah, Vermont, Virgin Islands, Virginia, Washington (state), and Wyoming. Hotels in such states should be aware that the safety standards promulgated and enforced by state safety and health agencies may in fact be more stringent than the federal OSHA standards.

OSHA Regulations on Bloodborne Pathogens

On December 6, 1991, the U.S. Department of Labor issued OSHA regulations on bloodborne pathogens.[16] Bloodborne pathogens are defined as "pathogenic microorganisms that are present in human blood and can cause disease in humans. These pathogens include, but are not limited to, hepatitis B virus (HBV) and human immunodeficiency virus (HIV)."

The OSHA regulations on bloodborne pathogens are oriented to the healthcare industry. However, aspects of the regulations apply to all industries, since OSHA mandates a trained first-aider on each work shift.

---

* Connecticut and New York cover only the state agencies and other government agencies.

Under the regulations, management determines those employees at risk of exposure. Hepatitis B vaccinations must be *offered* by an employer to those employees who have occupational exposure to blood or other potentially infectious materials. In addition, employers must provide certain employees with protective gear, clothing, and equipment. Employers must also maintain all records of on-the-job exposure incidents on file for thirty years, even if the employee involved in any of the incidents leaves the business's employ.

OSHA requires employers to schedule at least one employee who is trained in first aid on each work shift. Because such employees may come into contact with blood or body fluids, they must be *offered* hepatitis B vaccinations. They must also be provided with protective gloves, eye and face protection, and a tube-mouth mask unit, when necessary, for performing cardiopulmonary resuscitation (CPR).

Similarly, all staff members who are skilled in CPR must be *offered* hepatitis B vaccinations. Employees trained in first aid, security officers, and lifeguards are in this classification of employees.

A special response team of employees should be trained to clean up vomit from bar or dining areas, in the event that it becomes necessary, and should be offered the vaccination series and provided with the proper protective equipment.

If room attendants, housepersons, lifeguards, janitors, or other maintenance staff should be pricked by a discarded hypodermic needle when making up the guestroom, removing bagged trash, or patrolling lake or beach areas, those employees must be *offered* the vaccinations. They must also be provided with the proper protective equipment. This equipment includes protective gloves and face and eye protection.

The accidental pricking of a room attendant, houseperson, or any other employee by a discarded hypodermic needle requires that the employee be sent to a physician within twenty-four hours of the incident. The physician would make the decision as to the necessity for administering the hepatitis B vaccine. The employee may refuse the vaccine but must sign a waiver in the form required by OSHA.

If blood or body fluids are in bedding, sheets, pillowcases, or towels, not only must the room attendants be fully protected, but laundry workers *must* also be offered the vaccinations, special gloves, face and eye protection, and a dust respirator to eliminate the "dust" and particles from dried fluid or blood in the bed linens or towels.

Some hotels provide laundry services for facilities other than the immediate property. Whenever a hotel's laundry customers include clinics, hospitals, or nursing homes, the hotel's laundry staff must receive the full protection as explained earlier.

Several on-staff specialists must be designated and trained for the responsibility of "taking over" whenever a room attendant enters a guestroom and finds blood and body-fluid stains on bedding or towels, or discarded condoms. The specialist employees would be provided special training through a nearby hospital, clinic, or infirmary that serves the hotel. All employees with this special assignment would also be offered the hepatitis B vaccine and would be provided with full personal protection. This would include protective gloves, face and eye protection, a gown, shoe covers, and a dust mask that prevents the employee from ingesting particles when handling bedding or towels with caked blood or body fluids.

Whenever contaminated hypodermic needles are found, they are to be placed in appropriate containers, which are to be properly discarded when full. The local medical facility serving a property can often be a hotel's source or reference for purchasing such containers, as well as heavy-duty plastic bags bearing an OSHA-approved biohazard symbol or red bags bearing a similar symbol. A local medical facility might also provide contacts for or arrange for appropriate removal of medically contaminated waste from a property. Hotels should deal only with contractors licensed to remove medical waste to an approved medical waste disposal site.

It is recommended that consideration be given to establishing an emergency response team that would be called upon when a room obviously is contaminated. OSHA has agreed to this approach and it reduces the cost of personal protective equipment as well as the cost of the hepatitis B vaccination. However, it must be remembered that room attendants must be provided with gloves and eye and face protection for use while cleaning the bathroom area. A dust mask should be provided to supplement the eye and face protection when the room attendant is using any powdered cleaners or doing any overhead dusting or cleaning.

All occupational bloodborne pathogen exposure incidents (including needle-stick injuries, lacerations, or splashes) must be recorded on OSHA Form 300 (see Figure 1) if the incident results in: (1) medical treatment (e.g., immune serum globulin, hepatitis B vaccine, or other prescribed medical treatment); or (2) diagnosis of possible seroconversion (possible exposure to contaminated blood). In the instance of seroconversion, only the injury, such as "needlestick," should be recorded—*not* the serologic status of the employee.

In areas where there is continuing exposure, as in a laundry, there would be a need for an employer to offer vaccinations to all employees. In the laundry, a few key employees might be assigned to the sorting and laundering of all red bags or bags bearing the biohazard symbol, and such employees would be offered vaccinations and be provided with the protective clothing as noted earlier.

The hotel should prepare an exposure control plan, and all housekeeping, laundry, and security staff, lifeguards, and other employees who are trained in CPR and/or first aid should be advised of this plan.[17]

There are twenty-two states that administer OSHA-approved plans to implement the OSHA requirements. A property should verify whether its state has such an OSHA-approved plan that must be followed in that state.

Medical Emergencies

Hotels need to face the possibility of guests becoming seriously ill, becoming accidentally injured, or even dying. Management should create a policy for dealing with such problems. It should review with legal counsel and its insurance company an appropriate response to medical emergencies. It should also review with legal counsel the applicability of "Good Samaritan" laws, which protect, within limits, passersby who try to help.

The Occupational Safety and Health Act requires that a trained first-aider be present on each work shift in all hotels and motels, unless those properties have ready access to medical services on the premises or in close proximity. This may prove helpful in incidents involving guests, as the staff member trained in first aid will have some knowledge of how best to assist the guest. An important point is that first-aiders will also have a better idea of what *not* to do in certain situations.

The property should review with legal counsel the local regulations regarding calling an emergency medical service (EMS). This is important, for a guest may decline assistance and then later sue a property for its failure to provide appropriate aid. If legal counsel advises calling an EMS, the trained first-aider on staff should make the guest comfortable and only provide first aid assistance if a life-threatening condition or situation exists.

Hazard Communication Standard

Hotel and motel employers are responsible for complying with OSHA's Hazard Communication Standard. A violation has a minimum penalty of $5,000.

The following is an outline of the steps an employer must follow to comply with the standard. There is no right way to comply that is spelled out by OSHA, because this is a performance-oriented standard. OSHA thus requires that you develop your own program that complies with various elements it has outlined.

The primary elements of the OSHA Hazard Communication Standard include the following:

1. *Evaluate the hazards in your workplace.* Chemical manufacturers are required to report to companies that distribute or use their products information concerning any hazardous chemicals their products contain. Innkeepers are what OSHA calls "downstream employers" and can rely on these evaluations that come from a manufacturer or supplier. If you choose to evaluate the hazards yourself, you become responsible for the quality of the hazard determination.

2. *Prepare an inventory of all hazardous chemicals in the workplace.* You must do this in a centralized fashion for the entire property; then you can divide it by department for training purposes. Make sure that every product for which you have a material safety data sheet (MSDS) (see #3 below) is included in the inventory. Be sure to update the inventory if any new hazard is introduced into the workplace.

3. *Prepare a master MSDS file and keep a file by department in each department.* An MSDS is a material safety data sheet that the manufacturer or supplier is required to provide to you at the time of the initial shipment of a product.

    The MSDS is supposed to provide the necessary information on the chemical-containing product, including: health effects, exposure limits, whether it's a carcinogen, precautionary measures, emergency and first-aid procedures, and the name of the organization that prepared the MSDS.

    Copies of the MSDS must be readily accessible to employees. A copy of the master MSDS file should also be kept at the front desk for reference by any fire, police, or utility response service unit. When you receive a new MSDS for your master file, be sure a copy is placed in the file of the appropriate department(s).

The hotel is responsible for having an MSDS on each hazardous chemical product.

4. *Labels or a form of warning belong on all containers of hazardous chemicals.* This, once again, is the responsibility of the manufacturer or supplier. Your responsibility as an employer is to ensure the maintenance of the label, tag, or marking. The label should identify the product in such a way that an employee could readily find the MSDS for the product. It must also contain the appropriate hazard warning. Labels must be in English. Another language may appear on the label as long as the information also appears in English.

5. *You must develop a comprehensive written hazard communication program.* The program should include provisions for container labeling, MSDSs, an employee training program, and generally describe how your organization will comply with the hazard communication standard. It must also contain a list of the hazardous chemicals in each work area and the means you will use to inform employees of the hazards of non-routine tasks. The written program must be available to employees, employee representatives, and representatives of OSHA and the National Institute for Occupational Safety & Health (NIOSH). Your written program need not be lengthy or complicated.

6. *You must establish a training and information program for employees exposed to hazardous chemicals in their work area.**

OSHA Information Sources for the Hazard Communication Standard

OSHA has published numerous materials explaining various parts of the Occupational Safety and Health Act. These are available at www.osha.gov/pls/ publications/publication.html. Of particular relevance to the Hazard Communication Standard are the following publications:

Chemical Hazard Communication (OSHA 3084)
www.osha.gov/Publications/osha3084.html

Hazard Communication Guidelines for Compliance (OSHA 3111)
www.osha.gov/Publications/osha3111.html

Changes to the OSHA Hazard Communication Standard

In 2012 OSHA's Hazard Communication Standard was modified. As OSHA explained on its website, "The Hazard Communication Standard (HCS) is now

---

* In *Halterman* v. *Radisson Hotel Corp.* (2000 Va. Lexis 18, 259 Va. 171, Circuit Court of Alexandria, January 14, 2000) the court held that the hotel was not liable to a repairman who inhaled toxic fumes. The court held that under OSHA the hotel had a duty to do more than post a warning of hazardous materials—that the hotel had a responsibility to warn H&H (Halterman's employer). The court ruled that there was insufficient evidence in this case that the property had not properly warned H&H of the potential risk.

aligned with the Globally Harmonized System of Classification and Labeling of Chemicals (GHS). This update to the HCS will provide a common and coherent approach to classifying chemicals and communicating hazard information on labels and safety data sheets. Once implemented, the revised standard will improve the quality and consistency of hazard information in the workplace, making it safer for workers by providing easily understandable information on the appropriate handling and safe use of hazardous chemicals."

While a number of the changes to the HCS involve wording changes only, it can be anticipated that there could be other changes that will more substantially impact businesses. A discussion of frequently asked questions about the hazard communication changes can be found at www.osha.gov/dsg/hazcom/index.html. A more extensive examination of the changes can be found at www.osha.gov/dsg/hazcom/side-by-side.html.

The American Hotel & Lodging Association's Educational Institute has a video titled *GHS: Hazardous Communications* that discusses how the GHS works with existing hotel HAZCOM programs. More information about this resource can be found at www.ahlei.org/Products/Multimedia/DVD/GHS---Hazard-Communications.

Important Points for Management

- The Occupational Safety & Health Administration (OSHA) is a federal agency established to help ensure that employers provide a safe working environment for their employees. The agency sets standards, conducts inspections, requires that records be kept regarding work-related injuries and illnesses, and enforces the Occupational Safety and Health Act.

- Hotels are responsible for satisfying OSHA requirements, even though they are relatively safe places to work. Usually, hotels and motels are not a priority target industry for OSHA inspections. However, if operators do not follow safety practices, they may be subject to increased inspections.

- OSHA regulations require that by February 1 of the calendar year, an employer must conspicuously post in places where employee notices are generally posted an annual summary of the prior year's totals of work-related injuries and illnesses from the OSHA Form 300. A separate OSHA Form 300A must be used to present this summary information.

- Hotels must also post a notice furnished by OSHA that informs employees of their rights and obligations under the Act. The OSHA poster must be conspicuously posted in an area accessible to all employees.

- OSHA notices must be permanently posted under glass to ensure that such notices are not altered, defaced, or covered by other material.

- OSHA compliance officers are authorized to enter a business's premises *without delay* during regular working hours to inspect and investigate in order to determine compliance with OSHA regulations.

- An employer may deny entry to an OSHA inspector; however, OSHA can then obtain a search warrant authorizing an inspection. It is recommended that employers avoid using confrontational tactics when dealing with OSHA compliance officers.

- Advance notice of inspections may be provided only in the event of a reported dangerous condition requiring immediate attention. This condition usually would be reported by an employee.

- The OSHA compliance officer has the authority to take environmental samples; take relevant photographs; employ reasonable and necessary investigative techniques; and question privately any employer, owner, operator, agent, or employee.

- Under OSHA regulations on bloodborne pathogens, employers must offer hepatitis B vaccinations to any employee who has been exposed to bloodborne pathogens. The employee may decline the vaccine, but must sign a declination form whose specific wording is included in the regulations. Following an exposure incident, all records concerning that exposure must be maintained on file for thirty years.

- Hotel managers must prepare a master MSDS file and keep a file by department in each department. A copy of the master MSDS file should also be kept at the front desk for reference by any fire, police, or utility response service unit.

References

1. 29 U.S.C. § 651 *et seq.*
2. 29 U.S.C. § 651.
3. 29 U.S.C. § 654.
4. See 29 C.F.R., Part 1910 (2006) for a list of standards and information on guidelines.
5. Recording and Reporting Occupational Injuries and Illnesses, 29 C.F.R. Part 1904 (1993).
6. 29 C.F.R. § 1904.30; 1904.35; 1904.40.
7. 29 C.F.R. § 1904.33.
8. 29 C.F.R. § 1910.1020.
9. 29 C.F.R. § 1904.29(b)(6)–1904.29(b)(9); 1020.
10. 29 C.F.R. § 1904.39.
11. *Id.*
12. 436 U.S. 307 (1978). See also *Brock* v. *Emerson Electric Co.*, 834 F.2d 994 (11th Cir. 1987). But see *McLaughlin* v. *A. B. Chance Co.*, 56 U.S.L.W. 2547 (April 5, 1988).
13. 445 U.S. 1 (1980).
14. See 806 F. Supp. 47 (D.N.J. 1992).
15. *Ibid.*
16. 29 C.F.R. Part 1910.1030, *et seq.* (1993).
17. See 29 C.F.R. § 1910.1030(c) for requirements.

Case Study

Slipping Up—A Committee Catches Careless Acts

"Our mission is to provide a safe environment for employees, guests, and visitors and to ensure that the same accident never happens twice," said Abigail, the safety committee chair and executive housekeeper of the Seven Bungalows Resort. The resort boasted 1,500 rooms spread over 200 acres of tropical beach. The property catered to vacationers by pampering them with fine food, state-of-the-art fitness facilities, luxurious linens, skillful massage artists, and spacious rooms with awe-inspiring views.

It was 9 A.M. on a Tuesday morning and the safety committee had gathered for its monthly meeting. The top item on the agenda for the hour-long meeting was the orientation of two new members—Ryan, a laundry supervisor, and Brianna, the executive administrative assistant for the chief financial officer.

Around the table were the other members of the committee: Victoria from the front office; Jack, the executive chef; the dining room's maître d', Rachel; Jennifer, the banquet manager; the human resources representative, Tony; and Joseph, the security director. Each of them had been on the safety committee for a minimum of a year. A few, such as Abigail and Joseph, had been on it since its inception eight years ago.

"Victoria, why don't you explain to Ryan and Brianna the four functions that we serve as a security committee," Abigail suggested.

Victoria smiled as if the two were VIP guests and pointed to the orientation packet in front of them. "You'll find it all in your booklets, but in brief, we fulfill four very important purposes. First, we emphasize prevention by working together to identify hazards in each of our departments through safety inspections. Second, we are all conduits of safety information to and from this committee and our respective departments. Third, we act to create an awareness of safety issues in the hotel. Finally, we investigate accidents as they occur."

"Most of the hazard identification has been done," Jack said. "But new hazards are constantly being created and often the procedures we've put in place to protect people get bypassed. We'll show you how to do an inspection, what to look for, and what constitutes a hazard. After this meeting is over, you can accompany me as I do my weekly inspection of the kitchen. Abigail will then work with you to develop checklists for each of your areas."

"The things you find on your inspection can help you fulfill our second purpose," Abigail said. "You can let us know what hazards we need to deal with, and you can let your co-workers know what hazards exist and why certain safety precautions exist. This also helps create a greater awareness of safety at the resort. What sort of things come immediately to mind when you think about the safety information that all employees need to know?"

"Well, certainly the Material Safety Data Sheets for all the chemicals in the laundry," Ryan answered. "OSHA requires that everyone know where an MSDS is for each chemical. They're also very useful for knowing what sort of personal protective equipment should be worn when handling each chemical. I know I use them a lot."

"Good," Abigail said. "What about you, Brianna? What sort of safety information do the administrative employees need to know?"

"That's a tough one, and one I've been thinking about since I was asked to be on the committee. There just aren't a lot of hazards in the office—unless you count paper cuts," Brianna said, ending with a chuckle.

"Actually, you might be surprised at the hazards an office can present," Victoria said. "Two years ago, I would have agreed with you. But there are little things that people forget about when they're in a hurry that have the potential to cause great harm. File cabinets with a lot of files need to be secured so they don't tip over. People leave drawers open and then trip over them. Worse, you see people standing on chairs with wheels to reach things on shelves. Those are just a few of the hazards that your department might have to deal with."

"You're right," Brianna said, nodding thoughtfully. "Just yesterday our accounting clerk was cussing because she had tripped on a dangling mouse cord."

"It's the accident investigation aspect that we're going to concentrate on today," said Joseph, the security director. "It's the duty that requires the greatest amount of observation and judgment on your part—and also the duty that can be most critical in helping prevent any accident from occurring more than once. When investigating a scene, you want to look for unsafe acts and unsafe conditions. Unsafe conditions can be corrected by making a physical change to the process or area, usually through the generation of a work order. Unsafe acts must be corrected with additional training or by changing the way that the job is done."

Tony opened up his folder and handed Ryan and Brianna a blank accident investigation form. "We're going to do a miniature case study. It's one that we've put together based on an accident that actually happened a few years ago at the resort—and one that is the type that could happen any day. We'll describe the accident and then discuss the sorts of questions that you should ask when you arrive at the scene. You can then practice filling out the sheet based on the described scenario."

"The scenario starts with you getting a call to the banquet department," began Rachel. "One of the servers from the Sea Urchin Lounge was drafted to help with a banquet after she finished her eight-hour shift at the lounge. She's fallen and is complaining of leg and back pains."

Jennifer picked up the story. "You arrive on the scene. She's in a back-of-the-house hallway sitting on the floor, leaning up against the wall. One of the server assistants is picking up the dishes that fell off the tray that the server—we'll call her Jasmine—was carrying. Another employee is drying a spot of water on the floor. What sort of things are you going to look for right away? Ask questions and we'll answer according to what you see."

"How many dishes was she carrying?" Brianna asked.

"A lot. Without taking time to count them, you can tell that the large tray was pretty full and she was probably carrying around thirty-five pounds of dirty dishes," Jennifer responded.

"Thirty-five pounds?" Ryan asked. "Was her vision obstructed?"

"Probably," Jennifer said. "That's a question that you'll have to ask her directly, but you think it likely."

"Should she have been carrying the tray? If she was going down a hallway, then it was probably some distance to be carrying a tray of dirty dishes.

They can be awkward to carry. Shouldn't she have been using a cart of some type?"

"Very good. She was carrying the tray for about 300 feet when she fell," Abigail said. "What else do you look for?"

"What about her shoes?" asked Brianna. "Are they in good shape, are they working shoes?"

"Her heels are very worn—she's worked in them for a long time. You can even see the nails on her heel," Rachel said. "You also notice that there's the sheet to a pat of butter that is sticking to one of her shoes."

"Should she really have been working? Did she get a rest after her eight-hour shift? Maybe she's fatigued."

"What is the lighting like?" Ryan asked.

Joseph responded, "The lights are on, but you notice that two of the fluorescent tubes have burned out and things are a little dimmer than they should be."

"What about the surface of the floor?" Brianna asked. "Is it carpet? Tile? Is it level or is it a ramp?"

"And how close to the door was she when she fell? Is there any chance that she might have been hit by the door?"

The questions continued as the safety committee worked their way through the case, guiding the two new members into fully exploring the scene.

Two weeks later, Ryan had just finished programming the dilution levels for the new detergent they were using for table linens. He grabbed his clipboard to record the amounts when he noticed that Morgan, a new laundry attendant, was pouring bleach into the spotter at a table in the middle of the laundry room—and that she was wearing neither gloves, goggles, nor an apron.

Just as he was about to call out to her, Kyle, another laundry attendant who was pulling out a cart filled with dirty guestroom towels, backed into Morgan. She stumbled forward and the bleach she was pouring splashed into her eyes.

Discussion Questions

1. What factors contribute to the effectiveness of the safety committee of Seven Bungalows Resort?

2. Based on the description of the laundry incident, list the observations and questions that would provide information for completing an accident investigation form.

3. What items would go on an accident report checklist?

Case Number: 3877CA

The following industry experts helped generate and develop this case: Wendell Couch, ARM, CHA, Director of Technical Services for the Risk Management Department of Bass Hotels & Resorts; and Raymond C. Ellis, Jr., CHE, CHTP, CLSD, Professor, Conrad N. Hilton College, University of Houston, Director, Loss Prevention Management Institute.

Chapter 8 Outline

Accounting Control Procedures
    Inventory Control
    Payroll Procedures and Concerns
    Sequential Numbering Systems
    Bank Deposits
Physical Protection of the Accounting
   Function
Cashiering Procedures
Establishing Credit Policies and Procedures
    Payment Cards
    Checks
    Denying Credit to a Guest
    Guest Registration and Check-Out
Computer Security
    Accountability
    Auditability
    System Integrity
    Cost Effectiveness
    Ease of Implementation
    Policy Compliance
An Internal Audit Program

Competencies

1. Describe control procedures and physical protection for the accounting function. (pp. 257–260)

2. Summarize hotel cashiering procedures and credit policies and procedures. (pp. 260–271)

3. Explain key issues affecting computer security in a hospitality environment. (pp. 271–279)

4. Describe the benefits and objectives of establishing an internal audit program. (pp. 279–281)

8

The Protection of Funds and Information

WHETHER IN THE FORM of cash, payment card receipts, or incoming and outgoing checks, a lodging property regularly deals with substantial amounts of funds. If these monetary assets are not protected, profitability may be jeopardized. Protecting funds is a primary responsibility of the accounting department, though other departments—particularly the front office—play important contributing roles in protecting certain financial assets.

The accounting department (or accounting function in properties that do not have an actual accounting department) is responsible for overseeing the property's payroll, keeping careful records, and taking appropriate actions concerning accounts receivable and accounts payable. It also is typically at least partially (and sometimes solely) responsible for conducting inventories of the storerooms in the various departments of a property and for either overseeing or performing the purchasing and receiving functions. It also is sometimes responsible for working with management to establish the credit and cash handling policies for the business. Due to the use of computers for performing many of these tasks, computer security is another important concern of the accounting function.

Accounting employees play a significant role in protecting a property's financial assets. However, because of their central role in overseeing the financial transactions of every department and in discovering any theft of assets occurring on the premises, they themselves are often in a better position to embezzle assets than most other employees. For this reason, procedures need to be in place to make it difficult for accounting employees to abuse their position.

This chapter looks at how the accounting function protects the financial assets of a property and at certain procedures that may make the accounting function itself less susceptible to compromise.

Accounting Control Procedures

The accounting department, usually headed by a controller (or comptroller), relies on a number of procedural safeguards. One of the most important and basic is the **separation of duties**, sometimes called the segregation of duties. Under this concept, whenever possible, the various accounting functions should be handled by different staff members (in a smaller operation, it may not be economically feasible to provide the necessary staff). For example, all monies should be handled by one individual. Another member of the staff should process the bank deposit of monies. Bank reconciliation should never be completed by the same person who issues the bank deposit. Likewise, accounts receivable and accounts payable may be separate operations handled by different employees.

The same person should not be responsible for both purchasing and receiving (except when he or she is the owner/manager of a smaller property). This helps keep employees from misappropriating cash and charging the sums taken to false accounts.

Inventory Control

Every department that has an inventory of goods and/or supplies will inventory those goods and/or supplies occasionally as part of its effort to ensure continuing smooth operations. Inventories taken primarily for financial purposes, however, are often coordinated through the accounting department. Although some departments perform inventories of their supplies for their own benefit, major inventories should not be conducted by department heads or supervisors for their own departments. Better control is obtained when the inventory staff comes from outside the department having its stores and/or supplies inventoried.

Equipment inventory control may be enhanced through the use of serial numbers marked on the manufacturer's plate on many pieces of equipment. Consider implementing a system for permanently marking other items that do not carry a manufacturer's identification number. The markings should be a matter of record within the accounting office for inventory purposes and for identification when stolen items are recovered. With the increasing tendency to avoid placing logos or other identification attractive to "collectors" on hotel and motel goods, it is sometimes difficult to positively identify recovered property so that the police can release it to the hotel or motel. Some properties have solved this problem by sewing a colored thread into the corner of a hem or other appropriate place on linens, blankets, towels, flat-screen televisions, and so forth, which permits the identification and recovery of stolen goods.

A number of computer-based inventory control programs are available and should be considered.

Payroll Procedures and Concerns

The payroll process should be coordinated by as large a staff as may be required in relation to the number of employees and frequency of paydays. Master payroll files should be routinely matched with master personnel files to ensure that everyone on the payroll is currently employed by the property. Payroll theft may occur when someone either creates a fictitious employee or continues to carry an employee on the payroll who has departed. Unclaimed wages of departed employees may also be stolen. The possibility of collusion in this type of theft may also be lessened by separating the timekeeping and check distribution duties. There should be a payroll verification with photo identification every six months.

Payrolls may be padded when employees claim to have worked more hours than they actually did. This problem can be lessened or eliminated through the use of an effective timekeeping system.

Other concerns include keeping pay records in a secure storage area and providing appropriate physical security for payroll checks or electronic pay cards. Protection for *all* accounting records may be enhanced through the use of fire- and theft-resistant facilities. Computer controls such as keeping a separate record of on-premises computer data at an off-premises site should also be considered.

Sequential Numbering Systems

All order forms, blank checks, invoices, and other forms required for a specific function in the hotel or motel should be provided in a sequential numbering system. Every number should be accounted for, including voids and the reasons for any voids. Any variation from sequential control may allow an employee to misuse a purchase order, invoice, or check for his or her personal advantage. Check writing or printing equipment and signature plates or stamps should be secured. Some experts advise against using signature plates and stamps at all. Except in an operation run by an on-premises owner/manager, there should be a two-signature requirement on all checks.

Bank Deposits

Bank deposits are frequently handled by a member of the staff in smaller properties. Every effort should be made to avoid creating a routine route and time of delivery to the bank. When feasible, the member of the accounting department should be accompanied by another member of the property's staff. While security staff would seem logical for this assignment, an employee accompanied by a uniformed (and, in most cases, unarmed) security officer might be an equally vulnerable but more obvious target.

Larger properties, on the other hand, often have their bank deposits picked up by an armored car service. If a property uses an armored car service, that service should provide a list containing personnel signatures and photo IDs for verification purposes. When the armored car arrives to pick up a bank deposit, the property has the personnel sign for the deposit. The property then compares the signatures and photo ID with those on its list to ensure that they match *before* turning the deposit over.

Physical Protection of the Accounting Function

The accounting function, especially as it relates to the cashier, should be carefully protected. If at all possible, the general cashier and accounting offices should be located away from the public and guest areas of the property. Heavy-duty doors and locks should be installed in these areas. A silent alarm is advisable, particularly in the cashier area, where a significant amount of money may be kept. The general cashier's door should be locked whenever the safe is opened. If the safe has a day lock option (that is, it can stay unlocked even after it is closed), that option should not be used.

Consider adding an alarm to the general cashier's safe. In all cases where combination locks are used on safes, the combinations themselves should be made available only to those employees who have an absolute need for such information.

Whenever an employee who knows the combination is terminated, reassigned, or even simply leaves for five consecutive business days or more (such as on vacation), the combination should be changed. In addition, the safe should be counted on the day within the last few minutes before the individual leaves the property. Recorded combinations and the specific facilities to which they refer should be kept in a secure, double-locked box. The general manager and controller should each have half the combination in a sealed envelope. Access to this box should be restricted to the controller and general manager jointly. Periodic rotation of locks and combinations may also be considered.

Once the deposit is created, it should be kept in the main safe until taken to the bank or picked up by the armored car service. When banking is handled by the staff of the hotel or motel, the on-premises drop-safe should have an alarm and access should be limited to only authorized employees. The hotel should ensure the drop safe is secured to the floor and can't be removed. The removal of shift drops from the drop safe should be done by two individuals. The number of envelopes removed with both individuals' signatures should be recorded on the daily drop log.

Cashiering Procedures

The cashiering function is a critical aspect of accounting and requires special controls. For example, the amount of cash available in a cash drawer register should be limited by establishing a cash bank for use by cashiers at the front desk and at food and beverage and other sales outlets under the direct control of the hotel. Under such a system, each cashier is given the smallest amount of cash that will still allow the cashier to transact business normally. The cashier becomes responsible for this cash and for all the cash that is added to this starting amount by sales during the cashier's work shift. The cash drawer should be counted before and at the end of each shift. This should be documented.

The cashier should be instructed to close the cash register drawer between each transaction. If an employee works with an open cash register drawer, he or she may not record a transaction or may later ring up only a portion of it and then steal the extra money when closing out the drawer at the end of the shift. Occasionally, a member of the audit team within the accounting office or a supervisor should conduct an unscheduled audit of the register. Surprise counts should be conducted for all hotel banks on a monthly basis.

Ideally, only one person should have access to each cash drawer. Multiple users of a cash drawer make it difficult, if not impossible, to determine responsibility for any shortages.

All transactions should be immediately recorded upon payment. This is particularly important in beverage service. Failure to enter the payment right after the drink is mixed, served, and paid for may lead to the misappropriation of funds by bartenders and beverage servers. A policy should be established regarding the placement of currency during a cash transaction. Generally speaking, the employee should not place currency on the register ledge; doing so may make it easier for a thief to grab the money and run. Some organizations recommend that the money be placed in the cash drawer, but above the clip, until the transaction is completed. This can be helpful when a guest claims to have presented a bill of higher denomination than was actually presented. If the bill is under the clip, it is difficult to prove what denomination was actually received.

Cashiers should be instructed to complete any transaction in process before changing currency into different denominations for guests. This procedure helps deal with con artists who request different denominations of bills continually, making change requests until the cashier becomes so confused that he or she gives away more money than was received. Each request for a variation in denomination should be handled as a new, rather than as a continuing, transaction.

Cashiers should not be allowed to change out their tips for bigger denominations during their shift. If a tip jar is used, it should be at least one arm's length away from the cash drawer.

Establishing Credit Policies and Procedures

Whether a property has 20 rooms or 2,000 rooms, it needs a sound credit policy. Such policies will vary from property to property because each hotel and motel deals with a different location, clientele, and so forth. Each property must choose credit policies that best meet its needs. Remember, however, that one of a lodging property's needs is to provide hospitality. While a credit policy must be sufficient to protect the property, it should not so inconvenience or insult guests that it drives them away.

Credit policies may be chosen or set in a number of ways. For properties that are part of a chain operation, credit guidelines are almost always established by the corporate office. In stand-alone properties, sometimes the general manager will determine the policy and other times a credit committee or accounts receivable team will do so. Depending on the size of an operation and the number of employees it has, its committee could consist of the general manager, controller, front office manager, resident manager, director of sales, food and beverage manager, catering manager, and anyone else that an organization thinks should be involved.

After a chain or property determines a tentative credit policy, it should consult with counsel to ensure that the policy does not violate any state or local laws.

Whether the policy a property decides to follow is corporate, committee written, or established by the general manager, it should be introduced to and understood by sales department personnel—and everyone else who has anything to do with credit at the property—before it is implemented. The finest credit policy will not prevent losses if it is poorly implemented.

Payment Cards

Unfortunately, the illegal use of payment cards has become big business in the crime community. *More than half of all payment card fraud comes from the hospitality industry,* and the smallest merchants (defined as those making fewer than one million credit and debit card transactions per year) account for more than 85 percent of those fraud cases.[1] Payment card fraud may involve the use of stolen, counterfeit, and altered cards. Even when a patron offers a legitimate payment card, a property may be stuck with a bad debt if it does not follow the procedures for accepting the card that have been established by the payment card company. Special care should always be exercised by all employees who may be presented with payment cards. Employees should be trained (and retrained as necessary) about the restrictions and requirements of the individual cards that their property accepts.

In addition to meeting the payment card companies' requirements (which we will discuss further below), employees will need to be trained to meet their property's requirements. Exhibit 1 offers a list of general guidelines for preventing payment card fraud. In addition, many of the following procedures meet the requirements of both the property and the payment card company.

When a guest presents a payment card, the employee responsible for handling the transaction should immediately check both the signature block—to ensure that the card is signed—and the expiration date. If the card has expired, that fact should be pointed out to the guest so that another means of payment can be arranged. Payment card companies will not honor expired cards. The penalty for accepting one may be a bad debt loss for the entire amount charged.

Some properties will have their employees ask for some form of identification as well. While it is generally legal to ask for such identification, most payment card issuers have merchant provisions that do not allow a business to deny a card if

Exhibit 1   Guidelines for Preventing Payment Card Fraud

1. Avoid imprinting payment cards on hotel registration cards, folios, forms, and other paperwork to which hotel staff members may have access. There should be no documents that contain the entire payment card number.

2. Tighten security regarding the storage and recording of hotel guests' payment card information. Only authorized staff members should have access to such information. Cell phones should be prohibited from any area in which payment cards are present.

3. Use electronic data-capture machines that enter information directly into the computer, thereby reducing hotel personnel's access to that data.

4. Destroy documents containing payment card information, including unsigned payment card slips and computer printouts.

5. Restrict access to photocopying machines, especially during the night, and locate the machines in open, busy, and well-lit areas. No copies should be made of driver's licenses or payment cards.

6. Install closed-circuit television cameras in areas where guest information is kept, so that if it is determined that cards have been compromised, evidence may exist to begin tracking down those responsible.

7. Educate staff members to take fraud seriously and to report any suspicious actions or incidents to hotel security or law-enforcement agencies.

8. Review security procedures and devise operational systems to discover and prevent white-collar crime.

9. Cooperate with payment card companies, police, and agencies seeking to prevent counterfeiting.

the user refuses to provide identification beyond the signature on the back of the card. Failure to accept the card for this reason may violate the contractual agreement with the card issuer. Many businesses seem to be unaware of this fact. Furthermore, while it is usually legal to ask for identification, some jurisdictions have laws regarding the topic. Merchants should consult local counsel before requesting identification from payment card users.

Computer verification will not reveal the fraud when an illegal cardholder presents a card before the legal holder has noticed and reported the card lost or stolen. Nonetheless, verifying the card by electronic authorization for acceptance of the card will generally protect the property from loss if the use of the card later proves fraudulent.

If the card proves, after verification, to be invalid, the employee should follow the established procedures of the property and the individual card company. Most properties ask employees to alert either the front office manager or controller, who will handle the situation. In the case of a stolen card, security personnel might also be asked to be readily available. The fraudulent use of payment cards is usually a criminal offense. However, lodging properties should be wary of detaining guests they suspect of theft or fraudulently avoiding payment of their bills. Such detention, especially if unjustified or improperly instituted, might open the property to suits for false imprisonment and slander, depending on the circumstances of the case and applicable laws. Hotels and motels should check with their own counsel before establishing any procedures for detaining guests suspected of payment card fraud or other wrongdoing. Some properties insist that payment card companies indemnify them against such lawsuits. The holder of a stolen payment card will usually leave when he or she realizes the card is under special scrutiny.

Even when authorization is granted, payment card companies generally require that certain procedures be followed to reduce the possibility of the fraudulent use of cards before they are reported missing. The employee accepting the card should compare the signature on the card with the signature on the voucher and match the name of the person presenting the card with the name on the card. If the employee is suspicious, he or she should ask for additional identification. Many properties routinely ask all guests to provide positive identification during registration. If a payment is signed by someone other than the legal cardholder (for example, the holder's spouse or offspring), the payment card company will not pay if the legal holder contests the charge.

Making excessive charges or exceeding the hotel's established **floor limit** (the specific amount of credit per card that individual properties are allowed by payment card companies) is infrequent due to the use of computerized control systems, including point-of-sale (POS) systems. An account that is nearing an established limit is reviewed with the payment card company electronically, without involving the guest. The guest would only be involved should an increase in limit be denied, in which case the guest should be called into the office of the front office manager or other designated representative of the hotel. The hotel should then make the phone available for the guest to speak with the payment card company representative.

Some properties also set their own high balance limit for guests. Such properties usually check their guests' balances at least once a day. Computerized properties may perform this task every shift. When it occurs once a day, it usually is carried out during the night audit. The auditor lists on a high balance report the name, room number, and balance for those guests who have exceeded the established limit. The next morning, management studies the night auditor's report, checks individual folios to discover guests' payment plans, and makes decisions about which guests must be contacted to settle part or all of their bills before being allowed to charge any more services.

Some establishments program their computers to indicate the moment the guest goes one cent over (for example) $100 less than the credit card floor limit or $50 less than the high balance limit. For instance, if the floor limit for a particular credit card is $500, the front office manager will be informed as soon as a guest has spent $400.01; the manager can then keep an eye on the account so the property will be ready to get authorization on the account from the credit card company.

Some properties also train personnel such as front office cashiers, housekeepers, room service staff, and so forth to alert the management when a guest is spending wildly, tipping excessively, or charging even small items like a pack of cigarettes to his or her room number. All personnel who accept charges to a room number may quickly confirm electronically the legitimacy of a registered guest to avoid allowing others to use services for which they can never be billed. Some organizations provide a special guest identification card, passport, key, or other device to confirm that an individual is a registered guest. In properties that keep some guests on a cash basis, employees should be informed of, or trained to find out for themselves, which guests are not allowed to charge. A verification call for services charged to the room will cover this situation; the accounting or front office departments can immediately confirm that the guest can or cannot charge to the room account.

Management should also determine in advance the dollar level at which an interim bill will be presented to a guest on an extended stay. This especially applies to resort properties where guests are often present for a week or two. It is also applicable during conventions or meetings where food and beverage charges may be significant, particularly for the host.

Lodging establishments may consider reserving a specified amount of credit in a guest's credit card account to ensure payment for services rendered, but they must be aware of local laws regarding such procedures. Thus, if a guest comes into a property planning to stay eight days, and the property knows that the anticipated charges will exceed the authorized floor limit, the property may wish to reserve the amount of the anticipated charges in the guest's credit card account. But if the guest then decides to leave earlier than planned, his or her credit is now tied up. Laws vary, but in some jurisdictions, the property is obligated to notify the credit card company to release the unused credit that had been authorized.

PCI Compliance. Information security is a mounting concern among consumers, employees, and businesses alike due to the growing number of computer breaches, payment card fraud, and reports of identity theft. To combat these risks and protect cardholders, the major credit card companies (Visa, MasterCard, American Express, JCB, and Discover) have created a comprehensive data security standard called the Payment Card Industry Data Security Standard (PCI DSS).[2] This standard *requires* numerous changes to business processes, computer applications, and data storage (both electronic and paper-based). The issuing payment card brands can and do impose steep penalties on merchants failing to comply.

In simple terms, PCI DSS was created to reduce risk and prevent problems related to the misuse of cardholder data. As set forth in the PCI DSS, all merchants accepting payment in the forms of credit and/or debit (i.e., payment) cards must adopt a series of security measures to protect sensitive customer credit and debit account information.

Every business that accepts payment cards needs to complete a document called the Self-Assessment Questionnaire (SAQ) and submit it to its acquiring bank (sometimes called a "payment card processor" or "acquirer"). It must also submit a report from a certified vendor stating that the vendor has scanned all of the property's connections to the Internet and found no vulnerabilities. SAQs must be submitted annually. Network scans must be conducted quarterly.

According to Visa, the top five most common vulnerabilities surrounding payment card fraud are the following:[3]

1. Storing prohibited data (e.g., full track data, card verification values, and personal information number block information).

2. Unpatched systems.

3. Use of vendor default settings and passwords.

4. Poorly coded (i.e., unsecure) web-facing applications.

5. Unnecessary and vulnerable services on servers.

To address these threats, one should pursue three simple steps:

1. Eliminate the storage of prohibited cardholder data.

2. Protect cardholder data using secure payment applications.

3. Secure the environment according to PCI DSS.

The payment card–issuing brands enforce PCI DSS compliance with fines on merchants that fail to comply. These fines can be very steep. Visa's fine structure ranges $5,000 to $25,000 per month. American Express's fine structure begins at $50,000 and goes up from there. Fines are levied through the acquiring bank. In addition, each card-issuing brand can also deny the privilege of accepting its card brand to any business deemed to be an unacceptable security risk.

PCI DSS is not a law, but elements of PCI compliance have been incorporated into a variety of state laws dealing with information security breaches, and these laws subject the non-compliant merchant to further costs and potential lawsuits. It is, however, a contractual obligation and a matter of business ethics to comply with such a standard. If a business fails to comply, it may run the risk of losing the privilege of accepting payment cards to transact business. Given the popularity of payment cards in the lodging industry, it is simply not worth the risk of losing this payment option. It is hard to imagine how a hotel could operate in this day and age on a strictly cash basis.

PCI DSS is not just about technology (which is addressed later in this chapter), although that is an important part of it. PCI is about managing and controlling business risk by protecting guest payment card data. It is also about the organization, its culture and people, its information, and its business processes. It covers electronic data as well as data stored in paper-based files. PCI affects all merchants globally—regardless of size, industry, location, or type of business—that accept credit and/or debit cards and covers the collection, storage, transmission, and use of customer and account information embedded in these cards.

Payment cards contain a lot of sensitive data, such as track data, card verification values, and PIN block information. These data should be completely safeguarded, wherever and whenever they are used in the organization, and should not be stored unless absolutely necessary—and then, only for as long as necessary. In such cases, the organization must take all precautions to encrypt, secure, and control access to the data. The very essence of PCI compliance involves understanding what sensitive guest and payment card data are collected, where they are collected, by whom, how they are used and processed, the storage and transmission of these data, and how these data are disposed of after they have outlived their business usefulness. PCI compliance is about protecting and securing every facet of the business processes, technology, and personnel policies and training that play roles in any of these important business activities. The general rule regarding payment card data is that if you don't have a need to keep customer (or guest) data and payment information, then you shouldn't keep them. If you do need them, then you must carefully protect them (with secure and controlled access) and store them only as long as necessary—but no longer.

Checks

Many lodging companies do not accept checks or have limited and very specific circumstances under which they do accept checks. For those properties that continue to accept checks, this is an area that calls for careful control. This section addresses concerns that must be considered if a property accepts checks.

During registration, guests should be asked to indicate how they plan to settle their accounts. Initially, this is a function of the front desk agents, but if the guest indicates that payment will be by check, the front office manager may need to be notified. A number of check services and computerized check guarantee programs are available and should be reviewed as possible backup for a decision to accept checks. (Properties contemplating the use of such a service should ask the service for proof from the Federal Trade Commission that it complies with the Fair Credit Reporting Act.) These services are available around the clock and can be an invaluable aid to the lodging industry. Smaller properties, however, might find the cost of such programs prohibitive and discover that their own well-thought-out check cashing policies can adequately serve their particular needs.

Both the cashier and the front office manager must deal with guest identification when a check is presented for cash or services. Acceptable identification includes:

- Current driver's license or state-issued identification card
- Valid passport with photo ID
- Payment card with laminated photograph and signature

- Identification cards—such as those issued by the armed services, police departments, and some businesses—that include a photograph, a physical description, and a signature

The U.S. Small Business Administration recommends not accepting the following unless they are accompanied by a valid driver's license: Social Security cards, business cards, club or organization cards, bank books, work permits, insurance cards, learner's permits, letters, birth certificates, library cards, unsigned payment cards, or voter registration cards.

It is important to note that the property has no obligation to accept a check, regardless of whether the check is valid. However, a property cannot practice illegal discrimination in refusing to accept checks. Employees should never be instructed to refuse checks on the basis of race or gender, for instance. Such refusal would be a violation of federal discrimination laws.

Management should also define a policy on prosecution in the event of a returned check. Usually, upon re-submission a check returned for insufficient funds will clear. If it does not, few banks will accept the check a third time. The next step is to contact the individual who wrote the check and request immediate payment. A property should review with counsel the laws covering actions to seek recovery in its community. If, after repeated attempts, the property cannot collect, it may wish to consider prosecution. Generally speaking, it may be to the hotel or motel's advantage to establish a reputation for following up on bad checks and other guest or patron fraud. If a property becomes known as lax in its collection efforts, credit and income problems may sharply increase.

Reputable collection agencies provide an alternative to tying up staff time and effort in following up on bad checks or other guest accounts in arrears. While a percentage of the sums collected goes to the agency, that amount is generally less than the expense incurred by direct involvement of the property's staff.

Where the establishment accepts personal checks, electronic check verification (by subscription to various services) has become the favored method for check authorization. The popularity of the automated teller machine (ATM) has sharply reduced the request for check cashing privileges. Where the property has a policy of accepting personal checks, there are several questions to consider:

- Are checks accepted for room and taxes only?

- Are checks accepted for food, beverages, gift shop purchases, or other similar items or services?

- Will a check verification service be used for each transaction?

- Are checks drawn on foreign bank accounts acceptable?

- Will payroll checks, government checks, traveler's checks, money orders, or second- and third-party checks be accepted?

When a property accepts an advance payment by check from a guest who decides to leave the property earlier than planned, the property should not write a refund check unless the bank verifies that the guest's check has cleared. If the property still has the check, it should return it to the guest and ask for another check for the actual amount of the bill. Many properties do not refund cash for goods or services when the original payment was by check.

Checks written for payment of the guest's bill should be made out to the property, not to cash. On the other hand, if the property allows guests to write checks in return for cash, the checks should be made out to "cash," not to the property. This procedure will keep a guest who writes a check for cash from claiming that the property accepted the check as payment for the room and services.

Even properties that accept checks usually do not accept second- or third-party checks. Second-party checks are checks made out to the guest presenting the check. Third-party checks are checks made out to someone who has then signed the check over to the guest presenting the check. The hotel or motel accepting such a check may experience collection problems if the maker of the check stops payment. When properties that do accept second-party checks receive a check that has already been endorsed, they should have the guest sign the check again and then compare the signatures.

There are a number of things that front office personnel and cashiers should know and keep in mind when dealing with checks. A real check should have a perforation on at least one side and should state the name, branch, city, and state where the bank is located. A government check will have a distinct watermark and thread embedded within the paper. A payroll check usually has the name of the employer printed on it. In most instances, "payroll" is also printed on the check. The employee's name is printed by a check writing machine or typed. In metropolitan areas, properties often choose not to cash a payroll check that is hand printed, rubber stamped, or typewritten, even if it appears to be issued by a local business and drawn on a local bank.

Employees should not accept starter checks, illegible checks, or checks with erasures or overwritten amounts. Checks should be signed in ink in the presence of the property's employee. The guest's signed name should conform to the name as it appears on the face of the check. Checks that are marked "For Deposit Only," "For Collection," or with similar terms should not be accepted.

Employees should not accept checks from guests without identification. When identification is offered, employees should ensure that all signatures, photo IDs, and/or physical descriptions match the person offering the identification. If a property requires its employees to write identifying information on the check (such as a driver's license number), the information should be written on the face of the check; bank stamps and clearinghouse imprints will often make any entries on the reverse of the check illegible.

Most authorities recommend against accepting post-dated checks. A check should not be accepted if it is not dated at all; some authorities also suggest not accepting checks more than thirty days old. The written and numerical amounts on the check should agree. Some properties do not accept checks from intoxicated persons.

Studies have shown that checks numbered 400 and below are statistically more likely to bounce than checks with higher numbers.

Almost every check a property will ever see has a series of magnetic ink characters (numbers) starting at or near the lower left corner on the face of the check. On a good check, no light will reflect from these numbers when the check is tilted to the light. If the light reflects, the check was not printed by a bank and is very likely fraudulent. With the increasing sophistication of reproduction processes, checks may be reproduced that are extremely difficult to recognize as phony. Nonetheless, the numbers on many such copies will be shiny. Employees finding such checks should run a finger across the front. If the print smears, the check is fraudulent. Watermarks and paper quality should also be considered when judging the validity of the check being presented.

Although the widespread availability of ATMs has reduced the need for and use of traveler's checks (often spelled cheques), a property should also be alert for counterfeit checks. Traveler's check companies can inform a property how to spot fraudulent checks.

Denying Credit to a Guest

If a property checks a guest's credit properly, it greatly reduces the likelihood of subsequent trouble. But when a property has found a guest's credit to be poor or otherwise insufficient, how does it inform the guest of this fact?

When speaking to a guest about his or her credit, the hotel or motel employee should realize that more than money is involved. The guest may perceive his or her dignity, pride, even self-respect to be under attack. The employee should be as diplomatic as possible. His or her voice and manner should be friendly and calm, no matter how belligerent the guest is. This section contains a few tips on how to deal with this difficult task. They should be modified as necessary to fit the situation at hand, the guest involved, and the property's own philosophy.

When a credit card company will not allow a guest to charge a purchase to a card, the employee should not state this fact in a voice loud enough to be overheard by anyone other than the affected guest. The employee should not refer to the card as "bad" or "worthless." He or she should not ask the guest to leave the premises immediately or either threaten to or actually telephone the police. Instead, the employee should quietly ask the guest to step into an office or other area out of earshot of others; once there, the guest should be informed that further use of the credit card has not been approved by the card company. If the guest asks what that means, the employee is not obligated to explain a credit card company's policy. The property should, however, offer the use of its telephone so that the guest can speak with a credit card company representative to clear up the matter. The employee should also allow the guest a chance to explain or to provide another means of payment.

When a guest insists on presenting a check that, due to hotel/motel policy, cannot be cashed, the employee may note the availability of an ATM in the lobby of the hotel or at another nearby location.

Guest Registration and Check-Out

Reservations. Most guests make reservations through telephone contacts (often by calling a chain's toll-free central reservations system) or electronically via the Internet. If a property requires a deposit to hold a room for a late arrival, it should ensure that the guest knows when that payment is due. If the property will accept a check for this deposit, it should consider allowing enough time for the check to clear before the guest's arrival.

Registration. A hotel cannot reclaim lodging services already provided if the customer decides to leave without paying. When checking in, guests should be required to make acceptable payment arrangements. Certain registration procedures can reduce the potential for later problems.

If a property has its guests manually fill out its registration cards, it should require them to *print* the information legibly. If there are illegible numbers or words, the room clerk should ask the guest to state the information aloud. The clerk should then print the clarification next to the guest's writing. The clerk should also make certain that the guest signs the card. If the property pre-prints guest information on registration cards, guests should verify the information and sign the card.

Many properties ask for quite a lot of information at registration—for example, both home and business telephone numbers, home and business addresses, make of car, license plate number, and more. The purpose of getting so much information is to make it easier to find the guest if there are later collection problems.

Front desk agents should be trained to verify the completeness of registration information. For example, if a guest does not specify "Avenue," "Street," "Boulevard," "Drive," or so forth for a street address, the agent should ask for this information and complete the address. When possible, the property should compare the guest's actual automobile license plates with what he or she has provided.

When guests pay room charges and tax in advance, a property will need to decide whether it will require them to make a deposit toward telephone, valet, laundry, and other services provided by the property. Properties not requiring such a deposit may explain courteously to the guests that they should be certain to stop at the desk when they check out so that they can pay any accumulated charges.

Lodging properties should consider developing policies regarding guests wishing to pay cash. For example, many properties require payment in advance for such guests for at least the first night. The guests may also be informed that they are on a cash basis at the property. When cash-paying guests check in, there should be a procedure that will notify the property's various departments of this fact. In order to identify cash-paying guests quickly, some properties mark their folios "Paid in Advance," "Cash Only," or with some similar designation.

Checking Out. If reservation and/or check-in procedures have been handled carefully and guests' high balances have been monitored each day, checking out is in most cases a very simple procedure. Generally, guests appear at the front desk to return their room keys and report that they are checking out. The front desk agent should always ask whether a guest has had any late charges (telephone calls, breakfast or room service charges, and so forth). An increasing number of properties eliminate some of the doubt about late charges by using computers and POS terminals that record charges instantaneously to the guest folios. The cashier then presents the totaled bill, allows the guest to review it, and accepts payment (usually by the method determined during registration) or, if appropriate, reminds the guest that he or she will be direct-billed.

In an effort to expedite the check-out process, bills may be placed under the door on the morning of check-out, or the billing information may be available via the guestroom television. The guest may call a special telephone number or, using an interactive TV connection, check out of the room. The key may be left in the room, and the guest may leave the property without standing in line at the front desk. However, care must be taken that charges and other guest information are not compromised through failure to place the guest bill sufficiently under the door to avoid recovery by an unauthorized person who may have criminal intent.

Computer Security

Proprietary guest information and operational statistics are among the most valuable assets that a hospitality property can possess. We have already discussed the significant security procedures and requirements under the PCI DSS. Much of this standard concerns computer security.

Both paper and electronic records are subject to physical damage from fire, flood, and so forth. Electronic records may also be vulnerable to threats that are not as visible, but can be just as devastating. The flexibility and interconnectedness that make networked systems so valuable also make them subject to internal and external threats, both deliberate and random. There are three broad categories of system security threats:

- *Environmental.* Environmental threats include situations or events that threaten the infrastructure of the system. Major concerns include fire, flood, earthquake, power failure, and loss of external network connectivity. Hospitality properties need to protect all locations housing essential system components, as well as design and implement a disaster recovery plan that provides a detailed explanation of system maintenance in the event of a major catastrophe.

- *Electrical.* Data can be corrupted accidentally or on purpose through viruses, hacker attacks, and other malicious acts distributed across the network resources. The installation of an uninterruptible power supply, firewall protection, and anti-virus software is critical to system security.

- *Operational.* Accidental or intentional data entry errors, programming bugs, system circumvention, accidental deletions or modifications, and deliberate data corruption by current or former staff form a significant set of security threats. Restricting access through biometric identification, password authorization, or other means is important to data integrity and security.

Clearly, computer technology has given the lodging industry another security concern. Each lodging operation should regularly conduct a complete risk assessment and audit of all computer systems to uncover specific areas of vulnerability. This entails an assessment of the risk associated with the loss of each and all systems as well as all data stored on those systems. This assessment should be repeated annually or as new systems are brought online and legacy systems are replaced. Exhibit 2 presents the kinds of questions that an information systems audit should address.

Exhibit 2   Sample Information Systems Audit

Information Systems Audit
(Please comment on or explain any "No" responses.)

A. Computer Room/Physical Systems

1. Is the computer room in a quiet area, not on an outside wall, and not where it might be subject to flooding?

2. Does it have a self-closing, self-locking door? What kind of lock is fitted?

3. Who has access?

4. Is there a separate air-conditioning unit for the computer room?

5. Are temperature and humidity measured on a periodic basis to confirm that they are within specified ranges?
    a. Who performs the measurements?
    b. Attach copy of most recent page of log.

6. Is there a fire alarm/smoke detector in the computer room?

7. Is it a local alarm system? If not, where else does the alarm get indicated?

8. When was it last tested?

9. Is there a local fire extinguishing system in the computer room?
    a. What type?
    b. When was it last inspected? (Attach copy of log.)

10. Is the power for all critical systems on a separate electrical circuit with clearly marked outlets?

11. Are all critical systems on UPSs with sufficient battery backup for at least 20 minutes?
    a. When was the last check of the backup's reliability under full load performed?
    b. Do the battery backup systems provide automatic shutdown of the computer after a specified length of time?
    c. When was this last tested?

12. Are all peripherals (PCs, printers, scanners, etc.) connected to surge-suppressing power strips?

13. Are preventive maintenance inspections being performed regularly? (This includes physical hardware—filter changes, etc.—and any software preventive maintenance such as NT server re-boots, re-booting the PMS to reclaim memory, etc.)

14. Is the computer room kept clean?

15. Is all cabling tidy and clearly labeled?

16. Is there a network diagram? (Attach copy.) Are procedures in place to keep it current?

17. Is there an inventory of all computer hardware?
    a. How often is it checked, and by whom?
    b. What is done if something is missing?

Exhibit 2   *(continued)*

18. Is there an inventory of all software applications and operating systems?
   a. How often is it checked, and by whom?
   b. Do proper licenses exist for all software?
   c. What is done if the number of copies in use exceeds the number of legal licenses?

19. Are there full, written descriptions of all computer systems and interfaces, including configuration, support information, current version level and modification history?

20. Are procedures with regard to fire, flood, or other emergencies posted in the computer room and understood by all who have access to the room and equipment?

21. Is there a disaster recovery plan? (Attach copy.)
   a. When was the last time it was tested?
   b. Where is the plan posted?

B. Information Security

1. When are full/partial backups done? (Attach copy of plan.)
   a. Who performs the backups?
   b. Attach copy of log.

2. Where are the backups stored?
   a. In what type of container?
   b. Who has access to the media?
   c. Where is the off-site storage location?

3. How are verifications done to ensure the backup is working properly?

4. When was the last verification done?

5. Are downtime reports run to a specific schedule? (Attach copy.)

6. Are obsolete reports destroyed?

7. What redundancy is there for the critical computer systems?
   a. Are there complete backup computers/hardware?
   b. When were the computer/software maintenance contracts last reviewed for all critical systems?
   c. Is there an action plan for failure of the backup?
   d. When was it last tested?

8. Are all support contact numbers posted by the equipment?

9. Are the trouble logs kept with the systems or in an accessible location? (Attach copy.)

10. Are written procedures for manual operations posted at all appropriate locations?
   a. When were they last practiced?

(continued)

Exhibit 2 *(continued)*

---

   b. Are "crash kits" of office supplies, pre-filled forms, etc., kept available and fully stocked?

C. Network Security

1. How often are system and user passwords changed?

   a. Who determines the passwords?

   b. Are they secure? (At least 6 characters, mixed case and alphanumeric, not easily connected with any specific user.)

2. Is a procedure in place to ensure that employees leaving the company have no access to the systems?

3. Does the current password list match the personnel list?

4. Are all operating system patches/fixes up to date?

5. Is a network-wide anti-virus program installed?

   a. Are all the virus signatures/software updates current?

   b. How often are the servers scanned for viruses?

   c. Is there a written policy regarding the use of diskettes?

6. Are there any outside connections to the Local Area Network?

   a. If the connections are made using a modem on an individual computer, who has control over the connection(s) and the account(s)?

   b. If it is a direct connection into the LAN by a router or other similar device, who maintains the connection, hardware configuration, and passwords for the device?

   c. Is there a firewall?

   d. Who maintains it?

7. Have password cracking programs or external security consultants been employed to help determine the level of security?

D. Employee Security

1. Are new employees required to sign a written policy regarding computer usage and abuse?

2. Are there written procedures and policies for access to the Internet, including e-mail and browsing?

3. Are there written procedures for securing the computer systems when an employee is terminated?

   (Attach copies of all such policies and procedures.)

Source: Michael L. Kasavana, *Managing Technology in the Hospitality Industry,* Sixth Ed. (Lansing, Mich.: American Hotel & Lodging Educational Institute, 2011), pp. 314–316.

A strong information technology security program will cover a number of key areas, including:

- Accountability
- System auditability

- Integrity of systems and data
- Cost effectiveness
- Ease of implementation
- Policy compliance

Accountability

The structure and resources of lodging organizations usually require that one person carry the responsibility for overall computer system security. In many properties, this is either the controller or the director of management information systems (MIS) or information technology (IT). However, every user must be held accountable for protecting the information resources of the property and the corporation. Sharing system or file access passwords or providing other information that could allow unauthorized access to a property's systems is equivalent to company sabotage or theft. It becomes important, therefore, to limit access to information and systems to those users who require such access to perform their assigned duties.

Auditability

It is the responsibility of the designated systems security officer to know when users are accessing information, what they are accessing or modifying, and when and how unauthorized attempts to access a system are being made.

The use of unique passwords is one method of authorizing use and protecting computer data. When a property uses passwords, it should strongly encourage employees to avoid writing them down. Any master list of passwords—whether on paper or electronic—should be protected from unauthorized access. Some properties choose to change passwords at random; some computer systems prompt for new passwords at regular intervals. Passwords of employees who have left or been transferred or terminated should be permanently deleted from the system.

In order to maintain an audit trail and monitor system usage, system administrators should activate access, violation, and modification logs that track password use. Access logs provide an electronic record of each attempt to log on to a system. Violation logs record who attempted to violate system or file-level security, and modification logs record user information on all files that have been modified. In some systems, it is possible to have such logs activate an alarm when data gathered in the log fall outside established parameters. Such notification allows the system administrator the opportunity to locate the source of the potential security risk.

System Integrity

There is no security plan or system for computers that is 100 percent foolproof. Since unauthorized access can come from inside or outside a property, it is important to prevent hacking into a system on both fronts. It is the responsibility of the appointed systems security officer to perform due diligence as it relates to system integrity, keeping the system continuously operational without data loss or security incident.

Computer Viruses. Computer viruses are destructive computer programs that can "infect" a computer and damage data files, system files, and applications. Viruses can replicate themselves and can be transmitted as hidden files or programs from one computer to another. The most destructive way viruses are spread is over the Internet. Internet mail attachments are notorious for carrying computer viruses. These programs are attached to e-mail messages and then sent to numerous users. The unsuspecting user then opens the mail and carelessly infects the computer with a virus. It is also possible to pick up a virus simply by visiting an Internet site that has been compromised.

The most effective way to prevent the spread of computer viruses is to use an anti-virus computer program. These programs work as virus shields, scanning files for known computer viruses as they are opened or run. If a virus is detected, it is immediately cleaned from the system or otherwise quarantined. These programs can be set to periodically scan the entire computer for viruses. Virus protection programs are extremely effective when installed on a server and used in a local area network (LAN). In this situation, any data stored on the server can be scanned and cleaned on a regular basis. Because new computer viruses are constantly being developed and circulated, virus-protection software should be updated often to ensure the best protection possible. Most such programs check for updates automatically if the system administrator allows it to do so. Virus libraries are updated almost daily.

Internet Connectivity. When computers have access to the Internet as well as corporate and local area networks, it is important to protect data from unauthorized distribution over the Internet. It is especially critical to control Internet access centrally in any property where computers are connected to the hotel LAN and to the Internet via a modem. Anytime there is a modem on a PC, there is the possibility for unauthorized transmission of data. It is more secure to provide Internet access via the network so that a firewall can be put in place to protect the hotel's data and systems. **Firewalls** are communications filters that allow only authorized access and data transmission to and from a network.

Access Restrictions. The more people who have access to a computer, the greater the possibility for compromised security. Implementing certain access restrictions can help to maintain system integrity.

One type of restricted access involves the creation of different levels of authorization for access to different levels of information. Such systems limit the information available to employees to only those areas necessary for the performance of their jobs. Front desk staff, for example, would be limited to computer access relating to the check-in and check-out functions only.

In some hotels, it may be necessary to limit the time periods during which computers may be accessed. This can be managed through the user rights and privileges aspect of a network operating system. For example, users may be granted access to the network only between 9:00 A.M. and 5:00 P.M. This prevents access to data when there is no network administrator available to monitor data activity.

Embezzlement. Embezzlement is a major crime against which computers should be protected. With a little knowledge of programming, it is fairly easy to set up dummy accounts in order to embezzle money. Funds may be directed to such accounts for long periods of time before being detected. The use of passwords and restricted levels of access help to safeguard a property's assets, but it is not possible to completely eliminate the potential for someone to bypass these safeguards. Security systems can only make it difficult for unauthorized persons to gain access to the computer; authorized personnel may be in positions of authority that allow them access to important restricted information that they use for illegitimate purposes.

There are a number of ways to reduce the potential for embezzlement by computer. Some involve the same procedures used for preventing embezzlement of any sort. For example, just as there is in the accounting function, there should be a separation of duties. The computer programmer should not also be the computer operator. This separation of duties prevents the programmer from building loopholes into the program to permit access later for personal profit. Also, the computerized check writing operation should be separated from the department that authorizes checks, in order to keep false data from resulting in actual cash payments. A single individual should not be able to generate a payment. Some properties use a mandatory vacation policy to ensure that every employee's work—including that of potential embezzlers with access to the computer—is periodically reviewed by someone else (that is, the employee who substitutes for the vacationing employee).

Outside computer services. Perhaps somewhat surprisingly, protection from computer embezzlement and fraud may sometimes be enhanced through the use of outside computer services. Although this practice involves revealing internal information to persons outside the organization, the people seeing it will generally have little personal use for it—especially if the service is well organized and conscious of the security requirements of its clients. Employees within outside computer services seldom have the opportunity to gain the familiarity with a lodging property that is needed to effectively embezzle its assets. This is especially true when the lodging property assigns different computer responsibilities to more than one outside computer service. Contrast this with the situation in which corrupt or potentially corrupt internal employees have such detailed knowledge of the workings of the property that they are relatively well equipped to embezzle in ways that are hard to detect.

Of course, care should be taken in selecting an outside service. A property choosing a service should ensure that the service has an effective internal security program. This involves not only protecting the confidentiality of the information entrusted to the service, but also taking adequate precautions against hazards such as fire, flood, vandalism, civil disturbances, power blackouts, and more. The service also should be financially sound; services that are not may be more susceptible to the temptation to misuse their positions of trust. Also, there is the potential for records and documents to be tied up indefinitely if the service goes bankrupt.

Physical Access to Servers. The server room or main computer room in a property should be secured in an area separate from other operations, protected by adequate locks and double-door entry. All movement of personnel into the area should be controlled, and access should be granted only to those who work with the network. A log should be maintained in computer operating areas detailing any stoppages and any resulting problems. Such records should be maintained and reviewed regularly by supervisory personnel.

Physical Protection of the Computer. Computer security involves more than protecting against fraud or vandalism. The computer itself should be maintained and protected from numerous hazards that could temporarily or permanently incapacitate it.

The greatest danger is fire. Computer rooms should be constructed of fire-proof or fire-resistant materials. Sprinkler systems may be useful, although flooding is not good for computers either. Systems that use special gases that rapidly extinguish fires are available, but they are expensive to maintain. Review the local fire code requirements; some jurisdictions mandate water sprinkler systems in addition to or in place of chemical systems. Employees should be trained in how to react quickly and effectively to a fire in the computer room or a fire that may threaten the computer room. Because simple overheating can also be a problem, computer rooms are often air conditioned.

Properties also should take measures to protect against power failures that may disrupt computer functions. One strategy is to route all computer equipment through an uninterrupted power supply (UPS) unit. Common IT problems such as electrical outages should have recovery procedures detailed in a disaster handbook. These procedures should provide step-by-step instructions on how to maintain critical systems using backup power facilities and how to recover any transactions that were in process when the outage occurred.

Computer equipment, although increasingly affordable, is still coveted by many unscrupulous individuals. It is therefore paramount that desktop equipment be secured in place to prevent theft. Anti-theft systems include those that can be used to mount equipment to a base that is then secured to a desk or the floor, cable and lock systems, and systems that use fiber-optic cable and an integrated alarm system.

Finally, every hotel should develop a comprehensive disaster recovery plan that includes procedures for recovery from both natural disasters and premeditated, malicious attacks on critical information systems.

Data Backup. It is most important that all critical data on a hotel's network be backed up each day. Additionally, critical report information should be printed at regular intervals in case of emergency or system outage. For instance, room occupancy and guest information should be printed regularly (for each shift) so that room status can be determined in the event of the system going down.

In some instances, corporate policies will govern backup procedures and the storage of backup media. Otherwise, each property should develop adequate procedures that meet the needs of that property.

Cost Effectiveness

While cost effectiveness is important, it also is important to gain the commitment from senior management to invest in the appropriate level of resources to protect the information systems of the property. In all cases, the level of resources allocated to securing data should be directly proportional to the value of the data to the organization. Systems in student computer labs, for example, may hold data that can be easily replaced or reinstalled; therefore, data security is not a high priority. However, an organization with irreplaceable proprietary business information might use data encryption on all file transmissions, implement redundant data storage, and manage all security procedures closely; the financial life of the organization may depend upon it.

Ease of Implementation

Data and system security should be relatively easy to implement. An overly complex system may be underutilized or incorrectly set up because it is too difficult to work with, thereby compromising system integrity. A system should be flexible enough to assign access to system resources and information as needed without using extensive IT staff resources. Frequently, network operating systems allow system administrators to grant company-wide access by user type. Many hotel property management systems allow for the assignment of user rights by job function: the front office manager would have additional rights to those granted to the reservationist or the guest services representative who works the front desk. These are easily implemented user parameters that are controlled by the application or by the system software.

Policy Compliance

In addition to a well-designed security plan, complete with policies and procedures related to accountability, auditability, cost effectiveness, and ease of implementation, IT managers must be concerned with general safeguards against unauthorized access to data and continuous system operation.

Additional policies and procedures may be set to ensure data security. Password protection of system and file access is a classic example of a basic security parameter. Computer systems sometimes come with default passwords. Default passwords should be deleted once the system is configured and functioning properly. Once any password is revealed, it is useless as a security parameter. It is therefore important to implement policy associated with password management. The severity of the policy depends on the needs of the organization. For example, requiring users to change their password daily on a restaurant POS system would be counterproductive. However, implementing the same policy in the accounting department might be considered prudent, especially when any personnel with system administrative privileges leave the organization.

Computer security involves many aspects of the computer system. It is important that IT managers or the responsible party at the hotel property consider all aspects of computer security. Additionally, security managers should communicate to other hotel employees the importance of security and their role in the effectiveness of the overall security of the hotel's information systems.

An Internal Audit Program

Internal auditing has been defined as being the eyes and ears of an operation's owners or management.

An **internal audit** is an appraisal function set up to identify, examine and evaluate the effectiveness of an establishment's internal risk control system. An internal audit program should provide effective recommendations or solutions that will reduce the internal control risk The auditing process offers owners, investors, corporate staff, and the hotel managers a detailed analysis concerning the hotel's operations. Internal auditors examine every phase of operations to ensure that all company assets are properly recorded and safeguarded and that company operations are conducted in an efficient and businesslike manner. To be effective, the auditing process must span departments, encompassing financial activities and such areas as food and beverage, engineering, marketing and sales, and human resources.

Internal auditors are responsible for performing the following tasks:

- Determining that company policies are followed

- Determining that internal controls are adequate

- Suggesting improvements in practices and procedures to obtain increased efficiency or to lower operating costs

- Detecting fraud or manipulation of records or at least identifying red flags that indicate possible fraud or manipulation of records

- Providing recommendations for strengthening the organization's internal control environment

The internal auditor is ever watchful for any activity or failure that could cause a company to become party to a lawsuit or be subject to punitive action by a government agency.

Management has two options when it comes to obtaining an objective, analytical review of a specific operation. The internal audit team may comprise company personnel assigned to that task, or the hotel can outsource the internal auditing function to professionals trained in the art of analyzing records, controls, and procedures.

According to a survey conducted by the Institute of Internal Auditors, the primary reason hoteliers consider outsourcing is the perception of reduced costs. However, internal audit directors generally expressed the opinion that, as a permanent employee, an internal auditor develops a better understanding of organizational methods and can provide improved responsiveness and loyalty to the company's goals and vision. Outside contractors, such as CPA firms, rely on standardized checklists that apply to traditional operations. One weakness of CPA firms is that they are not familiar with the inner workings of hotels, therefore may not be able to recognize the possible "red flags" of fraud. Internal auditors, because they are involved in the day-to-day operations, are more familiar with the unique internal workings of the organization and are able to tailor their approach accordingly. In addition, because of their greater intimacy with the inner workings of their hotel's systems, staff auditors may be better equipped to detect fraud. On the other hand, staff auditors also will have close ties with others in the hotel, which may impair their ability to be wholly unbiased and honest. As a result, the hotel may be given a less-than-accurate appraisal, and significant problems may go unaddressed. Clearly, there are strengths and weaknesses to either approach that must be weighed.

Individual auditors may report to an audit committee, which may in turn report to the board of directors. If an outside agency is employed, that agency also would report to the audit committee.

Endnotes

1. Dorian Cougias, Securing Payments: What the Payment Card Industry Data Security Standard Means for Your Resort. Eighth Annual Resort Conference, San Diego, CA, April 18, 2008.

2. For more information, see Mark G. Haley and Daniel J. Connolly, *The Payment Card Industry Compliance Process for Lodging Establishments* (Washington, D.C.: American Hotel & Lodging Association, 2008).

3. Visa, Inc. (2008, February 27). *Security Best Practices for Level 4 Merchants and Franchise Operators: Payment System Security Compliance.*

Key Terms

firewalls—Communications filters on networked computer systems that allow only authorized access and data transmission to and from the network.

floor limit—The maximum amount of credit per credit card that is allowed by the sponsoring credit card company. Such companies may refuse payment for charges that exceed this limit, unless prior approval of the specific charges is sought. It is up to the hotel to know and observe the floor limit established by each credit card company.

internal audit—An appraisal function set up to identify, examine, and evaluate the effectiveness of an establishment's internal risk control system; it should provide effective recommendations or solutions that will reduce the internal control risk.

separation of duties—An element of internal control systems in which important multi-step tasks are divided among many people so no single person controls enough of the process to easily defraud or steal from the company.

Review Questions

1. Why should accounting functions be handled by different staff members?

2. What are some of the typical cashiering procedures?

3. What precautionary steps can employees take when presented with a payment card?

4. What is the Payment Card Industry Data Security Standard? Why is it critically important? To whom does it apply?

5. What is a second- or third-party check, and why do many properties choose not to accept them?

6. What questions must a property consider when accepting personal checks?

7. How should a guest's credit be denied, when necessary?

8. Why are incomplete or illegible guest registration records a problem?

9. What key areas are covered by a strong information technology security program?

10. What tasks are internal auditors responsible for performing?

Internet Sites

For more information, visit the following Internet sites. Remember that Internet addresses can change without notice. If the site is no longer there, you can use a search engine to look for additional sites.

Hospitality Financial & Technology
  Professionals
www.hftp.org

ISACA
www.isaca.org

The Institute of Internal Auditors
www.theiia.org

Case Study

Points of Internal Control at the Eastwick Resort

Scenario #1—Purchasing

Percy Purveyor, a hotel supplier, sat opposite the general manager of the Eastwick Resort, Guy Thorpe. Percy was meeting with him to satisfy his curiosity—and to air a grievance.

"I've been in business in this area for a few years now, Guy, and I know my competitors' products and prices well. Your property has been using Electrotel products all its life, and I know for sure that my goods are of better quality than theirs. Our price ranges are pretty close. I'm dying to know what kind of discount they're giving you to make you so faithful to them all this time."

"Discount? None but the usual one for the volume we purchase," said Guy.

"Not even a discount for timely payment?"

"Well, yes, that too, but those are the only two. Why are you so surprised?"

"That makes Electrotel's deal with you even worse. My volume discount and discount for timely payment are even better than theirs, and my rates are still comparable—for a better product." Percy leaned back and looked thoughtfully at Guy. "Your purchasing agent shows only a hint of interest when I make a pitch; it seems like he's just not listening. None of my solid arguments for considering my company's products reach him. It boggles my mind that someone could consistently choose a clearly inferior series of products at higher prices. Has your customer base changed to warrant lower-end products?"

Guy bristled. "Certainly not. This remains a property for the business traveler and upscale leisure market."

Percy shrugged. "It was just a thought. Your purchasing policies mystify me."

"I have noticed that our property lags behind comparable ones in purchasing efficiency," mused Guy. "By more than five thousand dollars some months. I'll tell you what: Let's meet again at the end of the month and talk about your products some more. Between now and then, there's some research I'd like to do."

Scenario #2—Check Cashing

The Eastwick Resort received two returned checks from the bank this week. One was a personal check for $250 that was dated March 18, and the hotel had tried to cash it March 17; and the other was a corporate check for $1,000.

The corporate check looked valid, with two signatures by financial officers and "Travel" in the memo space. When hotel staff called the corporation, they found that the check was indeed valid but only for authorized corporate agents, and the guest the hotel had hosted was not authorized.

Furthermore, the guest tricked the hotel into giving him almost $860 in cash by saying that though the corporation had prepaid his expenses for a week-long stay, he was going to leave after one night and would like to be reimbursed for the difference.

Scenario #3—Payroll

Almost all the housekeeping staff at the Eastwick Resort are part-time employees, and turnover is high. Recently, payroll expenses have increased significantly, but the general manager believes that the actual number of employees has dropped. When Guy Thorpe calls in his housekeeping manager, Jay, even Jay doesn't know for sure how many room attendants currently are (and should be) on the payroll. Some are on leave for various reasons, some have made it unclear whether they still want to work for the property, and so on. "We may have ghosting going on— someone could be setting up fictitious employees on the payroll and collecting their 'wages,'" Guy tells Jay.

Scenario #4—Linen Loss

The housekeeping department at the Eastwick Resort has been losing six to eight sheets per week. Jay and his assistant normally take inventory monthly, but they started taking it weekly when they noticed losses. Jay decided that the volume of loss is too high and too consistent to be attributable to guest theft, so he turns his attention to employees.

Scenario #5—Room Charges

Celia Sly has just treated several of her close friends to a hearty lunch at the Eastwick Resort's restaurant. When the server presents the check, Celia asks her to charge it to room 213. The server agrees to take care of it.

Scenario #6—Cash Drawers

The restaurant at the Eastwick Resort has been trying a new system of distributing cash drawers. In an effort to promote cooperation and to create an atmosphere of trust with and among its employees, it has made all three cashiers on a given shift responsible for all three cash drawers the restaurant uses. Managers hoped that cashiers would develop team spirit and that they might prevent other cashiers from stealing. This system worked fine at first, but recently, the cash drawers have been short by a total of about $20 after every shift. The cashiers have become suspicious of each other and have complained loudly to managers.

Discussion Questions

1. For each scenario, what policies and procedures could be implemented to prevent the type of loss concerned? What can managers do to deal with the situation before them?

2. Which of the scenarios would require action from the security department and which would require action from other departments?

3. Suppose that the Eastwick Resort's profit goal was 12 percent. If the operation managed to recover none of its losses from the events described above, how much would the operation have to achieve in sales to recoup its losses? Use the figures given below:

Scenario #1 Purchasing	$5,000/month × 12 months =	$60,000
Scenario #2 Check Cashing	$250 + $1,750 + $50 in fees =	$ 2,050
Scenario #3 Payroll	$200 in stolen wages per week × 52 weeks =	$10,400
Scenario #4 Linen Loss	$65 in lost sheet value per week × 52 weeks =	$ 3,380
Scenario #5 Room Charges	$85 meal × 52 weeks =	$ 4,420
Scenario #6 Cash Drawers	$20 × 14 shifts/week × 52 weeks =	$14,560

Case Number: 3875CA

The following industry experts helped generate and develop this case: Wendell Couch, ARM, CHA, Director of Technical Services for the Risk Management Department of Bass Hotels & Resorts; and Raymond C. Ellis, Jr., CHE, CHTP, CLSD, Professor, Conrad N. Hilton College, University of Houston, Director, Loss Prevention Management Institute.

Chapter 9 Outline

Competencies

1. Describe the role of an emergency management plan. (pp. 287–291)

2. Demonstrate knowledge of safety and security measures for responding appropriately to a variety of emergency situations, including bombs and bomb threats, fires, hurricanes and typhoons, tornadoes, floods, earthquakes, and tsunamis. (pp. 291–306)

3. Summarize procedures for handling blackouts, robberies, medical and dental emergencies, and terrorism. (pp. 306–318)

4. Outline a viable media relations response in the event of an emergency situation. (pp. 319–323)

9

Emergency Management and Media Relations

$\mathbf{A}$S THE HOSPITALITY INDUSTRY expands throughout the globe, it finds itself facing emergency situations somewhere on a regular basis. All hospitality managers must be prepared to effectively deal with, and fully recover from, emergencies of many kinds. Some emergencies involve natural forces (hurricanes, floods, etc.); others are caused by people (robberies, acts of terrorism, and so on). Managers must not only cope with these emergencies but also cope with the media attention that often follows. In the media-saturated world in which we live, media relations are certainly an important part of dealing with any emergency.

This chapter addresses an unfortunately long list of potential emergency situations that may affect hotels: bombs and bomb threats, fires, hurricanes and typhoons, tornadoes, floods, earthquakes and tsunamis, blackouts, robberies, medical and dental emergencies, and terrorism. The chapter will then explore constructive ways of working with the media to successfully recover from an emergency and rebuild a positive reputation. The Five P's should be the watchword for all managers preparing as best they can for the possible emergencies that they can foresee: Proper Planning Prevents Poor Performance.

Developing an Emergency Management Program

Emergency or contingency planning is an important element in the security of a lodging establishment. The degree of emergency preparation that is necessary or even feasible will vary from property to property. Management should consider: What resources, equipment, and staff members should be or can be directed to the property's emergency management program? Will community or governmental agencies be involved in achieving an acceptable program? Where will the control center be located? Who will be in charge? What is the order of command to cover situations when the top members of management may be unable to assume leadership roles? Questions like these are relevant to emergency management planning.

In developing an emergency (or contingency) plan for a hotel, management should consider the following items:

- The potential for various types of emergencies to occur

- Liaison possibilities with other lodging properties in the community; service organizations such as the Red Cross and Salvation Army; local governmental agencies, including police and fire authorities; and local utility companies

- Personnel needs, availability, and skills

- Equipment, supply, and communications needs

- Training opportunities to prepare the staff for an emergency

- Opportunities for emergency preparedness and simulated emergency drills at the community level

Managers should remember that each property is different. As with so many other aspects of the successful operation and administration of a hotel, the emergency program must be developed on an individual basis to take into account the unique attributes and needs of the property in question.

An initial step might be the formation of an executive-level committee within the property to help establish the emergency plan. This executive-level committee might include all department heads in addition to the general manager, assistant managers, and resident manager. In a small property, such a committee could include the owner and/or manager and at least one or two additional key personnel.

Once formed, the committee should begin by identifying possible emergencies the property might face, taking into account such factors as the property's location, size, and other factors. The following emergencies and any others that may be appropriate to a given property should be reviewed to determine whether any are likely to affect the hotel: bomb threats or bombings, fire, hurricanes, tornadoes, floods, earthquakes, blackouts, blizzards, ice storms, kidnappings, hostage situations, medical or dental emergencies, snipers, workplace violence, riots and other civil disorders, mudslides, contaminated water supplies, food poisoning, elevator emergencies, lightning, forest fires, hazardous materials spills, etc., etc. Of course, some emergencies are impossible to predict.

After a hotel's managers decide which emergency events have the most potential to occur at the property, they should then determine which local agencies will provide support in the event of an emergency. Such agencies may provide resources and backup prior to, during, and after an emergency, which can be coordinated with the property's emergency program. The ten regional offices of the Federal Emergency Management Agency or FEMA (a division of the Department of Homeland Security) have established emergency programs under the direction of the national FEMA office. On the Internet, the regional FEMA offices maintain a continuing reporting service on various emergencies within the ten regions, along with various resources to assist an individual property and its community in meeting an emergency. The FEMA emergency programs are an ongoing coordinated effort to prepare the public for emergency situations. Lining up support from FEMA and other agencies "before the fact" is the difference between merely having a written plan sitting on a shelf somewhere and effective, active planning. The FEMA publication *Emergency Management Guide for Business and Industry* is a resource managers and others can use to help them with their emergency management planning.[1]

A number of other local organizations can be contacted and included in a hotel's emergency planning. Managers should consider including the American Red Cross, the Salvation Army (or a similar organization with emergency housing, clothing, and feeding capabilities), the local civil defense or integrated emergency management systems office, local utility companies, police and fire departments, the weather forecasting service, National Guard units, the building inspector's department, and various local service organizations (such as the Lions Club or Rotary Club) and fraternal organizations (such as the Masons, Shriners, and Knights of Columbus).

Another critical element in the development of an emergency response plan is the assessment of the property's personnel. Managers should inventory the skills of staff members and find out whether any employees are certified in first aid, lifesaving (water rescue), or cardiopulmonary resuscitation (CPR); or skilled in carpentry, electrical work, plumbing, mechanical work, or food preparation under emergency conditions (for example, preparing food over a wood fire).

After this information has been compiled, emergency program planners may ask themselves various questions about the possible circumstances that may be faced at the hotel during an emergency. What staff will be available if a natural disaster involves the whole community? How many of the staff will be able to reach the hotel? Will it be possible for staff members with special skills to reach the hotel? What will the on-site alternative be if skilled staff persons are unable to reach the property? Are there provisions to allow key staff to bring family members with them to avoid having to cover responsibilities in two different locations? Is there a plan for handling an emergency when only one key staff member is on duty? What backup is feasible, and how soon can backup be provided? Can cooperative agreements be arranged in advance with other lodging properties in the area?

As a result of thinking about such questions, management can then consider the formation of emergency response teams. Generally, the composition of an emergency response team will vary according to the nature of the emergency. Management should consider staff and material needs on an emergency-by-emergency basis. A natural disaster that affects the entire community puts the hotel into a different position than a fire, bomb threat, or hostage situation on the premises. The concentration of effort by the local fire and police authorities will be entirely different when responding to a single emergency at a hotel than it will be when responding to a community-wide problem, such as a flood or tornado.

When managers are structuring an emergency response team, the following elements should be addressed:

- Consider establishing responsibilities by department for appropriate response by the staff within the department.

- Consider establishing a command center with a pre-arranged chain of command; the front desk and PBX (or phone facility at the front desk in small properties) can serve as that command center. If the front desk is put out of commission as a result of an emergency, alternative command centers might be set up in the executive offices, security director's office, or chief engineer's office.

- In a community-wide emergency, the property itself may have to provide technical, mechanical, and even fire-fighting capability. Consider defining and assigning to specific personnel such responsibilities as food service, hous-ing, laundry, first aid, and construction repair as required by the nature of the particular emergency.

• It should be clearly explained to staff members that there is a single desig-nated spokesperson for the hotel. All employees should understand that they are not to talk to reporters or camera operators.

A review of equipment needs, including special equipment needs, should also be undertaken. Some possible equipment and supply needs include:

• Emergency lighting (including flashlights and light sticks); auxiliary genera-tors with reserve or alternative fuel supplies; sump pumps for relieving flood-ing problems; and emergency communications equipment.

• Food and water reserves. Consideration should be given to menu alternatives for times when cooking facilities are minimal or totally unavailable.

• Gas, battery, or manually operated tools for use in the event of power failure; and tools for cutting, lifting, and moving debris in the event of building col-lapse due to flooding, wind, or earthquakes.

• Shutters for covering glass surfaces.

• Bedding, cots, and bed linens, if the property is designated as a housing cen-ter in a community-wide incident.

• Diapers and infant formula.

• Gasoline for hotel and guest vehicles.

Properties should have an inspection and maintenance program in place for equipment assigned for emergency use. Managers should review the equipment they expect to operate during an emergency and the length of time they might need to operate this equipment. A key need will be an adequate supply of fuel to operate the emergency generator(s). If on-site fuel storage or availability is a prob-lem, plans should be in place to have supplemental fuel delivered. Keep in mind that massive power outages can also result in an inability of some fuel stations to operate if they also lose power. The following quote from a study done in the after-math of the Northeast Blackout of 2003 is unfortunately probably still true: "What I learned from that study [of the blackout] is that much of the hospitality industry was not and still is not prepared for unexpected events such as a protracted power failure. A tremendous effort by employees made it possible for hotels to continue to provide hospitality during the blackout, but the fact remains that service sys-tems remain largely vulnerable to unexpected events."[2]

A program that is tailored to deal with a variety of emergencies is more effec-tive if it is in writing (OSHA mandates that the fire emergency program *must* be in writing). The written plan should be flexible, but should also provide enough information and detail that each employee knows what his or her responsibilities are in the event of an emergency.

Once written programs are developed, they should be disseminated. How will all members of the staff be trained in their individual roles in implementing the emergency action plan? Investigate first aid, CPR, lifesaving, and emergency response training opportunities within the community. Managers should not limit the training to management and supervisory personnel. The more trained staff present, the more likely an effective response will be provided in an emergency. Some properties may want to consider expanding the training to permit key members of the property's staff to participate at the community level in emergency-preparedness drills and in simulated exercises.

As mandated by OSHA, fire drills and rehearsals must be conducted. Many lodging operations have full fire drills during the day or on an early evening shift. All guests are advised of the drill and may even be invited to participate to a limited degree. For example, they may be requested to go to the nearest exit, but not to use the exit stairway to leave the floor. Guest involvement is an opportunity for employees to actually direct guests in a simulated emergency evacuation.

Community rehearsal for a natural disaster provides an opportunity for a hotel's managers to deal realistically with a number of people—establishing emergency shelters or converting existing accommodations to provide for a large number of people, administering first aid for simulated injuries, and meeting any other requirements connected with a specific emergency. Properties interested in a community-wide exercise should advise local police, fire, and emergency management authorities of their interest. Some hotels may wish to volunteer their premises for housing, feeding, etc., as part of the community plan if the property is not directly affected by the emergency.

On-premises emergency-training sessions with local authorities may also be considered. These authorities should be invited to evaluate the operation as an integral part of the community emergency action plan.

Bombs and Bomb Threats

In recent years there have been a number of bombing incidents (and certainly many bomb threats) throughout the globe. Almost all of the bombs that have been detonated in the past ten years have been in locations outside the United States, with the bombing of the Boston Marathon on April 15, 2013, being a notable exception. A significant number of the international bombing incidents have targeted U.S. citizens, corporations, or the government.[3] U.S. and other lodging chains have found their overseas properties targets of bombs, resulting in substantial loss of life and property damage. This illustrates the need for hotels to have procedures in place to deal with bombs and bomb threats.

U.S. hotels are subject to a number of bomb threats every year. This can be illustrated by a simple Internet search using the phrase "hotel bomb threat." Unfortunately, such a search commonly reveals many recent examples of bomb threats made against hotels in the United States and elsewhere. Most of these threats are not related to terrorism, but are threats made by disgruntled or disturbed individuals with no political agenda. Because bomb threats are not as rare as some hotel managers might assume, procedures for responding to bombs and bomb threats should be included in any lodging property's emergency plans. These procedures should be in writing. (Hotel managers can review Exhibit 1 for help in establishing a similar checklist for use at their properties.) All staff members who are most likely to receive a bomb threat by phone should have copies of the bomb threat

Exhibit 1   Sample Bomb Threat Checklist

1. Date: _____   2. Origin of call:
   Time of call: _____   Local _____ Long Distance _____
   Time caller hung up: _____   Internal _____
3. Exact words of caller:

   _____

   _____

   (CONTINUE ON BACK IF NECESSARY)

4. Ask the following, if possible:
   a. When is the bomb set to go off? _____
   b. What kind of bomb is it? _____
   c. Where did you place the bomb? _____
   d. Why did you place the bomb? _____
   e. What is your name and address? _____

   _____

   f. What does the bomb look like? _____

5. Caller: Male _____   Female _____   Adult _____   Child _____
              Age _____   Suspect _____
6. Speech: Slow _____   Excited _____   Disguised ____   Rapid _____
              Loud _____   Accent _____   Normal _____   Sincere ___
              Drunk _____   Deep _____   Soft _____   Nasal _____
7. Have you received a bomb threat before?   Yes _____   No _____
8. Do not discuss call with other employees.
9. Immediately notify the following: General Manager
                                       Manager-on-Duty
                                       Security
10. Person taking call: Name _____
                         Department _____
                         Home Phone # _____

procedures on hand. That may include switchboard staff members and personnel in the executive offices, security office, and front desk area.

The person who receives the bomb threat should be instructed not to use a cell phone, radio, or beeper system to communicate the threat to others; the electrical impulse from these devices might cause certain types of bombs to detonate. Rather, this person should contact the general manager, manager-on-duty, or the security department on a regular telephone or hardwired intercom so that the situation can be quickly assessed and the appropriate authorities (police, fire

Boston Bombings Impact Hotels

On Monday [April 15, 2013], two bombs went off near the finish line of the Boston Marathon, as runners were on their way to wrapping up the highly publicized 26.2-mile race.* The explosions occurred on Boylston Street, a commercial corridor in the city containing several hotels and restaurants.

Mark Hagopian, owner of the Charlesmark Hotel, a 40-room boutique property located at 655 Boylston St., experienced the event firsthand. The hotel was hosting its annual Marathon Party, and Hagopian was standing on the property's first-floor patio when the first explosion happened. "It was about 35 to 40 feet from me. It knocked people over and there was a big surge of wind," he said. "We didn't know what it was—we didn't know if it was a cannon or fireworks or an electrical explosion. But then, when the second bomb went off about 10 seconds later, people started crying. We knew that it was terrorism."

Hagopian explained that he and the hotel staff yelled for all the guests to get back in the hotel and to stay down. He and two of his hotel managers ran out onto the sidewalk and saw the carnage that resulted from the attack. "It must have been 30 seconds after the explosion—and there were just people that were torn apart," he said. "There were people on the ground missing their limbs and bleeding. Immediately, runners and police started putting tourniquets on them."

Bar manager Jefferson Ryder and operations manager Curt Butcher helped police and event spectators remove the barrier that was in place between the road and the sidewalk so that doctors and emergency professionals could get access to the victims.

"Our employees were really courageous and smart," Hagopian said. "It's natural instinct, I guess. You go out to help or you run and hide. We went out to help. It's our job—to make sure that the hotel guests were safe."

All Charlesmark hotel staff and employees are safe and accounted for, but Hagopian reflected that if the bombing had happened earlier, things might have turned out differently. "Earlier in the day, we'd all been to that area, which we walked by to watch the finish line," he said. "We just feel lucky. We weren't there at the wrong time."

Several other hotels in and around the crime scene put emergency plans into place immediately following the bombings. The Lenox Hotel, located across the street from the Charlesmark, was evacuated, and the Fairmont Copley Plaza, located two blocks from the explosions, was put on lockdown. The Mandarin Oriental Boston was also evacuated as a precaution.

On Twitter, the Lenox Hotel thanked its followers for their support during the aftermath of the event and wrote, "It is times like these that unite a community and bring us together." The property announced that it would open to guests Tuesday morning, so those who were staying at the property during the race could collect their belongings. The hotel is not yet fully operational.

In a statement, the Fairmont Copley Plaza said that all hotel employees were safe but asked guests to stay inside while the Boston Police Department investigated the area. Following Monday's attack, the hotel set up the St. James Room for guests to use as a place to relax and get in touch with loved ones. The hotel will continue to check guest identifications and room keys to ensure that the property remains secure.

(continued)

(continued)

> In response to the events, Starwood issued a statement that said, "The Westin Copley Place and Sheraton Boston are in full operation and were not damaged by the explosions near the finish line of the Boston Marathon. Both hotels, the closest Starwood properties to the marathon finish line, are providing support to authorities as well as runners, area workers, and others in addition to guests." Starwood also said that as race officials closed off the last mile of the course following the bombings, runners were directed to the Sheraton, where hotel employees assisted by providing water and towels to the race participants. Starwood is waiving penalties for cancellations and early departures due to the event.
>
> The city of Boston has set up an information center at the Park Plaza Castle so that displaced hotel guests and residents can find shelter and re-connect with family and friends.
>
> As for the Charlesmark, the boutique property remains closed to employees and guests, and Hagopian said he is trying to relocate guests to his other downtown hotel, The Harborside Inn. He is cooperating and waiting for information from the police department regarding when he will be able to get back into the property, and he is unsure when the hotel will resume operation.
>
> "There is a 13-block radius that they are calling a crime scene," Hagopian said. "I live next to the hotel, and I can't get back to my house. A lot of people are displaced. It's a difficult time for everybody."
>
> *This article was written on April 16, 2013, a day after the bombing took place.

Source: Adapted from Deidre Wengen, "Boston Bombings Impact Hotels," *Lodging,* April 16, 2013; http://lodgingmagazine.com/PastIssues/PastIssues/Boston-Bombings-Impact-Hotels-2736.aspx.

department, bomb squad) notified. The individual receiving the bomb threat should also be instructed to obtain as much information as possible from the caller and should listen closely for voice characteristics and background noises; these details may be of great value to investigating authorities.

Once the police have been called, some properties will begin a search of the premises. Engineering, security, and housekeeping supervisory personnel are often the sources for members of a search team. These staff members work throughout the entire property and are likely to notice suspicious items or changes in the arrangement of equipment, furnishings, or other items that might indicate the presence of a bomb. The scope of the search will depend on the information provided by the caller. However, the members of the team should not touch, handle, or move any suspicious object they might find.

While this initial search is in progress and before the police arrive, management will have to decide whether to evacuate the property. The policy in this regard should be carefully reviewed by top management with the advice of legal counsel. If the caller specified the bomb's placement, management may decide to evacuate only those areas surrounding the alleged location of the bomb. If the caller did not specify the bomb's placement and an evacuation is deemed necessary, some properties will limit the evacuation to public areas within the establishment, since guests may be safer in their rooms than they would be passing through public areas during an evacuation. This is one of the most difficult decisions for management to make. Unfortunately, there is no rule of thumb. Even when the police arrive, they may leave the decision to evacuate to management, although they may make recommendations. Most properties do not evacuate on a verbal threat alone. Usually an evacuation is ordered only after a suspicious package or device is located, or when the threat is very specific to an event being held at the hotel.

A single evacuation team with alternate escape routes mapped out can meet most of the emergency evacuation needs of a lodging establishment. The members of this team should receive training in the various alternate evacuation strategies that might be employed, depending on the nature of the emergency.

If, in spite of every effort, a bomb does explode on the premises, the response plan should include procedures for providing emergency medical services as needed; evacuating the injured to a medical facility; cooperating with police, fire fighters, and other responders as they search the bomb site and remove structural elements that may have trapped individuals at the time of the explosion; and removing debris and making repairs to return the hotel to operational status as soon as is deemed appropriate. Hotel managers must remember that local authorities may need time to examine the bomb site. Permission from the authorities may be required before repair work can begin.

Fires

Written plans must be formulated for possible fire emergencies. The OSHA standard for "Means of Egress"[4] mandates that employee emergency plans and fire prevention plans must include:

1. Emergency escape procedures and emergency escape route assignments

2. Procedures to be followed by employees who remain to operate critical hotel operations before they evacuate

3. Procedures to account for all employees after emergency evacuation procedures have been completed

4. Rescue and first aid duties for those employees who are to perform them

5. The preferred means of reporting fire and other emergencies

6. Names or regular job titles of persons or departments who can be contacted for further information or explanation of duties under the plan

Staffing for a fire emergency is an important consideration. A property should carefully evaluate its needs and realistically establish appropriate responses and emergency teams. Emergency team members may come from various parts of the property. The team's general responsibilities may include evaluating the situation when a fire is reported, extinguishing small fires if this can be done safely, assisting the fire department, maintaining calm and order with guests and employees, and assisting in any necessary evacuation. The task of maintaining calm and order among guests involves establishing procedures for communicating with them. Survivors of some hotel fires have voiced concerns over the lack of information available at the time about the fire and what they should do.

A Tale of Two Hotels

What follows are two articles about fire-related incidents at two hotels (thankfully, one incident turned out to be a false alarm). As you will see, the very different reactions of the hotels left very different impressions on their guests.

Hotel #1: False Alarm Fumble

Having a strong crisis communications plan in place at your hotel is a paramount priority, but ensuring your staff knows what to do when an incident occurs is even more critical. For many hotels, the entire concept of a crisis communications plan seems esoteric, something strange and obscure. Too many times I've heard stories of plans created at hotels by brand or management good intentions that simply wind up gathering dust on a shelf somewhere.

That's not an acceptable scenario. It's inevitable that a hotel's staff will need to snap into action and manage an unexpected event eventually. Recently I experienced such a situation. A fire alarm when off after eleven at night on a Sunday. And how the hotel handled this episode was shocking and disappointing.

From the moment the alarm rang, confusion gained an immediate stranglehold on the property. Pajama-clad guests poked tired heads out of their rooms, looking at each other and trying to decipher if the emergency was real or a false alarm. It became a question of who would blink first and begin the hotel exodus.

After five or so minutes, guests began filtering down the emergency stairwell, arms filled with semi-conscious kids, making molasses-like progress to the outside. Once outside, people began gathering in the parking lot adjacent to the hotel, questioning each other as to what was happening. No one from the hotel staff directed people as to where to stand or explained what was happening. Eventually a hotel staffer did stand in front of the hotel's entrance, seemingly with the sole purpose of telling people they could not re-enter the building.

Meanwhile, back inside, several employees gathered in the lobby and chatted (I had snuck back in and observed them from the second-floor landing). More than ten minutes after the alarm went off, an announcement was made over the loudspeakers to evacuate the hotel. Ten minutes! They had the ability to communicate with the entire property and did not utilize that tool immediately? This property was in the middle of a kid-centric family resort town. I was floored that they had the ability to tell all of the guests in the hotel to clear out, yet chose not to do so for ten critical minutes. How many little ones were still sleeping in their rooms, oblivious to this situation? How many grandparents, perhaps needing additional help, were wondering what was happening? Sounds to me like grounds for a lawsuit if an injury occurred because the hotel waited so long.

Shortly thereafter the fire department arrived, investigated, and let everyone back inside. It also upset and disappointed me that the next morning there was no note from the GM under my door—or a voice mail waiting on my guestroom telephone—explaining what had happened. I had to ask several employees before I was told a guest had microwaved the popcorn a little too overzealously. Another lack of communication that was simply unacceptable.

"This is the perfect example of why a crisis communication plan is critical," said Chris Daly, a vice president with Daly Gray Public Relations. Daly, who handles hotel crises on a regular basis and guest-lectures on the subject at New York University, said GMs must make sure their staffs know how to handle an emergency. "A GM needs to prepare for any eventuality. A hotel is really a public space housing transient visitors, and management needs to have the ability to deal with anything that comes up. It is not a question of maybe, it is a question of when. If you are not ready, you are doing your guests a disservice."

Every hotel should have a crisis plan in place and it should be reviewed regularly. Plans typically feature step-by-step actions that must take place during an emergency. Additionally, regular drills should take place for employees, so they too know the correct policies and procedures.

Communicating with guests during an emergency is also important to quell the fear and anxiety that can instantly wash over a parking lot full of customers. Knowledge instills comfort and allays concern. Arm your guests with as much information as possible.

Meanwhile, back at the hotel, I was awash with frustration that the hotel failed on its mandate. I voted with my feet and checked out the next day—two days ahead of schedule. I also asked if the GM could please call me so I could discuss the situation with him. Nearly two weeks later I still haven't heard anything. I'm not surprised—earlier that evening it took three tries to get my room service order right and it was still terrible.

I'm not sure why things went wrong at this hotel, but I do know seeing a parking lot full of scared and crying children is not something I need to see again. The hotel's staff may not be to blame for the situation they were thrust into, but they were certainly culpable for the unprofessional way it was handled.

Hotel #2: High Praise for High-Rise Hospitality

What a way to get a hotel-room upgrade.

When Steven and Randie Siegel arrived at the Monte Carlo on January 24, they checked into one of the hotel's standard rooms on the 25th floor. But a fire the next day forced the Maryland couple out of the Monte Carlo—and into some seriously posh digs at MGM Mirage's Signature high-rise development at the MGM Grand. Their new accommodations featured a flat-screen television, a Jacuzzi tub, and a kitchenette, among other amenities. And the Siegels didn't have to pay a dime for the suite, as MGM Mirage picked up the tab for the rest of the couple's five-day stay.

Disasters can cost a company legions of customers and imperil its survival. Handled poorly, a calamity can send clients fleeing to competitors. But catastrophes also provide businesses with opportunities to show off their best customer-service chops. Companies who get it right can secure loyal customers for life, experts say. The secret: being equitable and honest, and communicating with employees in advance about processes during a disaster.

"There's one overriding command, and that's to treat the customer like you'd like to be treated," said Don Peppers, a founding partner of customer-service consulting firm Peppers & Rogers Group in Connecticut. "That might mean giving up a short-term opportunity to make a profit in exchange for being open and fair with customers."

Earnings were the last thing MGM Mirage executives worried about in the Monte Carlo fire's aftermath, said Alan Feldman, senior vice president of public affairs for the company. The company had to transfer roughly 5,000 guests to other local hotels, and keep them happy in the process. To understand customers' needs, MGM Mirage's managers asked themselves what they'd need in similar circumstances, Feldman said. New rooms, medications, and clothes topped their list. The company

(continued)

(continued)

gave fresh hotel rooms gratis to Monte Carlo guests, and employees worked past midnight picking up prescriptions for customers who'd left their medications in their luggage inside the hotel. For the few Monte Carlo guests who couldn't retrieve their belongings before late Saturday, MGM Mirage told them to buy necessary clothes and submit an expense claim to the hotel. The few receipts that have trickled in have all been reasonable, Feldman said, and some of them have come attached to "the nicest" letters praising the company's professionalism during the fire.

The assistance hasn't been cheap, but Feldman and other MGM Mirage executives consider it an investment in protecting the company's customer base. "If you make the mistake of trying to control the financial hit you're going to take, you might as well try to hold a wave on the sand," he said. "You're much better off thinking about the long term, and thinking about how you'd want to be treated in those circumstances."

For the Siegels, the Monte Carlo's customer care following the fire didn't end with the upgraded room. The company bought and delivered a thirty-day supply of the couple's medications—an expense of about $700 for out-of-plan purchases, Randie Siegel said. And a porter accompanied the couple up to their room on the 25th floor to help them collect and carry their bags late Friday night. "I personally thought they did an excellent job, and that everyone was as kind and as helpful as they could be," Siegel said.

Christina Redden, an Indianapolis resident staying at the Monte Carlo with friends and family for her 23rd birthday, also appreciated her alternate hotel. MGM Mirage transferred Redden's party to Mandalay Bay, where they "had a really good experience" and were "treated very well," Redden said.

Peppers, who doesn't have a business relationship with the Monte Carlo or parent company MGM Mirage, called the resort operator's offer to comp guests' stays in other, sometimes-upgraded rooms "terrific, and above and beyond."

"There's a lot of academic research into how customer trust is lost and recovered, or not recovered," Peppers continued. "One of the main findings is that good behavior is the only sure and true way to recover trust. It doesn't matter what you say and don't say, or how many things you promise."

Source: Adapted from Glenn Haussman, "When Crisis Strikes," *Hotel Interactive,* April 5, 2007; and Jennifer Robison, "MGM Mirage Receives High Marks for Treatment of 5,000 Displaced Guests Following Monte Carlo Fire: Advance Planning, Communication, Being Equitable and Honest Keeps Customer's Trust and Future Business," *Las Vegas Review-Journal,* February 4, 2008. © McClatchy-Tribune Information Services. All rights reserved. Reprinted with permission.

As part of a property's emergency action plan, OSHA requires an employer to designate and train a sufficient number of persons to assist in the safe and orderly evacuation of employees. In addition, the plan must be reviewed with each employee covered by the plan when it is initially developed, whenever the employee's responsibilities or designated actions under the plan change, and whenever the plan itself is changed. Although OSHA requirements apply directly to employees, not guests or the general public, they undergird the hotel's program for emergency evacuation of guests and the public.

Two important points concerning the nature of fires and injuries due to fires need to be made. First, there are three main classes of fire that a lodging property should prepare for. Class A fires involve ordinary combustibles such as wood, paper, and cloth. Class B fires involve flammable liquids and grease, paints, oils, and so forth. Class C fires involve electrical equipment. (Class D fires involve combustible metals and are rare in a hotel environment. Class K fires, involving cooking oils and grease, are a particular concern for hotels with food and beverage operations.) Although a fire can begin with any single type of fuel source, it can and most often does spread to fuel sources in other classes. For example, an electrical fire near an open can of paint and a bag of old rags can become an "ABC" fire in a matter of seconds. Each class of fire requires a specific type of extinguishing agent. Managers should inform employees of where fire extinguishers are located and train them in how to use the type or types of fire extinguishers available on the premises.

The second point is that most injuries and deaths are caused by the smoke and gases that are released during a fire and not by the actual flames. Keeping close to the floor increases the chance for survival of people caught in a fire. If it is necessary to move through or into a smoke-filled room, the person doing so should place a wet towel over his or her head and mouth, if possible; the towel will act as a filter, making breathing easier.

Fires may start in various ways. One cause of fire is arson. It is difficult to establish a profile of a typical arsonist, as motives vary. Fires may be started out of spite; fires have been started by discharged employees; and fires have been started by patrons angry because they were evicted from a property's bar or lounge. Fatal fires have also been traced to individuals with psychological and physiological problems. Within legal limits, every effort should be made to screen new employees to avoid employing an arsonist.

When a fire occurs, there should be immediate action. The fire alarm should be sounded to alert guests and employees of the fire, and the fire department should be immediately notified. Employees should learn the location of fire alarm boxes and how to operate them *before* an emergency occurs. Some alarms send an automatic alarm signal to the local fire department, but a follow-up telephone call may still be advisable to confirm that the fire department has indeed received the alarm. Anyone in immediate danger should be evacuated from the area if possible.

It is sometimes said that the first five minutes of fire fighting may be worth more than the next five hours of fire fighting. Once a fire has been discovered and reported, the time that passes while awaiting the arrival of the fire department may be crucial. During this period, prompt and effective action by trained personnel on the scene may contain or extinguish the fire. Of course, personnel should be trained not to take risks that unnecessarily endanger themselves or others; it may be beyond the ability of the staff to fight some fires.

After a fire has occurred, a property manager may complete a fire report that records what is known about the fire and any damage or injury it caused. (A sample fire report form is shown in Exhibit 2.) A fire report form should be developed and adapted to meet a property's specific needs.

Managers should review their property's fire protection program and capabilities with local fire authorities and remain current on local code changes that

Exhibit 2   Sample Fire Report Form

This report must be completed for ALL fires regardless of the dollar loss and forwarded to the appropriate management.

Date _____   Time fire was discovered _____

Time fire department was notified _____

Name of person notifying fire department _____

Guest name & room number _____

Manager—describe exactly what happened _____

_____

_____

Where did fire start? _____

What burned? _____

Fire damage: Building _____

                    Contents _____

Number and kind of portable extinguishers used _____

Did sprinkler system operate? _____

_____

Did dry chemical or CO_2 system operate? _____

Action taken by fire brigade _____

_____

Action taken by fire department (including time of response) _____

_____

Injuries: Employee _____

                Guest _____

Name and phone number of fire department office/investigator _____

_____

may apply to their lodging facility. Fire protection requirements specified by the Occupational Safety and Health Act should be carefully reviewed for compliance.

Some communities require the fire authority to review and approve a hotel's emergency fire programs. Some fire departments have the capacity to assist in training hotel employees in fire emergency procedures. Establishing working relationships with local fire authorities can be very helpful.

Hurricanes and Typhoons

Coastal areas in the United States and other parts of the world can be subject to tropical cyclones, which, depending on their location and strength, may be termed hurricanes, typhoons, tropical storms, cyclonic storms, tropical depressions, or simply cyclones.[5] Tropical cyclones are large storms with high winds and large amounts of rain that can cause extensive damage and, tragically, sometimes a large loss of life. The damaging effect of these storms can extend a substantial distance inland from coastal areas. (See Exhibit 3 for a list of different types of hurricanes and the types of damage they cause.) The cost of a tropical storm can run into many billions of dollars.

Hotels located in areas where hurricanes, typhoons, and other tropical storms may strike should have very complete plans to cope with their impact. Modern weather forecasting provides the ability to follow the development of a hurricane or typhoon threat over several days, so a property can adjust its emergency response to the level of the threat. Since property employees may have their homes impacted by the storm, too, employees need to take appropriate action as well as the hotel.[6] Hotels need to be aware of the issues presented by hurricanes or typhoons for their employees and recognize that employees may not be available for duty at the hotel for a period of time after a storm strikes, due to blocked roads and other effects of the storm.

Exhibit 3   Hurricane Scale and Effects on Property

Category	Definitions and Effects
ONE	*Winds 74–95 mph:* No real damage to building structures. Damage primarily to unanchored mobile homes, shrubbery, and trees. Also, some coastal road flooding and minor pier damage.
TWO	*Winds 96–110 mph:* Some roofing material, door, and window damage to buildings. Considerable damage to vegetation, mobile homes, and piers. Coastal and low-lying escape routes flood two to five hours before arrival of center. Small craft in unprotected anchorages break moorings.
THREE	*Winds 111–130 mph:* Some structural damage to small residences and utility buildings with minor amount of wall failures. Mobile homes are destroyed. Flooding near the coast destroys smaller structures, with larger structures damaged by floating debris. Terrain continuously lower than five feet above sea level may be flooded inland eight miles or more.
FOUR	*Winds 131–155 mph:* More extensive wall failures with some complete roof structure failure of small residences. Major erosion of beach areas. Major damage to lower floors of structures near the shore. Terrain continuously lower than ten feet above sea level may be flooded, requiring massive evacuation of residential areas inland as far as six miles.
FIVE	*Winds greater than 155 mph:* Complete roof failure on many residences and industrial buildings. Some complete building failures with small utility buildings blown over or away. Major damage to lower floors of all structures located less than fifteen feet above sea level and within 500 yards of the shoreline. Massive evacuation of residential areas on low ground within five to ten miles of the shoreline may be required.

This data from the National Oceanic and Atmospheric Administration (NOAA) provides the Saffir/Simpson Hurricane Scale by which the storm's intensity is measured.

Hotels will need to develop hurricane and typhoon procedures specific to their property and setting. At a minimum, their procedures should address the following elements (with special attention to those elements that should be addressed when a storm that might threaten a property has been identified):

- Employee training
- Securing of mobile property (e.g., trash cans, planters, chairs)
- Protection of internal equipment (e.g., computers, televisions, appliances)
- Protection of the hotel structure (doors, windows, etc.)
- Plans for protection and use of stored food
- Security of key business records and assets (computer backup, guest information, employee information, financial data, cash)
- Communication with guests
- Communication with staff
- Equipment and supplies for emergency operations (emergency generators, potable water, flashlights, radios)
- Aid agreements with other businesses (covering, for example, fuel, transport, water, food, and equipment)
- Plans for recovery and restoration

This list is only a representative sampling of the many procedures that a specific lodging property preparing for a tropical storm must consider. For example, resorts with extensive marina facilities will have their own unique concerns. The Caribbean Hotel Association recognized the need for its members to have a hurricane procedures manual to help them prepare for hurricanes and therefore solicited the development of such a manual.[7] Many other resources are available for hotels. For example, chain hotels can turn to corporate headquarters for resources to help them prepare their hurricane or typhoon emergency procedures.

While there is clearly a major concern associated with hurricanes and typhoons, there is also concern associated with other, weaker tropical storms. While wind levels are lower with these types of storms and therefore wind damage is not as extensive or does not occur at all, the potential for large amounts of rain still exists and therefore the risk of flooding is still present and should not be ignored.

Tornadoes

Tornadoes occur inland and require many of the same preparations and procedures that hurricanes require. Frequently, tornado action will occur as an aftermath of a hurricane's movement from the ocean or gulf onto land. In all instances, being prepared and having a plan are of vital importance. Assigning duties to personnel is an important part of planning, and this will be more successful if done without the pressure of an impending emergency. The most important duty for everyone is the protection of lives.

If possible, a tornado shelter should be established in a basement area, tunnel, underground parking facility, or other below-grade location removed from glass windows, doors, or panels. When selecting a shelter, managers should avoid atrium-style lobbies and locations in the building where there is a long-span roof (such as over a large convention or meeting room).

A battery-operated radio in operative condition should always be on hand. In a tornado emergency, the radio might provide the only communication with the outside world.

Floods

Floods are a risk that is faced by hotels in many areas of the world. The impact of flooding can be severe, and floods can occur with a relatively short warning time. The potential severity of flooding is illustrated by the extensive flooding of the Opryland Hotel in 2010. The 2,800-room hotel, located in Nashville, Tennessee, was inundated with as much as ten feet of water, resulting in its closure for months; it cost more than $200 million to repair the flood-related damage.[8] Within the United States, the flood risk for a specific location can be identified through the use of flood maps issued by FEMA.[9]

Flooding can, and often does, result from the lingering effects of hurricanes and other tropical storms. These storms can produce long periods of heavy rainfall that can overwhelm a property's storm water systems as well as impacting local rivers and flood-prone areas. In the northeastern United States, the late summer of 2011 saw Hurricane Irene deliver large amounts of rain that caused flooding in many inland areas.[10]

Properties located in areas where floods occur should have an emergency plan for use in the event of a flood. All necessary pump equipment should be accessible and in working order. All supplies required for caulking, barricading, etc., should be stored in such a way that they are available for immediate use. Telephone numbers for emergency supplies, information, and assistance should be conspicuously posted and updated when necessary.

When any property manager becomes aware of the possibility of flooding or receives a flood warning from local authorities, the general manager should be immediately notified. He or she should verify the report by calling the local Civil Defense agency or the police. If the possibility of flooding is verified, the general manager can then contact those employees involved in flood emergency control. The general manager, or his or her designee, may then assume responsibility for coordinating all departments in flood control procedures. Consider the following plan of action if there is a danger of flooding.

The front desk, which may serve as the communications link to outside agencies, can make all employees and guests aware of the possible emergency, evacuate rooms as needed, and relocate guests moved from rooms in endangered areas. The housekeeping department can attend to guests on lower levels of the property and supply necessary materials, such as old bedspreads, to be used for sealing small openings to prevent water seepage.

The engineering and maintenance department can at this time issue to appropriate employees any foul-weather gear on hand; set up a large flood-control pump; load a van with emergency flood control equipment (door barriers, sandbags, caulking guns); install any additional standby sump pumps; verify the working condition of gas-operated pumps; check the operation of any emergency generators; clear the basement of any objects that may get lost, damaged, or clog sump pumps; and test the operation of flood emergency warning lights. Additional measures may include erecting flood-control barriers when water reaches the barrier marking-stake and notifying guests via posted bulletins and oral instructions to move vehicles to higher ground, wherever possible.

Security department staff members should secure the property and its assets, moving as much as possible to a secured location away from the anticipated flood level. They should also patrol guest areas, reassure guests, assist as needed in relocating guests to upper floors of the property, and coordinate activities on the premises with those of local authorities, as necessary.

Earthquakes and Tsunamis

Internationally, the past decade has seen a number of particularly devastating earthquakes.[11, 12] None of these major earthquakes directly affected the United States, although when a small earthquake hit the eastern United States in 2011 it was a reminder of the country's potential vulnerability. For example, recently there has been more attention paid to the existence of the New Madrid Fault in the south-central United States and the potential for earthquakes in this area. New Madrid was the site of four major earthquakes that occurred from mid-December 1811 to early February 1812; at that time the region was sparsely populated, so, despite the quakes' high magnitudes, property damage and casualties were low. Of course, the potential for earthquakes in California along the San Andreas Fault and the state's other active faults is well known.

Hotel managers should investigate whether an earthquake is likely to occur in the community where their hotel is located. Where such a danger exists, planning might include:

- Establishing a command center and assigning personnel to emergency response teams.
- Supplying the center with portable radios and additional batteries.
- Keeping first aid supplies on hand for use by trained staff members.
- Establishing food and water reserves.
- Keeping appropriate wrenches available for turning off gas and water valves. The security staff as well as the engineering staff should know the location and proper method for turning off such utilities.
- Providing flashlights and extra batteries. Managers should schedule an occasional maintenance check to be sure flashlights and batteries are operative.

A general recommendation during an earthquake is to suggest that employees and guests remain indoors and get under a substantial piece of furniture, such as a desk or table. A door frame may also provide some protection. Individuals should be instructed to stay away from windows and to find an inside location where there is minimal danger of being struck by falling objects such as books from shelves or stored items from shelves in storerooms or display areas. Shelf units or other items of furniture that might tip and injure a person should be anchored to the floor or to a wall.

If staff or guests are outside the building, they should get to an open area and stay away from buildings and overhead power lines.

Following an earthquake, a property's search team (often made up of security, engineering, and housekeeping personnel) should immediately check around the property for anyone who might be injured and provide appropriate first aid until medical assistance can be obtained or the injured can be safely moved to a medical facility. The team should also check for spills or leaking water, gas, or chemical containers on the premises that could result in physical harm, fire, or explosion. Toilet facilities should not be used until the integrity of the sewage system is verified.

Food and water supplies should be inspected and necessary steps taken to protect such supplies for use during the emergency. Where refrigeration has been interrupted, consider preparing as much of the food as possible with the use of outdoor cooking equipment such as grills or charcoal broilers.

The property should take appropriate steps to prevent injuries from broken windows, doors, curtain walls, and so forth. Employees should be careful around shelving, doors to storage areas, and closets where materials may have piled up against the door, creating a hazard.

After the earthquake is over, any pre-arranged emergency program with local agencies and authorities should be implemented. If the property has sustained minimal damage, it may serve as an emergency center for the community. If regular communication channels have been knocked out, communication by messenger, two-way radio, ham radio, or CB radio can keep the hotel in contact with local authorities and the community.

In recent years, the world has become more aware of the risk to coastal areas of the flooding caused by tsunamis. A tsunami is a series of large ocean waves generated by sudden displacements in the sea floor, landslides, or volcanic activity.[13] The 2004 Indian Ocean tsunami resulted in the deaths of hundreds of thousands of people, billions of dollars of property damage, and heavily impacted hundreds of coastal areas. In 2011, the Tohoku earthquake off Japan resulted in the deaths of thousands, extensive property damage, and radioactive leaks from nuclear reactors as the resulting tsunami inundated coastal areas.

Beach resorts and communities located in coastal areas should be aware of the potential tsunami risk and have plans in place for notifying and evacuating guests if a tsunami occurs. As awareness has grown about tsunami risks, warning systems have improved. A major source for tsunami information and warnings is the website operated by the National Oceanic and Atmospheric Administration (NOAA). However, information gathered from NOAA must trigger notifications and actions at the local level if this information is to be truly useful. It should be noted that while many tsunamis provide some time for notification (sometimes several hours), some develop so quickly that notification times are very brief.

Bali hotels have developed a "Tsunami Ready" program to help hotels prepare for tsunami events and to assure guests of their preparation.[14] Other hotels in locations with the potential for a tsunami event may rely on local civil defense resources to help in developing their tsunami-preparedness programs.

Blackouts

Guests, employees, hotel operations, and the assets of the hotel and its guests may all become affected by a blackout. Security should be a top consideration when a hotel puts together a plan for what to do when the power fails.

Of course, a battery-operated emergency lighting system is very helpful during a blackout. Hotels that can afford it should check into the feasibility of purchasing emergency generators. If backup lighting is not working, the security staff

---

Lessons from the Northeast Blackout of 2003

Affecting perhaps as many as fifty million people in eight U.S. states and the Canadian province of Ontario, the Northeast Blackout of 2003, which started during the late afternoon of August 14, was the most widespread blackout in U.S. history. It demonstrated that almost any hotel needs to plan for the eventuality that it might have to operate without its utilities, including electricity and running water, for a period of anywhere from many hours to many days. While it is not possible to prevent utilities from failing, hotel operators can mitigate the effects of a blackout by planning ahead. The experience of hotels that remained in operation during the 2003 blackout provides a road map for disaster preparedness. The following checklist is distilled from the lessons these hotels learned about their preparedness (or lack thereof):

Facilities and Process Management

- Know where you are vulnerable if the power goes down.
- Document this examination of the service delivery system.
- Perform "what-if" scenarios and simulations, and plan appropriate responses.
- If your hotel does not have standby power, price out a generator set. If your hotel does have standby power, price out expanding its capacity.
- Provide support beyond the National Electric Code (NEC) for emergency systems.
- Investigate adding at least some air conditioning and lighting functionality to standby systems.
- Locate and mark phone lines that are not susceptible to power loss.
- Keep the tools needed to ensure the functionality of manual processes (manual payment card imprint machines, battery-operated calculators, etc.) in a secure location.

Emergency Planning and Management

- Formulate or revise emergency plans.
- Run drills and tests.
- Train and retrain staff on emergency plans.

or other management staff must be ready to use flashlights to help them secure money and valuables on the premises.

As necessary, security personnel should work with the engineering department and local police and fire authorities in freeing guests or employees from stalled elevators. Management should consider providing auxiliary equipment for light and communication to a stalled elevator. Ideally, emergency generators will provide sufficient power to move elevator cars to the next floor for evacuation. If feasible, sufficient power should be generated to maintain the services of one car during a blackout.

It is most important to have patrols operating during a blackout to reassure guests and staff and to minimize any acts of vandalism or sabotage on the premises. The potential for looting should be recognized and a plan of action formulated to deal with it. Managers should consider having a supply of light sticks and/or flashlights on hand for use by guests during a blackout.

If sufficient security staff is available, perimeter patrols should be increased, especially at the hotel's access points. While the blackout persists, managers should consider whether hotel access should be reduced to a single location at the main entrance of the property. Where courtesy cars and employees' personal vehicles are on the premises, such vehicles could be strategically located to temporarily provide perimeter lighting.

Robberies

Unfortunately, because lodging properties typically have at least some cash on the premises, cashiers are sometimes confronted by armed robbers. While it is easy to simply tell cashiers to be calm, more detailed suggestions concerning their behavior during a robbery will help them respond appropriately under the circumstances. Cashiers should comply with a robber's demands and make no sudden movements that might be perceived by the robber as an attempt to thwart the crime. Cashiers should not do anything to jeopardize their lives or the lives of other persons. Amateur criminals may be extremely nervous, and professional criminals may have little regard for others; in either case, unexpected actions or a lack of cooperation might cause a weapon to be used.

Management should consider having a silent alarm in the cash drawer that may, for example, be activated when a predetermined packet of bills is removed from a certain clip. Generally, the serial numbers of the bills in this packet are recorded and the bills are not used in regular business transactions. When complying with a robber's demand for money, the cashier can remove this packet of money with the rest of the money, thus setting off the silent alarm. No comment should be made and the cashier should avoid the appearance of setting off an alarm.

A property's management should consider developing a robbery description form (see Exhibit 4). Whether or not such a form is used, the cashiers and other employees should observe the robber carefully, noting physical characteristics such as height, weight, build, color and length of hair, eye color, facial hair, complexion, scars, tattoos, piercings, clothing, and anything unusual. Attention should also be given to the voice and mannerisms of the robber and to the type of weapon he or she is using.

Exhibit 4   Sample Robbery Description Form

1. Male or female _____
2. Approximate age _____
3. Race and nationality _____
4. Height _____
5. Weight _____
6. Build _____
7. Color and length of hair _____
8. Color of eyes _____
9. Facial hair:
   A. Beard _____
   B. Mustache _____
   C. Goatee, etc. _____
10. Tattoos _____ Piercings _____
11. Complexion—light, dark, etc. _____
12. Speech—accent, impairments, etc. _____
13. Clothing worn:
   A. Hat _____
   B. Shirt _____
   C. Coat or jacket—length and color _____
   D. Trousers—color and style _____
   E. Shoes _____
14. Outstanding physical characteristics—limp, deformities, etc. _____
15. Description of vehicle, if used _____
16. License number _____
17. Direction of escape _____
   WITNESS NAME _____
   _____
   _____

If it can be done without danger, employees should try to observe the robber's direction of escape and the type and license number of the escape vehicle (if any). If the robber leaves behind any evidence such as a note, the cashier should carefully set it aside for the police. Similarly, employees should refrain from touching, and prevent others from touching, articles or places the robber may have touched or evidence he or she may have left from which fingerprints may be taken.

As soon as possible following the incident, the property should notify the police.

Medical and Dental Emergencies

Managers of lodging properties need to face the possibility of guests becoming seriously ill, accidentally injured, or even dying while at the property. The security staff should be ready to deal appropriately with any of these unfortunate incidents. Managers should review with legal counsel and the property's insurance company an appropriate response to foreseeable medical and dental emergencies that might occur on-site. They should also review with legal counsel the applicability of "Good Samaritan" laws, which protect, within limits, passersby who try to help.

First Aid and Emergency Medical Services

The Occupational Safety and Health Act requires that someone trained in first aid be present on each work shift in all hotels, unless those properties have ready access to medical services on the premises or close by. Staff members trained in first aid will have some knowledge of how best to assist those who need help. An important point is that they will have a better idea of what *not* to do in certain situations.

The property should review with legal counsel any local regulations regarding calling an emergency medical service (EMS). Managers should be aware that a guest may decline assistance and then later sue the hotel for its failure to provide appropriate aid. If legal counsel advises calling an EMS, the trained first-aider on staff should make the guest comfortable while waiting for EMS personnel to arrive, and only provide first aid assistance if a life-threatening condition or situation exists, such as severe bleeding, poisoning, or the loss of consciousness due to choking or some other condition affecting the ability of the guest to breathe. (See Exhibit 5 for sample procedures to help someone choking.) Cardiopulmonary resuscitation (CPR) training may also be valuable in helping a guest who may be having a heart attack. The arrival of EMS personnel shifts the responsibility to them for caring for the guest and properly transporting him or her to a medical facility. Except in major community-wide emergencies, property employees should never move a guest to a medical facility in anything other than an ambulance.

It should be noted that providing CPR is not a requirement of OSHA, nor is it required by law for hotels in the United States. If hotel personnel choose to provide CPR, they must be properly trained. Hotels may wish to provide automated external defibrillators (AEDs) as an additional element of their medical emergency procedures. The position of the American Hotel & Lodging Association on AEDs is shown in Exhibit 6. The Red Cross provides information about AEDs as well as CPR procedures to address cardiac arrest.[15]

When a property chooses to offer medical and dental services to guests through the use of house physicians and dentists, it should ensure that those house physicians and dentists are qualified. For reasons relating to liability, many hotels, instead of offering house personnel, keep lists obtained from legitimate local medical and dental associations of physicians, dentists, and medical facilities to allow guests to make their own choices. When a guest is incapacitated and does not have a close relative on the premises, medical decisions should be made by a responsible member of the management staff or by a paramedic or other medically trained person.

Exhibit 5   Information for Helping Choking Victims

CONSCIOUS CHOKING
Cannot Cough, Speak, Cry or Breathe

After checking the scene for safety and the injured or ill person, have someone CALL 9-1-1 and get consent. For children and infants, get consent from the parent or guardian, if present.

1 GIVE 5 BACK BLOWS
■ Adult: ■ Child: ■ Infant:

2 GIVE 5 ABDOMINAL THRUSTS
■ Adult: ■ Child: ■ Infant: (chest thrusts for infant)

TIP: For infants, support the head and neck securely. Keep the head lower than the chest.

3 REPEAT STEPS 1 AND 2 UNTIL THE:
■ Object is forced out.
■ Person can cough forcefully or breathe.
■ Person becomes unconscious.

WHAT TO DO NEXT
■ IF PERSON BECOMES UNCONSCIOUS — Carefully lower the person to the ground and give CARE for unconscious choking, beginning with looking for an object.
■ Make sure 9-1-1 has been called.

American Red Cross

Copyright © 2011 by The American National Red Cross

Source: American Red Cross.

In coordination with the property's top management and its food service management, the security or medical staff should consider a plan of action for dealing with food poisoning incidents.

Exhibit 6   AH&LA Statement on Automated External Defibrillators (AEDs) in Hotels

Like every business in which the public is served, the lodging industry views guest and employee safety as a top priority. At the present time, lodging facilities in the United States do not uniformly provide training and AEDs on-site.

Currently, there are several concerns with respect to widespread implementation of AEDs in U.S. hotels, including:

- Liability concerns for both individuals and businesses in the absence of strong national Good Samaritan protections;

- Conflicting guidance on the acceptable number of AEDs, response time, maintenance, staffing, and training;

- Uncertainty as to staffing and AED training in an industry with historically high levels of employee turnover.

Though not empowered to set standards, AH&LA encourages the industry to continuously review and re-evaluate their policies and procedures as they relate to guest and employee safety. AH&LA has been in contact with several AED advocacy organizations, such as the Sudden Cardiac Arrest Association, and plans to continue to assist in ensuring appropriate safety standards in U.S. hotels.

A property should also consider developing procedures for advising callers of a guest's illness and/or hospitalization. Usually, the police will provide information about incidents in which they are involved; an emergency medical service or a hospital may be less likely to notify the family or business associates of the guest. Rather than simply saying a guest has checked out or providing details as to the nature of an illness or injury, PBX and front desk personnel should consider the following: advise the caller that the guest was moved to a hospital due to an injury or sudden illness; provide the name and number of the hospital (and attending physician, if possible); and connect the caller with any friend, relative, or associate of the guest if such a person is available.

It is important for the director of security or another representative of management to record any known facts or circumstances relating to the illness or injury. If possible, the property should obtain statements from any witnesses to an accident. Managers should carefully examine the accident site, noting the condition of stairs, floor surfaces, carpeting, or any other factor involved in the accident. Any number of questions may be asked. Was the guest wearing slippers, shoes with worn heels, clogs, sandals, or other footwear that may not provide adequate protection for the foot or which might have reduced the guest's stability? Were there physical disabilities or limitations that might have been a factor in the accident? What was the weather? Had moisture from rain or snow been tracked into the area where the accident occurred? Was too much or too little lighting involved? Management should record any statements made by the guest and, if possible, photograph the area. Employees in the area of the accident should be instructed not to speak to the guest about whether the guest or the property is at fault. Until all the facts are known, management should make no statements and draw no conclusions.

Infectious Diseases

As public buildings serving a large and very mobile population, hotels have always had the potential to be locations where disease transmission might occur. Proper housekeeping and maintenance practices help to reduce the potential for disease transmission. However, as is illustrated by the *Legionella* bacteria,[16] it is certainly possible that bacteria and diseases that are broadly present in society may have outbreaks in hotels. In addition, disease outbreaks elsewhere in society can significantly impact hotel operations and indeed can affect entire tourism regions.

Legionella outbreaks have continued in the decades since the discovery of this bacteria in a Philadelphia hotel in 1976. Because this bacteria is rather widespread, hotels have the potential to have *Legionella* infections break out from property locations as wide-ranging as cooling towers and air handling systems to hot tubs and spas. The Centers for Disease Control and Prevention (CDC) has a location on its website that provides information for hotels and health professionals to help them identify and deal with a *Legionella* outbreak.[17]

Legionella is not just an American problem and certainly is not just found in hotels. The European Centre for Disease Prevention and Control has done regular monitoring of outbreaks within the European Union and identifies thousands of outbreaks each year, with mortality identified as approximately 10 percent of those infected. About 20 percent of the overall European cases are labeled as "travel related."[18]

Almost thirty years after the first *Legionella* outbreak in the United States, the outbreak of SARS (Severe Acute Respiratory Syndrome) from 2002 through 2003 in Asia and elsewhere illustrated again how disease outbreaks can impact hotels and can be associated with a hotel. SARS is believed to have begun in Guangdong Province in China in November of 2002. It eventually spread to several dozen countries, with the largest number of cases in China (5,327 cases), Hong Kong (1,755), Canada (251), and Singapore (238). A total of 916 deaths were attributed to SARS.[19] A hotel became a SARS focal point when the spread of SARS outside Hong Kong was attributed to infections of guests at the Metropole Hotel in Hong Kong. Other transmissions were traced to the spread of the disease by airline travelers. Given the uncertainty and rapid onset associated with this new disease, the World Heath Organization (WHO) and numerous governments took a variety of actions, including quarantines, to attempt to control its spread.

The human suffering by those infected and the loss of life from SARS was tragic. In addition, the impact of SARS on the travel economy of many locations was substantial. Tourism revenue losses were estimated in the billions of dollars, with China and Canada having the largest losses.

In 2009–2010, an outbreak of swine flu (H1N1 Flu) was reported in many locations around the globe, including the United States. H1N1 was declared a pandemic by WHO, with estimates of the human impact being 61 million infected, 274,000 hospitalized, and 12,470 deaths.[20] A number of resources were assembled to address this outbreak and, given the severity of the earlier SARS outbreak, the U.S. lodging industry took direct action. For example, the American Hotel & Lodging Association created a section on its website to disseminate information to hoteliers about the H1N1 disease, with links to other resources on the Internet.[21]

Travelers need to be aware of the potential health risks they may encounter while traveling. *Legionella*, SARS, and H1N1 are just a subset of the potential diseases that may be encountered by the traveling public. Organizations such as the CDC publish health-related information for various travel destinations and provide other information about health issues of interest to travelers. Obviously, for many moral, business, and legal reasons, hotels must take appropriate action to help ensure the health of their guests.

Death of Guests

It is an unfortunate fact of life that sometimes deaths happen unexpectedly, and at times these deaths occur in hotels. Hotel managers should review with the police or the coroner the appropriate response in the event of a guest's death. Generally speaking, the police should be called immediately and the guestroom or other affected area secured until their arrival. Neither the body nor any personal effects should be touched. The police usually take charge of the situation and provide instructions for handling the guest's personal effects. If hotel personnel are instructed to prepare the guest's possessions for removal, an inventory should be made and retained as a matter of record in case survivors later raise questions as to the items turned over to the police. Careful records should be made regarding the death, including when the guest was last seen by the staff, the time of discovery of the body, and any data provided by the police, coroner, or other authorities.

Terrorism

Terrorism is a growing worldwide problem that may affect any number of lodging companies, especially those with properties overseas.[22] Terrorist acts can include bombings, arson, sabotage, kidnappings, hostage situations, rioting and civil disorders, and almost any criminal act calculated to achieve some sort of political or ideological objective. We have already discussed procedures for dealing with bombings and fires. This section will look at sabotage, kidnappings and hostage situations, and riots and civil disorders. We will focus on these acts in relation to terrorism, though clearly these tactics may be used by people other than terrorists (for example, kidnappers who merely seek a ransom).

With the international holdings of many hotel corporations, special attention should be given to the safety of hotel executives while visiting foreign lodging properties. Often the best advice for these executives is to keep a low profile. Hotel executives should consider the following points: American embassies and consulates will advise any American citizen or business representative who requests information on possible terrorist threats in foreign countries; traveling executives may wish to avoid types of cars or actions that might identify them as American, rich, or important; and potential victims of terrorist acts should make all necessary emergency financial arrangements for dependents, and designate an individual or office to contact in the event these plans must be implemented. Updated overseas security advisories are available on the Internet from the Bureau of Diplomatic Security at http://www.state.gov/m/ds/.

Ten Keys to Designing More Secure Hotels

The horrific terrorist attacks on the Taj and Oberoi Hotels in Mumbai, India, in 2008 served as chilling reminders of the need for more effective security in hospitality facilities. But enhancing security at hotels is not simple. Hotels go to extraordinary lengths to welcome both individual guests and large gatherings of people; this atmosphere of hospitality makes it easier for a criminal or terrorist to slip past watchful security officers.

While it is necessary for hotel managers to ensure that guests can rely on hotels to watch out for their physical safety, managers must also preserve the equity of a hospitality brand that has been painstakingly created over the years. Tough, tight, visible security might reassure guests, but it could also damage brand equity. One of the key challenges of hospitality security, then, involves balancing security measures with expected guest experiences.

The first step in tightening security is to make an assessment of the perceived threat, which will vary with geography and hotel type. A boutique hotel in the arts district in Fort Worth, Texas, faces small risks compared to a major hotel near Capitol Hill in Washington, D.C., that is frequented by members of Congress, wealthy businesspeople, and celebrities. Each type of hotel requires different security treatments.

Whatever the treatment, however, building design can help deliver effective security that doesn't significantly compromise the experience promised by a brand. Here are ten building design concepts that enhance security without compromising the hospitality experience:

1. **Perimeter.** The perimeter of a hotel is the first line of defense against an attack, and an effective security design will subtly but firmly control access to a building, especially by vehicles. Secure perimeter design separates the building from streets and parking areas and forces vehicles (which might be equipped with bombs) to remain at standoff distances of fifty to one hundred feet. Standoff design tools include bollards, lighting standards, and collapsible pavement ("Tiger Traps"). Landscaping elements such as low walls, planters, and water features can also keep vehicles back. These landscaping features are security measures with aesthetic appeal.

2. **Lighting.** Lighting tailored to security can also appeal to guests. Entrances, walkways, and potential hiding places outside the hotel need adequate lighting to facilitate observations by patrolling security officers and video surveillance cameras, as well as guests out for a stroll. Loading docks and delivery entrances also need lighting, which need not show concern for aesthetics. One caution: While bright lighting facilitates observation, overly bright lighting creates glare and limits visibility. Variable intensity systems, smart controls, and motion detection can minimize energy use and mitigate aesthetic disadvantages created by lighting.

3. **Parking.** As the first attack on the World Trade Center in 1993 showed, parking structures below buildings invite attention from terrorists. Vehicles carrying bombs that detonate under buildings can cause extensive damage to the structures above. To prevent this problem, parking structures can be placed adjacent to rather than beneath a hotel. When conditions require putting a

(continued)

parking structure under a hotel, it is important to institute strict controls over the size of vehicles permitted into the garage. In addition, a security officer monitoring a security gate should facilitate positive identification of vehicles and drivers entering the structure.

4. **Ballrooms, auditoriums, and gathering spaces.** Hotels provide large and small gathering spaces. When filled with people, ballrooms, auditoriums, lounges, and restaurants make attractive targets. Locating these spaces away from exterior walls, perhaps facing interior courtyards or other secure but attractive spaces, can make them difficult to attack from the outside.

5. **Glazing.** Expanses of glazing should face away from streets and parking areas and look out on protected, interior gardens and courtyards. When exterior glazing must face a street, special film coating the glass can minimize lethal flying shards in the event of a blast. At locations presenting extreme risks, walls facing unsecured areas may eliminate glass altogether in favor of reinforced masonry or concrete. The security benefits justify the added cost.

6. **Access points.** In terms of securing a hotel, the fewer points of access, the better. In addition, placing entrances at locations offering clear lines of sight make it easier for security officers, hotel staff members, or video cameras to monitor comings and goings. Spaces requiring easy access for vendor trucks, trash trucks, and other large vehicles should be located away from the guestroom tower, main lobby, conference rooms, restaurants, lounges, and other gathering spaces. For example, the lobby might work well as a freestanding pavilion so an attack there could be contained outside of the hotel's main structure; this would also protect the hotel from a blast occurring in the lobby. Such a design would likely move a porte cochere (and the vehicles typically parking there) further from the main structure.

7. **Air intakes.** To help protect against chemical or biological attacks, designers can place air intakes for heating, ventilating, and air conditioning equipment high up on building facades. This technique provides the additional benefit of fresher air. To protect intakes that must, of necessity, be placed near the ground, designers can specify equipment with tops that slope steeply downward to make it more difficult and more time-consuming for an attacker to inject contaminants.

8. **Guestroom tower.** The guestroom tower needs sufficient standoff distance from major streets to add insurance against the progressive collapse of the structure should a bomb go off on the street. If a setback or standoff is impractical, structural reinforcement might be necessary.

9. **Floor plan.** Designers should develop interior floor plans that make it easy to monitor and control access to elevator lobbies and guestroom floors. Techniques include allowing natural lines of sight to entrances and public spaces to make it easy for security personnel as well as hotel staff—reception, concierge, housekeepers, and others—to keep watch. A secure floor plan also enables staff to lock down the facility incrementally to contain dangerous activity. It might be necessary, for example, to isolate lobbies and lounges, pre-function spaces, ballrooms, meeting spaces, the loading dock, and various back-of-house spaces.

(continued)

(continued)

> 10. **Technologies.** Security technologies can supplement and improve the performance of security people. If considered from the outset of the hotel's design, metal detectors, explosive material detectors, and video surveillance cameras can be integrated unobtrusively into a building's design. Emerging technologies are expanding the available options as well. For instance, video analytics, embedded in chips inside cameras, can be programmed to recognize certain actions: a vehicle parked beside a building for an unusual length of time; people running; people fighting; speeding vehicles; and a host of other shapes and movements that may indicate trouble.
>
> Classic security practice combines design, technology, and staffing with operational policies and procedures. Together, these components make it possible to identify problems early enough to mount an appropriate response. Procedures include an emergency response plan that includes alarm, containment/lock-down, evacuation, and communications capabilities that can maintain contact among staff, guests, security staff, and law enforcement.
>
> No guest will feel comfortable in a hotel that fails to address the potential problems associated with fire, theft, and, increasingly, terrorism. Security design can address these issues without detracting from the experience offered by the hotel or the equity of a hospitality brand.

Source: Adapted from Jim Suggs, "10 Keys to Designing More Secure Hotels," http://web. archive.org/web/20101102180358/http://lhonline.com/design/lighting/security_design_ lighting_parking_technology_0223/. Jim Suggs is a principal with RTKL Associates Inc. Founded in 1946, RTKL is a global architecture, planning, and design firm consistently ranked among the world's top design companies. RTKL's award-winning portfolio spans six continents and includes projects in the retail, entertainment, residential, healthcare, civic and public, workplace, mixed use, hospitality, urban planning, and technology sectors.

Sabotage

Sabotage is a terrorist technique that can be guarded against in a number of ways. Some of these involve simply adhering to sound security procedures. For example, security personnel should thoroughly investigate anything unusual or abnormal on the premises. Employees alert to security concerns may deter a potential saboteur or discover attempted sabotage before any substantial damage has occurred.

Effective personnel procedures may also be useful. It is essential to perform a thorough pre-employment reference check of all applicants. Suspicious background information may be elicited and questionable job candidates weeded out through the use of pre-employment personality tests. Employers must realize, however, that such checks will not catch all types of dangerous individuals, because in some cases the applicants are highly intelligent and well aware of how to give the "right" answers in order to get hired.

Another security tactic that may prevent sabotage is dispensing equipment and supplies under a very strict accounting procedure. Double sets of signatures can be required for obtaining certain materials and equipment. Two persons can be required to unlock a door to a restricted area. This team approach discourages unauthorized use of materials or the presence of unauthorized individuals in an area. Collusion between the potential saboteur and another employee would be necessary for the destructive act to be carried out.

Saboteurs may attempt to destroy a property's equipment and machinery, especially that related to its power supply. Therefore, electric cabinets and motor rooms should be locked and restricted to authorized personnel only. Employees using equipment should check it before starting work. This may reveal sabotage before any injuries or destruction actually takes place.

Kidnappings and Hostage Situations

Executives and their families are particularly vulnerable to terrorist kidnappings. Few people are ready to deal with a kidnapping situation without an emotional or physical reaction, least of all children.

Potential kidnapping victims can be told of certain protective tactics in advance. Past kidnappings indicate that kidnappers generally keep victims under surveillance for substantial periods of time in order to discover travel patterns and arrange a suitable time and place for the crime. Unpredictability is one of a potential victim's best weapons, as is being discreet on the telephone (which may be tapped) when discussing information concerning travel plans. When preventive actions fail and a kidnapping occurs, kidnapping victims should:

1. Remain calm and be alert to situations which they can use to their advantage.

2. Not attempt to fight back or struggle physically. No matter how reasonable their captors may appear to be on the surface, they cannot be trusted to behave normally and their actions may be unpredictable.

3. Comply with the instructions of their abductors as fully as possible.

4. Mentally note the time spent in transit, direction, distances, speeds, landmarks along the way, special odors, and distinctive sounds and voices—even when blindfolded.

5. Mentally take note of the characteristics of their captors, including their habits, surroundings, speech mannerisms, and what contacts they make.

6. Not expect a good opportunity for escape. No attempt should be made unless it has been carefully calculated to ensure the best possible odds for success.

7. Not provoke their captors. They may be unstable and react irrationally.

8. Request special medicines or medical attention immediately if they have a disease or physical condition that requires treatment.

9. Try to establish some kind of rapport with their captors.

Lodging property staff members and guests may also be subject to being held hostage on the premises. Many of the suggestions concerning kidnapping situations also apply when dealing with terrorists taking hostages at the hotel. Some properties have chosen to train certain key staff members at the local and, when appropriate, corporate levels in hostage negotiation. It has been found in some cases that terrorists will refuse to negotiate with the police or a government negotiator; instead, they compel the staff to negotiate.

Every property must determine for itself the likelihood of its being the target of terrorist acts. Depending on the property and its location, the likelihood may be remote. On the other hand, international chains with a large number of properties may find the possibility to be great enough to warrant concern and advance planning. A corporate contingency plan for dealing with kidnappings and hostage situations might necessitate determining which members of the corporate staff should go to an emergency site. Operations, security, insurance, fire protection, safety, communications, and public relations personnel are all possible candidates for an initial corporate response team. Even with such a team in place, there should be only one official spokesperson for the property in any kidnapping or hostage situation.

Riots and Civil Disturbances

Two aspects of terrorism that should not be overlooked are riots and civil disturbances. Management should develop a feasible plan of action that will be implemented whenever a riot or civil disturbance occurs within a certain distance of the lodging property. Such a disturbance cannot be ignored, even if it originates at some distance from the establishment.

Perimeter protection should be focused primarily on buildings rather than the grounds. Basement and ground-level windows should be secured, as should all entrances except the main entrance to the lobby, which should be protected by security throughout the duration of the emergency. Security personnel should check for tunnels and utility connections to the property to prevent unwanted access.

Properties should consider installing fire-retardant wood or metal shutters on windows. This is especially helpful in the event of fire bombing efforts by rioters. A roof security detail may also be considered for neutralizing fire bombs that may be thrown onto the roof or other elevated surfaces.

If at all possible, properties should keep unwanted individuals out of the hotel. If forced entry is made, an effort may need to be made to negotiate for the safety of guests and employees. Preparation for the responsibility of such negotiations should be coordinated with local authorities and legal counsel. This is especially important if a hotel representative is to assume the role of negotiator.

Cash on hand should be reduced at the initial warning of a riot or civil disorder. If possible, monies should be moved by armored car to a bank.

A plan for food rationing might be considered. If guests and employees are trapped on the premises, an emergency food plan would be helpful. Alcoholic beverages should be secured during the emergency and should not be served.

If possible, vehicles should be protected by moving them into a secured area on the property or to a location away from the property and the riot or civil disorder.

Security staff may be supplemented by personnel from other departments to provide a security presence throughout the property. Patrols of each floor on a continuing basis may be required throughout the emergency.

Media Relations

Emergencies and bad news involving a hotel may negatively affect the public's perceptions of a property. While good news is often forgotten, bad news may create a lasting impression, and its effects on business may be devastating. Effective media relations can help to minimize these effects.

Public relations plays an important part in an emergency response program. The ties between public relations and security may be critical. Unless instructed by management, the security director should not meet with the media, but may serve as a resource for the public relations director and staff as they prepare a statement for the designated property spokesperson.

What to Tell the Media

In handling emergencies and bad news with regard to public and media relations, management should exercise discretion based on the circumstances and the nature of business operations and policies. Employees as well as managers should know how to address the media *before* an emergency occurs. Every property should consider preparing its own public relations manual (with advice of legal counsel) and educate all employees on the proper procedures to follow. Once a manual has been printed, it should be distributed to supervisory personnel. Then, all employees should be informed of the property's policy regarding communications with the news media. In addition, employees may be reminded of the manual's key elements from time to time.

This section does not (nor could it) present a comprehensive media relations policy for all lodging properties to follow. However, it does discuss points that all properties might consider in preparing their own crisis communication manuals:

- The owners or managers of the property should contact their attorneys and corporate communications department (if the property is part of a chain) for advice on whether any statement should be made to the media. The property may wish to ask counsel to help in preparing such a statement, so that neither legal rights nor the outcome of future litigation are jeopardized.

- Before answering any questions about an incident, a property should quickly and accurately determine the facts surrounding the incident.

- If a property and its attorneys decide that communication with the press is appropriate in the given situation, *there should be only one spokesperson for the property.* The spokesperson should be fully briefed on responses to any questions that may arise and should be instructed not to deviate from the prepared responses. A fairly popular technique of some media reporters is to seek out and interview people, including employees, whom the incident affects or who saw the incident, instead of or in addition to interviewing the organization's spokesperson. All employees should be notified and reminded through their department heads or supervisors that they should not respond to inquiries by reporters or guests, but rather should refer all inquiries to management or the official spokesperson. The property's owner, manager, and appointed spokesperson should be available to respond to such referrals.

Organizations such as the Public Relations Society of America (www.prsa.org) offer a variety of resources, networking, and professional development opportunities for anyone who works regularly with the media to create and maintain a positive corporate image.

- Reporters should not be allowed to wander unescorted through the property, take pictures or video, or interview guests or other witnesses, especially if there has been a fire, explosion, or other event which may have caused structural damage. (Managers should be aware, however, that there is little they can do to control guests taking pictures or videos and making them available to the media.)

- If appropriate, communications to the media should be made at a scheduled news conference so that all reporters receive the same information at the same time.

In the event of a serious incident at a property, all media inquiries should be referred by management or the appointed spokesperson to the appropriate investigating authorities (for example, the police or fire department).

Responding to reporters' questions with "No comment" is never acceptable. It creates the perception that facts are being hidden and may provoke an investigative reporter into creating unnecessary and misleading reporting of an incident. All questions should be answered by the official spokesperson. In order to avoid "No comment," some properties find it preferable to explain why no comment can be made. For example, in the event of a fire or suspected arson, the inquiries should be referred to the fire chief. The property spokesperson should explain that he or she is unable to comment on the cause of the fire because it is under routine investigation by the fire department, which will release its own findings.

If there are casualties resulting from an incident, reporter inquiries should be referred to the fire chief, police chief, and local hospitals for confirmation. The names of victims or supposed victims should not be released to the media by the hotel. Rather, such information properly comes from the investigating authority after notification of next of kin.

When reporters request immediate estimates from management on the extent of physical damage to the property, they may be informed by the spokesperson that any quick damage assessment would only be a guess. Reporters can be truthfully told that the property's insurance company investigators have been notified and that the dollar amount of damage will have to be determined by them.

There may be any number of details concerning some incidents that the property may wish to tell authorized investigators but not the media. These details will obviously vary from incident to incident. For example, a property that has been robbed may choose not to inform the media of the exact amount of money taken or whether any cash was overlooked by the robbers. It may not wish to discuss the types of alarm systems it uses (or whether it uses any at all) and if they functioned properly. It may withhold the identity of any witnesses who can accurately describe or identify the criminals.

Suicides, bombings, and other irrational actions of unstable people may happen, on rare occasions, in a hotel. Properties faced with such occurrences should immediately contact legal counsel regarding their proposed statements to the media. It may be appropriate for the spokesperson to request in those cases that the name of the property not be mentioned by the media, since lodging industry experience and psychological studies have shown that when a depressed or disturbed person learns of this type of activity, he or she may be drawn to the same place to commit a similar deed. The media can be asked to refer to the property as "a downtown hotel" or "a motel north of town," for example.

When possible, the property's spokesperson can describe the positive actions taken in coping with an emergency to ensure ongoing guest services and comfort. This information and cooperation with the media may result in more sympathetic media coverage. Reporters may subsequently be more inclined to report only the facts, avoiding the temptation to sensationalize because of an uncooperative spokesperson. Also, efforts to accommodate displaced or inconvenienced guests are positive news that the property may use to combat any negative inferences that the public might draw from the emergency, regardless of its cause. The Las Vegas Palace Station Hotel & Casino made such a positive publicity effort when lightning and heavy thunderstorms caused major property damage in the summer of 1998. The initial press release, available the day following the incident, presented the situation clearly and straightforwardly:

> Early this morning, a portion of the casino roof collapsed during a heavy thunderstorm that struck the Las Vegas Valley. The collapsed area impacted approximately 25 percent of the 85,000-square-foot casino. In addition to the roof collapse, the storm also knocked out all electrical power within a 10-square block area of Palace Station and sent floodwater through several entrances of the casino.
>
> A few hours following this incident, a four-alarm fire broke out in a building facade at the top of the hotel tower. Damage was confined to the outside of the building at the roof. The Las Vegas Fire Department attributed the fire to lightning or rain that short-circuited wiring atop the hotel tower. It was extinguished approximately 30 minutes later while hotel security personnel evacuated approximately 2,200 guests. Injuries were minor in both incidents.
>
> The 21-story hotel tower is fully functional with the exception of the rooms on the 21st floor that underwent more substantial smoke and water damage. The casino portion of the facility is currently closed as the company evaluates its alternatives.

The press release went on to include a quote from the property's Executive Vice President and Chief Financial Officer Glenn C. Christenson: "We are fortunate that none of our guests or team members suffered any serious injuries.... We are working with our insurance representatives, construction consultants, and engineers to determine the extent of damages, a realistic timetable for repairs, and when we can completely re-open." The next day's follow-up release announced the re-opening of several gaming facilities and four restaurants.

According to Director of Corporate Communications Jack Taylor, the key is to have "a good plan—and stick to it. Whenever you are offering any product to the public, you have to be prepared for anything that could occur. We developed our communications plan over five years ago; as our company grew, we found we needed to expand our crisis management strategies. Today, we have a written plan on the shelf at every one of our properties." That plan enabled the Palace Station to take swift action on the day of the emergency. "We had TV crews live on every side of the hotel. Our crisis response team hit the ground running, and we literally did a news conference in the parking lot. We had to act extremely quickly to make sure everyone was 'on the same page,' getting the same information. Your messages must be continuous, consistent, and accurate."

Once Taylor and his department felt the press releases had run their course, they turned to paid advertising. "Once the news aspect runs out, ads can step in and play a key role in communicating your message." The property also prepared a video news release to distribute to local media that had covered the original crisis, showing off the improvements and repairs and the hotel's series of re-opening celebrations. They also brought one of the local TV news crews back to the property for a walk-through with the city's fire chief, who explained how well-prepared the hotel was and how smoothly the emergency had been handled.

Dealing with Group Disturbances

Problems involving group disturbances might include picketing or aggressive activity by organizations critical of the property's hiring or employment policies; consumer groups taking issue with one or more of the property's services; political groups protesting the presence of a controversial guest; and more.

The bad publicity associated with such disturbances can be aggravated when the group has informed the media of its intentions ahead of time. This means reporters, television cameras, and photographers may be on the scene before the property is aware of what is happening.

Once the property is aware of what is going on, it can prepare a statement to make to the media with regard to the demonstration. It should be approved by legal counsel, if possible, and should be brief, factual, and as objective as possible. Also, the property should consider notifying the police.

If the group disturbance is well-organized and members have contacted the media in advance, it is quite likely that they will have prepared their own written information to release to the media. A property is justified in asking for a copy of this material from either the media or the protesting group. This may help in the preparation of the property's statement. If the property cannot obtain this information, either in writing or orally from a group leader, it is reasonable for its spokesperson to respond to media questions by saying that the property cannot comment on something about which it knows nothing.

Endnotes

1. http://www.fema.gov/library/viewRecord.do?id=1689.

2. R. J. Kwornik, "Preparing for Disaster: Recommendations Based on the Blackout of '03," *Cornell Quarterly*, 2005, 46:47–51.

3. http://www.infoplease.com/ipa/A0001454.html.

4. Occupational Safety and Health Standards, Subpart E—Means of Egress. Code of Federal Regulations, Title 29, Chapter XVII, Part 1910, Subpart E; Revised as of July 1, 1979; Amended as 45 FR 60703—September 12, 1980. Section 1910.38 Employee emergency plans and fire prevention plans.

5. For more information about cyclones, please see the website for the National Hurricane Center (part of the National Oceanic and Atmospheric Administration [NOAA]) at http://www.nhc.noaa.gov.

6. A good source for general information on how individuals can prepare for tropical cyclones can be found at *Tropical Cyclones: A Preparedness Guide*, created by the Federal Emergency Management Agency (FEMA), the American Red Cross, and the National Weather Service; http://www.nws.noaa.gov/os/hurricane/resources/TropicalCyclones11.pdf.

7. *Hurricane Procedures Manual*, Caribbean Disaster Mitigation Project; http://www.oas.org/cdmp/document/chaman/chaman.html.

8. http://www.bizjournals.com/nashville/stories/2010/05/31/daily13.html.

9. https://msc.fema.gov/webapp/wcs/stores/servlet/CategoryDisplay?catalogId=10001&storeId=10001&categoryId=12001&langId=-1&userType=G&type=1&future=false.

10. http://www.insurancejournal.com/news/national/2011/12/05/226211.htm.

11. http://www.mapsofworld.com/world-major-earthquake.htm.

12. Hotels in earthquake-prone areas may find FEMA 400, *Incremental Seismic Rehabilitation of Hotel and Motel Buildings* (April 2005) to be a useful resource. www.fema.gov/library/viewRecord.do?id=1433.

13. An excellent source for information about tsunamis is the National Oceanic and Atmospheric Administration's tsunami web page at http://tsunami.noaa.gov/basics.html.

14. http://www.tsunamiready.com/index.php.

15. http://www.redcross.org/www-files/Documents/pdf/Preparedness/AED_FAQs.pdf.

16. In late July 1976, the Bellevue-Stratford Hotel in Philadelphia had a number of guests become ill with flu-like symptoms. Eventually, 221 guests became ill, of which 34 died. A bacteria was identified as the cause and given the name *Legionella* (most of the sickened guests had been attending an American Legion convention). Since this event, infections involving this bacteria have been identified at other hotels as well as in other residential and commercial settings. More information can be found at http://en.wikipedia.org/wiki/1976_Philadelphia_Legionnaires%27_disease_outbreak.

17. http://www.cdc.gov/legionella/.

18. http://ecdc.europa.eu/en/publications/Publications/1109_SR_Legionnaires'%20disease_Europe_2009.pdf.

19. http://www.who.int/csr/sars/country/country2003_08_15.pdf.

20. http://www.cdc.gov/h1n1flu/estimates_2009_h1n1.htm.

21. http://www.ahla.com/flu/.

22. The Department of Homeland Security and the American Hotel & Lodging Association partnered to produce two anti-terrorism resources for the lodging industry: the *Protective Measures Guide for the U.S. Lodging Industry*, published in 2010; and the "If you see something, say something" security campaign featuring videos, posters, and other training materials.

Review Questions

1. What are some of the different types of emergencies lodging operations might have to deal with?

2. Why is emergency planning an important element in lodging security?

3. What items should management consider when developing an emergency management program?

4. What are the categories of hurricanes and what are the effects of each category?

5. What are some typical precautions lodging properties should take, regardless of the type of emergency?

6. How should medical emergencies be handled?

7. Should a property offer medical service through the use of house physicians and assistants? Why or why not?

8. When preventive actions fail and a kidnapping occurs, what are some things kidnap victims should do?

9. How do media relations play a part in a property's emergency response system?

10. What should be included in a property's media relations policy?

Internet Sites

For more information, visit the following Internet sites. Remember that Internet addresses can change without notice. If the site is no longer there, you can use a search engine to look for additional sites.

American Red Cross
www.redcross.org

Bureau of Diplomatic Security
www.ds.state.gov

The Crisis Coalition
www.crisiscoalition.com

Federal Emergency Management
Association
www.fema.gov

Hart Media (Media Training/
Crisis Communication)
www.hartmedia.com

International Association of Business
Communicators
www.iabc.com

National Fire Protection Association
www.nfpa.org

National Oceanic and Atmospheric
Administration
www.noaa.gov

National Safety Council
www.nsc.org

Opryland Hotel
www.opryhotel.com

Overseas Security Advisory Council
www.ds.state.gov/osacmenu.cfm

Public Relations Society of America
www.prsa.org

The Salvation Army
www.salvationarmy.org

Case Study

Terrorist on the Telephone

PBX Operator Carolee Tomlinson glanced at the clock. "Noon," she thought as the phone rang with yet another call. She was eager to help the caller and leave for a very well-deserved lunch break. It seemed everything at the Northpoint was especially hectic that day. It was the first day of the hotel's first large convention since a major renovation project was completed. With over 1,000 nationally respected guests on site, everyone wanted to make the best impression possible.

"Thank you for calling the Northpoint Hotel. How may I direct your call?"

"There's a bomb at your hotel."

Carolee gulped. "I beg your pardon, sir?"

"Your hearing better improve fast unless you want to see a lot of people get blown up."

Carolee took a deep breath and tried to keep her nerves under control as she reached for the Northpoint's printed list of bomb-threat procedures. "I'm sorry, sir, we seem to have a bad connection. If you're on a cell phone, it might be best to—"

"I'm not on a cell phone, I'm in a ph—." The caller stopped abruptly. "Just listen. There's a bomb in your hotel and you'd better do something about it."

"What time is it going to go off?" Carolee asked, reading from the bomb-threat checklist.

"Forty-five minutes from now."

"12:45," she said, taking notes.

"That's what I said."

"Where is it?"

"Why don't we just say that's for me to know and you to find out. More fun that way, don't you think?"

"What kind of bomb is it?"

"The kind that sends a very, very loud message." The caller laughed, and Carolee noted the sound of traffic in the background.

"Why are you doing this?"

"You've got a lot of nerve, asking me that. I think it's time all those so-called scientists came face-to-face with the fact that there are some things they just can't fix. Maybe they won't keep thinking they can play God with people's lives."

The convention, Carolee thought. The Cancer Research Society of America. Who in the world could possibly hold a grudge against cancer researchers? And then Carolee remembered something. "Is this Dale?"

The line went dead.

Carolee glanced up at the clock. It was 12:07. Amazing how quickly your whole world can change, she thought as she dialed the police. After informing them of the threat, she notified the property's general manager, Marisa Hingle.

Marisa quickly appeared at Carolee's workstation. "What was your impression of the caller?" she asked.

Carolee reviewed her notes from the conversation. "It was a man, no accent to speak of. I think he was calling from a phone booth; I heard traffic in the background."

"No location or description of the device?" Marisa asked.

"He just said it would send a very loud message." Carolee paused. "You know, I think it was Dale Edgar. The caller specifically said he wanted to get back at our conference attendees because they were 'playing God with people's lives.' I know Dale's wife died of cancer about two weeks after he quit to care for her, and I sort of recognized his voice. But I didn't really know him well, so I don't know if it's something he's really capable of or whether he's just bluffing."

"Thanks, Carolee," Marisa said as she hurried away, glancing at her watch. "No matter who it was, we're taking every precaution. Make the evacuation call now."

For the Northpoint Hotel, "every precaution" meant an evacuation and a complete search of the property for any packages, luggage, or other devices that looked suspicious, out of place, or unclaimed.

Carolee referred to her bomb-procedures sheet again and dialed into the public-address system that went into all of the rooms in the hotel.

"We apologize for this inconvenience," Carolee read over the PA, "but an emergency situation has arisen. We must ask that you evacuate the premises immediately, taking with you your valuables and personal belongings, and proceed to the park located across the street from the hotel. Please use the stairwells, if necessary. Do not use the elevators. Thank you. Safety code 319."

"Safety code 319" was the Northpoint's code for a bomb threat, which every staff member at the hotel would recognize. Even as people were beginning to hurry out of the conference rooms and guestrooms, hotel staff were assembling in their assigned areas.

The food and beverage and sales managers began moving through the seminar rooms and meeting spaces being used by the conference attendees. Room attendants checked linen closets and other storage areas to be sure they were indeed locked and that there were no signs of suspicious activity. Engineering employees worked their way through the mechanical rooms, checking all equipment for anything that looked unusual.

Marisa and her staff were standing at the entrance ushering guests into the parking lot when three police cars screeched down the driveway. The Channel 10 news van and a car from the *Suburban Sun-Sentinel* were close behind. Marisa knew that once the call went out over the police bands it would only be a question of "when," not "if," the news media would arrive. She also knew that herding 1,000 eminent doctors and scientists across the street and into the park was bound to create images too intriguing for the TV broadcasters and newspaper photographers to ignore. She searched the growing crowd for the hotel's director of public relations and the property's designated spokesman, Roger Carr.

Discussion Questions

1. Did the general manager make the right choice in evacuating over 1,000 guests to the park? What factors influenced her decision?

2. Based on this year's experience, should the Northpoint Hotel take any steps to prepare for bomb threats against this convention group in future years? If so, what steps might it take?

3. What points might Roger Carr make when he makes a statement to the local media? When should that statement occur?

Case Number: 3876CA

The following industry experts helped generate and develop this case: Wendell Couch, ARM, CHA, Director of Technical Services for the Risk Management Department of Bass Hotels & Resorts; and Raymond C. Ellis, Jr., CHE, CHTP, CLSD, Professor, Conrad N. Hilton College, University of Houston, Director, Loss Prevention Management Institute.

Chapter 10 Outline

Competencies

1. Explain how insurance can help properties minimize their financial expenses due to losses, summarize considerations in purchasing insurance, and discuss insurance industry regulation. (pp. 329–334)

2. List and describe the types of coverage found in commercial package policies and in additional types of coverage available to lodging properties. (pp. 335–342)

3. Demonstrate the proper procedures used for managing claims. (pp. 342–344)

10

Insurance

RISK MANAGEMENT is the protection of people and assets through the identification, determination, and management of the risks a corporation faces. The goal of risk management is to achieve the most economical use of resources in order to minimize or control risk. One way to protect a hotel from certain types of risk is to purchase insurance coverage.

We will begin the chapter with a general discussion about insurance, then move to a discussion of commercial package policies and other types of insurance for hotels (flood insurance, umbrella coverage, and legally mandated coverage). The chapter concludes with a look at insurance claims management.

Insurance: An Overview

Correct decisions regarding insurance purchases can help properties minimize their financial expenses due to losses, reducing not only the monetary cost of loss, but the potential anxiety and worry that may accompany uncertainty regarding the ability to survive these losses. Insurance providers, through their in-house loss prevention resources (consultant site visits, training webinars and videos, vendor recommendations, etc.), can also be highly beneficial in reducing potential losses. Finally, knowledge of insurance can assist in securing the correct coverage at a reasonable cost, thereby controlling the cost of risk financing while still providing the coverage needed. Insurance may be purchased by hotels in order to provide funds to pay for losses resulting from natural disasters, workplace injuries, and other events that may be encountered in the course of business, such as auto accidents, theft, and liability claims.

Insurance Purchase

The purchase of insurance involves both risk transfer and risk sharing. **Risk transfer** occurs when all or part of the financial costs of a loss are transferred from the insured to the insurer, who is typically in a stronger financial position to pay the loss than the insured. This transfer of risk has an identifiable cost: premium payments and, if a claim is made, deductible payments. **Risk sharing,** or **pooling,** occurs when the group policy holders agree to share the risk costs of the group via a payment by all to a fund shared by the group. For example, the hospitality niche of a large mid-market insurance broker developed a master insurance program tailored to the needs of several smaller (twenty hotels or less) hotel management companies. Utilizing the economies of scale (overall, the broker had over $600 million of premiums placed with insurance carriers for hospitality clients), the master program was able to reduce each company's total cost of insurance and increase their coverage limits.

Also inherent in an insurance purchase may be an element of risk retention, since many insurance policies will require the payment of a deductible by the insured. In some instances the policies may only cover losses in excess of certain amounts (in effect a deductible, but generally not called so). This approach is very effective for a well-run company with a mature loss prevention and risk management program.

Viewed from a risk standpoint, the company purchasing insurance can be thought of as trading off a potentially large, unpredictable cost for a generally smaller but highly predictable cost. And, while the unpredictability of loss for a single business can be high, insurance combines the losses of a large number of firms into a group that is large enough that losses become much more predictable. For example, the potential losses due to a fire at an individual hotel could be as much as the entire building itself or as little as no damage. And the probability of a fire at any given hotel is very low. This combination results in a potentially large and highly unpredictable loss for a hotel owner. However, the total number of hotel fires in the United States and the total property losses from those fires are relatively predictable from one year to the next. Insurance takes advantage of this fact and allows all hotels to pay a relatively small amount of money (the premium) to cover the losses of a relatively small group of hotels (those with fires).

Not all possible risks are insurable, for a variety of reasons. Insurance experts cite four key prerequisites that make a risk insurable:

- There must be a sufficiently large number of roughly similar exposure units to make the losses reasonably predictable. The large number of units argument is a result of the laws of probability providing higher levels of predictability as the number of units grows.

- The loss produced by the risk must be definite and measurable. The need for a definite and measurable loss is necessary in order to determine the amount of money that needs to be paid in premiums.

- The loss must be accidental and unintentional. Providing insurance for a loss that could be a decision of the insured would obviously open the door for fraud. For example, if the owner of a building deliberately burned it down, that person could not collect on an insurance policy.

- The loss must not be catastrophic. Avoiding insuring of catastrophic losses (i.e., to a large number of the insured units at the same time) is necessary if the financial viability of the insurer is to be sustained. One example of insurers avoiding catastrophic losses is when they exclude damages "due to acts of war" from their insurance policies. Such damage could be so widespread and so unpredictable that insurance could clearly not be written to provide coverage.

When contemplating the purchase of insurance, hotel managers should be aware that there are a number of options available. While most insurance is purchased from private insurance companies, some insurance, such as workers' compensation coverage (in some states) or flood insurance, is available from public (governmental) sources.

Private insurance purchases may be from **stock insurers** (a corporation owned by stockholders who participate in the profits and losses of the insurer) or **mutual insurers** (a corporation owned by the policyholders). There are many additional forms of these types of insurers as well. The Blue Cross and Blue Shield Association and health maintenance organizations (HMOs) are types of insurance that provide medical coverage. Insurance companies themselves purchase insurance through **reinsurers,** firms that transfer potential risk from a single insurance company to a number of insurance companies.

The purchase of insurance is done through agents or brokers. **Agents** legally represent the insurer and have the authority to act on the insurer's behalf. Agents will normally issue a **binder,** which is temporary evidence that insurance exists until a policy is issued. **Brokers** legally represent the insured. A broker solicits applications for insurance and then attempts to place the coverage with an appropriate insurer; upon acceptance, the policy is issued. A broker with a large hospitality business can leverage that volume with insurance carriers. In many cases, the broker can recommend target pricing for a specific risk. Brokers are active in many aspects of insurance, often focusing on specific forms of insurance coverage and providing specialized services (such as loss control and claims management).

When calculating the cost of insurance premiums, the insurance carrier underwriter uses an assortment of "truth tellers" to rate the account:

- Does the prospective client have a top-down safety culture? Do senior managers rate the importance of safety on a par with quality and productivity? Do they "walk the talk" by providing clear examples of the importance of loss control and risk management?

- Does the organization have a designated risk manager—someone who monitors the loss control program, reviews claims, tracks loss trends, etc.?

- Is there a formal, comprehensive, written safety program that all managers and properties must follow?

- Is there an active, respected, and empowered safety committee that meets on a regular basis? Are all departments represented? Are both hourly workers and managers represented?

- Is there an active return-to-work program? Is every effort made to design and provide transitional duties for injured employees? Has local management established a relationship with their assigned primary healthcare facility? Have the local healthcare providers been given job descriptions and a list of light-duty jobs available?

- Are all levels of management held financially accountable for meeting assigned safety goals? Do these goals take into account the frequency and severity of injuries, number of lost work days, timeliness of claim reporting, use of preferred healthcare providers, and regularity of safety committee meetings?

What to Seek in a Broker

Due to the complexity and changing nature of insurance, it is quite likely that hotel owners and operators will look to the services of an insurance broker when making insurance decisions. A broker typically considers several insurance firms before placing the actual insurance itself. The broker for a hotel company should have experience with the hotel industry and be of a size that is appropriate for the business being insured, so that the hotel company receives the needed insurance services in a timely manner. It is important for the hotel's representatives to spend time with the broker so that the broker understands the hotel's business activities and the hotel understands the broker's industry experience and approach to insurance.

Small hotels may wish to deal with a local insurance broker company or even an agent. Care must be taken that the wide range of risks associated with the hotel are properly addressed in the insurance that is purchased. Brokers experienced in dealing with hotels are most likely to be able to help a hotel identify the appropriate types of insurance coverage, determine the dollar limits that are needed for this coverage, and find the right insurance programs and carriers to provide bids and coverage. Since small hotels are unlikely to have loss control or risk management departments, the expertise of the broker (and the insurance company) in loss reduction can be particularly valuable to small hotels. The same is likely to be true when it comes to claims management.

Some specific areas of common insurance "gaps" that have been identified by insurance professionals, which hoteliers should be aware of, include the following:

- Failure to review policy limits and covered property when renewing policies. Insurance policies can change over time in subtle but sometimes substantial ways, resulting in coverage exclusions that can be devastating.

- Failure to retain copies of insurance policies after their expiration. Some claims are based on the date of occurrence of the injury or damage, and expired policies may apply to the time period in question.

- Insuring property for values that are substantially lower than actual replacement costs.

- Failure to have adequate levels of business income coverage to enable the hotel to continue through times of business interruption and recovery.

- Failure to identify contractual obligations that the hotel has outside of normal business obligations as well as policy exclusions that may exist. For example, if a hotel has a spa operation on its premises, hotel managers must make sure they have the proper insurance coverage. The scope of the needed insurance coverage will depend in part on whether the hotel operates the spa facilities or the spa operation is outsourced.

- Failure to include specific insurance requirements (coverage and limits) in contracts for events meeting at the hotel, and failure to ask the event planner

(continued)

(continued)

> to have the hotel named as an additional insured in the policy the event planner purchases. Hotels also need to make sure that the group holding the event actually purchases the insurance coverage and provides documentation.
>
> - Hotel having excess liability coverage limits that are too low. Franchise agreements often require excess liability coverage of $3 to $10 million. Excess liability coverage provides a large amount of protection for what is usually a very low cost.

Industry Regulation

Purchasers of insurance, whether through an agent or broker, want to be sure that the company providing the insurance is legitimate and has the financial capability to cover losses. The government recognizes this and provides a rather extensive regulatory system of state insurance departments that provide oversight on the operation of insurance companies. Besides legislation applying to all firms, insurance companies must comply with industry-specific legislation at both the state and federal level. The National Association of Insurance Commissioners provides general guidance and communication regarding insurance issues.

An insurance purchase decision should include consideration of the insurer's rating. Ratings involve a review of the insurer's financial exposures, the income from premiums, and the various assets of the firms. A.M. Best Company and Standard & Poor's (among others) provide ratings of insurers. Ratings firms use letter grades to rate companies. Be sure to understand the meaning of the letters, since an "A" from one company may be the top grade, while at another it may be somewhat less than the top. With insurance purchasing, you not only "get what you pay for," you also "pay for what you get." To be sure that you have adequate coverage at a reasonable cost, it is important to correctly specify your needs when contacting insurance providers. Exhibit 1 outlines the importance of insurance specifications.

Given the potential complexities of decisions regarding coverage and the costs of coverage, some hotels may opt for participation in **group coverage.** Groups exist for all types of properties (luxury, independent, ski resorts), as well as for state associations. Most large hotel chains purchase group coverage for their hotels rather than allowing each hotel to negotiate coverage individually. Benefits of purchasing insurance in this manner include lower prices and rate stability. The larger number of participants in the group provides a more predictable loss base and therefore more stability in the pricing of premiums. Also, purchasing groups focusing on the industry itself will provide opportunities to customize insurance policies to the specific needs of the industry. For example, ski resorts looking to purchase insurance for ski lift–related incidents should be able to find more specific coverage at a lower cost through a ski industry group.

Exhibit 1   The Importance of Insurance Specifications

The single most important document in arranging a competitive and comprehensive insurance program is the specifications that are submitted to the insurance company. This document should be composed of the following sections:

Corporate History
It is important that the underwriters are given a clear picture of your company, its past as well as what is being planned for the future.

Exposures
Depending on the coverage you are applying for, full disclosure of your current exposures, such as sales, payroll, vehicles, property values real and personal by location, loss of income potential, rental value, rental expense, etc., should be provided. In addition to your current exposures, your exposures for the past three to five years are also an intricate part of the underwriting process. As a subsection to exposures, you will need to supply the construction, occupancy, and protection information (COPE) on all locations.

Loss Information
Three to five years of detailed loss history by coverage is required. A separate report on large losses with more complete detail should also be included.

Program Design
It is always better to outline the type of program you feel will best suit the needs of your company than to let the underwriters dictate one which will not accomplish the goals you have set forth. You need to indicate the type of limits, deductibles, and cash flow options you wish to see in this section. You also need to outline the parameters for claims reporting and loss control engineering requirements.

Safety and Management Programs
From an underwriter's point of view, management's commitment to safety has a direct bearing on the extent of losses likely to occur in the course of the policy year. If possible, include any and all safety manuals, employee training information, company guidelines, etc. If this is not practical, identify the types of programs in place and offer to make the manual or personnel available upon inspection.

Contingent Exposures/Contractual Obligations
You will need to provide detail on contractual obligations that may go outside of the general coverage parameters. You will also need to identify those contingent exposures which could affect you, but for which you do not have direct control (e.g., concessionaires and vendors who come onto your property).

As stated at the outset, this is a very important document. It can also be somewhat intimidating. It is important that you and your broker, in partnership, assemble it and are in agreement as to its contents. Full disclosure of all possible exposures as well as past and current loss history eliminates any misunderstanding with the underwriters and will allow for a mutually beneficial relationship.

Source: George Kearon and Carey O'Connor, *The BottomLine,* April/May 1997, p. 14. Used with permission.

Commercial Package Policy

A common way to provide property coverage is through purchase of a **commercial package policy (CPP).** The CPP has common provisions suitable for various business types, but can also be modified to cover the needs of a specific business. The CPP also includes coverage for various liability exposures. Combining property and liability exposures in a single package can result in lower insurance costs and a coverage that has fewer gaps (and fewer possible difficulties in determining coverage if a loss occurs). The CPP contains two or more forms of insurance coverage that may include:

- Commercial property coverage
- Commercial crime coverage
- Boiler and machinery coverage
- Inland marine coverage
- Commercial general liability coverage
- Commercial automotive coverage

The components of the CPP include a **common policy declarations component** and a **common policy conditions component.** The declarations component involves an identification of the insured, the property insured, policy period, summary of coverage, and premium. The conditions component includes statements regarding transfer provisions, rights of the insurer to conduct property inspections and surveys, rights of the insurer to examine books and records, and cancellation and change provisions.

There are many aspects of the CPP and its coverage that should be carefully reviewed with the insurance broker or agent. The purpose of this discussion is to provide an introduction to the CPP; details of specific insurance policies and coverage options are beyond the scope of this chapter.

Commercial Property Coverage

Commercial property coverage commonly includes building and personal property components. The building includes physical structures, machinery, and equipment items that are permanently installed, such as light poles and mailboxes. Equipment used to maintain or service the building, such as floor buffers and fire-extinguishing equipment, is also included. Personal property includes property of the insured (such as furniture and fixtures), as well as personal property of others in the care, custody, or control of the insured.

A variety of additional coverage can be included that expands the property coverage. For example, additional coverage can be purchased for a fire department service charge, debris removal, and building ordinance coverage that includes increased costs of construction coverage. Hoteliers should make certain they guard against hidden costs, such as the demolition of the undamaged portion of the building (which may be required by law), refurbishment of the part(s) not destroyed, and any construction costs that may be required to bring a new building into compliance with current building codes.

Extensions of coverage can also be purchased. A building insurance extension, for example, includes new structures on the premises or newly acquired buildings at other locations—insured automatically up to a specified limit and time. Other provisions of commercial property coverage include deductibles, the process for determining the value of the losses, and coinsurance. **Coinsurance** is a provision of some policies that requires the insured to carry insurance equal to a specified percentage of the property's value—or receive less than full reimbursement for a loss. Exhibit 2 shows coinsurance calculations to determine the insurance amount to be paid on a claim. A **causes of loss form** identifies the specific types of perils

Exhibit 2   Coinsurance Calculations

Failure to insure property up to proper coinsurance levels (typically 80 or 90 percent of the property's value) is the most common problem encountered in property insurance policies. If your operation is underinsured, the insurance company will penalize you by paying less than the face amount on your policy.

To determine the insurance amount to be paid on a claim:

$$\frac{\text{Amount of insurance carried}}{\text{Amount of insurance to be received}} \times \text{Actual loss} = \text{Amount to be paid}$$

Example 1:

The replacement value of your property is $111,000 and your policy requires you to insure to at least 90 percent (or about $100,000), but you only insure $80,000. You sustain $40,000 in fire damages. How much would you recover?

$$\frac{\$80,000}{\$100,000} \times \$40,000 = \$32,000$$

The unreimbursed $8,000 would come out of your own pocket.

Example 2:

You insure the required $100,000. You sustain $40,000 in fire damages. How much would you recover?

$$\frac{\$100,000}{\$100,000} \times \$40,000 = \$40,000$$

This formula is not perfect, however. It doesn't work if you have insured to the required amount but sustained a *complete* loss. In that instance, you would only recover the amount to which you had insured—in this case, $100,000. Because you only insured to $100,000, you would incur $11,000 in unreimbursed damages. It is for this reason that experts recommend insuring to full value—that way you always get paid 100 percent of your loss.

Abridged from Phillip M. Perry, "Don't Let Your Fire Insurance Go Up in Smoke," *Restaurants USA*, October 1997.

(fire, lightning, etc.) that are covered under the policy; an earthquake is one peril which isn't covered in the basic insurance.

Business owners also generally purchase **business income (extra expense) coverage.** This coverage recognizes that property damage and other events may result in loss of business income, and that certain expenses may continue during the recovery period. Well-structured business income coverage can mean the difference between the survival and death of the business. Specifically, it is designed to cover the loss of business income, expenses that continue during the shutdown period, and extra expenses because of a direct physical loss to insured property. The loss of business income provision of these policies involves the net profit or loss that would have been earned plus continuing normal operating expenses, including payroll. The coverage also includes extra expenses incurred (such as rental of substitute equipment), action of civil authority (such as denial of use of a facility due to rioting), and extended business coverage (recognizing that a period of time may be required to fully recover from the event). Business owners should investigate the potential value to the firm of various optional coverages, including the maximum **period of indemnity,** monthly limit of **indemnity,** agreed value, and extended period of indemnity. Finally, business owners should be aware of coinsurance provisions in their policies that require minimum amounts of insurance coverage and function similar to coinsurance provisions for property insurance.

Commercial Crime Coverage

Commercial crime coverage recognizes that the assets of the firm include cash and securities and that these are potentially at risk from the acts of people. Besides concern about the loss of cash and securities of the operation itself, potential liability for guests' property in safe deposit boxes is a concern of lodging operations. Exhibit 3 lists types of crime insurance.

Boiler and Machinery Coverage

Boiler and machinery coverage applies to many types of equipment including boilers, refrigerating systems, engines, turbines, and generators that are not covered under the property component of the CPP coverage. With the critical nature and large quantity of such equipment that may be present in hotels, resorts, and even some restaurants, it is important to consider the value of this coverage. The insurance can be purchased to include not only direct losses to the equipment, but also losses due to lost business income, spoilage, and extra expenses necessary to keep the hotel operating in case of equipment failure (such as renting a piece of portable equipment).

Inland Marine Coverage

Inland (and ocean) marine coverage may seem like unnecessary insurance for most hotels and restaurants. However, inland marine coverage provides protection for goods shipped on land. Operations that take title to goods (such as furniture and equipment for a renovation) at the time of shipment from the supplier may wish to purchase inland marine coverage. Any property relying on shipment

Exhibit 3   Types of Crime Insurance Available

- Form A—Employee Dishonesty
- Form B—Forgery or Alteration
- Form C—Theft, Disappearance, and Destruction
- Form D—Robbery and Safe Burglary
- Form E—Premises Burglary
- Form F—Computer Fraud
- Form G—Extortion
- Form H—Premises Theft and Robbery Outside the Premises
- Form I—Losses of Safe-Deposit Boxes
- Form J—Securities Deposited with Others
- Form K—Liability for Guests' Property—Safe-Deposit Box
- Form L—Liability for Guests' Property
- Form M—Safe-Depository Liability
- Form N—Safe-Depository Direct Loss

of materials or supplies by water (e.g., an island resort) may also wish to consider marine coverage.

Commercial General Liability Coverage

Businesses can incur legal liability for a variety and growing number of reasons. Providing coverage for such liability is an important decision, since these liabilities can be for large sums of money. The **commercial general liability (CGL)** policy addresses the various sources of loss exposure of business firms and the various types of losses that may be incurred.

Premises and operations coverage involves legal liability that can arise out of ownership and maintenance of the location where the firm does business. This would include slips and trips by guests, injuries due to the collapse of a chair, and similar mishaps.

Products liability coverage involves injury to guests or damage to their property from defective products. While hotels may not think that they produce "products," food produced for a banquet or wedding reception could receive coverage under this option.

Completed operations coverage involves liability losses that occur away from the premises and arise out of the insured's product or work after the insured has relinquished possession of the product or the work has been completed. Hospitality operations certainly want this sort of coverage to exist for those doing work on or in their property, as well as for the manufacturer of products they purchase. Contractual liability coverage is desired if liability has been assumed from another party by written or oral contract.

Contractual liability coverage concerns instances where the business incurs some legal liability as a result of a contract with another firm. A common element of coverage would exist for leased space where the lease agreement calls for the lessee to assume liability for use of the property. As a general rule, liability assumed under a contract is not covered unless specifically stated.

Contingent liability coverage addresses the potential liability that can occur as a result of the work of independent contractors. While the business is generally not legally liable for work done by contractors, there are some circumstances when liability does exist. An example would be when the work done by the contractor is inherently dangerous—such as may be involved with some types of construction or demolition activities.

Many liability loss exposures require the purchase of additional insurance coverage (or may not be insurable). Among the excluded loss exposures are items such as liability of directors and officers, liquor liability, pollution, war, and employer-related practices. Where available, separate coverage for these exposures may be purchased.

Insurance purchasing should not be a "do it and forget it" activity. Good record-keeping is essential. Information about major items acquired (cost, date of purchase, description), copies of insurance policies (including expired policies), financial records, and correspondence related to insurance and claims should all be stored in a safe location. This may mean storage off the hotel property, since you may need this information the most following a fire or other disaster at the property.

Commercial Automotive Coverage

Commercial automotive coverage provides a combination of liability and physical damage coverages. Physical damage coverage can include collision coverage, comprehensive coverage (loss from any cause *except* collision or overturn), and specified causes-of-loss coverage (only losses from specified perils are covered). Hotels which provide valet services—or even parking lots—should consider the purchase of **garage coverage** that provides liability, parking attendant, and physical damage coverage.

Additional Types of Coverage

Flood Coverage

Flood insurance began as a federal government insurance program developed to provide coverage for a difficult-to-insure class of properties—those located in flood-prone areas. This has subsequently been broadened to allow private insurers to sell insurance that is underwritten by the federal program. Flood insurance provides low-cost coverage from damage resulting from the overflow of inland or tidal waters, the unusual or rapid accumulation of runoff, or mudslides that are proximately caused by flood.

Umbrella Coverage

Umbrella coverage provides insurance above and beyond that of the primary insurance policies that the hotel might have. The concept behind this coverage is

Are You Getting Your Insurance Premium Dollar's Worth?

The insurance premium you pay each year for your property, liability, workers' compensation, and other business coverage includes a commission, unless you have agreed to pay your agent or broker a fee for services. That commission or fee entitles you to a good deal of service. Some of those services are listed here:

1. Insurance Without Gaps
2. Competitive Quotes
3. Explanation of Coverages Available/Provided
4. Timely Delivery of Policies and Endorsements
5. Claims Reporting and Monitoring
6. Periodic Loss Reports
7. Loss Prevention/Loss Control Assistance

1. Insurance Without Gaps

The most important service you deserve from your professional insurance person (agent or broker) is a thorough analysis of your insurable exposures to loss or claims. To accomplish this, he or she must have clear and complete understanding of your business and everything for which your business is responsible through ownership, contract, or lease. Without this information, your insurance professional cannot do the best job for you. For instance, if you have a warehouse where you store furniture, supplies, and computers, then you have an exposure to a liability loss for injury or damage to someone else, as well as an exposure for loss or damage to your property. Or, if one of your employees uses his or her car to take deposits to the bank, then your business has a "non-owned auto" liability exposure and an exposure to loss of the deposit through off-premises holdup or robbery.

Once your agent or broker knows what's involved in your business activities, he or she needs to design an insurance program that has no gaps or uninsured exposures. You may not choose to buy insurance for all your exposures, but it should be your choice: when you choose not to buy insurance for an aspect of your risk, you are essentially "self-insuring" that exposure. Consider whether or not you could stay in business if you have a loss under that self-insured risk.

2. Competitive Quotes

Around sixty to ninety days before your policies expire, it pays to reinvest time in your renewal. On your own, ask others in your industry about their insurance and jot down the names of preferred insurers. Spend time with your agent or broker to bring him or her up to date on what is going on in your business, as well as what services you expect regarding your renewal. Mention the "preferred insurers" of which you have heard, and ask your agent to include them in the competitive process. You should get quotes from two or three insurance companies on each policy, but you may not want to do this every year. Compare coverage as well as price to be sure you know what you are selecting. Ask what is excluded from each quote to see what's covered.

(continued)

3. Explanation of Coverages Available/Provided

Even "plain English" insurance policies need translation into lay terms to spell out what is covered when and for how much. Your insurance professional should help you understand what coverages and options are available, what is being recommended, and what are the trade-offs. Once you have purchased insurance, you need an explanation of what you bought and how to use it, when and if the need arises.

4. Timely Delivery of Policies and Endorsements

Once you order policies, your insurance professional should receive them from the insurance company, review, and deliver them within sixty days. Hold on to your expired policies, especially those covering auto and general liability. If years from now you get notice of a claim for something that occurred in the expired year, you still have coverage under the old policy if it was on an "occurrence" form (most liability coverages are on this form).

5. Claims Reporting and Monitoring

When a loss occurs, getting it correctly and promptly reported to the insurer is very important. Your broker or agent can review your claim and help provide all the pertinent information. If it is a loss to your property, your broker can facilitate with the claims adjuster for payment from the company. For claims involving injury or damage to others, monitoring is needed to assure that claims are closed as promptly and favorably as possible. Your broker can provide that service.

6. Periodic Loss Reports

Your broker or agent can also obtain loss runs or consolidated reports of all claims you have had (i.e., your loss history). This is often needed if you choose to change insurers in the future. Providing competing insurers complete loss experience can determine whether or not you get favorable quotes on your insurance premiums.

7. Loss Prevention/Loss Control Assistance

Finally, the best way to improve your claims experience and "appeal" to an insurer as a profitable client is to have an effective loss prevention and/or loss control program in place. Loss prevention requires that fire and life safety issues, security precautions, industrial hygiene issues, and safety procedures be intertwined in management's philosophy and practice. The expertise needed to assist you in developing a loss prevention/loss control program to fit your operation can be obtained from your agent, broker, or insurance company. The insurers recognize that helping you prevent claims protects their bottom line, so they do want to help. Some agents and brokers have safety professionals on their staff for you to use.

Should you find that you are not getting all you deserve for your insurance premium dollar, just discuss your concerns with your broker or agent. If, for any reason, your current insurance professional is unwilling to provide the services described, there are many others around who would jump at the chance to serve you and your business.

Source: Sherry Z. Terao, *Risk Management Bulletin,* AH&MA Risk Management Committee, April 1994.

that hospitality firms may be jeopardized by potentially catastrophic liability judgments (or in some instances, property losses). Umbrella coverage could be written for as little as a few million dollars for a small firm to several hundred million for a large firm.

Legally Mandated Coverage

While some insurance is optional, some coverage is legally mandated. Some coverage is mandated for all operations, such as automobile insurance, while other insurance is the result of contracts signed related to the operation, such as a franchise agreement.

Insurance coverage required by contracts can exist in a variety of forms and for a variety of coverages. Franchise agreements require coverage for a variety of things during the lifetime of the franchise, including insurance during construction, comprehensive-commercial general liability coverage during operation, workers' compensation and employers' liability insurance (also usually required by law), property insurance, and business interruption insurance. Management agreements are also likely to include insurance provisions.

Workers' Compensation. The most common and for some employers the most costly type of legally mandated insurance is **workers' compensation.** This insurance exists to provide a source of benefits for workers who are injured in the workplace. Coverage includes medical expenses, disability payments, survivor's death benefits, and rehabilitation benefits. Disability payments involve a replacement of income lost as a result of the injury. The disability may be total or partial, temporary or permanent. A critical element of the workers' compensation system is that no determination of fault by the employer is necessary. Workers' compensation insurance may be provided by state programs, private insurance, or self-insurance.

Employers' Liability Insurance. Besides workers' compensation, firms are likely to want to purchase **employers' liability insurance.** While workers' compensation insurance provides employers with coverage for claims from the injured employee, claims from other parties (such as a spouse) as a result of the injury are not covered. There are also other circumstances when a workplace injury covered by workers' compensation can result in a potential liability for the employer. For example, the employee may sue a third party and this third party may sue the employer. Employers' liability insurance provides coverage for a large number of these circumstances.

Other legally mandated insurance coverage may be provided by separate policies, by inclusion in other policies, or by the government itself.

Claims Management

In spite of vigorous efforts to reduce the possibility of a loss, losses do happen. This can be an injury to a guest or an employee, or the loss of or damage to guest or hotel property. Before any of these losses occur, the hotel should have clearly established the **claims management** process, or the procedures that will be used to manage claims. This should include proper documentation, procedures

---

Providing Workers' Compensation

Workers' compensation insurance may be provided by state programs, private insurance, or self-insurance.

Firms utilizing state programs may be doing so because of their small size or high risk characteristics. Private insurance coverage is commonly purchased with a large number of insurers providing the coverage. (In some states, private insurance for workers' compensation is not permitted and is instead provided from a monopoly state fund.) It is also possible to purchase workers' compensation insurance through industry organizations.

The uniform classification and rating system that state programs and private insurance rely upon as their pricing basis is developed by the National Council on Compensation Insurance (NCCI). Using this system as a starting point, the actual base premium rates are then established by state governments. A variety of modifications to this base rating method are available, especially for larger firms. These modifications—which include experience rating, participating or dividend plans, retention programs, and retrospective rating plans—move the cost basis of the workers' compensation from a fixed rate per dollar of payroll (varied for type of job) to a cost based more on the overall claim level experienced by the business itself.

Some larger companies may elect to self-insure. Where allowed by state law, firms can receive approval to provide workers' compensation coverage from their own cash flows. These firms may hire outside administrators to manage these programs or they may handle them internally.

---

regarding the incident, and settlement policies. Some of these claims may be filed with the insurance company for reimbursement, while others may be assumed at the property level or charged against a corporate insurance account.

Proper documentation of incidents is an important step in claims management. Use of a standardized reporting form at the property level helps to ensure proper documentation. There may be different forms or components of the same form used, depending on the nature of the incident. Incidents involving injury to guests may require information that is much different than that involving a robbery or assault. Prompt capture of this information is critical, since transient hotel guests and employee turnover make data gathering very difficult if it is undertaken too long after the fact. The key components of these forms solicit the information necessary to answer the questions:

- What (happened)?
- Where?
- When?
- Who (was involved)?
- How (did the event happen)?

Another key element of good claims management involves proper procedures regarding the incident itself. Showing a proper level of concern on guest or employee claims—without overtly indicating or accepting responsibility—

requires training for employees and management. Ignoring the guest's or employee's concerns at the time of the incident can turn a simple slip, for example, into a major claim. Local management must take ownership of claims and, with the assistance of corporate resources (if available) and the insurance company, bring them to closure.

A strategy is needed in settling claims. Hotel managers must decide if they want to fight every claim that is made, only those that are potentially significant, or none of them. Keep in mind that insurance companies will have their own approaches to claims that may be different from the hotel's. Discussion and coordination with the hotel's insurance providers can help to align their claims management methods with the hotel's. Decisions about legal services in relation to claims are also potentially important. Some firms will elect to allow the insurance company's counsel to represent them in the claims process unless the dollar amount is particularly large or the claim involves something particularly damaging to the company's reputation (such as a food-related liability claim in a restaurant).

A good insurance broker with an established hospitality portfolio will be invaluable in assisting the claim management process. Such brokers have an experienced claims advocate as part of their support staff whose duties involve working closely with clients to ensure that they receive timely, fair, and accurate claims handling that fully compensates them for their losses.

Many property-related claims will involve only the property and the insurance company. The insurance company includes information in its policies that defines the responsibilities of the insured when making a claim. The first step is prompt notification of the insurer that a potential loss has occurred. The insurance company will then investigate the claim. The insurance company's interests include whether the policy was in effect when the loss occurred, whether the policy covered the peril that caused the loss, and whether the type of loss was covered by the policy. The insured party may be asked to substantiate the loss that is claimed. For example, if a property is decorated with rare historical photos and furnished with expensive antiques, documentation of this may be required. If loss of business income is claimed, financial records will need to be provided for documentation.

With the introduction of centralized claims management centers in large hotel chains and similar services from insurance providers, incident reporting is sometimes done online or via phone. Prompt reporting of incidents is critical to prompt and cost-effective settlement of claims.

Finally, it must be recognized that claims reporting is mandatory for injuries serious enough to warrant workers' compensation claims. Since the potential seriousness is not always known at the time of an injury, a log for minor injuries (initially requiring only first aid) is also recommended. Proper procedures will vary by state due to the nature of the workers' compensation process.

🔑 Key Terms

agents—Legal representatives of the insurer who have the authority to act on the insurer's behalf. Agents will normally issue a binder, which is temporary evidence that insurance exists until a policy is issued.

binder—Proof that insurance exists during the interim period before a policy has been issued.

boiler and machinery coverage—Insurance that applies to equipment including boilers, refrigerating systems, engines, turbines, and generators that are not covered under the property component of the commercial package property coverage. It can include not only direct losses to the equipment, but also losses due to lost business income, spoilage, and extra expenses incurred to keep the hotel operating when an equipment breakdown occurs (such as renting a piece of portable equipment).

brokers—Legal representatives of the insured who solicit applications for insurance and then attempt to place the coverage with an appropriate insurer. Brokers are active in many aspects of insurance, often providing specialized services and focusing on specific forms of insurance coverage.

business income (extra expense) coverage—Insurance that recognizes that property damage and other events may result in loss of business income, and that certain expenses may continue during the recovery period.

causes of loss form—Identifies the specific types of perils (fire, lightning, etc.) that are covered under an insurance policy.

claims management—Process and actions to be taken when an event occurs that may result in a loss.

coinsurance—A provision of some policies that requires the insured to carry insurance equal to a specified percentage of the property's value—or receive less than full reimbursement for a loss.

commercial automotive coverage—Insurance that provides a combination of liability and physical damage coverages, including collision coverage, comprehensive coverage, and specified causes-of-loss coverage.

commercial crime coverage—Insurance that recognizes that the assets of the firm include cash and securities and that these are potentially at risk from the acts of people.

commercial general liability (CGL)—An insurance policy that addresses the various sources of liability loss exposure of business firms and the various types of losses that may be incurred.

commercial package policy (CPP)—A common way to provide property coverage; an insurance policy that includes coverage for various property loss exposures.

commercial property coverage—Insurance that includes the firm's building(s) and personal property components.

common policy conditions component—An insurance component that includes statements regarding transfer provisions, rights of the insurer to conduct property inspections and surveys, rights of the insurer to examine books and records, and cancellation and change provisions.

common policy declarations component—An insurance component that involves an identification of the insured, the property insured, policy period, summary of coverage, and amount of premium.

completed operations coverage—Insurance that involves liability losses that occur away from the premises and arise out of the insured's product or work after the insured has relinquished possession of the product, or the work has been completed.

contingent liability coverage—Insurance that addresses the potential liability that can occur as a result of the work of independent contractors.

contractual liability coverage—Insurance that concerns instances where the business incurs some legal liability as a result of a contract with another firm.

employers' liability insurance—Insurance that provides coverage for claims from other parties (such as a spouse) as a result of a workers' compensation injury.

flood insurance—Insurance that provides low-cost coverage for damage resulting from the overflow of inland or tidal waters, the unusual or rapid accumulation of runoff, or mudslides that are proximately caused by flooding.

garage coverage—Insurance that provides liability, parking attendant, and physical damage coverage for hotels that provide valet service.

group coverage—Insurance that allows large chains to purchase coverage for all their hotels rather than allowing each hotel to negotiate coverage individually; benefits include lower prices and rate stability.

indemnity—Compensation for a loss.

inland (and ocean) marine coverage—Insurance that provides protection for operations that take title to goods at the time of shipment from the supplier.

mutual insurers—A corporation owned by the policyholders.

period of indemnity—In an insurance policy, the time frame in which the policy holder's loss is covered.

pooling (risk sharing)—A provision of insurance in which the group policy holders agree to share the risk costs of the group via a payment by all to a fund shared by the group.

premises and operations coverage—Insurance that involves legal liability that can arise out of ownership and maintenance of the location where the firm does business.

products liability coverage—Insurance that covers injury to customers or damage to their property from defective products.

reinsurers—Insurance firms that transfer potential risk from a single insurance company to a number of insurance companies.

risk sharing (pooling)—A provision of insurance in which the group policy holders agree to share the risk costs of the group via a payment by all to a fund shared by the group.

risk transfer—A provision of insurance that transfers the risk associated with policy-covered losses from the insured to the insurer.

stock insurers—An insurance corporation owned by stockholders who participate in the profits and losses of the insurer.

umbrella coverage—Insurance above and beyond that of other underlying insurance coverages.

workers' compensation—The most common type of legally mandated insurance, it exists to provide a source of benefits for workers who are injured in the workplace. Coverage includes medical expenses, disability payments, survivor's death benefits, and rehabilitation benefits.

 Review Questions

1. What is the purpose of insurance?
2. What is risk transfer? risk sharing?
3. What is an example of government regulation of the insurance industry?
4. Why do many hotels purchase a commercial package policy?
5. What types of losses are covered by business income (extra expense) coverage?
6. How can properties far from marine areas benefit from inland marine coverage?
7. What precautions should be taken when storing insurance policies?
8. What is the purpose of workers' compensation insurance?
9. When should properties establish claims management procedures?

 Internet Sites

For more information, visit the following Internet sites. Remember that Internet addresses can change without notice. If the site is no longer there, you can use a search engine to look for additional sites.

A.M. Best Company
www.ambest.com

American Hotel & Lodging Association
www.ahla.com

American Insurance Association
www.aiadc.org

American Risk and Insurance
Association
www.aria.org

Blue Cross and Blue Shield Association
www.bcbs.com

Business Insurance Magazine
www.businessinsurance.com

Insurance Information Institute
www.iii.org

Insurance Services Office
www.iso.com

Insure.com
www.insure.com

National Association of Insurance
 Commissioners
www.naic.org

National Council on Compensation
Insurance
www.ncci.com

National Fire Protection Association
www.nfpa.org

Occupational Safety & Health
 Administration
www.osha.gov

Property Casualty 360°
www.propertycasualty360.com

RiskandInsurance.com
www.riskandinsurance.com

Risk and Insurance Management
 Society, Inc.
www.rims.org

RiskINFO
www.riskinfo.com

Self-Insurance Institute of America,
 Inc.
www.siia.org

Standard & Poor's
www.standardandpoors.com

Index